Thanks to you readers, **Beet, the Vandel Buster** has become incredibly popular, and the second volume is already here. It seems like this series is going to be a long one (LOL), so I'll have Beet continue to do his best. There are a lot of hardships I've faced lately, and I struggle each month, trying to develop Beet into the type of hero whose words of courage can make anyone's pain vanish, despite the fact that he's in as much trouble as I am. Please continue to cheer me on!
— Riku Sanjo

Author Riku Sanjo and artist Koji Inada were both born in Tokyo in 1964. Riku began his career writing a radio-controlled car manga for the comic **Bonbon**. Koji debuted with **Kussotare Daze!!** in **Weekly Shonen Jump**. Riku and Koji first worked together on the highly successful **Dragon Quest–Dai's Big Adventure**. Beet, the Vandel Buster, their latest collaboration, debuted in **Monthly Shonen Jump** in 2002 and was an immediate hit, inspiring an action-packed video game and an animated series on Japanese TV.

BEET THE VANDEL BUSTER
VOL. 2
The SHONEN JUMP Graphic Novel Edition

STORY BY RIKU SANJO
ART BY KOJI INADA

English Adaptation/Shaenon K. Garrity
Translation/Naomi Kokubo
Touch-Up & Lettering/Mark McMurray
Cover Design/Sean Lee
Graphics/Andrea Rice
Editor/Richard Kadrey

Managing Editor/Elizabeth Kawasaki
Director of Production/Noboru Watanabe
Editorial Director/Alvin Lu
Executive Vice President & Editor in Chief/Hyoe Narita
Sr. Director of Licensing & Acquisitions/Rika Inouye
Vice President of Sales & Marketing/Liza Coppola
Vice President of Strategic Development/Yumi Hoashi
Publisher/Seiji Horibuchi

Printed in the U.S.A.

Published by VIZ, LLC
P.O. Box 77064
San Francisco, CA 94107

SHONEN JUMP Graphic Novel Edition
10 9 8 7 6 5 4 3 2 1
First printing, November 2004

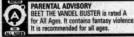

PARENTAL ADVISORY
BEET THE VANDEL BUSTER is rated A
for All Ages. It contains fantasy violence.
It is recommended for all ages.

THE WORLD'S
MOST POPULAR MANGA
SHONEN JUMP
GRAPHIC NOVEL
www.shonenjump.com

www.viz.com

Beet

THE VANDEL BUSTER

Volume 2

Story by **Riku Sanjo**

Art by **Koji Inada**

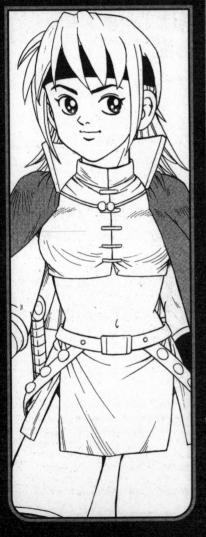

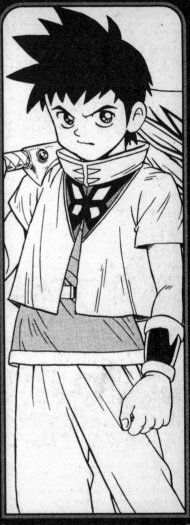

BEET
The hero of this story.
Believing in justice, he sets out on a journey to save the world. He received five Saiga weapons from the Zenon Warriors.

POALA
Beet's childhood friend.
She has an unyielding spirit. Poala joins Beet in his journey as the second of the Beet Warriors. She is skilled at attacking enemies using her Divine Attack.

STORY

CHARACTERS

BELTORZE
Known as the "King of Tragedy," he is a five-star Vandel, feared by humans. He always wants to fight against the strongest human warriors.

the ZENON WARRIORS
From left to right: Zenon, Cruss, Bluezam, Alside and Laio. After a battle against Beltorze, they disappeared. No one knows if they're still alive.

"Vandels" ... In this story, that's what we call the evil creatures with magical powers. One day they appeared on the surface of the Earth, releasing monsters and destroying the peace and order of the nations. People called this seemingly endless era "The Dark Age."

Beet is born at this time in the history of his world. He's a pure-hearted boy who believes in justice. Idolizing the Zenon Warriors, a team of Vandel Busters whose occupational goal is to conquer the Vandels, Beet binds himself to a contract and becomes a Buster.

That's when Beltorze, a five-star Vandel, comes to Beet's village. Inadvertently stumbling into the midst of a battle between the Zenon Warriors and Beltorze, Beet suffers a fatal injury. He miraculously survives due to the quick wits of the Zenon Warriors, who give him their lives, along with their Saiga, or spiritual weapons.

Three years later, Beet completes his training as a Buster, just as the Zenon Warriors wished him to do. Now he sets out on a quest with his childhood friend, Poala, who is also a Buster, to annihilate all Vandels from their world.

Beet THE VANDEL BUSTER™

2

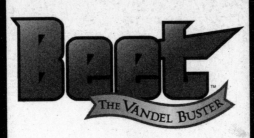

Chapter 4: The Arch-Enemy Arises!

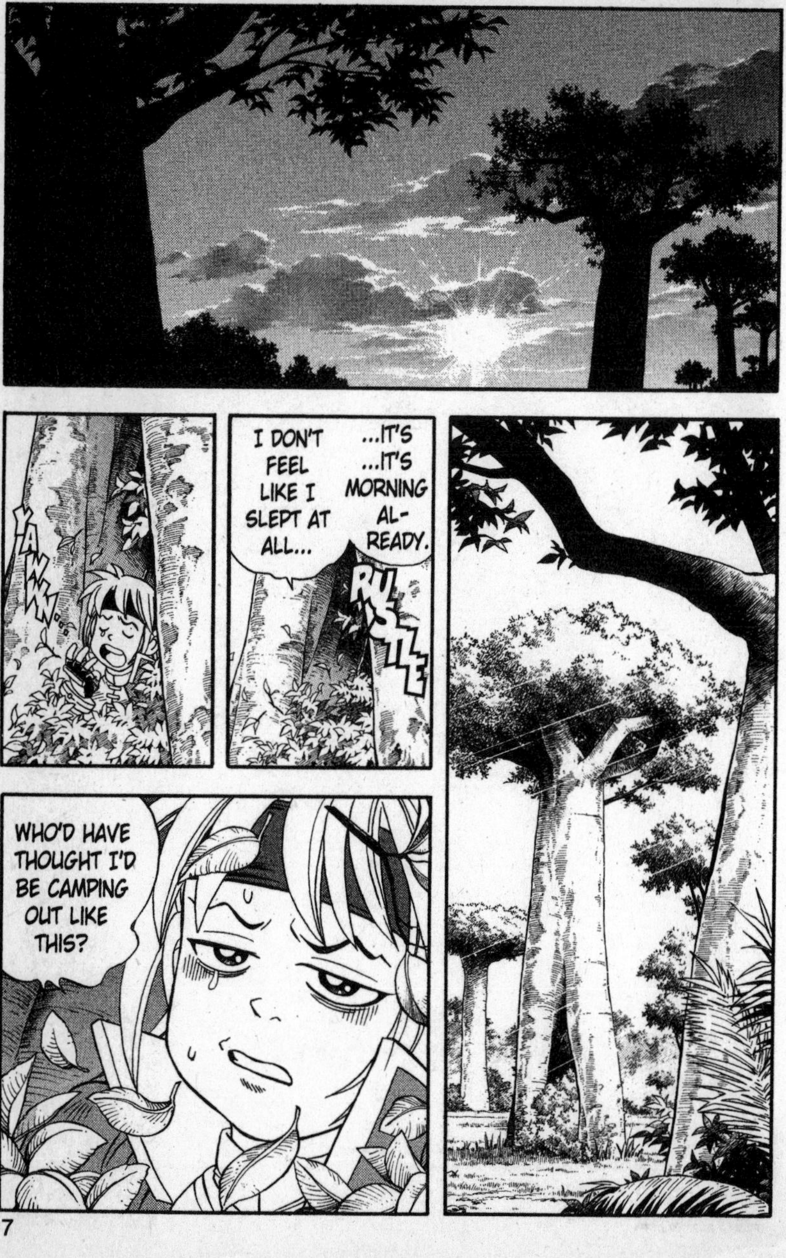
...IT'S ...IT'S MORNING AL-READY.
I DON'T FEEL LIKE I SLEPT AT ALL...
RUSTLE
YAWWN...
WHO'D HAVE THOUGHT I'D BE CAMPING OUT LIKE THIS?

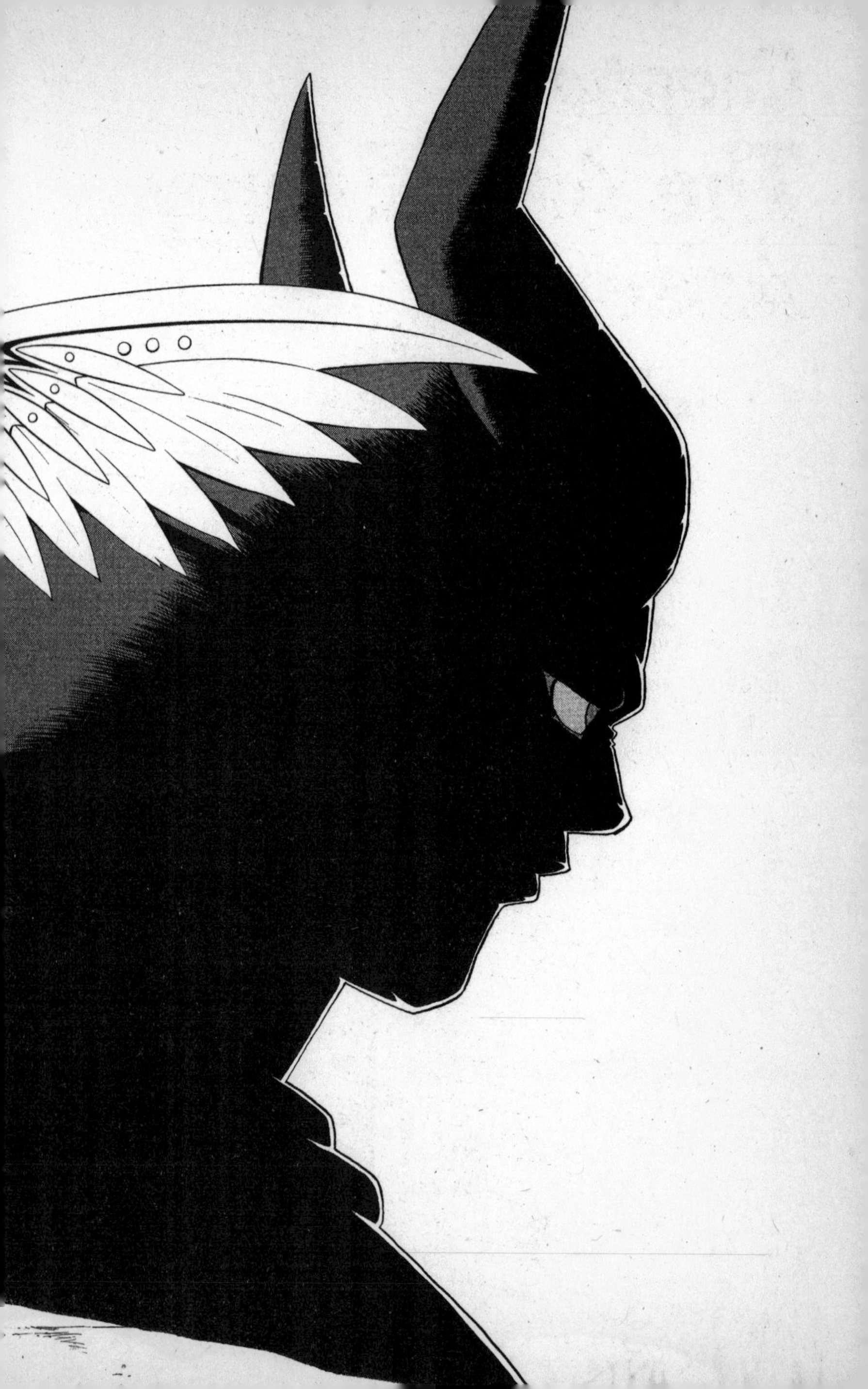

Chapter 4: The Arch-Enemy Arises!

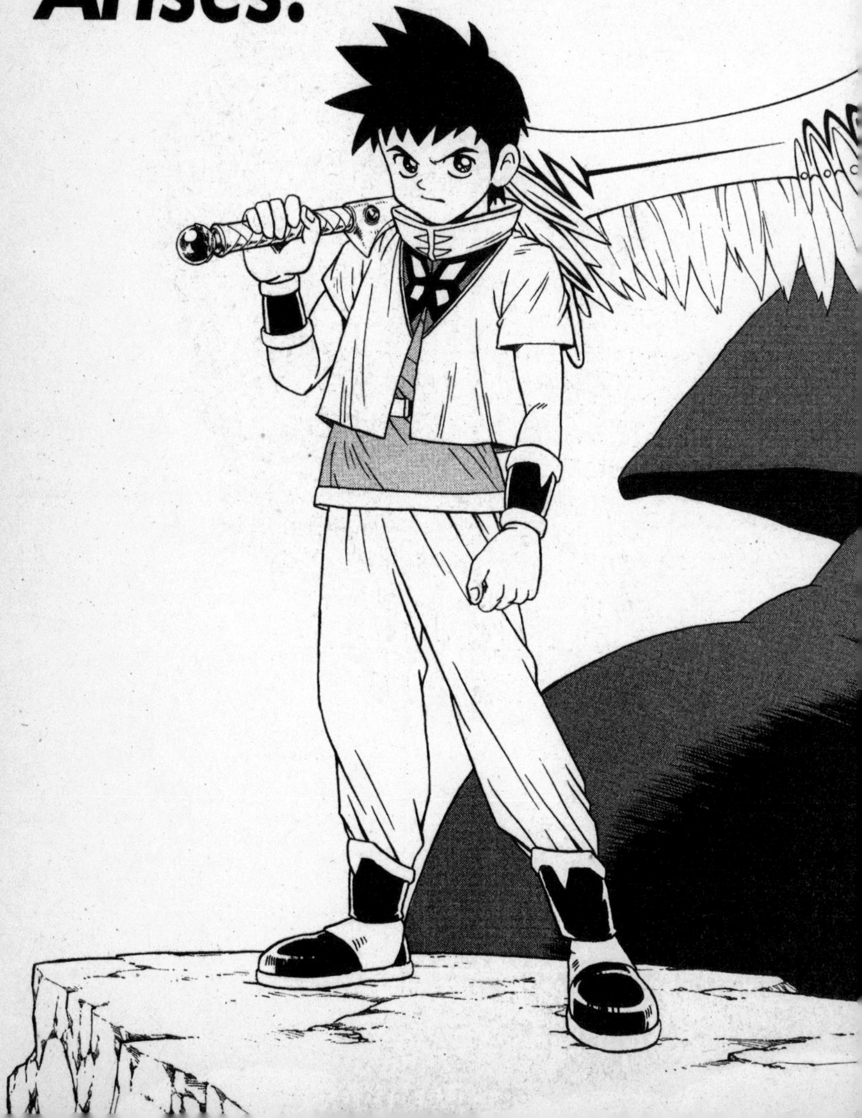

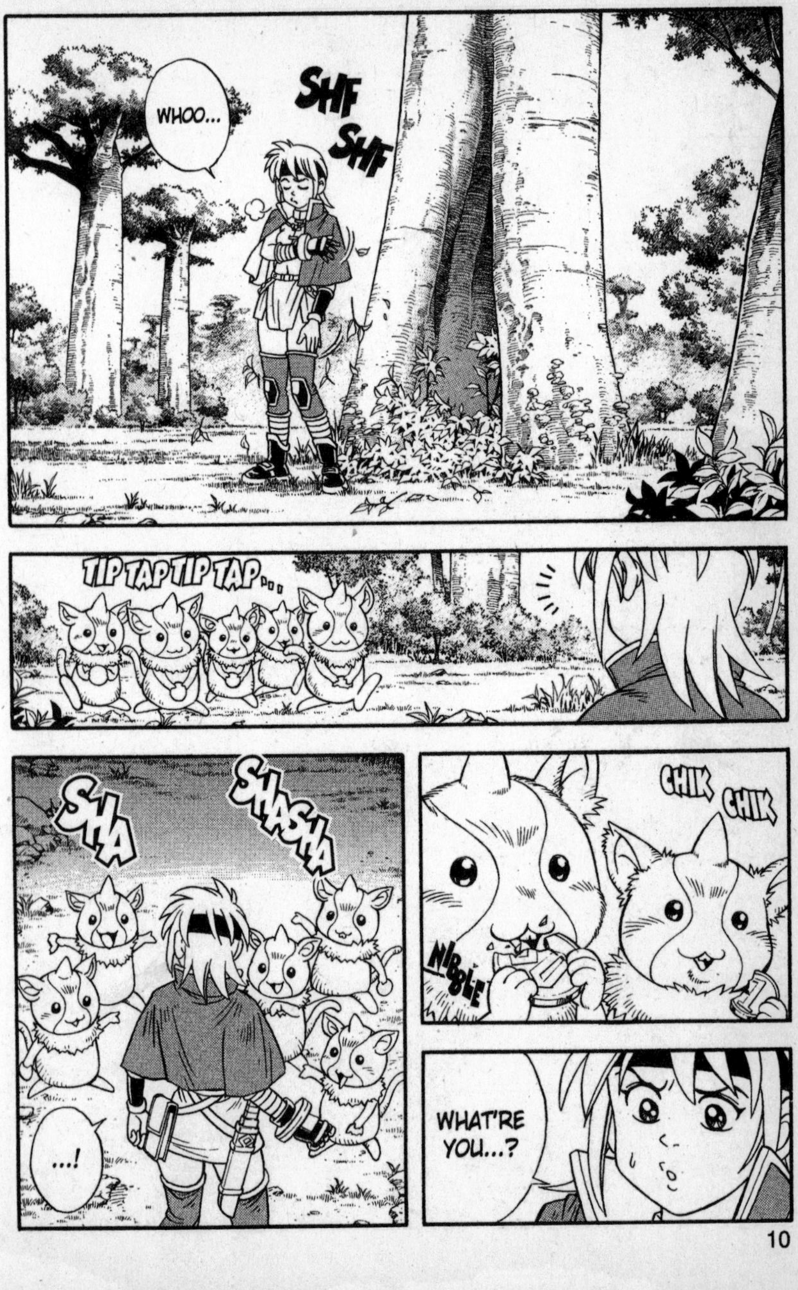
WHOO...
SHF
SHF
TIP TAP TIP TAP...
CHIK
CHIK
NIBBLE
WHAT'RE YOU...?
SHASHA
SHA
...!

READ THIS WAY

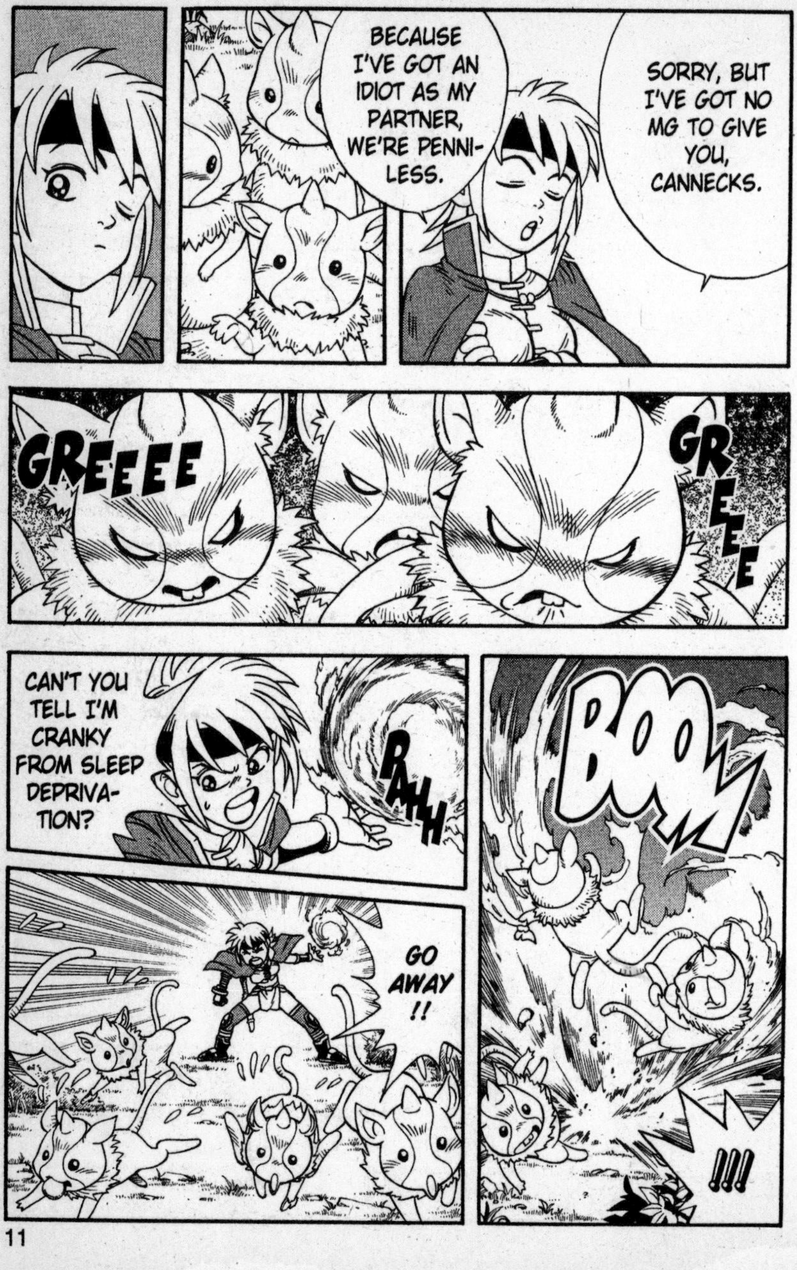

SORRY, BUT I'VE GOT NO MG TO GIVE YOU, CANNECKS.
BECAUSE I'VE GOT AN IDIOT AS MY PARTNER, WE'RE PENNI-LESS.
GREEE
GREEEE
BOOM
!!!
CAN'T YOU TELL I'M CRANKY FROM SLEEP DEPRIVA-TION?
RAHHH
GO AWAY !!

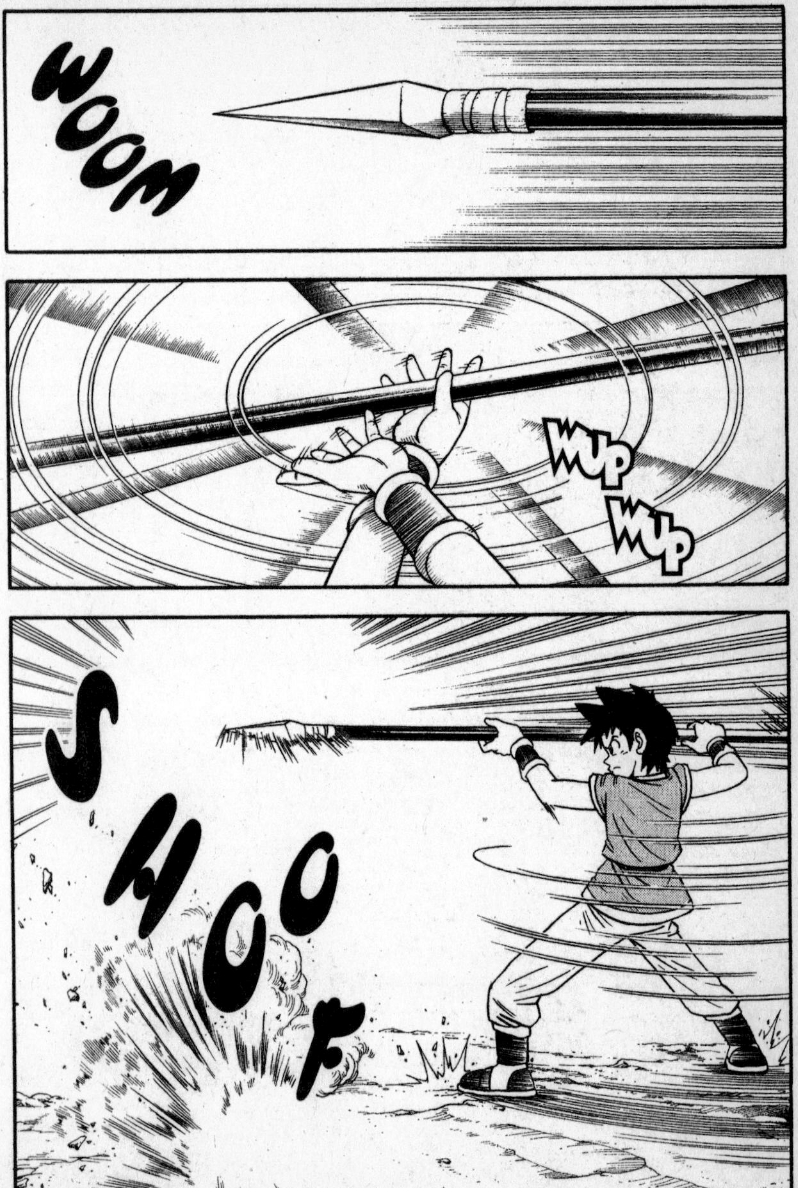
WOOM
WUP
WUP
SHOOF

READ THIS WAY

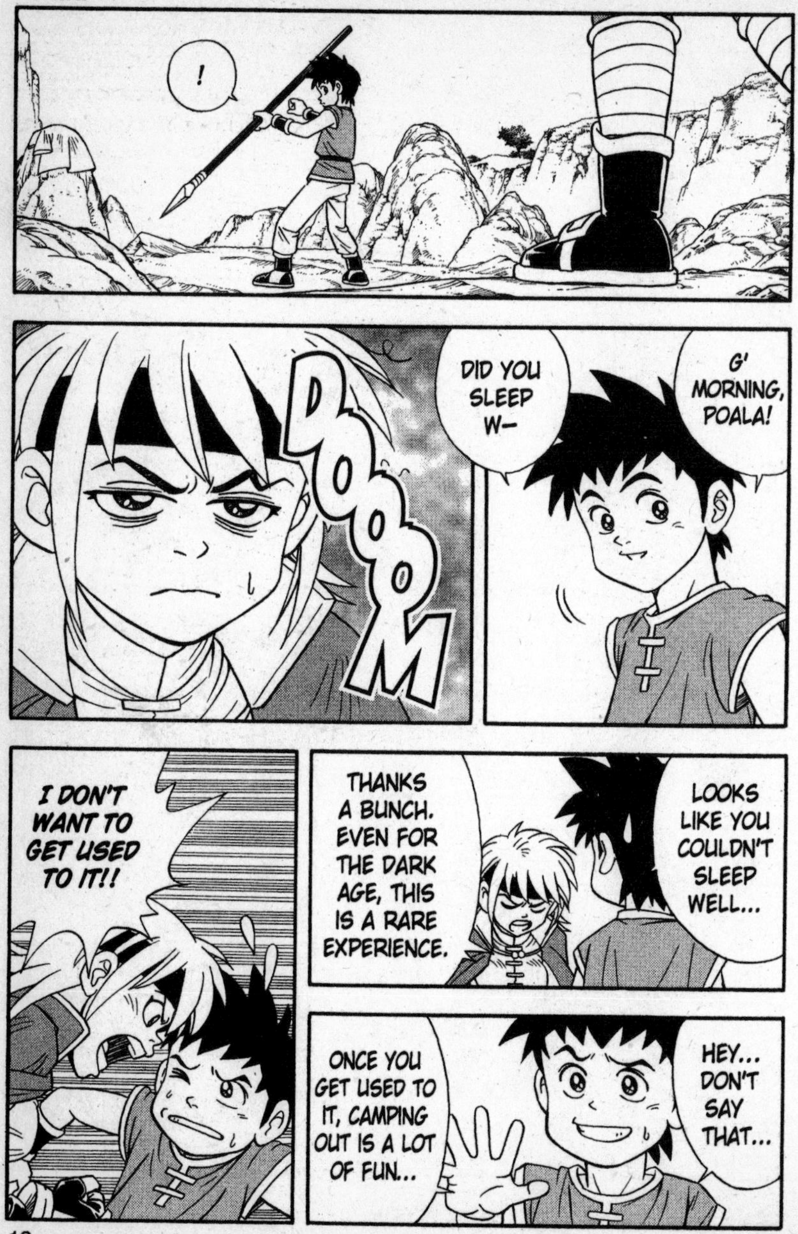

!
G' MORNING, POALA!
DID YOU SLEEP W—
DOOOOM
LOOKS LIKE YOU COULDN'T SLEEP WELL...
THANKS A BUNCH. EVEN FOR THE DARK AGE, THIS IS A RARE EXPERIENCE.
HEY... DON'T SAY THAT...
ONCE YOU GET USED TO IT, CAMPING OUT IS A LOT OF FUN...
I DON'T WANT TO GET USED TO IT!!

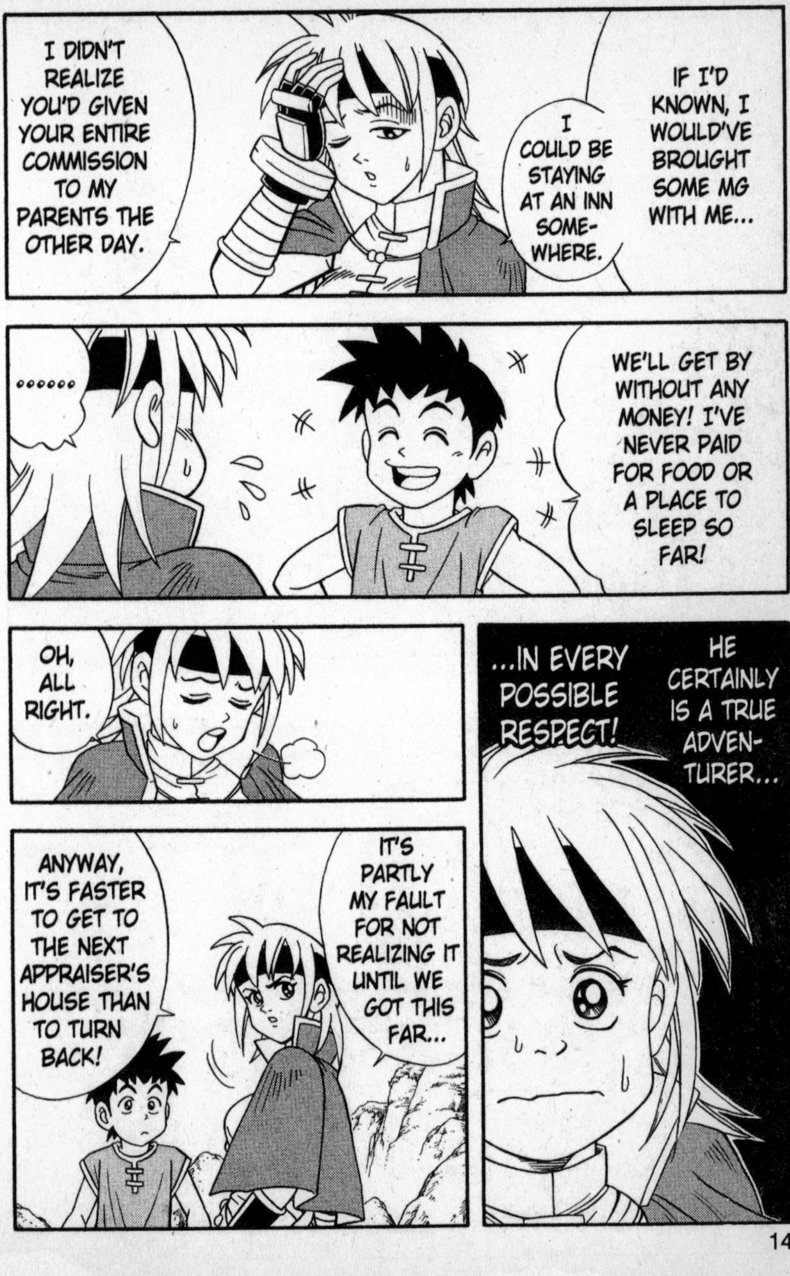
IF I'D KNOWN, I WOULD'VE BROUGHT SOME MG WITH ME...
I COULD BE STAYING AT AN INN SOME-WHERE.
I DIDN'T REALIZE YOU'D GIVEN YOUR ENTIRE COMMISSION TO MY PARENTS THE OTHER DAY.
WE'LL GET BY WITHOUT ANY MONEY! I'VE NEVER PAID FOR FOOD OR A PLACE TO SLEEP SO FAR!
......
HE CERTAINLY IS A TRUE ADVEN-TURER...
...IN EVERY POSSIBLE RESPECT!
OH, ALL RIGHT.
IT'S PARTLY MY FAULT FOR NOT REALIZING IT UNTIL WE GOT THIS FAR...
ANYWAY, IT'S FASTER TO GET TO THE NEXT APPRAISER'S HOUSE THAN TO TURN BACK!

READ THIS WAY

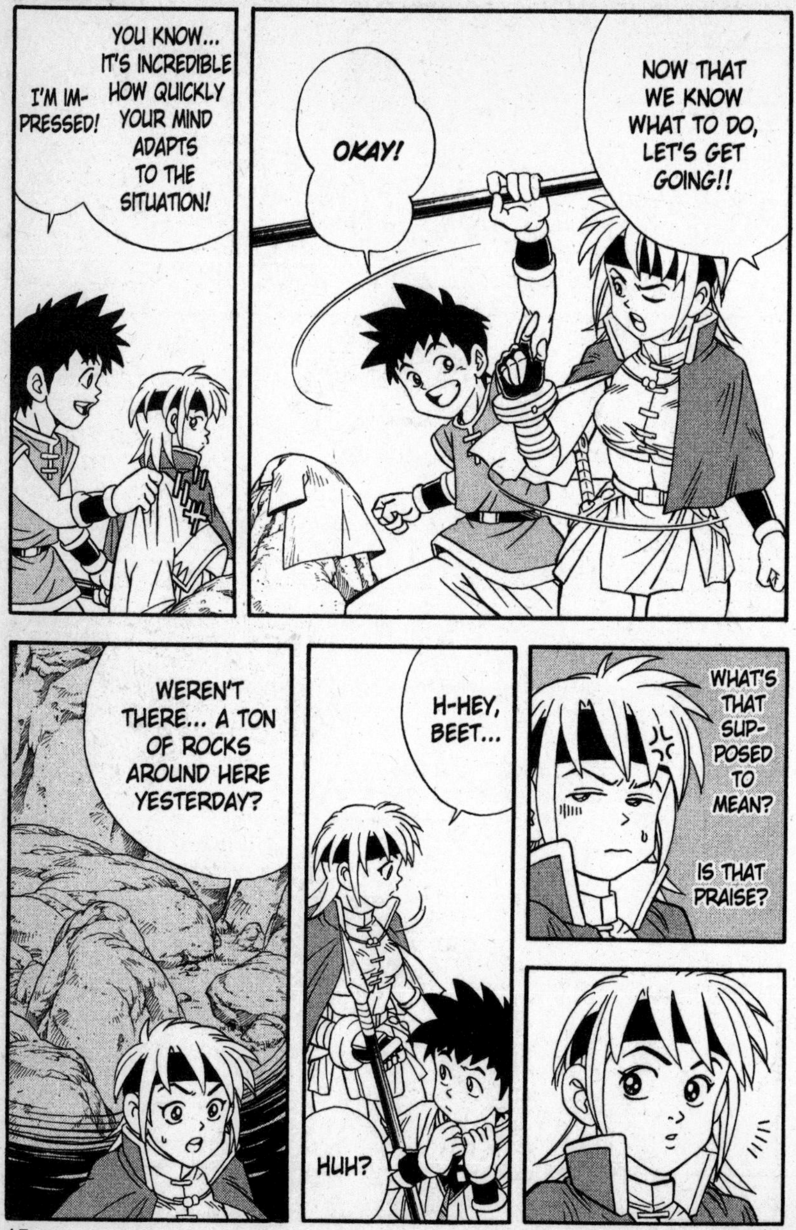
NOW THAT WE KNOW WHAT TO DO, LET'S GET GOING!!
OKAY!
YOU KNOW... IT'S INCREDIBLE HOW QUICKLY YOUR MIND ADAPTS TO THE SITUATION!
I'M IM-PRESSED!
WHAT'S THAT SUP-POSED TO MEAN?
IS THAT PRAISE?
H-HEY, BEET...
HUH?
WEREN'T THERE... A TON OF ROCKS AROUND HERE YESTERDAY?

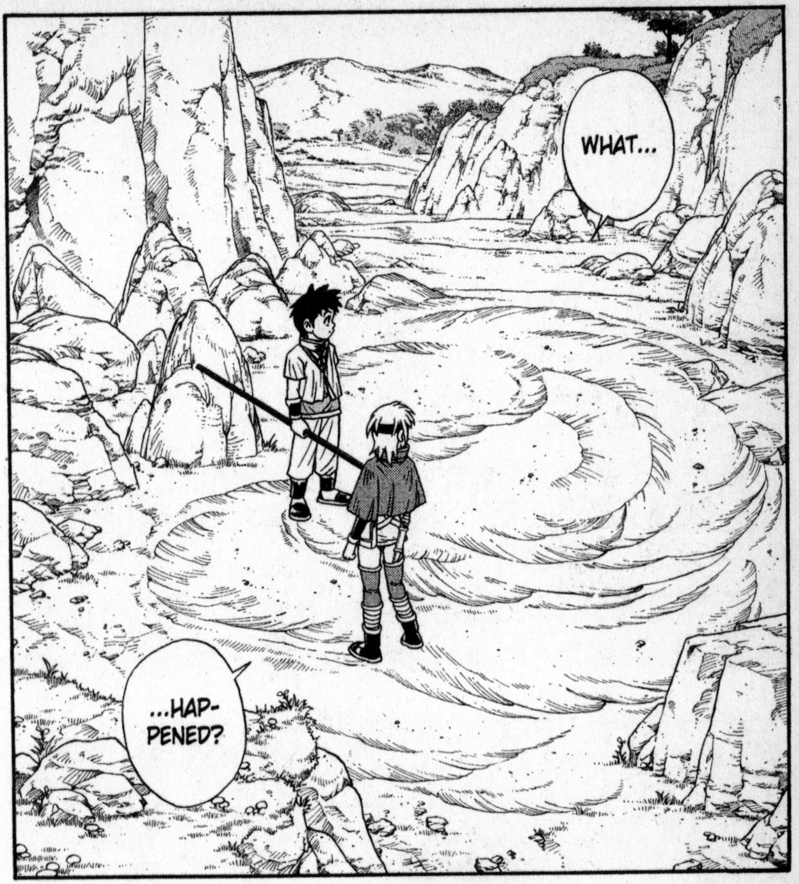
WHAT...
...HAP-
PENED?

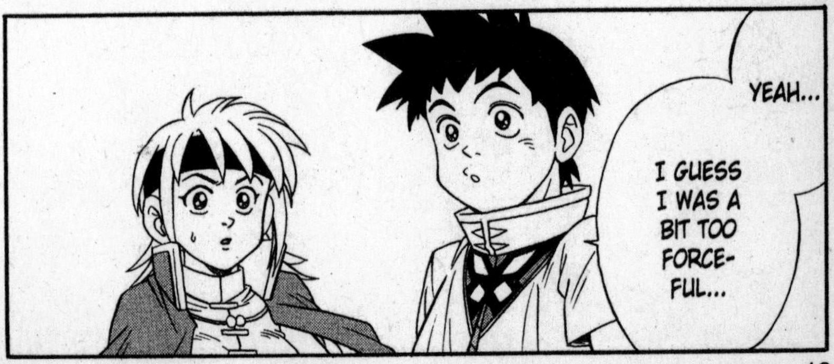
YEAH...
I GUESS
I WAS A
BIT TOO
FORCE-
FUL...

READ THIS WAY

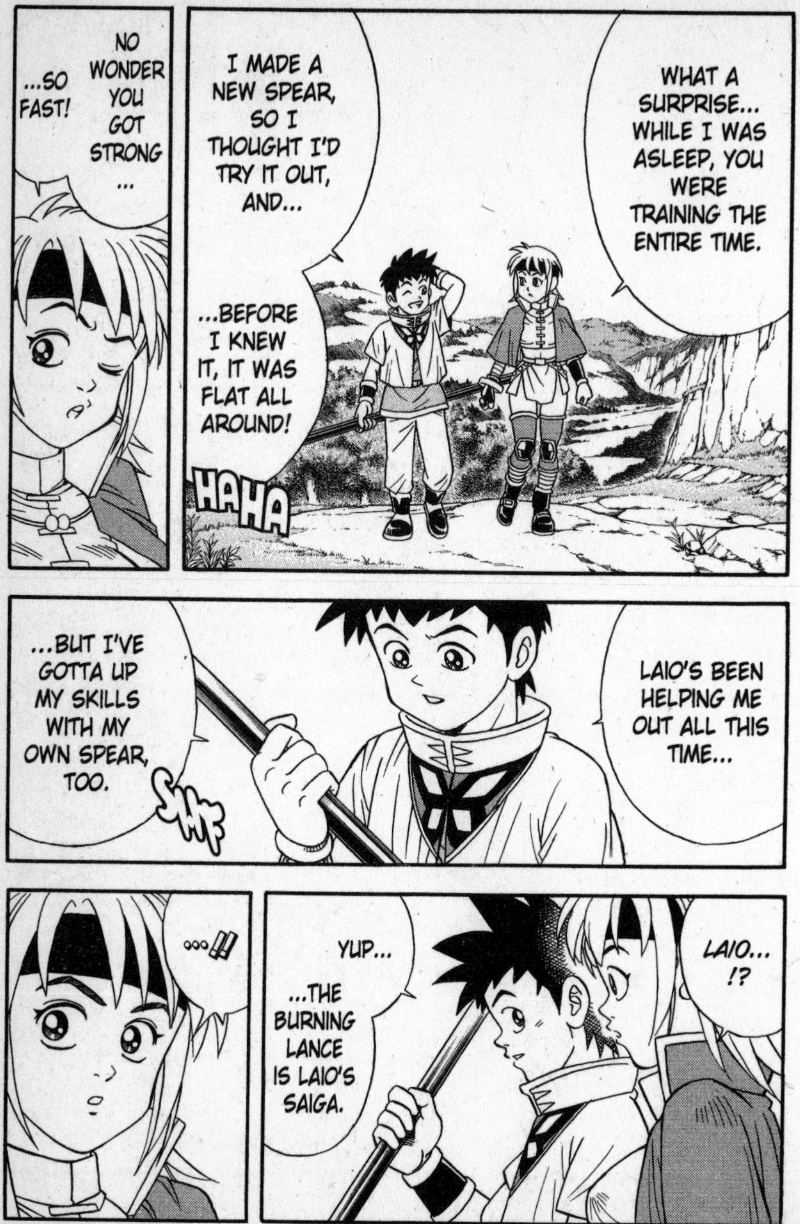
WHAT A SURPRISE... WHILE I WAS ASLEEP, YOU WERE TRAINING THE ENTIRE TIME.
I MADE A NEW SPEAR, SO I THOUGHT I'D TRY IT OUT, AND...
...BEFORE I KNEW IT, IT WAS FLAT ALL AROUND!
HAHA
NO WONDER YOU GOT STRONG ...
...SO FAST!
LAIO'S BEEN HELPING ME OUT ALL THIS TIME...
...BUT I'VE GOTTA UP MY SKILLS WITH MY OWN SPEAR, TOO.
LAIO... !?
YUP...
...THE BURNING LANCE IS LAIO'S SAIGA.
...!!

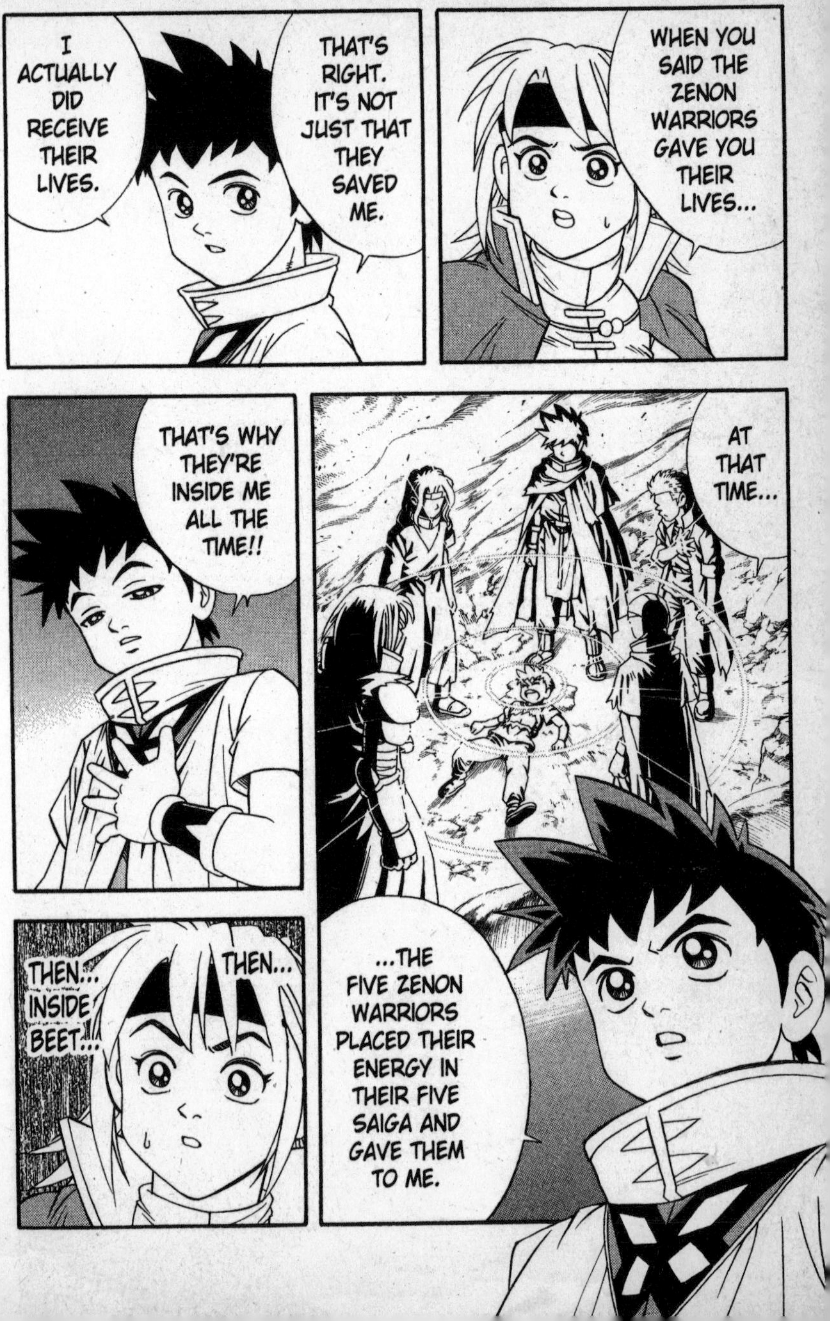
WHEN YOU SAID THE ZENON WARRIORS GAVE YOU THEIR LIVES...
THAT'S RIGHT. IT'S NOT JUST THAT THEY SAVED ME.
I ACTUALLY DID RECEIVE THEIR LIVES.
AT THAT TIME...
...THE FIVE ZENON WARRIORS PLACED THEIR ENERGY IN THEIR FIVE SAIGA AND GAVE THEM TO ME.
THAT'S WHY THEY'RE INSIDE ME ALL THE TIME!!
THEN...
THEN... INSIDE BEET...

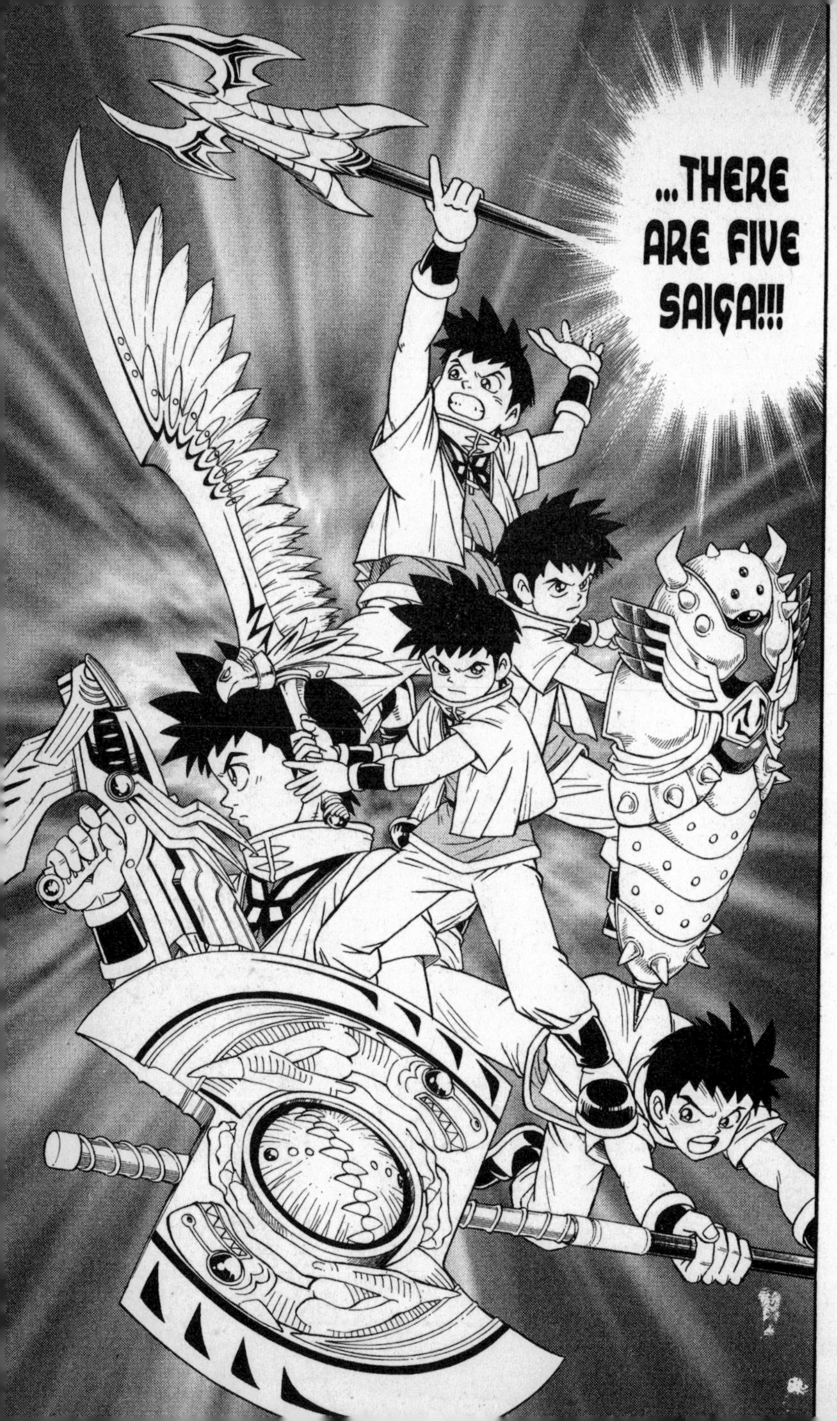
...THERE ARE FIVE SAIGA!!!

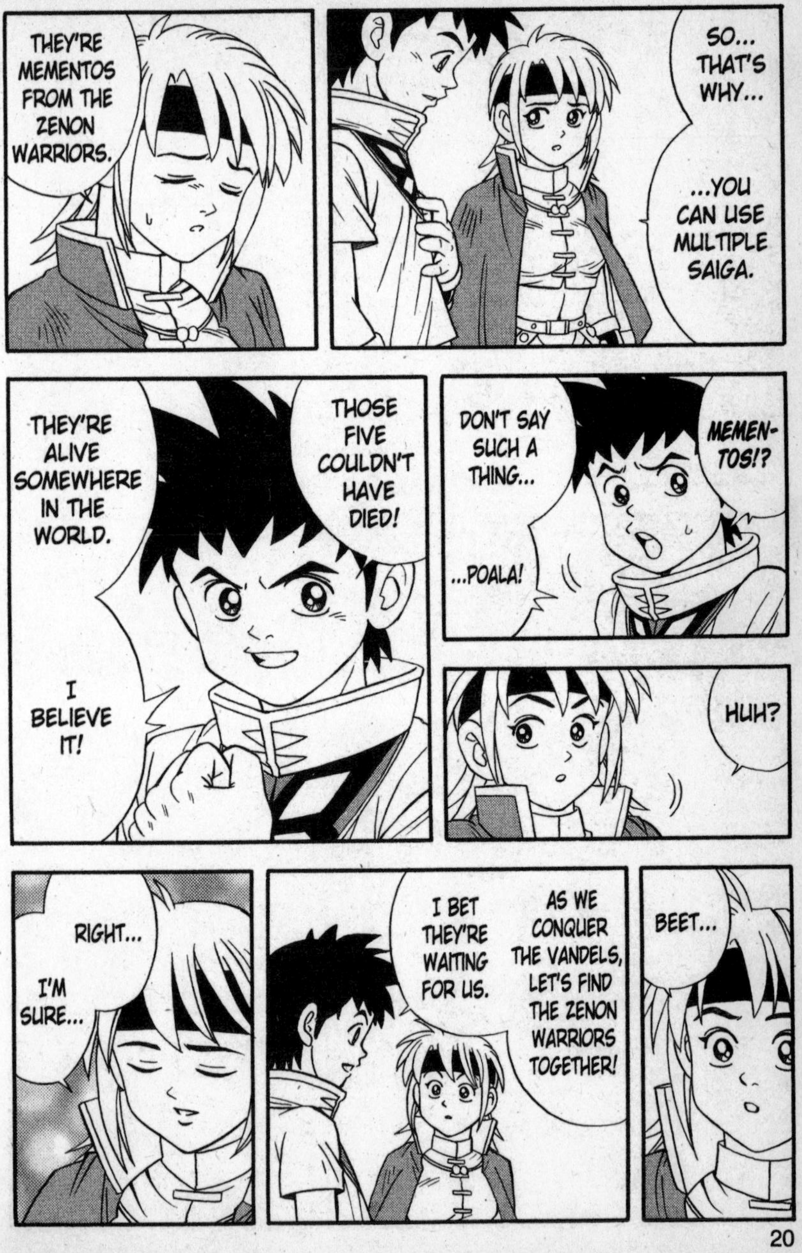
SO... THAT'S WHY...
...YOU CAN USE MULTIPLE SAIGA.
THEY'RE MEMENTOS FROM THE ZENON WARRIORS.
MEMEN-TOS!?
DON'T SAY SUCH A THING...
...POALA!
HUH?
THOSE FIVE COULDN'T HAVE DIED!
THEY'RE ALIVE SOMEWHERE IN THE WORLD.
I BELIEVE IT!
BEET...
AS WE CONQUER THE VANDELS, LET'S FIND THE ZENON WARRIORS TOGETHER!
I BET THEY'RE WAITING FOR US.
RIGHT...
I'M SURE...

READ THIS WAY

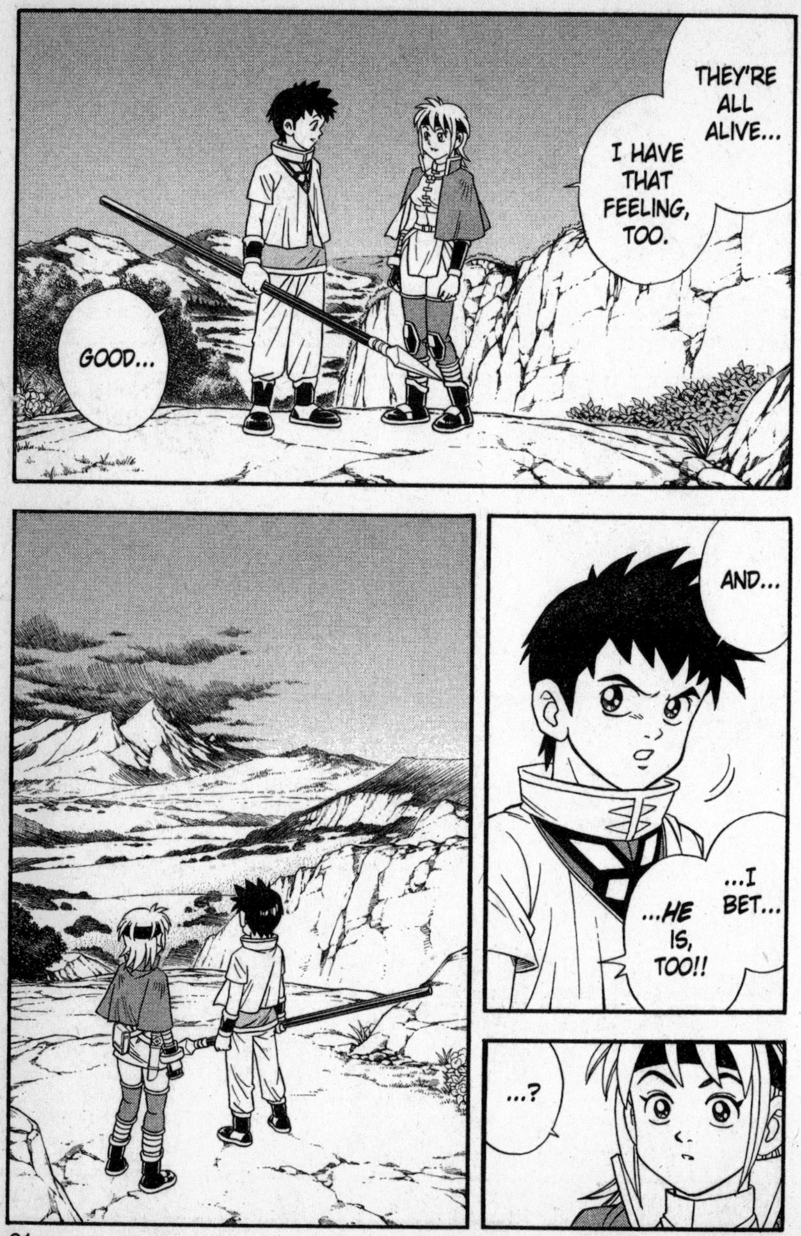
THEY'RE ALL ALIVE...
I HAVE THAT FEELING, TOO.
GOOD...
AND...
...I BET...
...HE IS, TOO!!
...?

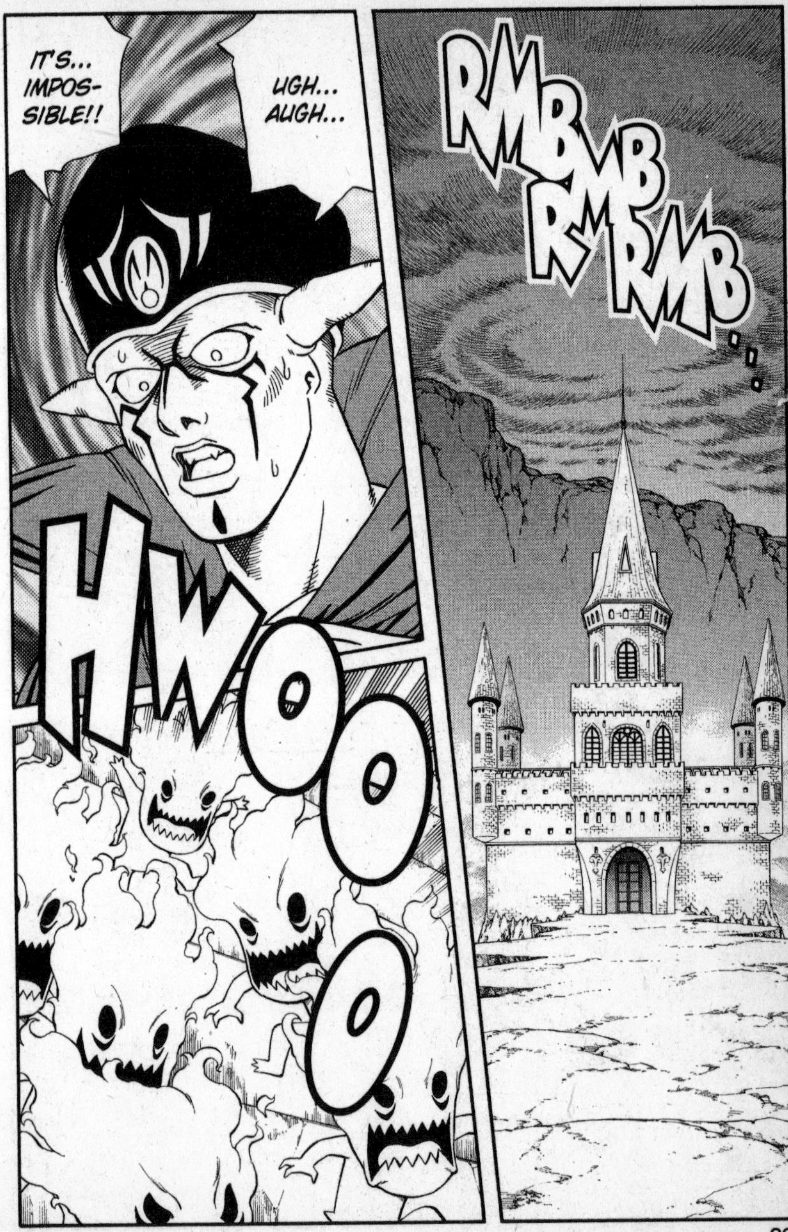
RMBMB
RMRMB...
UGH... AUGH...
IT'S... IMPOS-SIBLE!!
HWOOOO

......

I TOLD YOU...

...CAN-BAL...

...EVEN FIVE AGAINST ONE...

...MY MINION WOULD WIN!

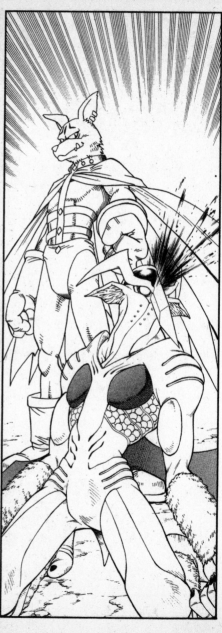

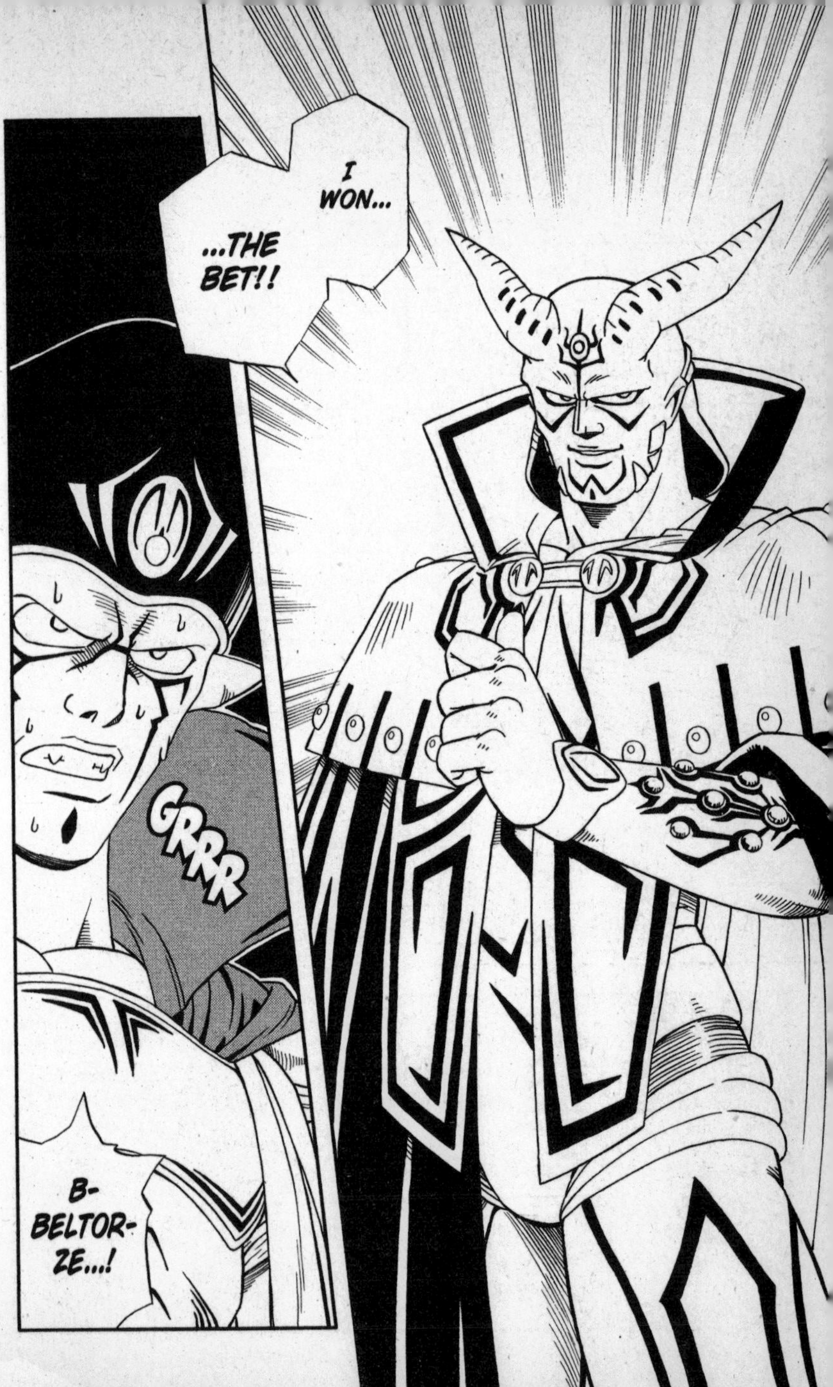
I WON... ...THE BET!!
GRRR
B-BELTORZE...!

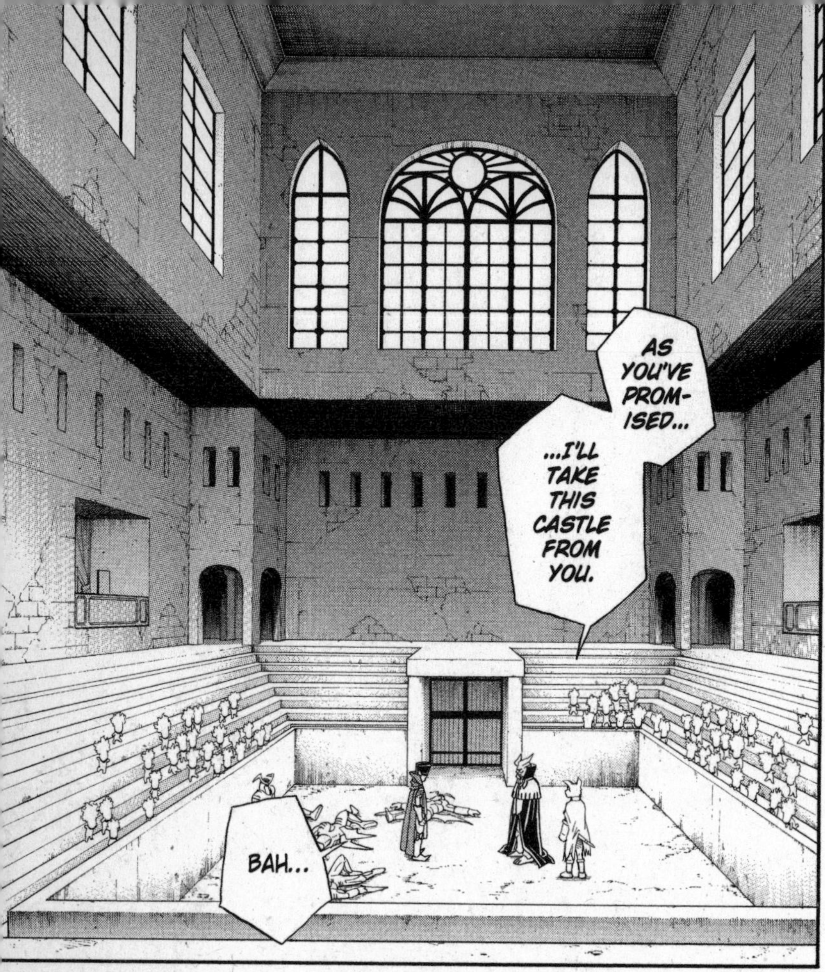
AS YOU'VE PROMISED...
...I'LL TAKE THIS CASTLE FROM YOU.
BAH...
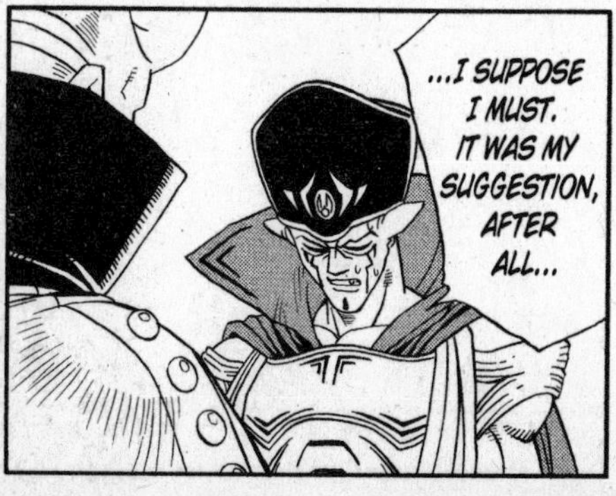
...I SUPPOSE I MUST. IT WAS MY SUGGESTION, AFTER ALL...
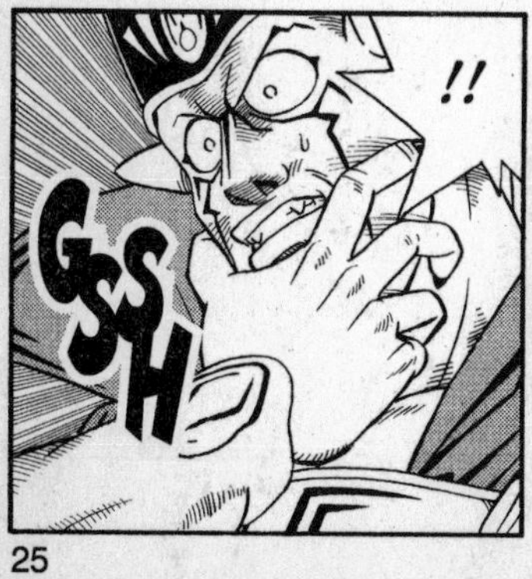
!!
GSSH

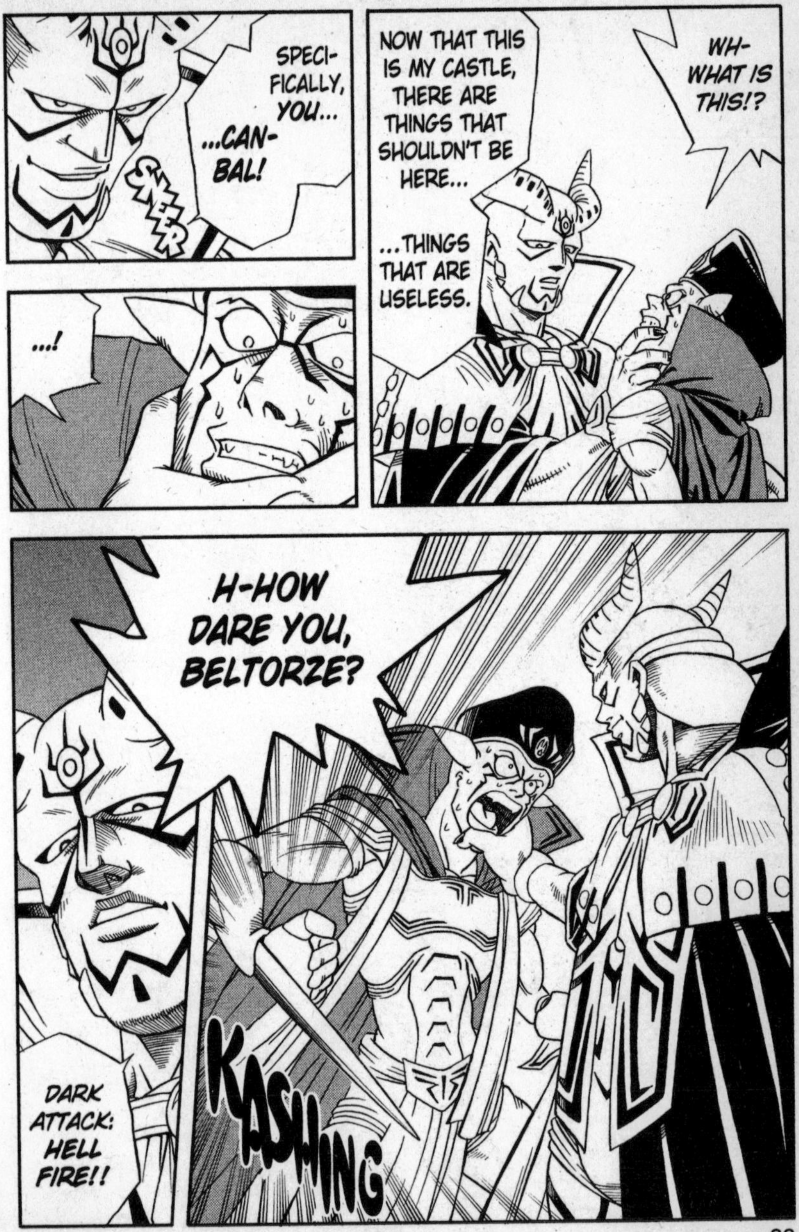
WH- WHAT IS THIS!?
NOW THAT THIS IS MY CASTLE, THERE ARE THINGS THAT SHOULDN'T BE HERE...
...THINGS THAT ARE USELESS.
SPECI- FICALLY, YOU...
...CAN- BAL!
SNEER
...!
H-HOW DARE YOU, BELTORZE?
KASHING
DARK ATTACK: HELL FIRE!!

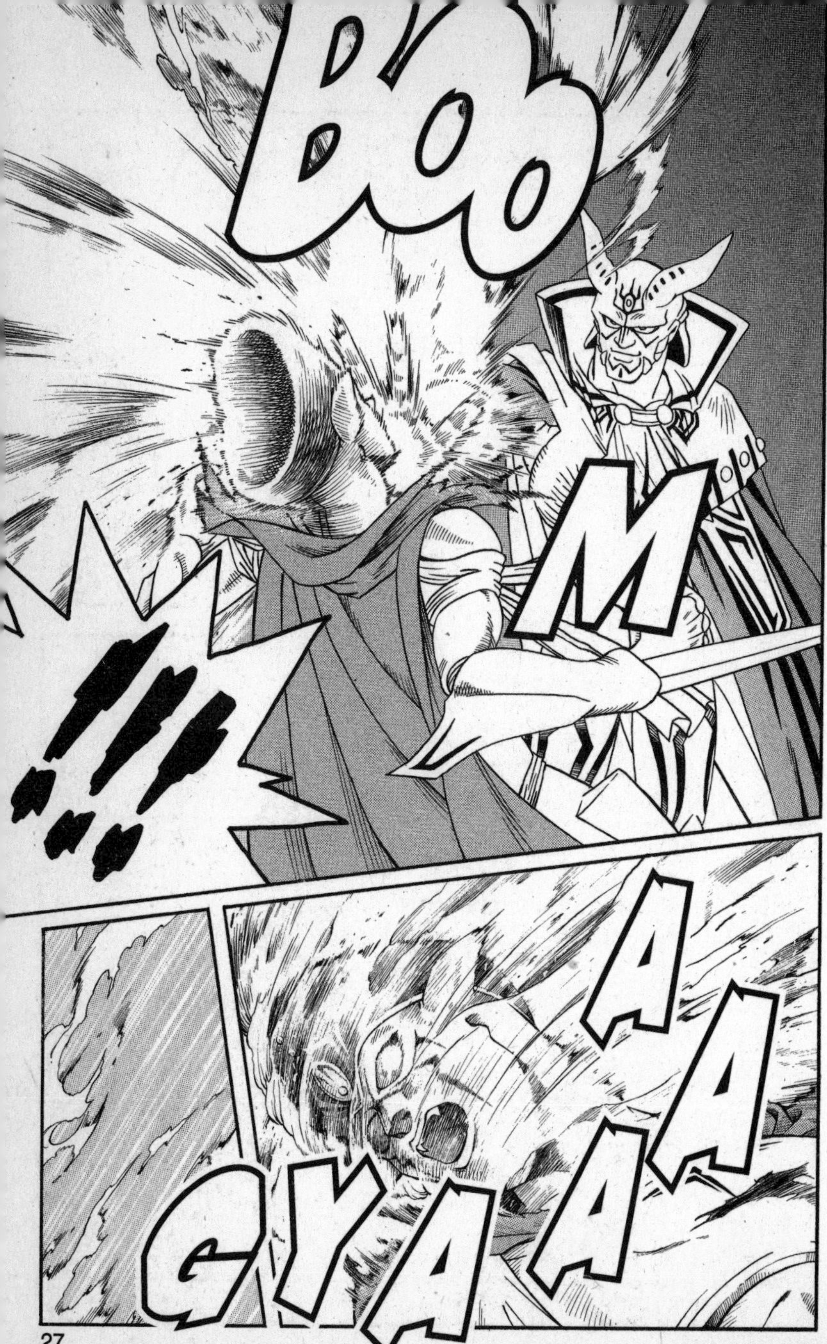
DOOO
M
!!!
GYAAAAA

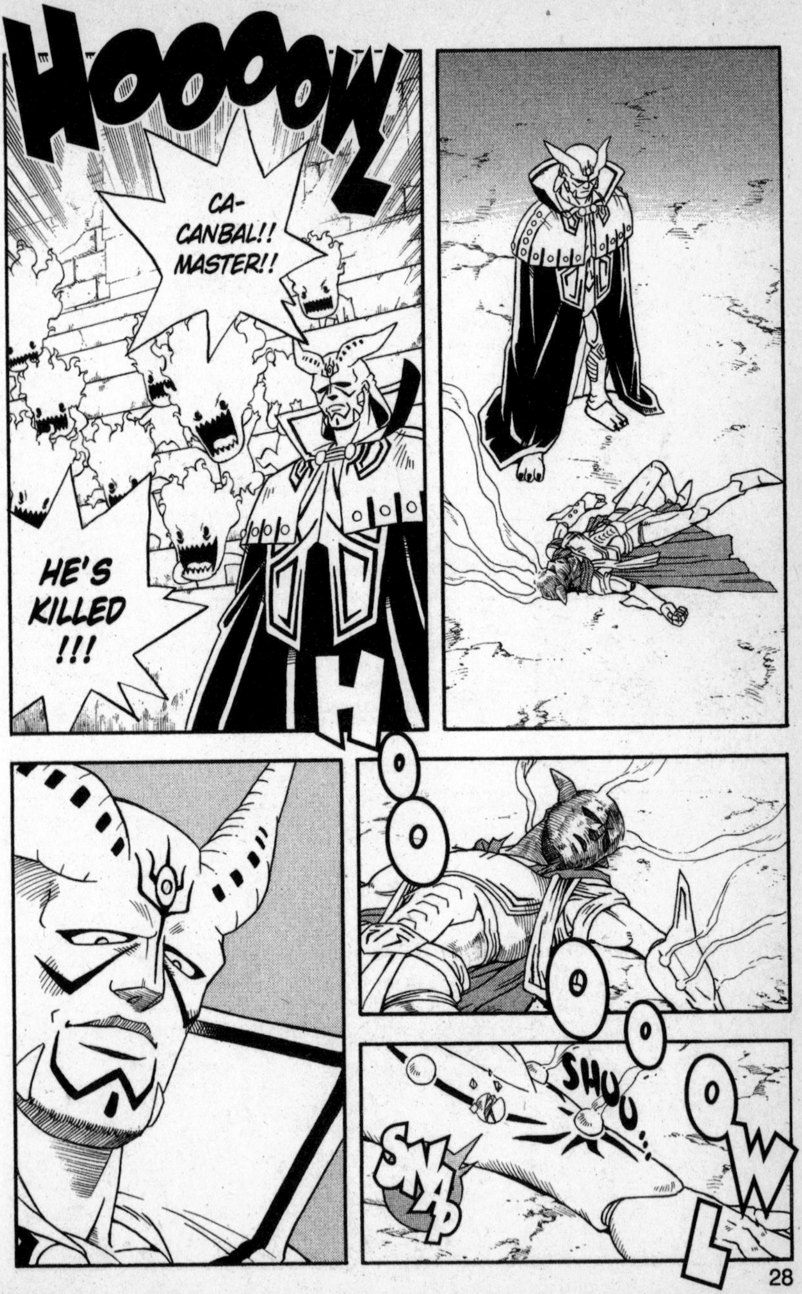
HOOOOWL
CA-
CANBAL!!
MASTER!!
HE'S
KILLED
!!!
HOOOOOWL
SHUU...
SNAP

READ THIS WAY

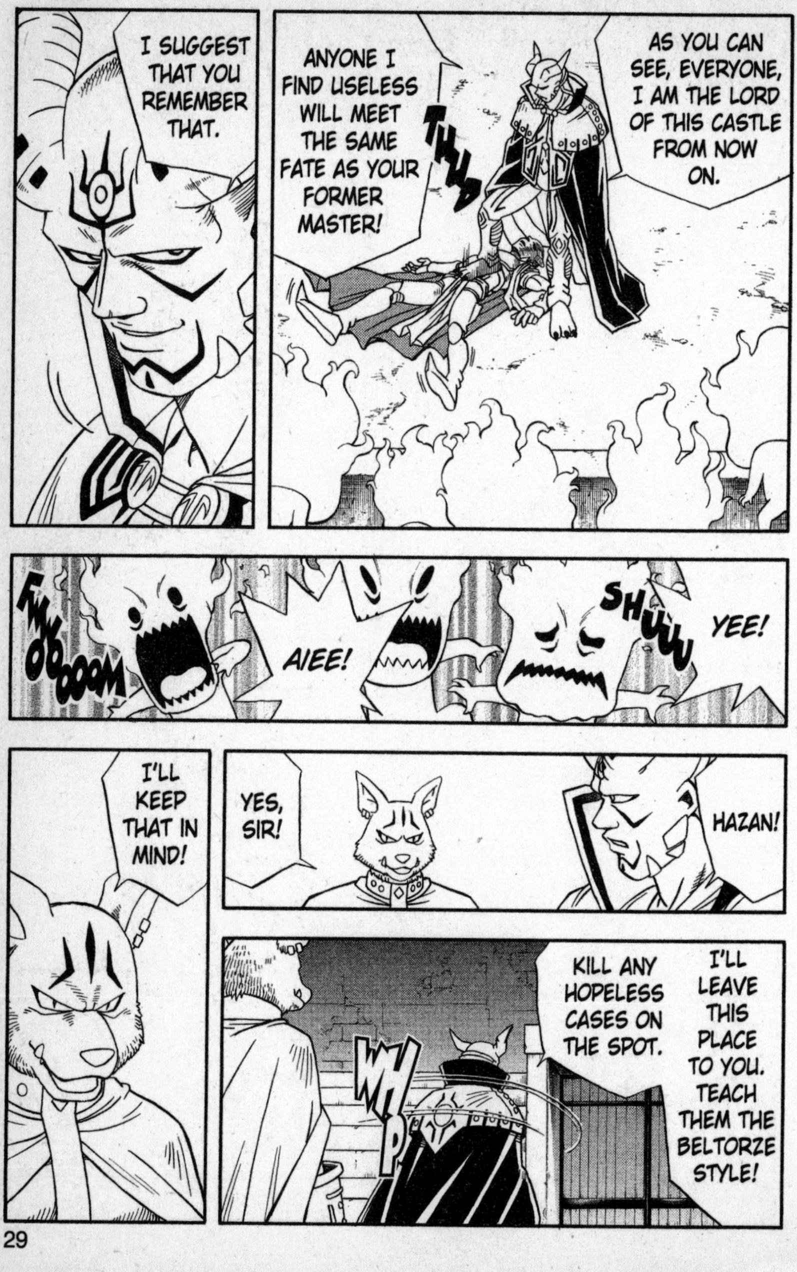

AS YOU CAN SEE, EVERYONE, I AM THE LORD OF THIS CASTLE FROM NOW ON.
ANYONE I FIND USELESS WILL MEET THE SAME FATE AS YOUR FORMER MASTER!
THUD
I SUGGEST THAT YOU REMEMBER THAT.
YEE!
SHUUU
AIEE!
FWOOOOOM
HAZAN!
YES, SIR!
I'LL LEAVE THIS PLACE TO YOU. TEACH THEM THE BELTORZE STYLE!
KILL ANY HOPELESS CASES ON THE SPOT.
WHIP
I'LL KEEP THAT IN MIND!

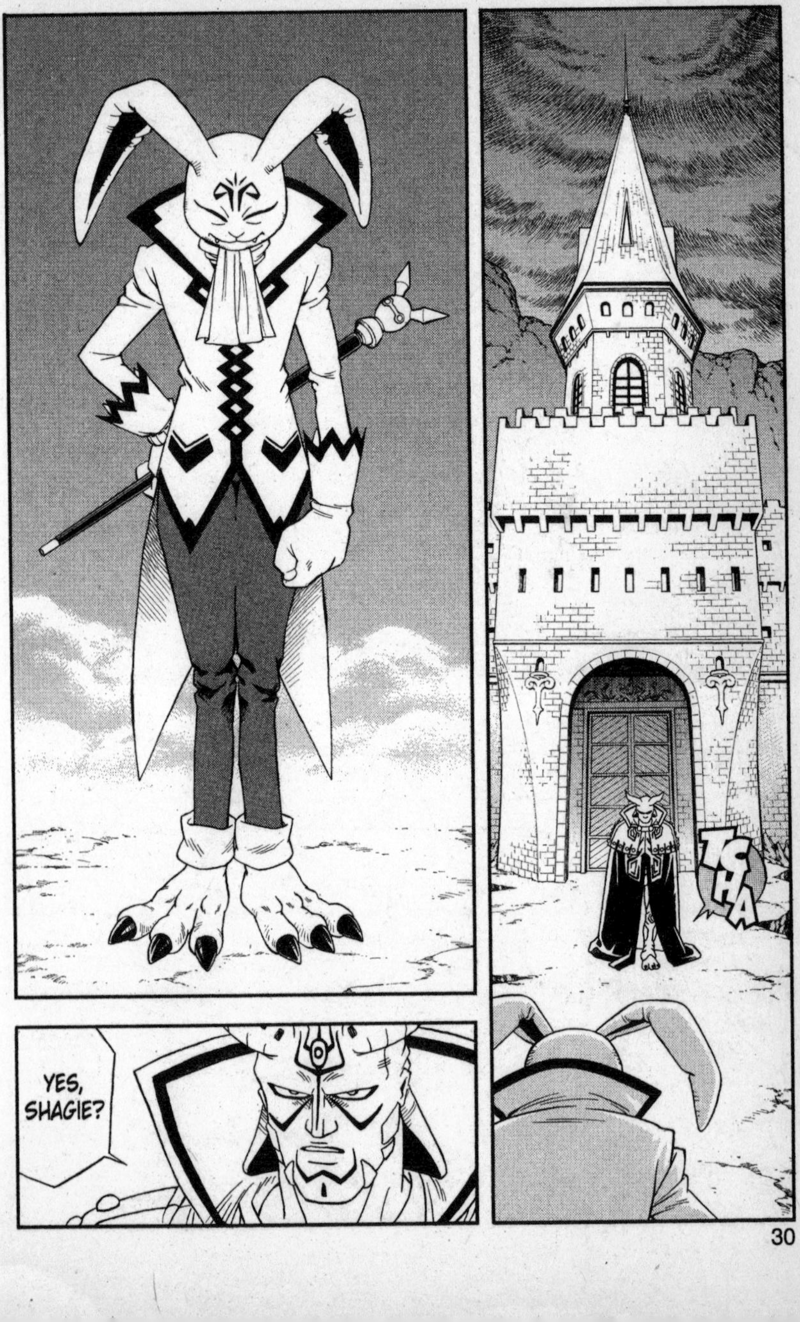
TCHA
YES, SHAGIE?

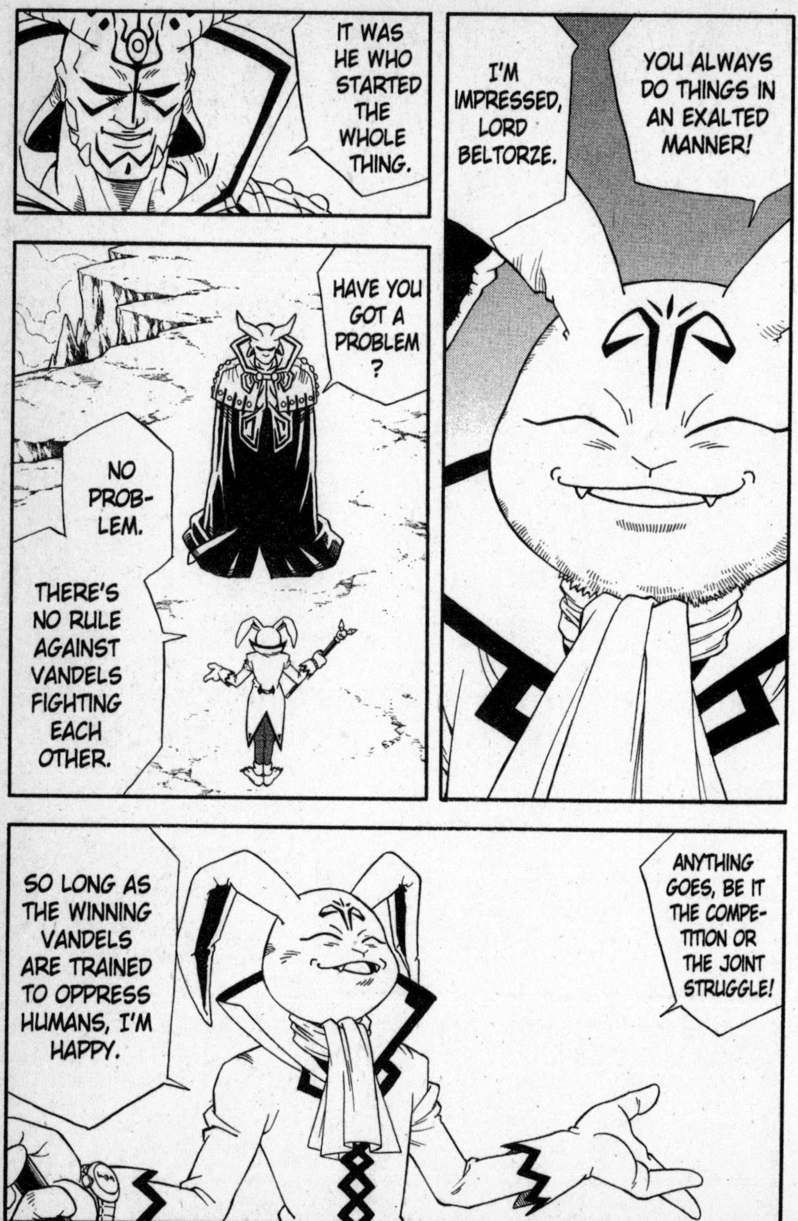
YOU ALWAYS DO THINGS IN AN EXALTED MANNER!
I'M IMPRESSED, LORD BELTORZE.
IT WAS HE WHO STARTED THE WHOLE THING.
HAVE YOU GOT A PROBLEM?
NO PROB-LEM.
THERE'S NO RULE AGAINST VANDELS FIGHTING EACH OTHER.
ANYTHING GOES, BE IT THE COMPE-TITION OR THE JOINT STRUGGLE!
SO LONG AS THE WINNING VANDELS ARE TRAINED TO OPPRESS HUMANS, I'M HAPPY.

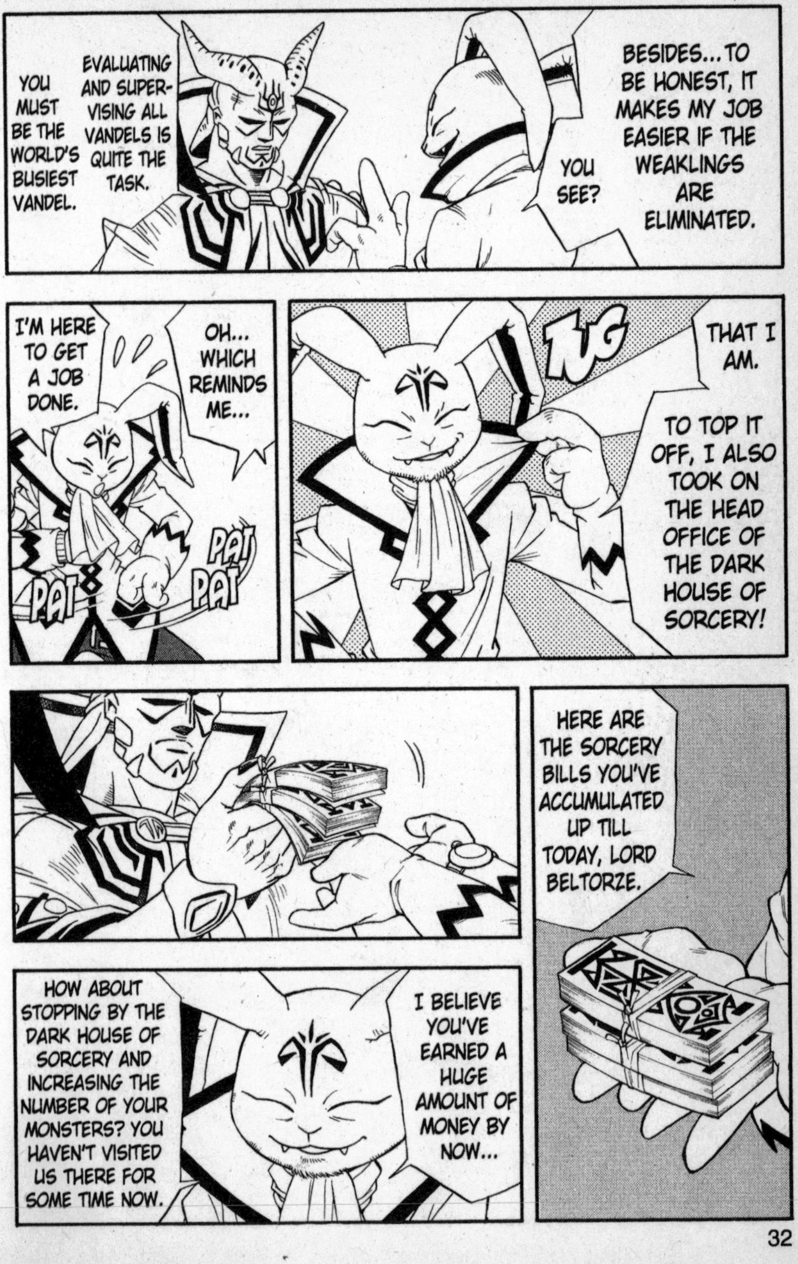
BESIDES... TO BE HONEST, IT MAKES MY JOB EASIER IF THE WEAKLINGS ARE ELIMINATED.
YOU SEE?
EVALUATING AND SUPER-VISING ALL VANDELS IS QUITE THE TASK.
YOU MUST BE THE WORLD'S BUSIEST VANDEL.
THAT I AM.
TUG
TO TOP IT OFF, I ALSO TOOK ON THE HEAD OFFICE OF THE DARK HOUSE OF SORCERY!
OH... WHICH REMINDS ME...
I'M HERE TO GET A JOB DONE.
PAT PAT
PAT
HERE ARE THE SORCERY BILLS YOU'VE ACCUMULATED UP TILL TODAY, LORD BELTORZE.
I BELIEVE YOU'VE EARNED A HUGE AMOUNT OF MONEY BY NOW...
HOW ABOUT STOPPING BY THE DARK HOUSE OF SORCERY AND INCREASING THE NUMBER OF YOUR MONSTERS? YOU HAVEN'T VISITED US THERE FOR SOME TIME NOW.

READ THIS WAY

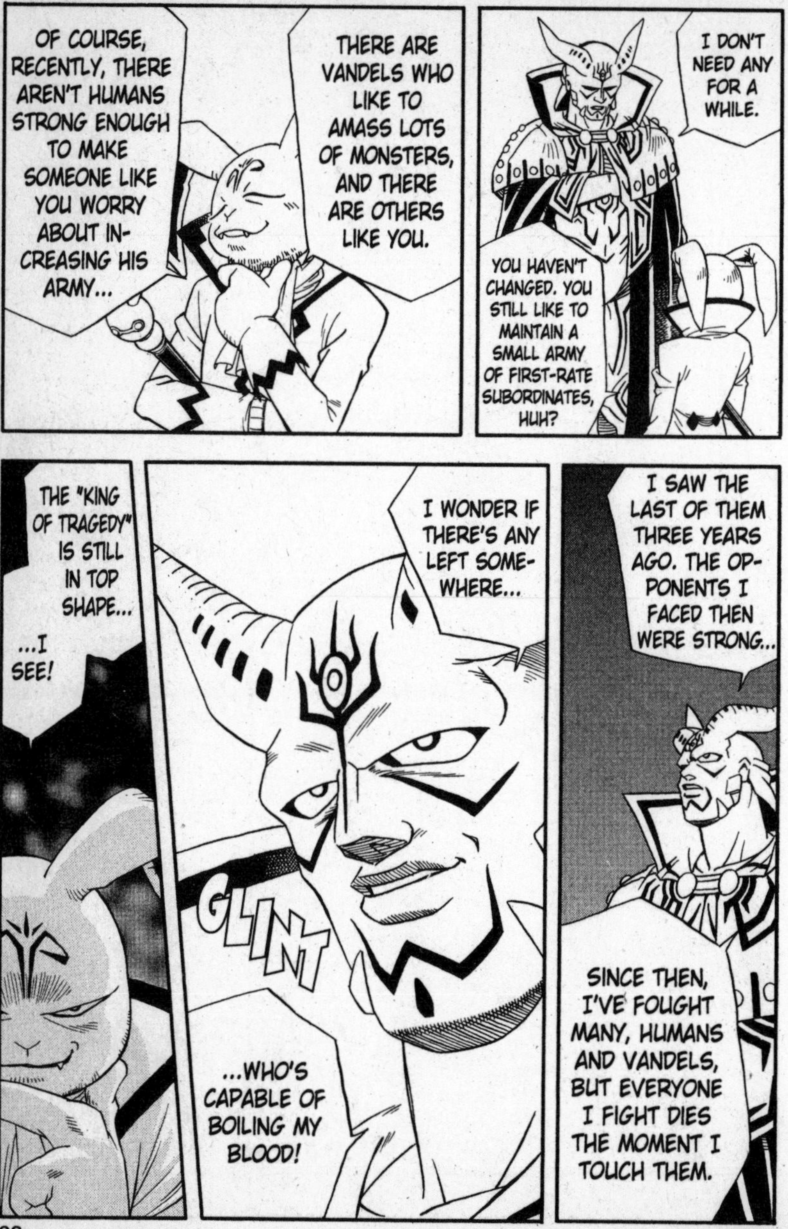
I DON'T NEED ANY FOR A WHILE.
YOU HAVEN'T CHANGED. YOU STILL LIKE TO MAINTAIN A SMALL ARMY OF FIRST-RATE SUBORDINATES, HUH?
THERE ARE VANDELS WHO LIKE TO AMASS LOTS OF MONSTERS, AND THERE ARE OTHERS LIKE YOU.
OF COURSE, RECENTLY, THERE AREN'T HUMANS STRONG ENOUGH TO MAKE SOMEONE LIKE YOU WORRY ABOUT IN-CREASING HIS ARMY...
I SAW THE LAST OF THEM THREE YEARS AGO. THE OP-PONENTS I FACED THEN WERE STRONG...
SINCE THEN, I'VE FOUGHT MANY, HUMANS AND VANDELS, BUT EVERYONE I FIGHT DIES THE MOMENT I TOUCH THEM.
I WONDER IF THERE'S ANY LEFT SOME-WHERE...
GLINT
...WHO'S CAPABLE OF BOILING MY BLOOD!
THE "KING OF TRAGEDY" IS STILL IN TOP SHAPE...
...I SEE!

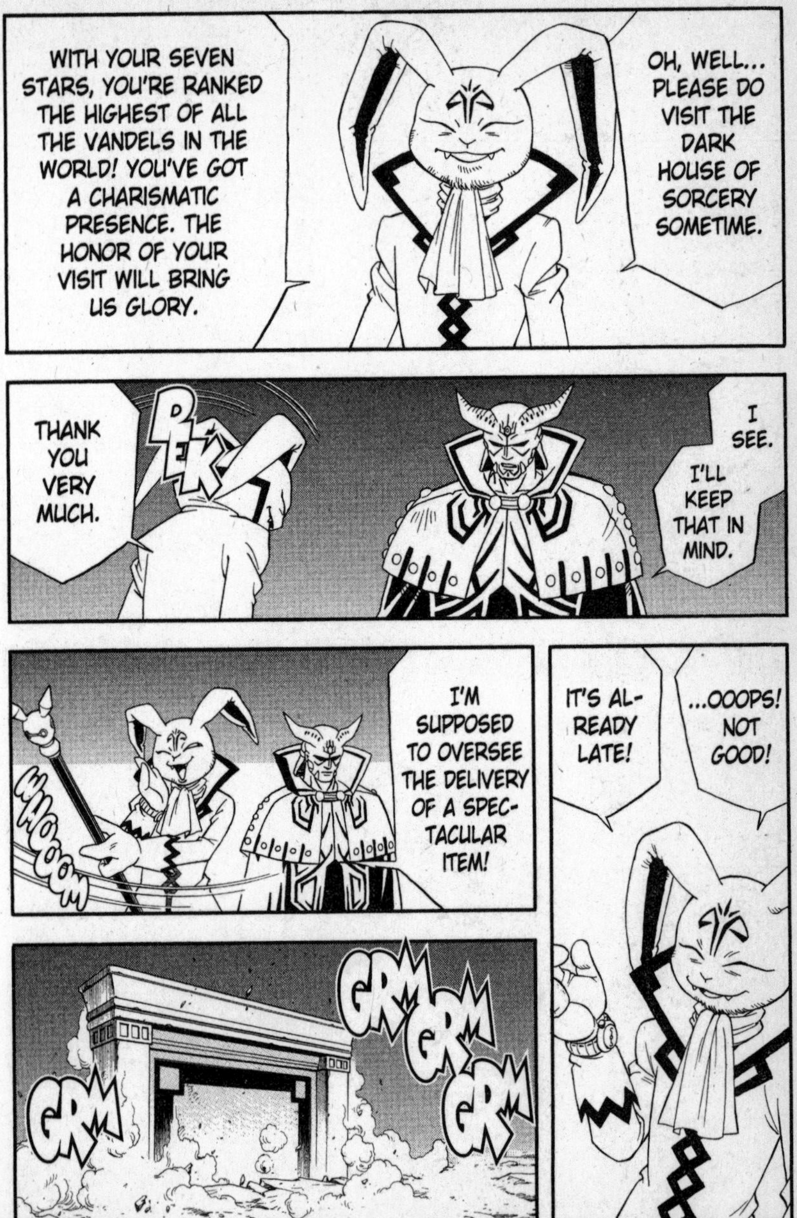
OH, WELL... PLEASE DO VISIT THE DARK HOUSE OF SORCERY SOMETIME.
WITH YOUR SEVEN STARS, YOU'RE RANKED THE HIGHEST OF ALL THE VANDELS IN THE WORLD! YOU'VE GOT A CHARISMATIC PRESENCE. THE HONOR OF YOUR VISIT WILL BRING US GLORY.
I SEE. I'LL KEEP THAT IN MIND.
PEK
THANK YOU VERY MUCH.
...OOOPS! NOT GOOD!
IT'S AL-READY LATE!
I'M SUPPOSED TO OVERSEE THE DELIVERY OF A SPEC-TACULAR ITEM!
WHOOOOM
GRM
GRM
GRM
GRM
GRM

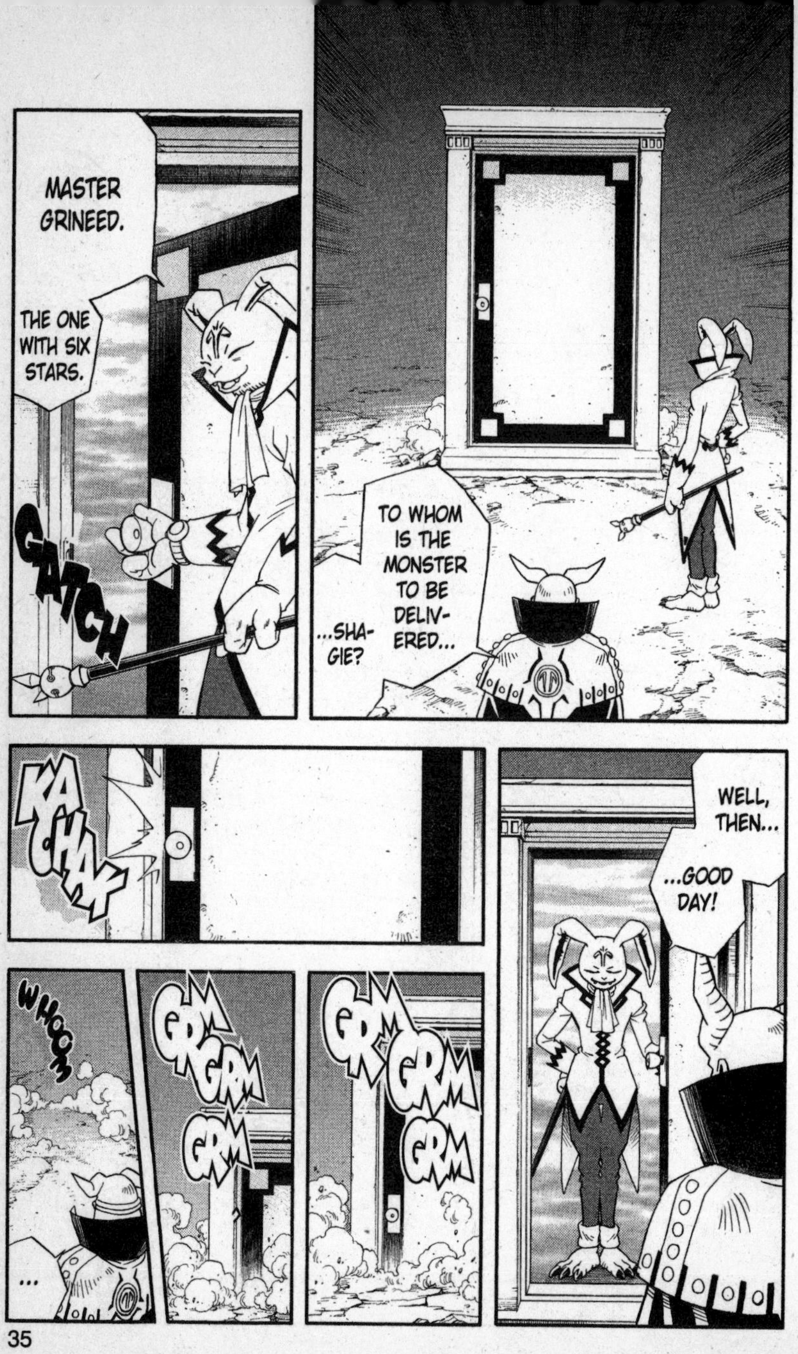
TO WHOM IS THE MONSTER TO BE DELIVERED...
...SHAGIE?
MASTER GRINEED.
THE ONE WITH SIX STARS.
GATCH
WELL, THEN...
...GOOD DAY!
KA CHAK
GRM GRM GRM GRM
GRM GRM GRM
WHOOM
...

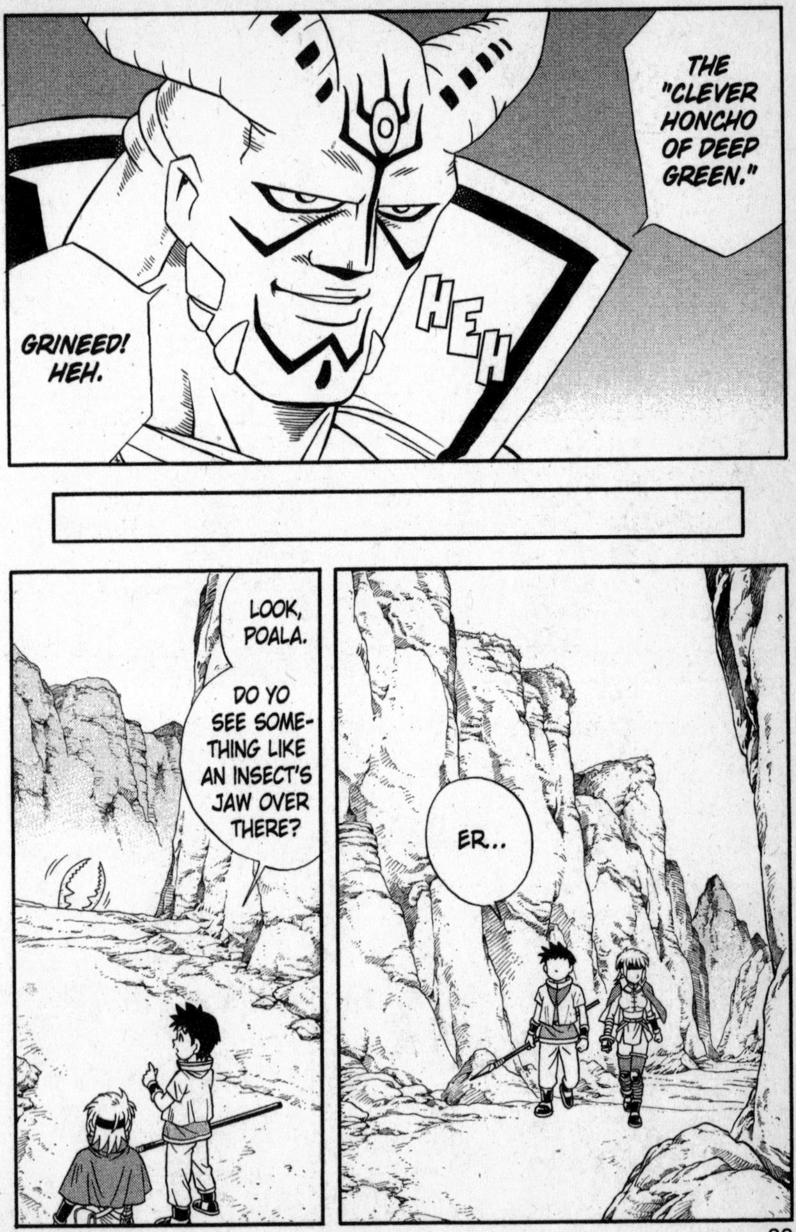
THE "CLEVER HONCHO OF DEEP GREEN."
HEH HEH
GRINEED! HEH.
ER..
LOOK, POALA.
DO YO SEE SOME-THING LIKE AN INSECT'S JAW OVER THERE?

READ THIS WAY

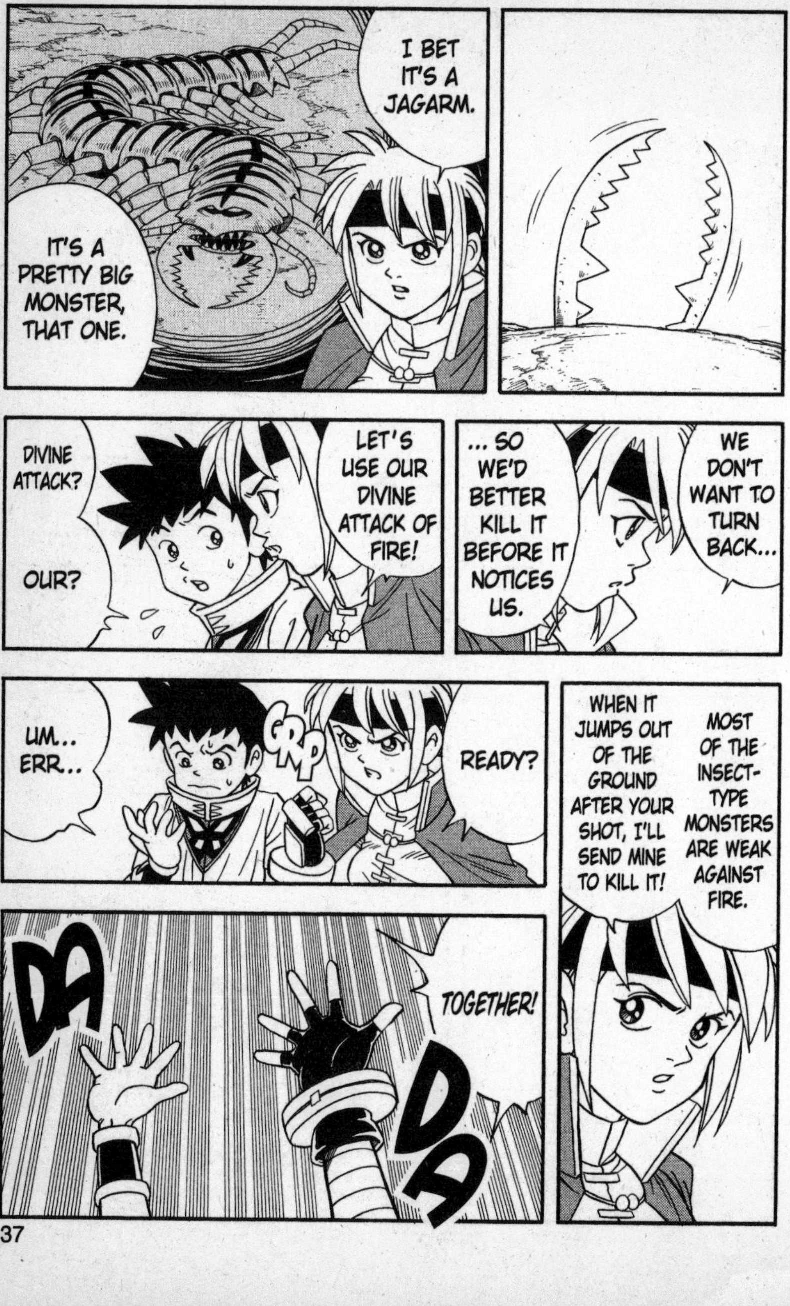

I BET IT'S A JAGARM.
IT'S A PRETTY BIG MONSTER, THAT ONE.
WE DON'T WANT TO TURN BACK...
... SO WE'D BETTER KILL IT BEFORE IT NOTICES US.
LET'S USE OUR DIVINE ATTACK OF FIRE!
DIVINE ATTACK?
OUR?
MOST OF THE INSECT-TYPE MONSTERS ARE WEAK AGAINST FIRE.
WHEN IT JUMPS OUT OF THE GROUND AFTER YOUR SHOT, I'LL SEND MINE TO KILL IT!
READY?
GRP
UM... ERR...
TOGETHER!
DA
DA

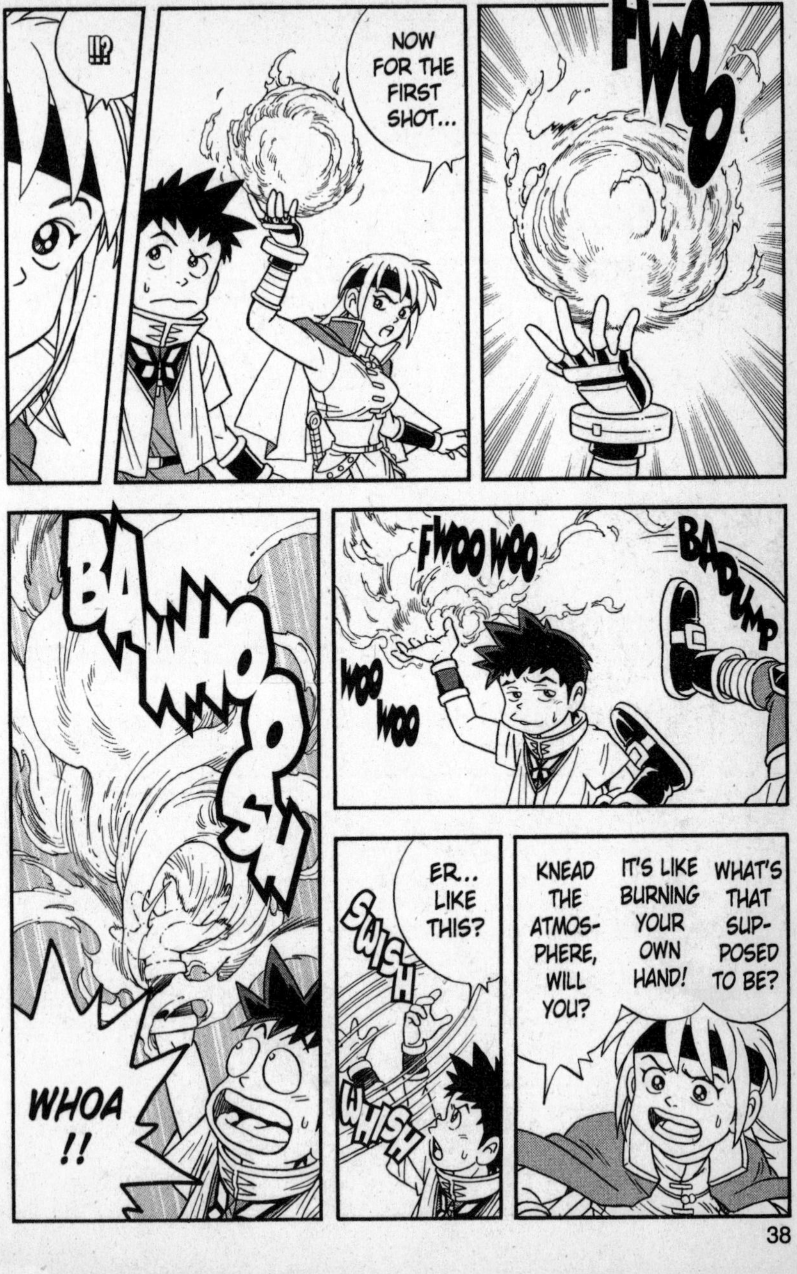
FWOO
NOW FOR THE FIRST SHOT...
!!?
FWOO WOO
BADUMP
WOO WOO
WHAT'S THAT SUP-POSED TO BE?
IT'S LIKE BURNING YOUR OWN HAND!
KNEAD THE ATMOS-PHERE, WILL YOU?
ER... LIKE THIS?
SWISH
WHISH
BAWHOOSH
WHOA !!

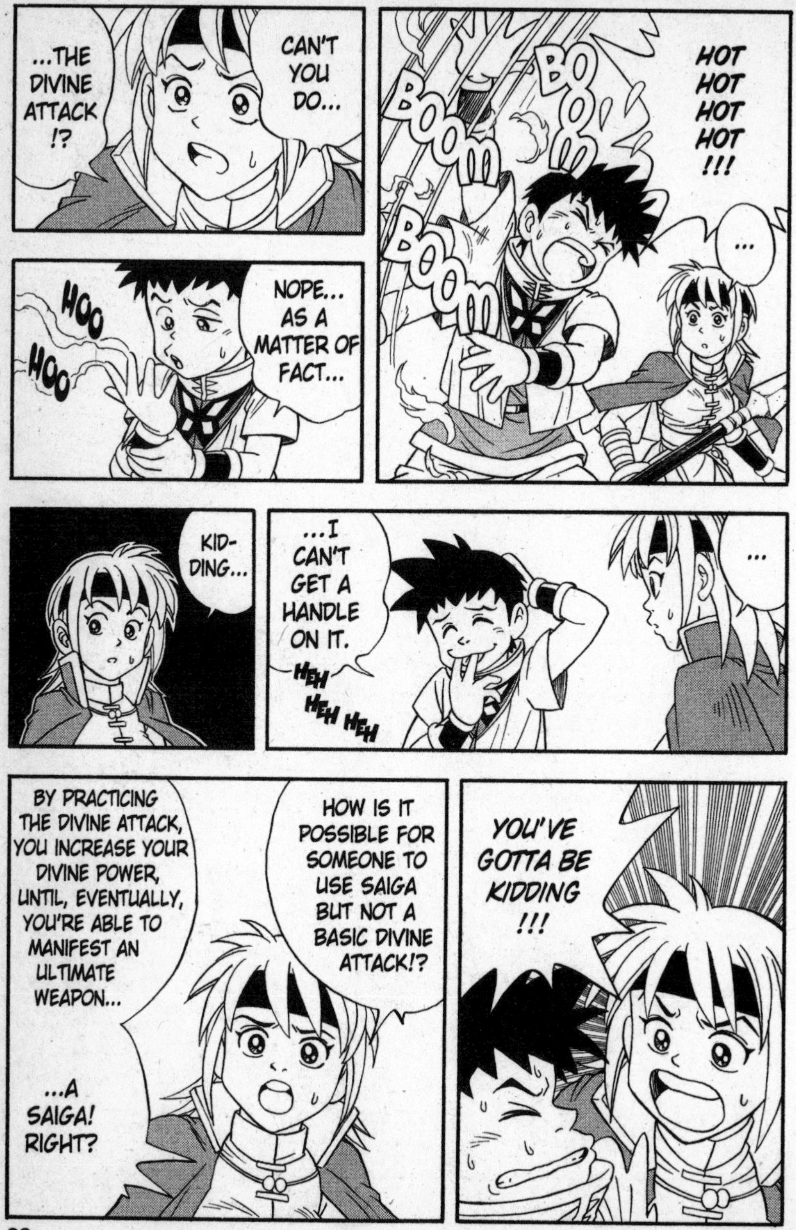
HOT HOT HOT HOT !!!
BOOM
...
BOOM
BOOM
CAN'T YOU DO...
...THE DIVINE ATTACK !?
NOPE... AS A MATTER OF FACT...
HOO
HOO
...
...I CAN'T GET A HANDLE ON IT.
HEH HEH HEH
KID-DING...
YOU'VE GOTTA BE KIDDING !!!
HOW IS IT POSSIBLE FOR SOMEONE TO USE SAIGA BUT NOT A BASIC DIVINE ATTACK!?
BY PRACTICING THE DIVINE ATTACK, YOU INCREASE YOUR DIVINE POWER, UNTIL, EVENTUALLY, YOU'RE ABLE TO MANIFEST AN ULTIMATE WEAPON...
...A SAIGA! RIGHT?

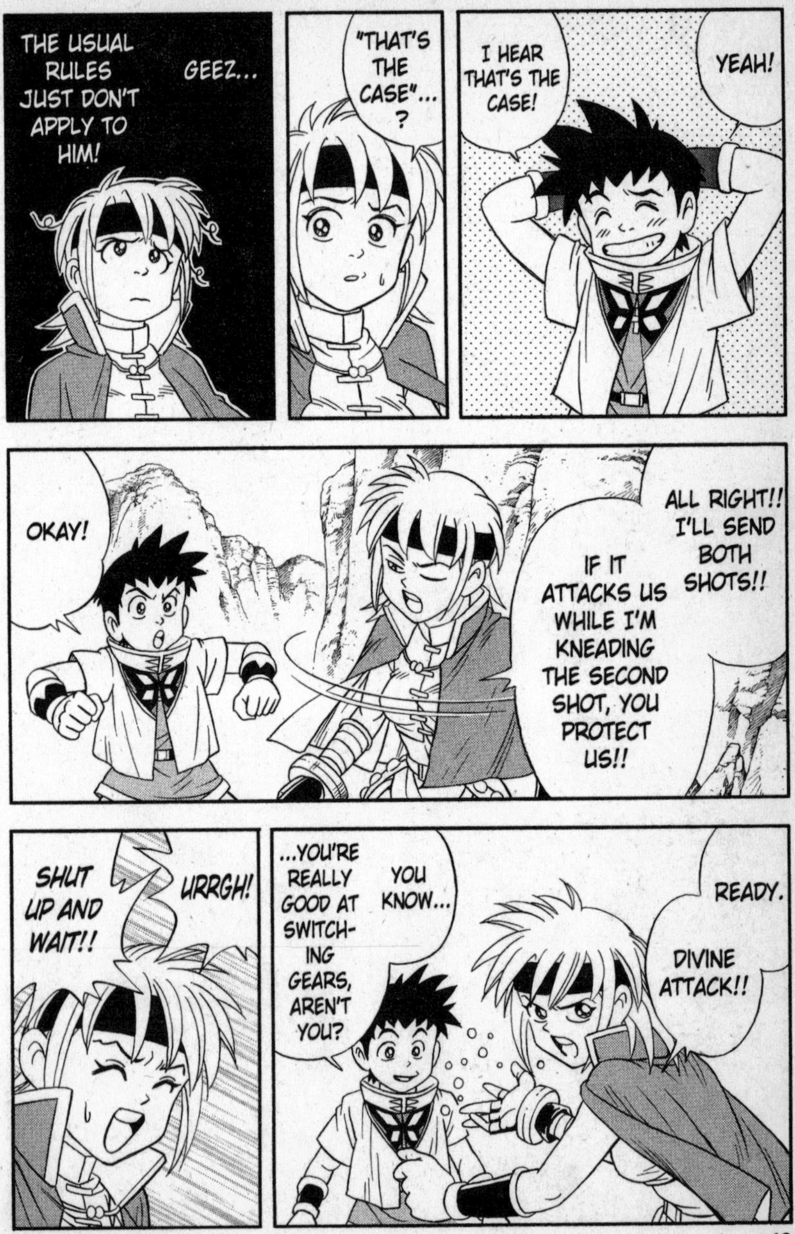
YEAH!
I HEAR THAT'S THE CASE!
"THAT'S THE CASE"... ?
GEEZ...
THE USUAL RULES JUST DON'T APPLY TO HIM!
ALL RIGHT!! I'LL SEND BOTH SHOTS!!
IF IT ATTACKS US WHILE I'M KNEADING THE SECOND SHOT, YOU PROTECT US!!
OKAY!
READY.
DIVINE ATTACK!!
YOU KNOW...
...YOU'RE REALLY GOOD AT SWITCH-ING GEARS, AREN'T YOU?
URRGH!
SHUT UP AND WAIT!!

READ THIS WAY

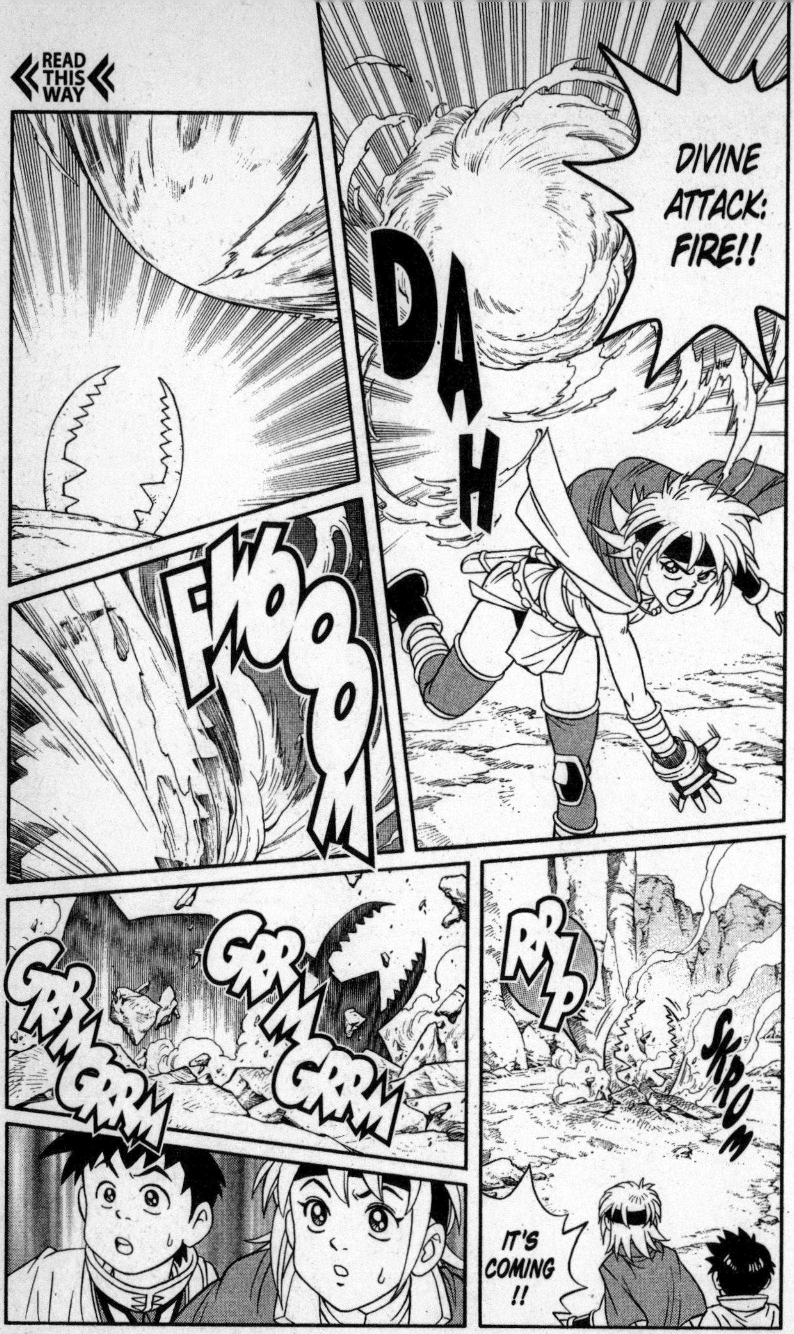

DIVINE ATTACK: FIRE!!
DAH
FWOOOOM
RRRIP
SKRUM
IT'S COMING !!
GRRM GRRM
GRRM GRRM

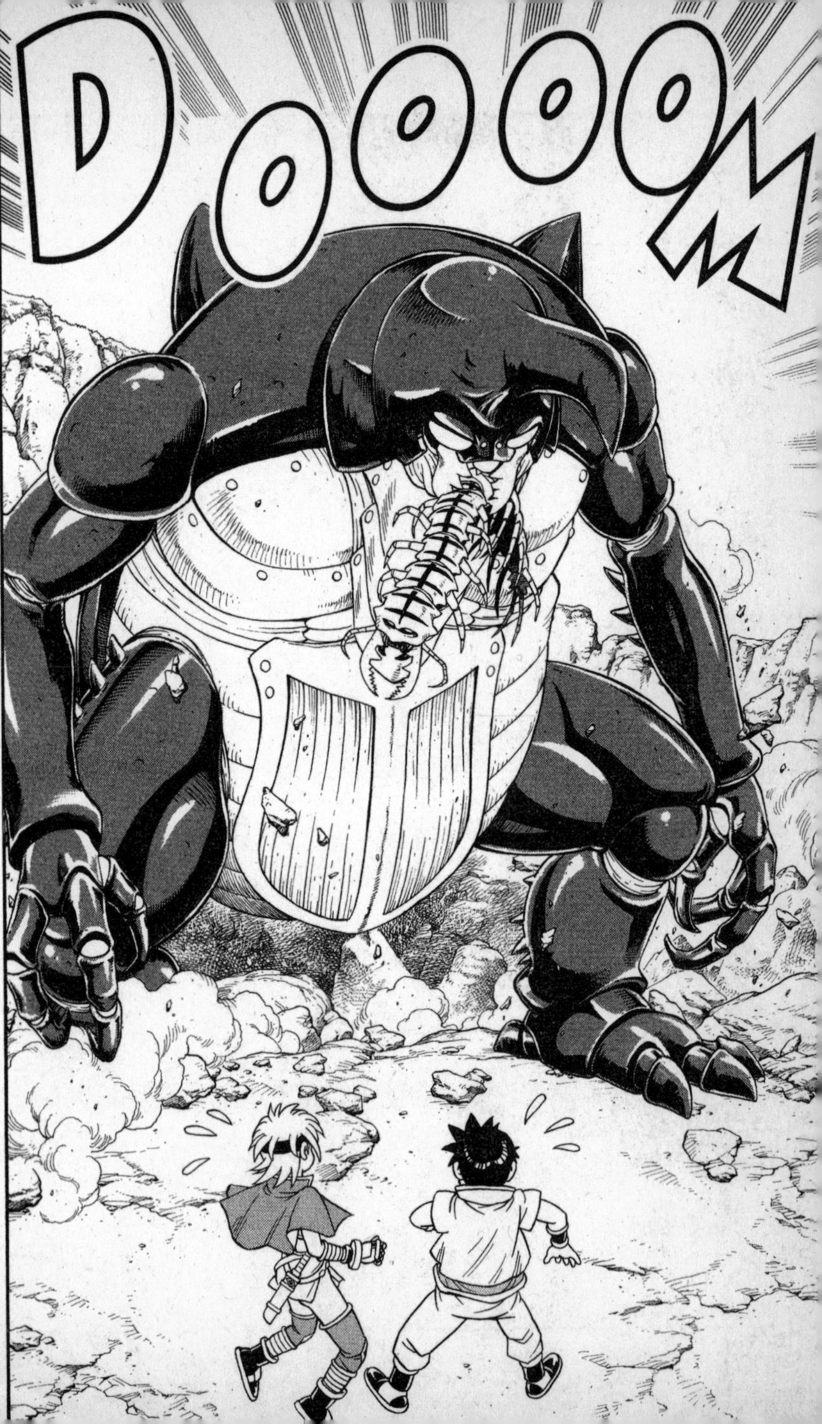
DOOOOOM

READ THIS WAY

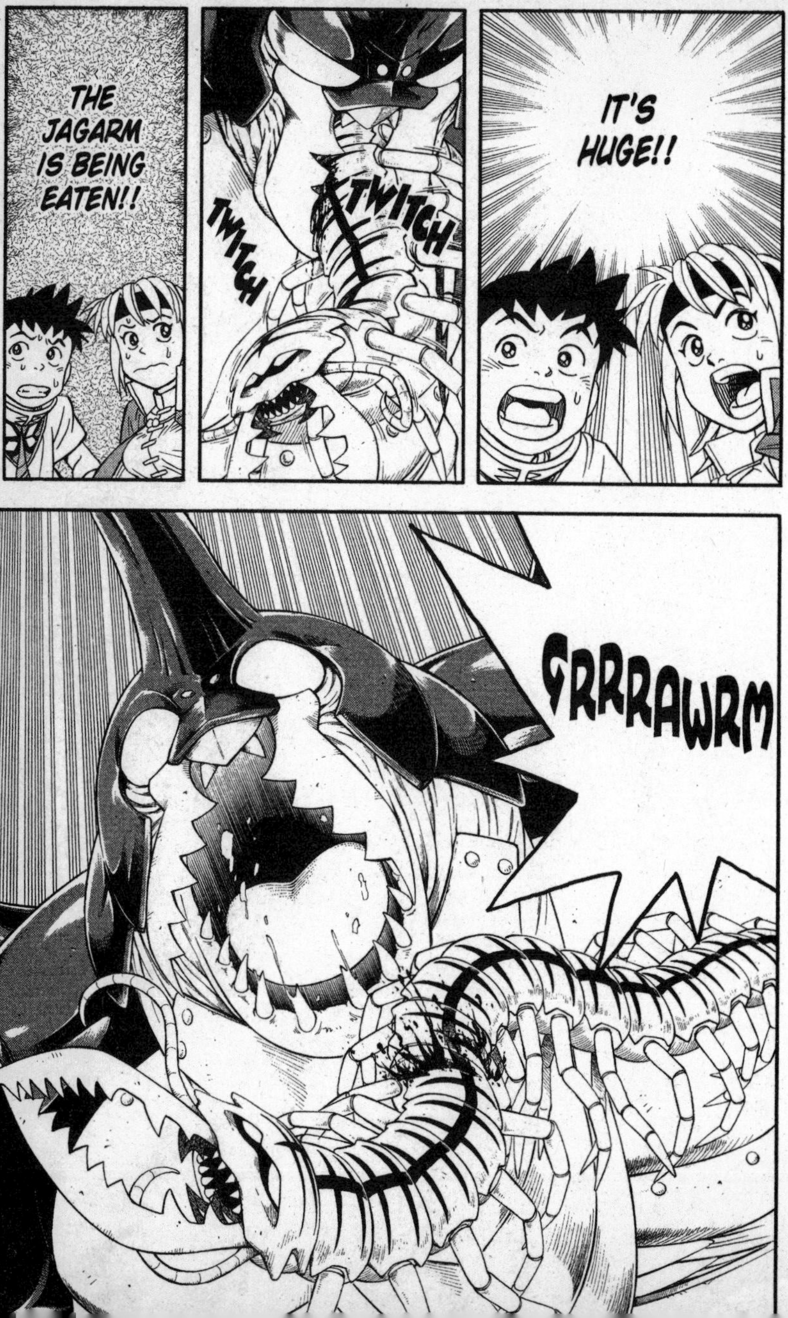
IT'S HUGE!!
TWITCH
TWITCH
THE JAGARM IS BEING EATEN!!
GRRRAWRM

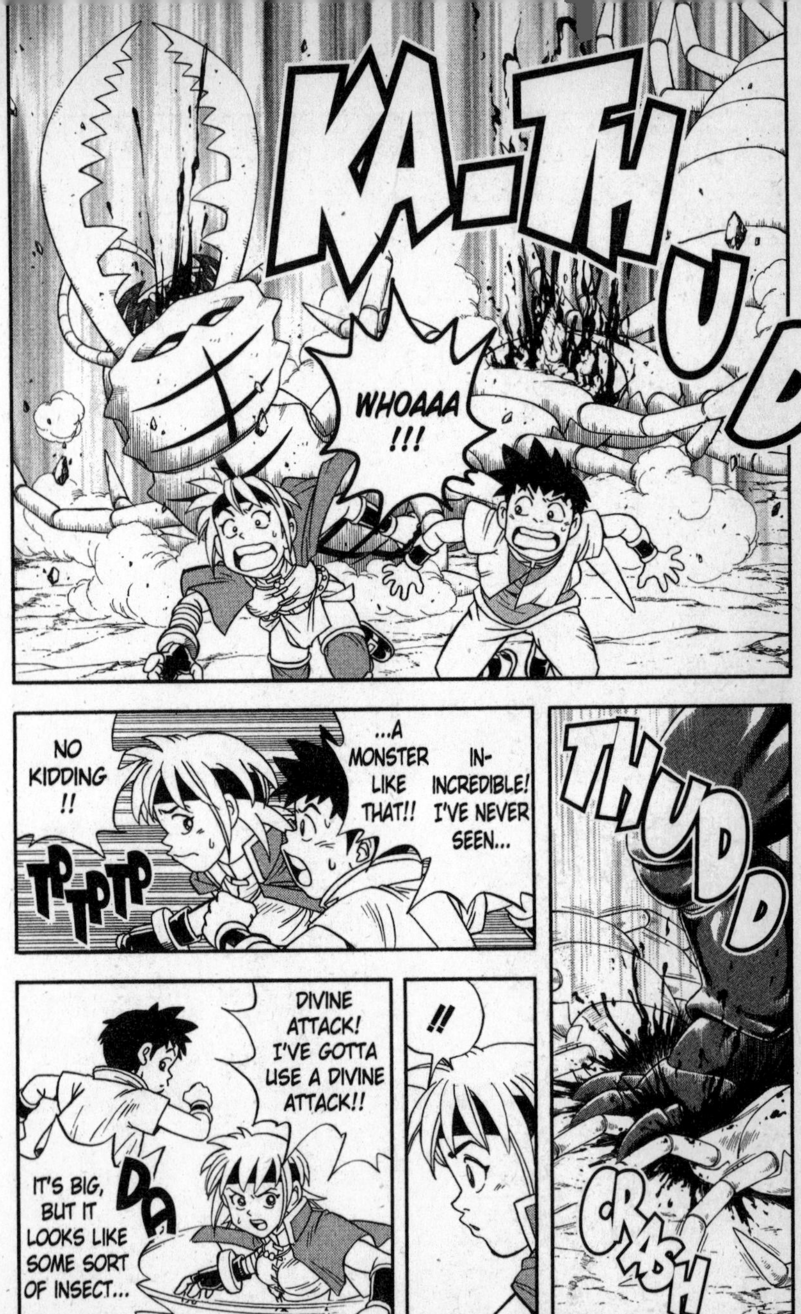
KA-THUD
WHOAAA!!!
THUDD
CRASH
IN- INCREDIBLE! I'VE NEVER SEEN...
...A MONSTER LIKE THAT!!
NO KIDDING!!
TPTPTP
!!
DIVINE ATTACK! I'VE GOTTA USE A DIVINE ATTACK!!
DA
IT'S BIG, BUT IT LOOKS LIKE SOME SORT OF INSECT...

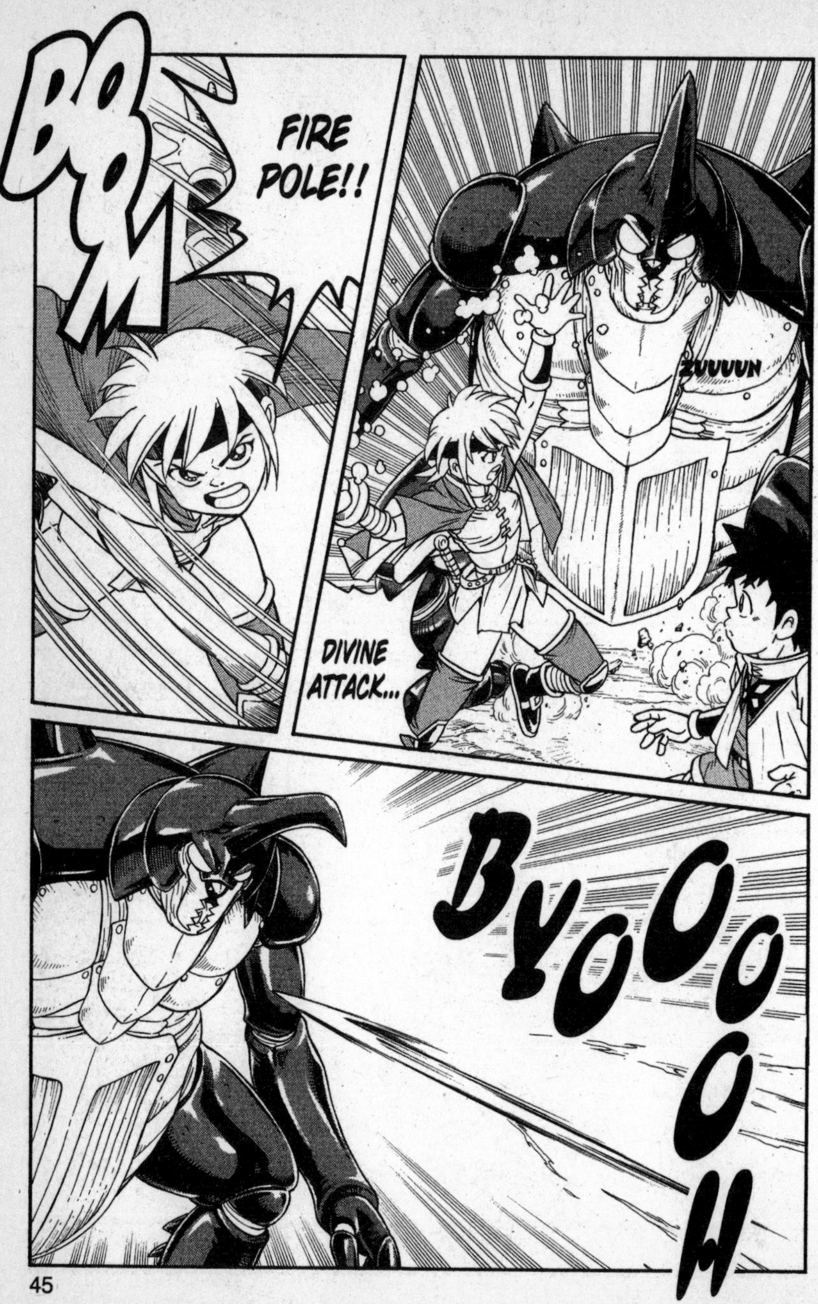
ZUUUUN
DIVINE ATTACK...
FIRE POLE!!
BOOM
BYOOOOOOOH

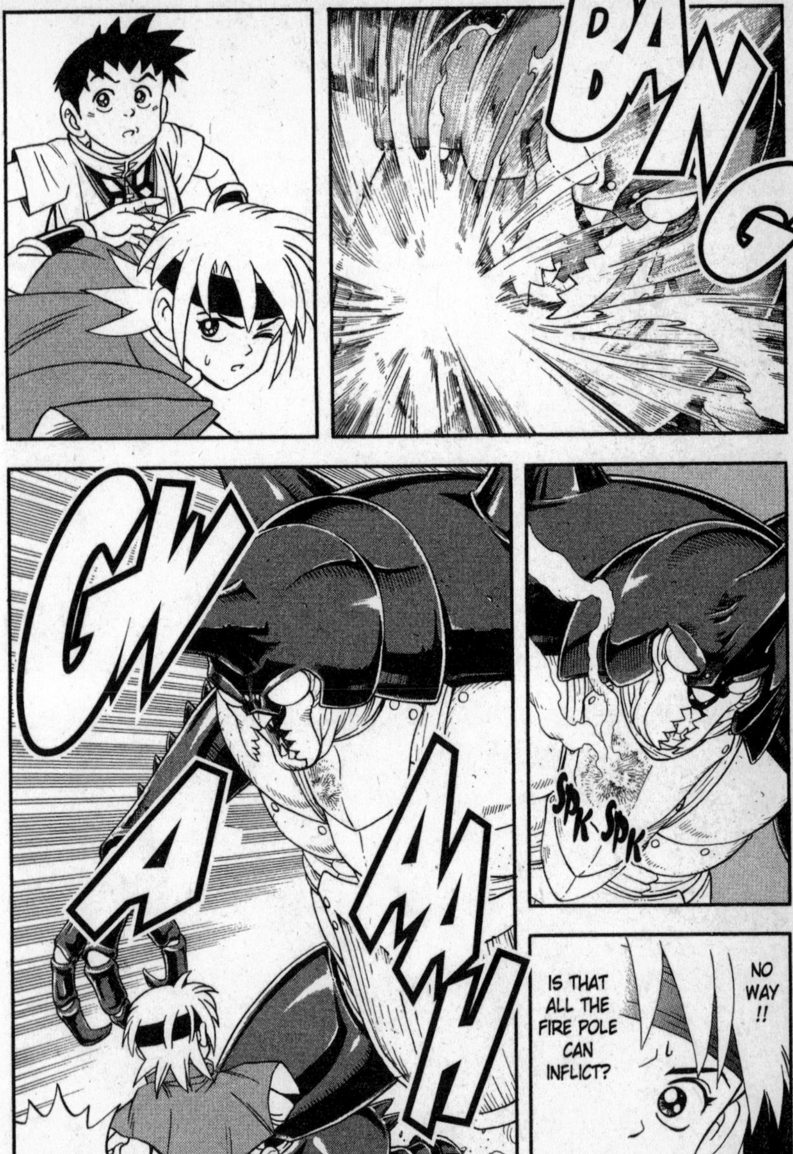
BANG
SPK SPK
NO WAY !!
IS THAT ALL THE FIRE POLE CAN INFLICT?
GWAAAH
!!

«READ THIS WAY«

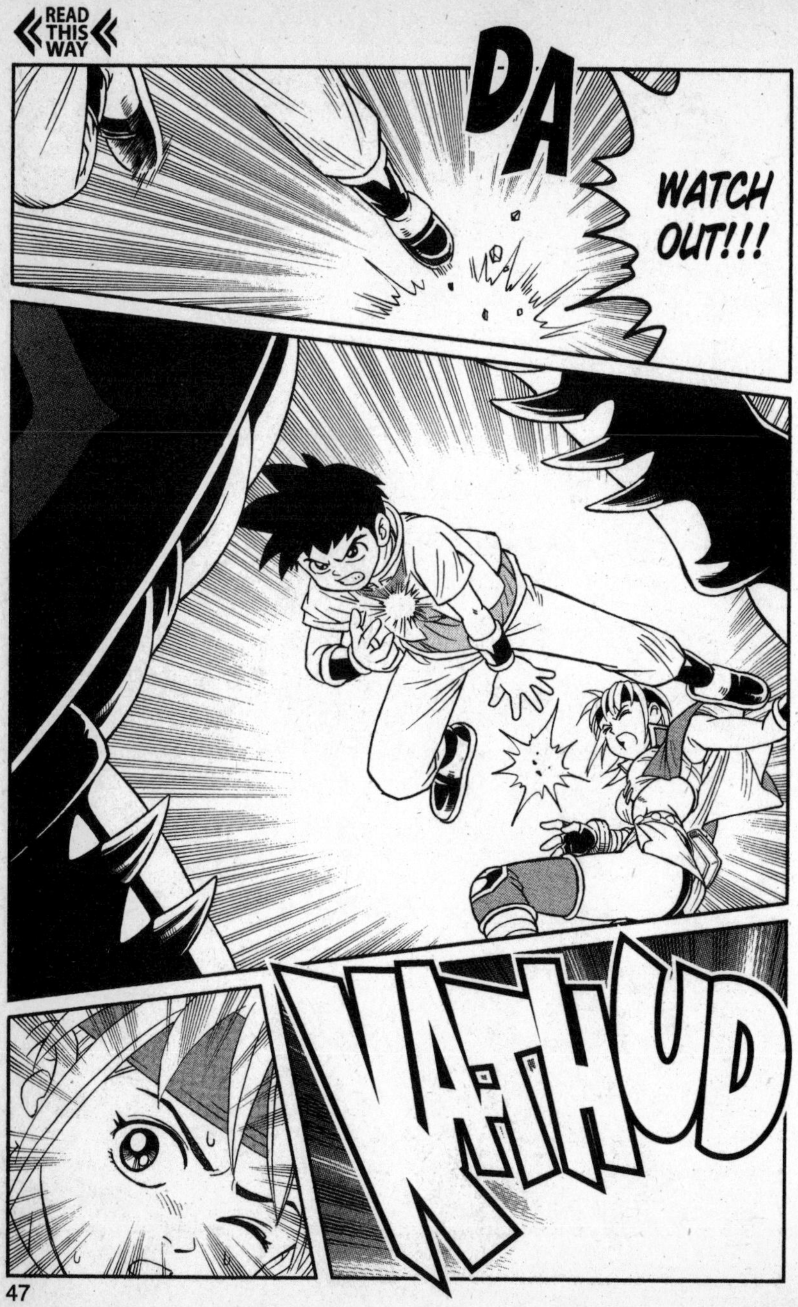
DA
WATCH OUT!!!
KA-THUD

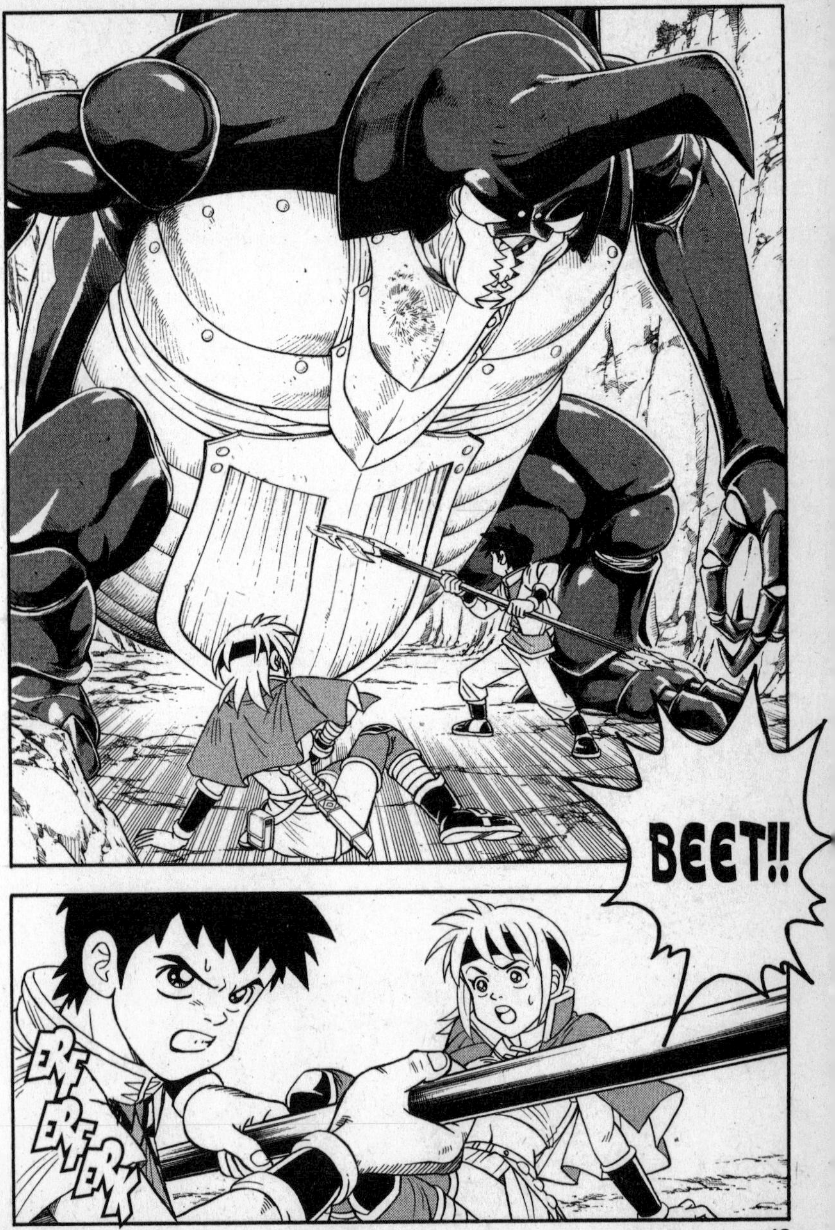
BEET!!
ERF ERF ERK

READ THIS WAY

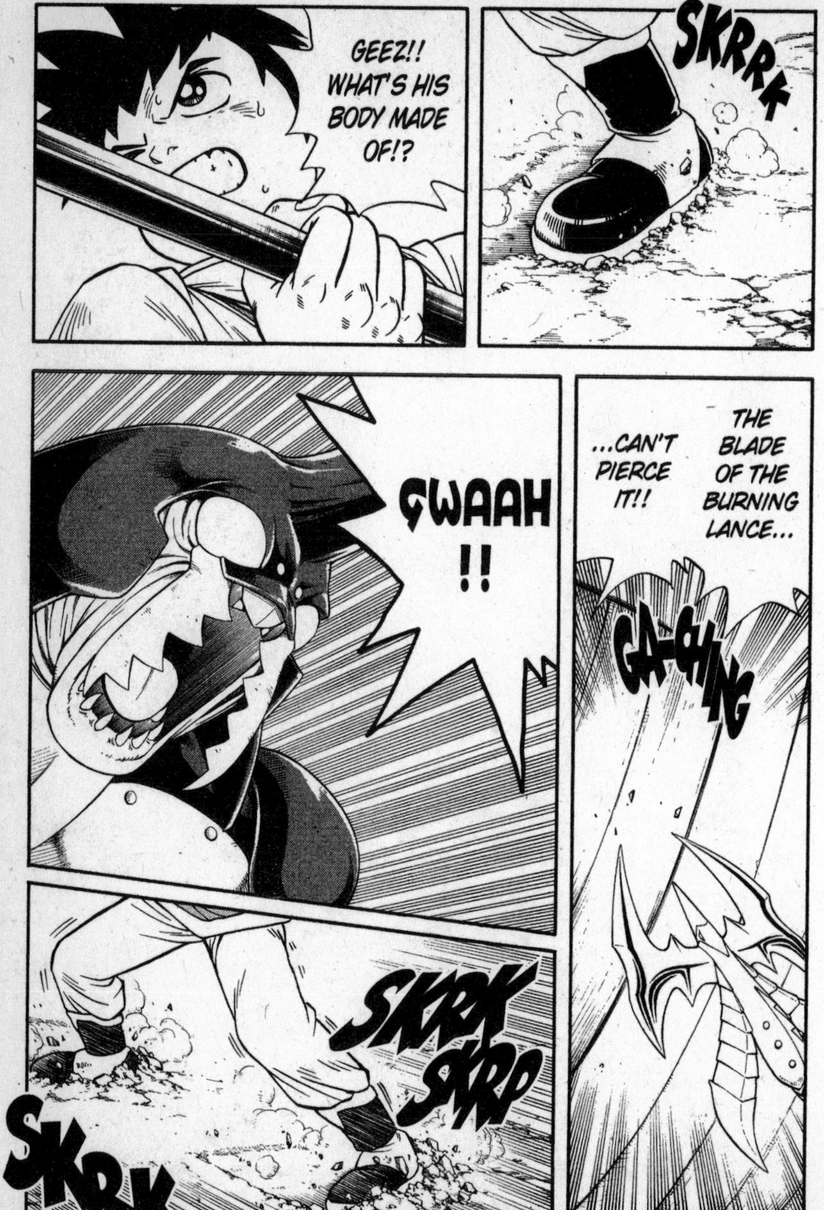
SKRRK
GEEZ!! WHAT'S HIS BODY MADE OF!?
THE BLADE OF THE BURNING LANCE...
...CAN'T PIERCE IT!!
GA-CHING
GWAAH!!
SKRK SKRP
SKRK

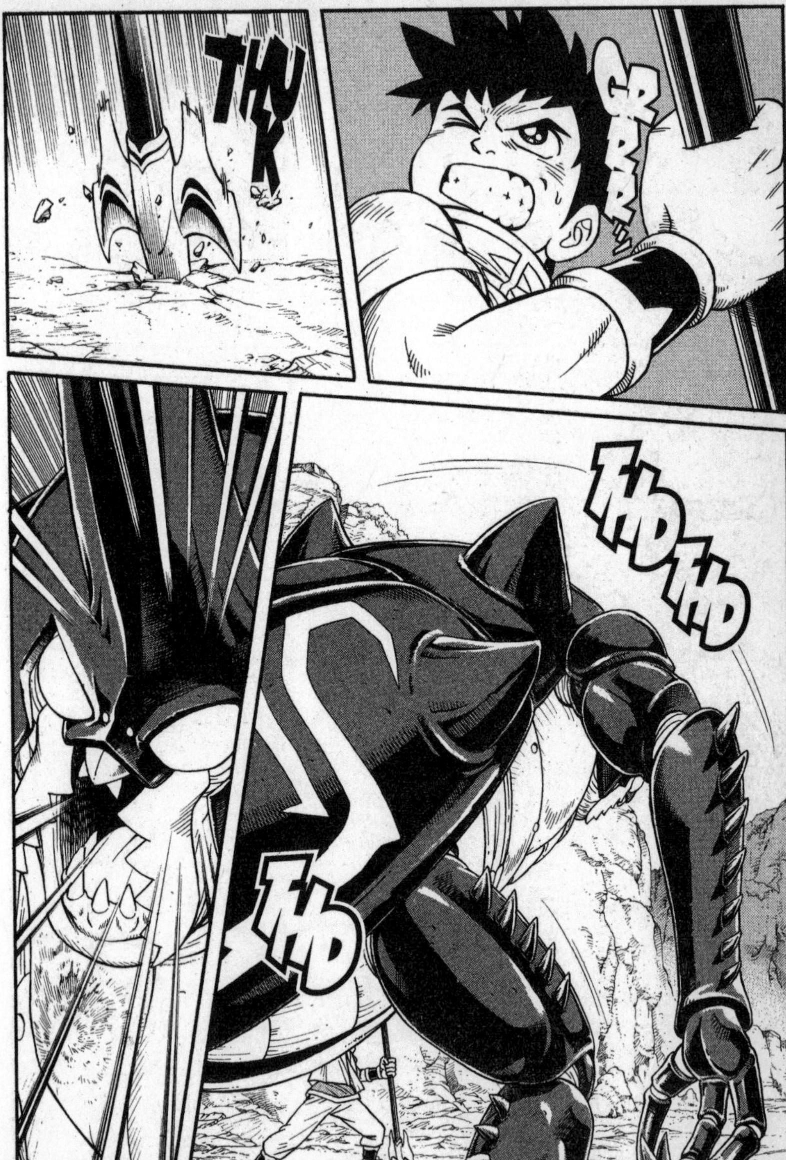
GRRR...
THUK
THD THD
THD

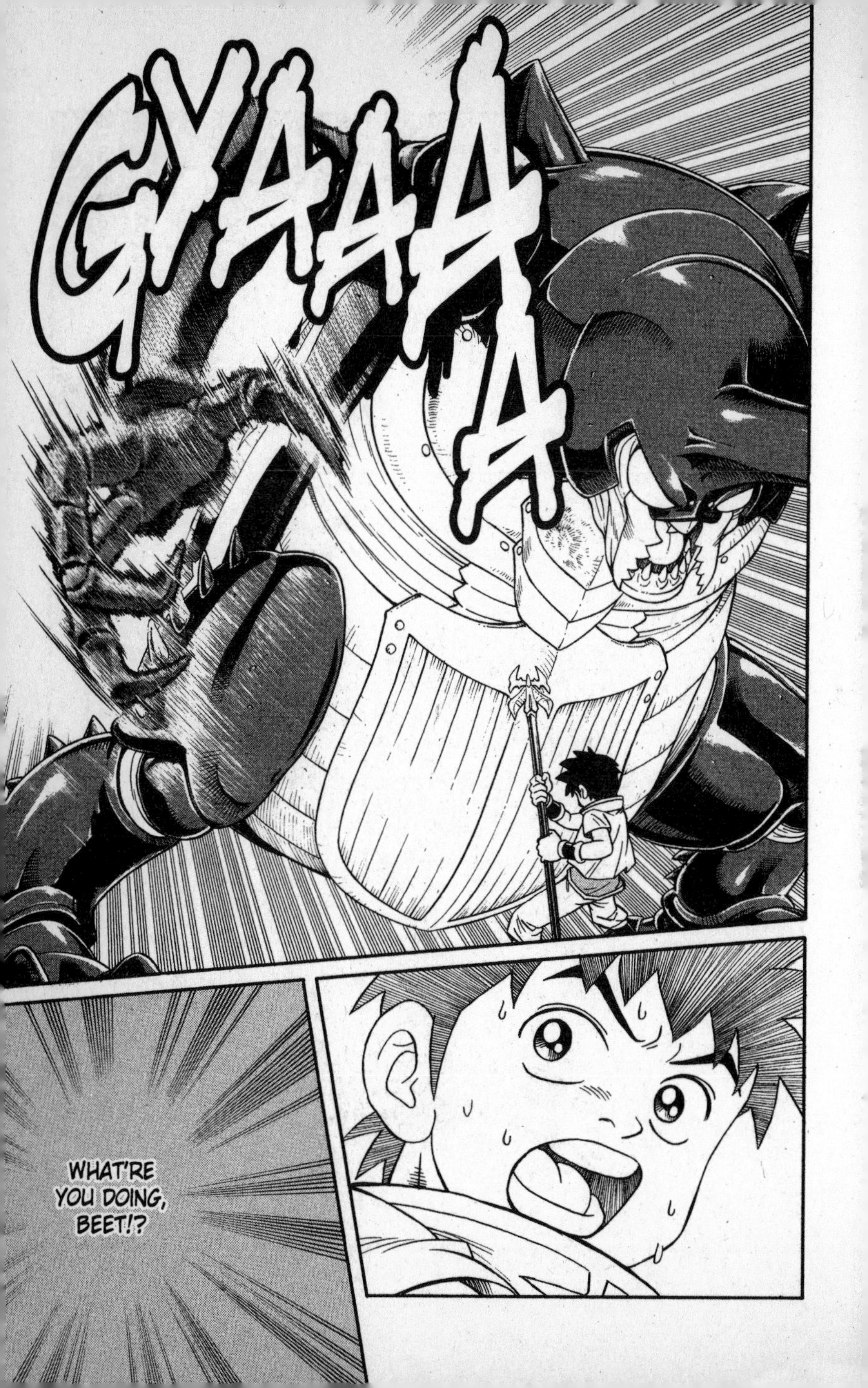
GYAAAA
WHAT'RE YOU DOING, BEET!?

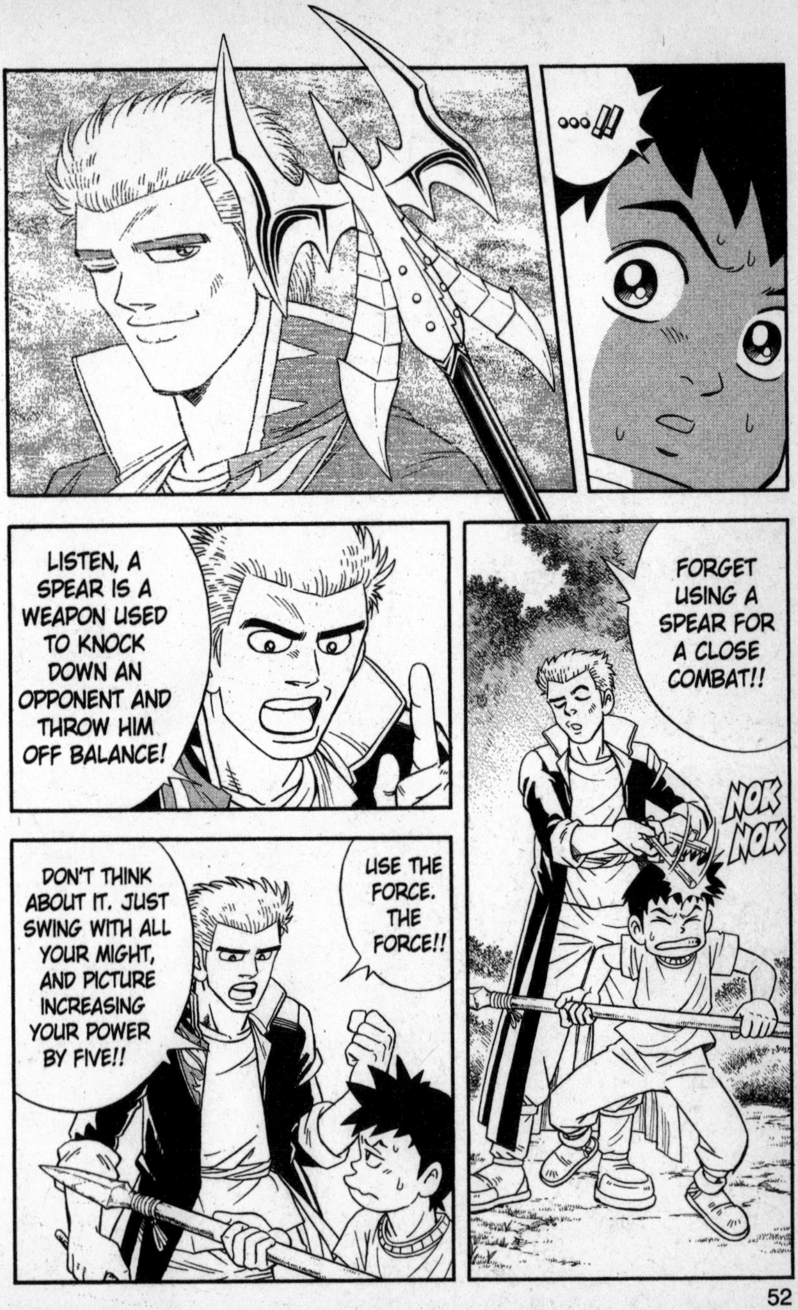

...!!
FORGET USING A SPEAR FOR A CLOSE COMBAT!!
NOK NOK
LISTEN, A SPEAR IS A WEAPON USED TO KNOCK DOWN AN OPPONENT AND THROW HIM OFF BALANCE!
USE THE FORCE. THE FORCE!!
DON'T THINK ABOUT IT. JUST SWING WITH ALL YOUR MIGHT, AND PICTURE INCREASING YOUR POWER BY FIVE!!

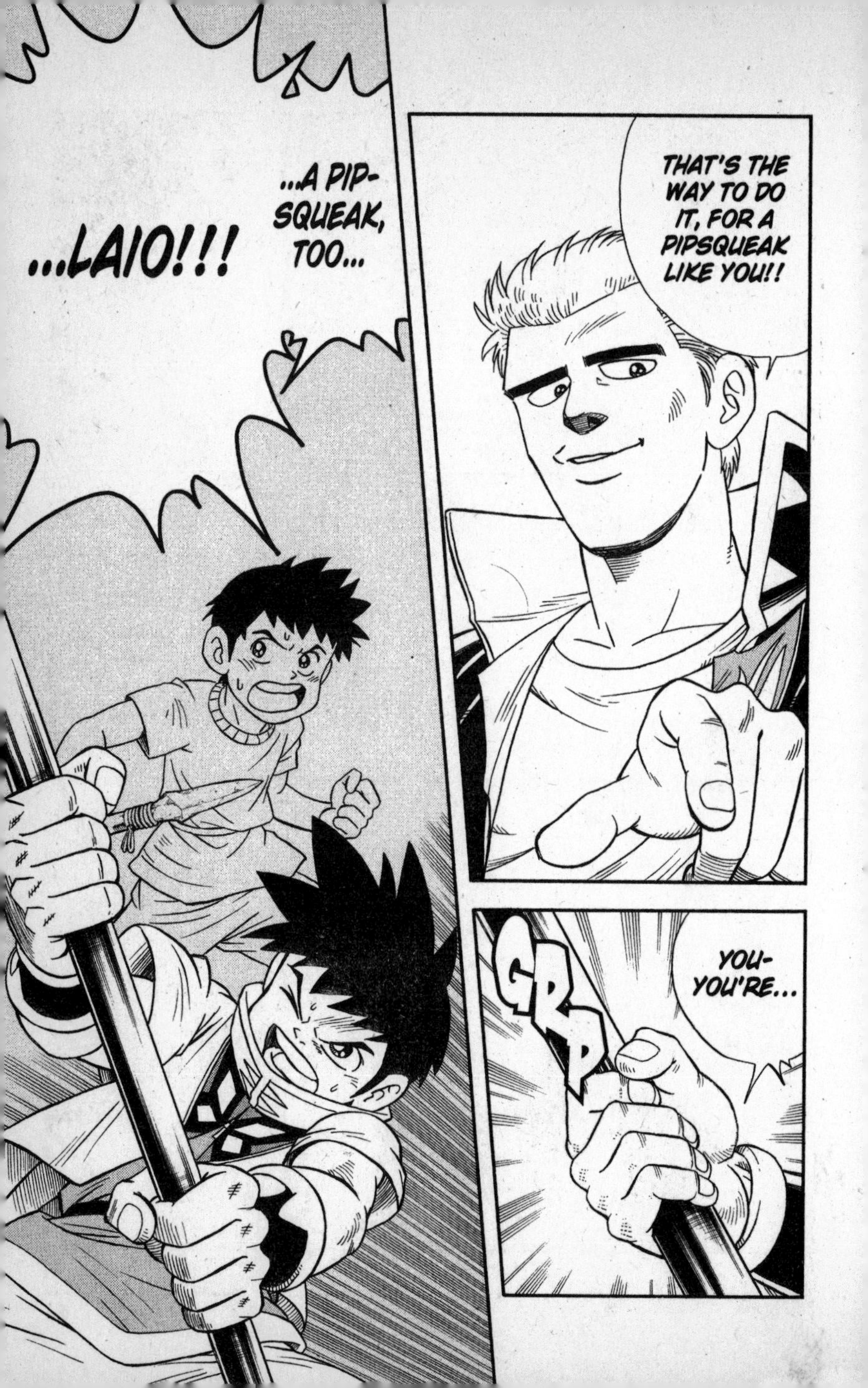
THAT'S THE WAY TO DO IT, FOR A PIPSQUEAK LIKE YOU!!
GRP
YOU-YOU'RE...
...A PIP-SQUEAK, TOO...
...LAIO!!!

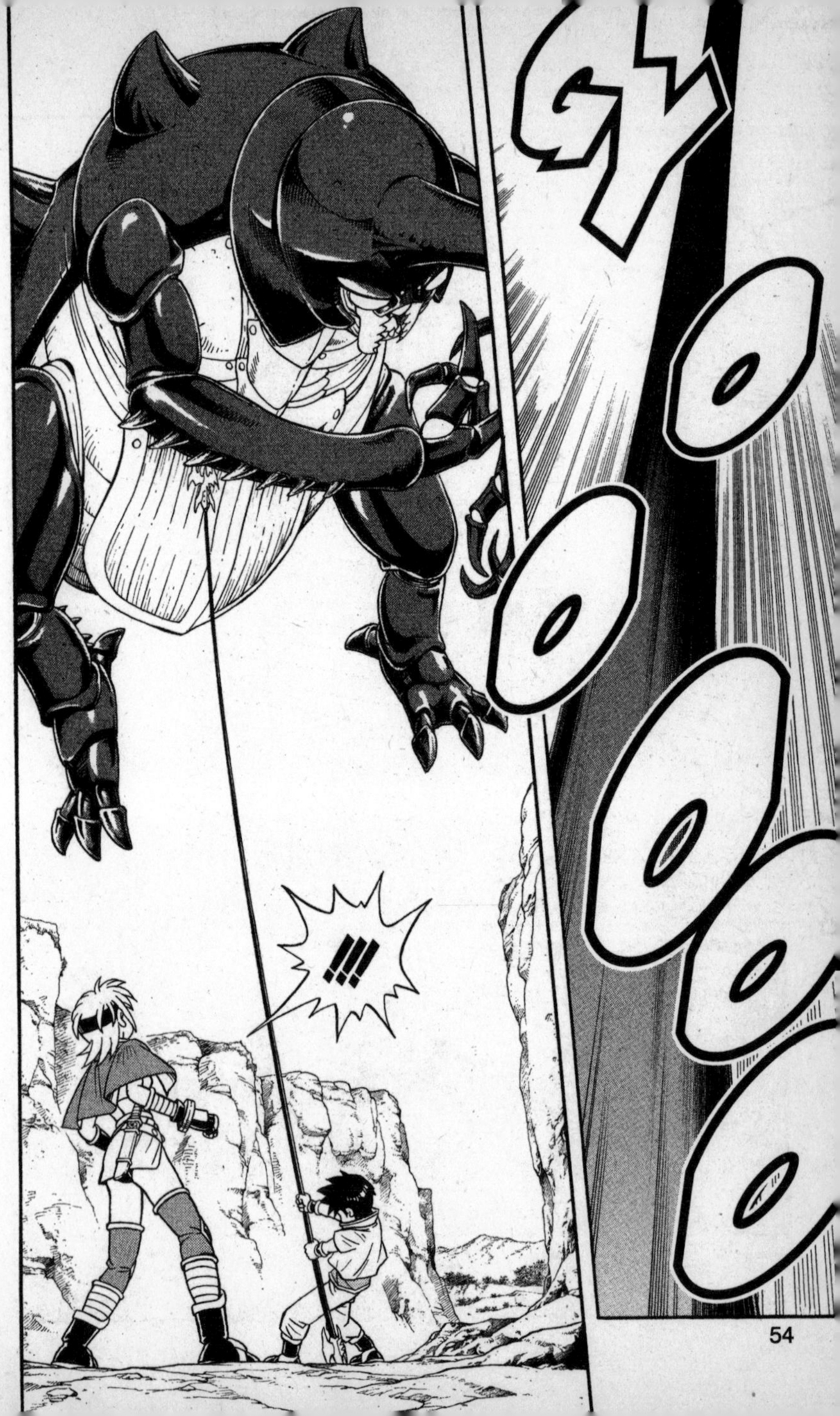
GYOOOOO
!!!

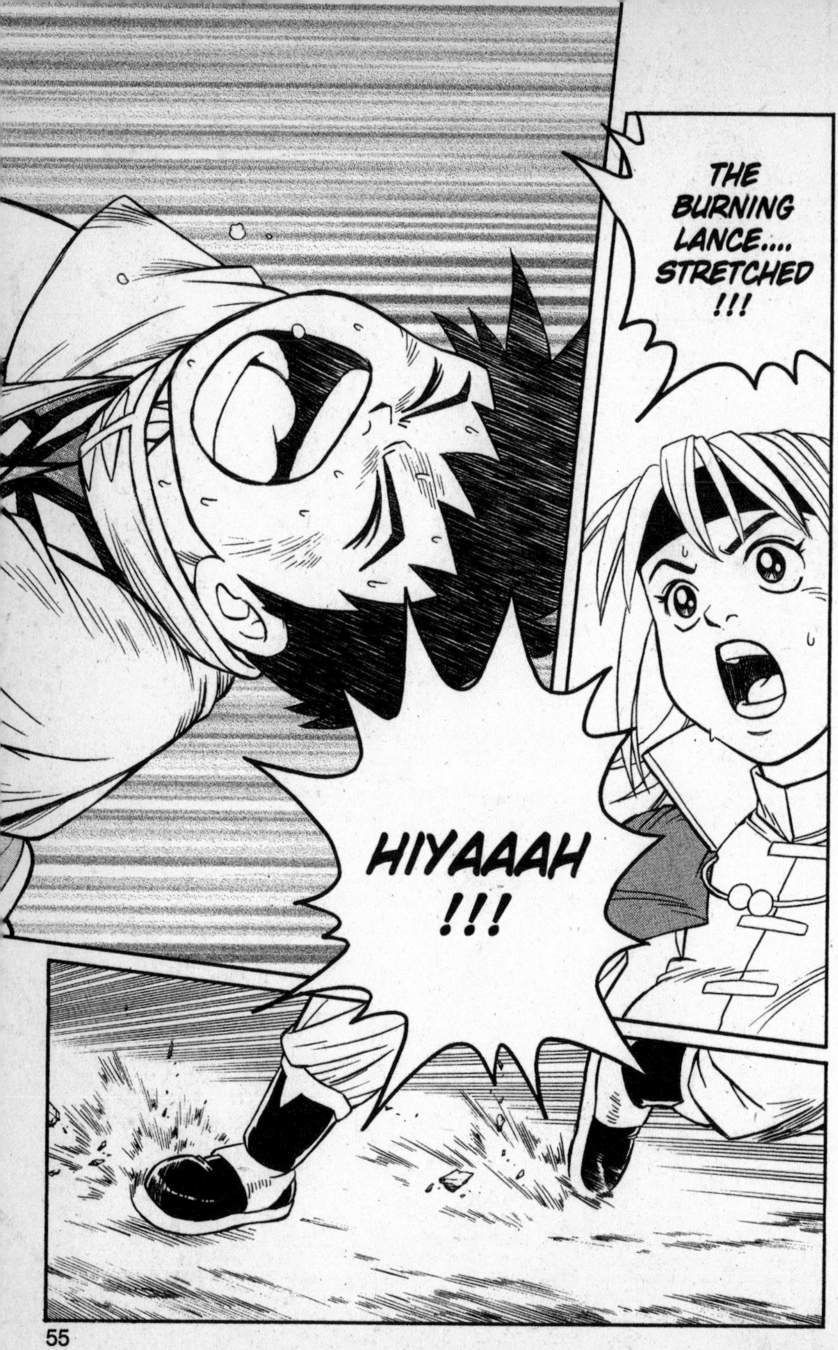
THE BURNING LANCE.... STRETCHED !!!
HIYAAAH !!!

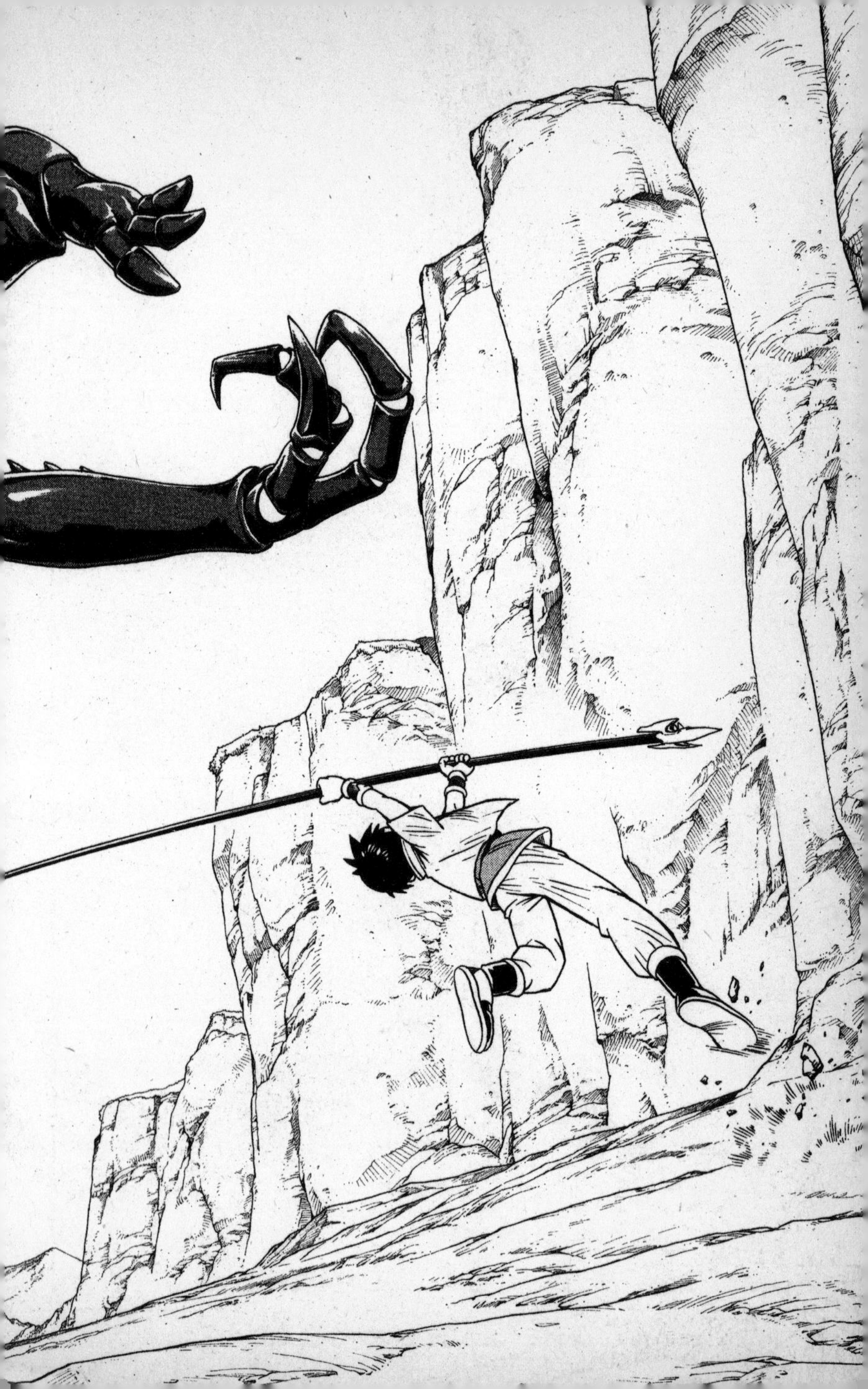

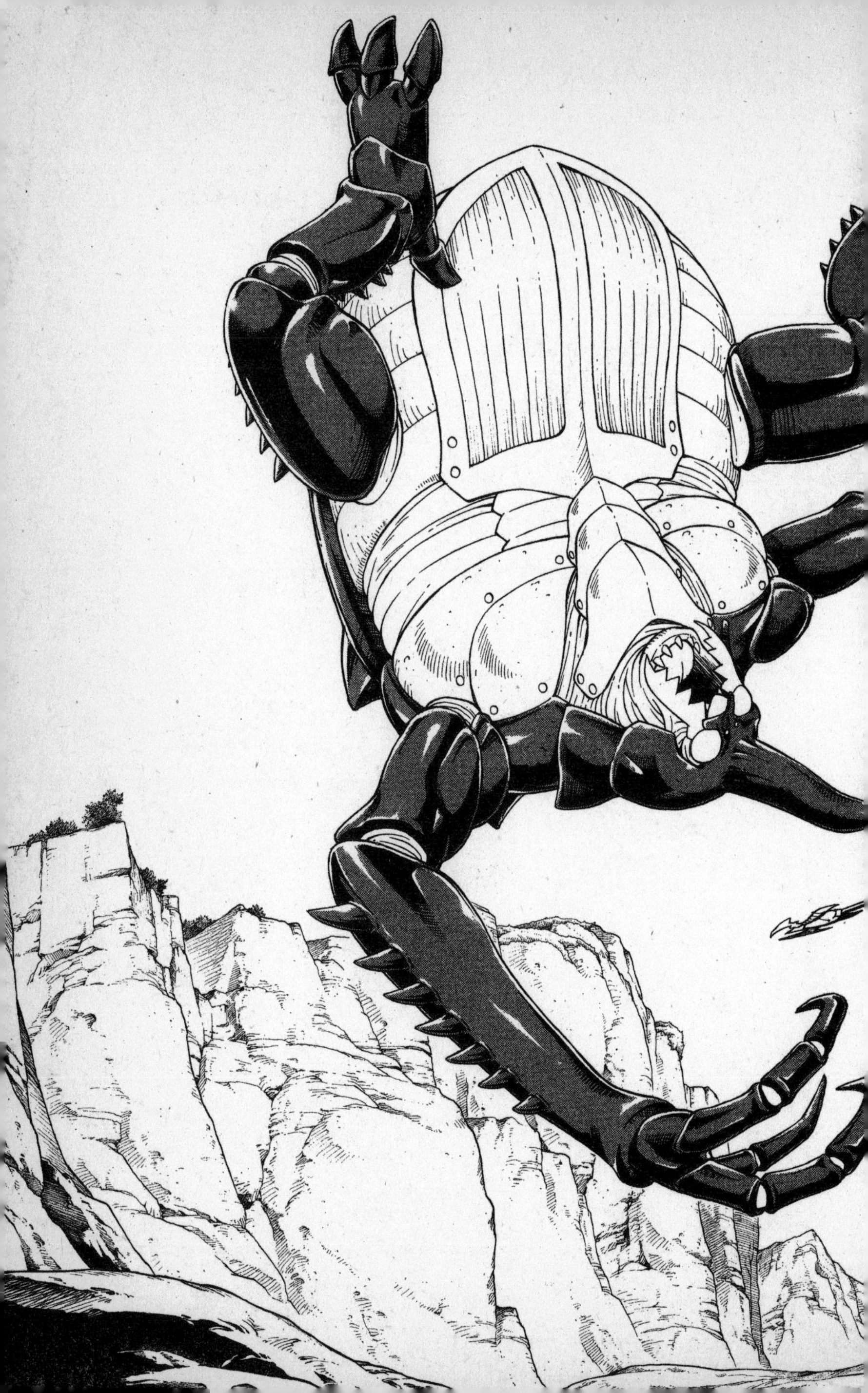

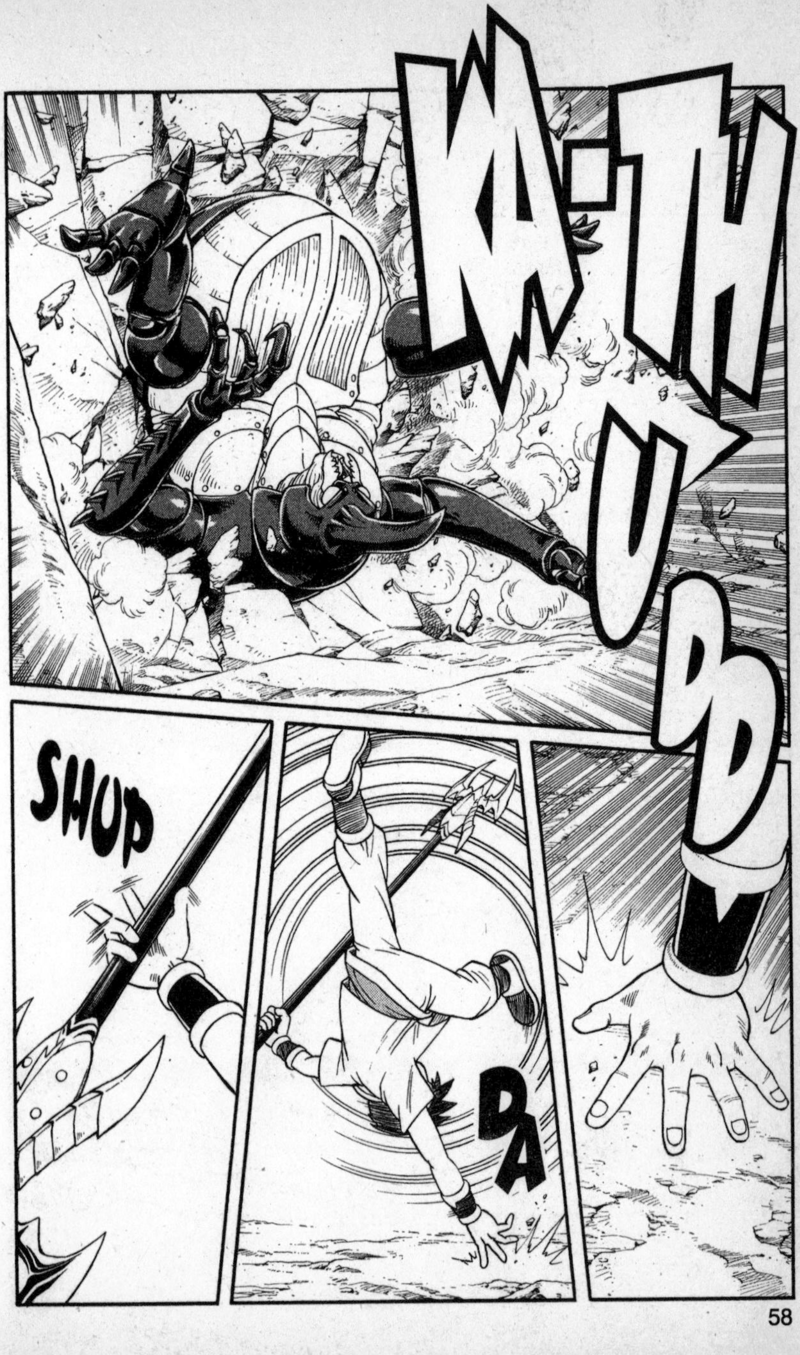
KA-THUD
SHUP
DA

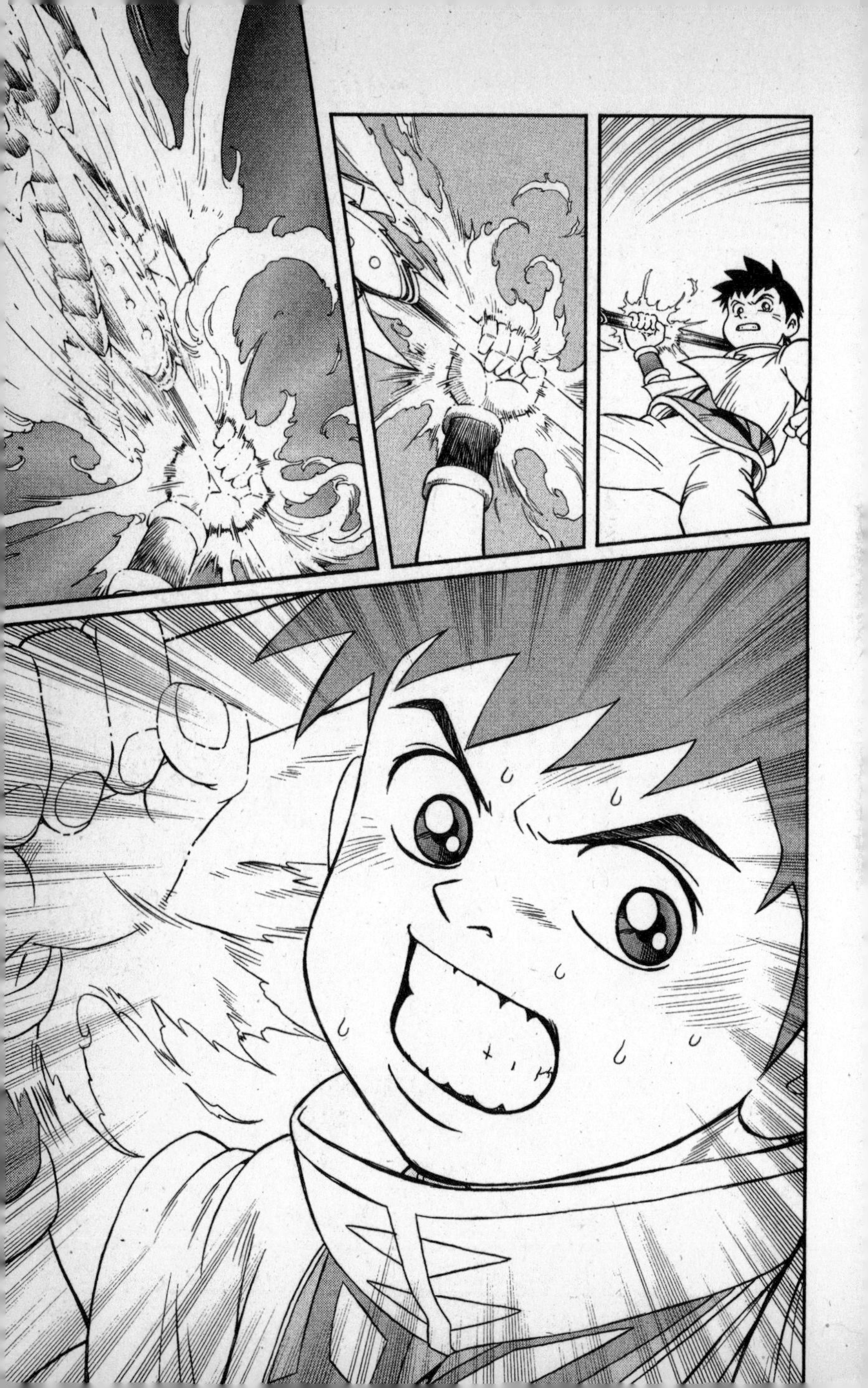

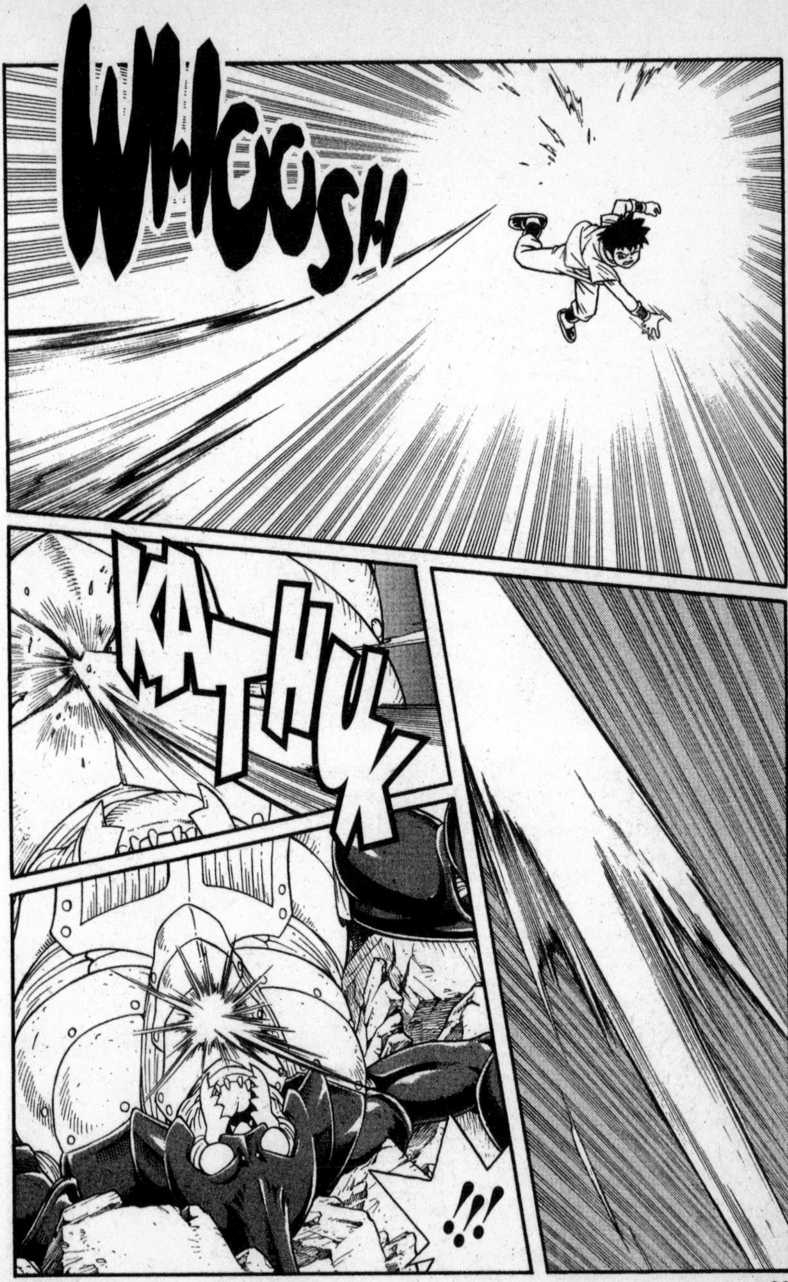
WHOOSH
KA-THUK
!!!

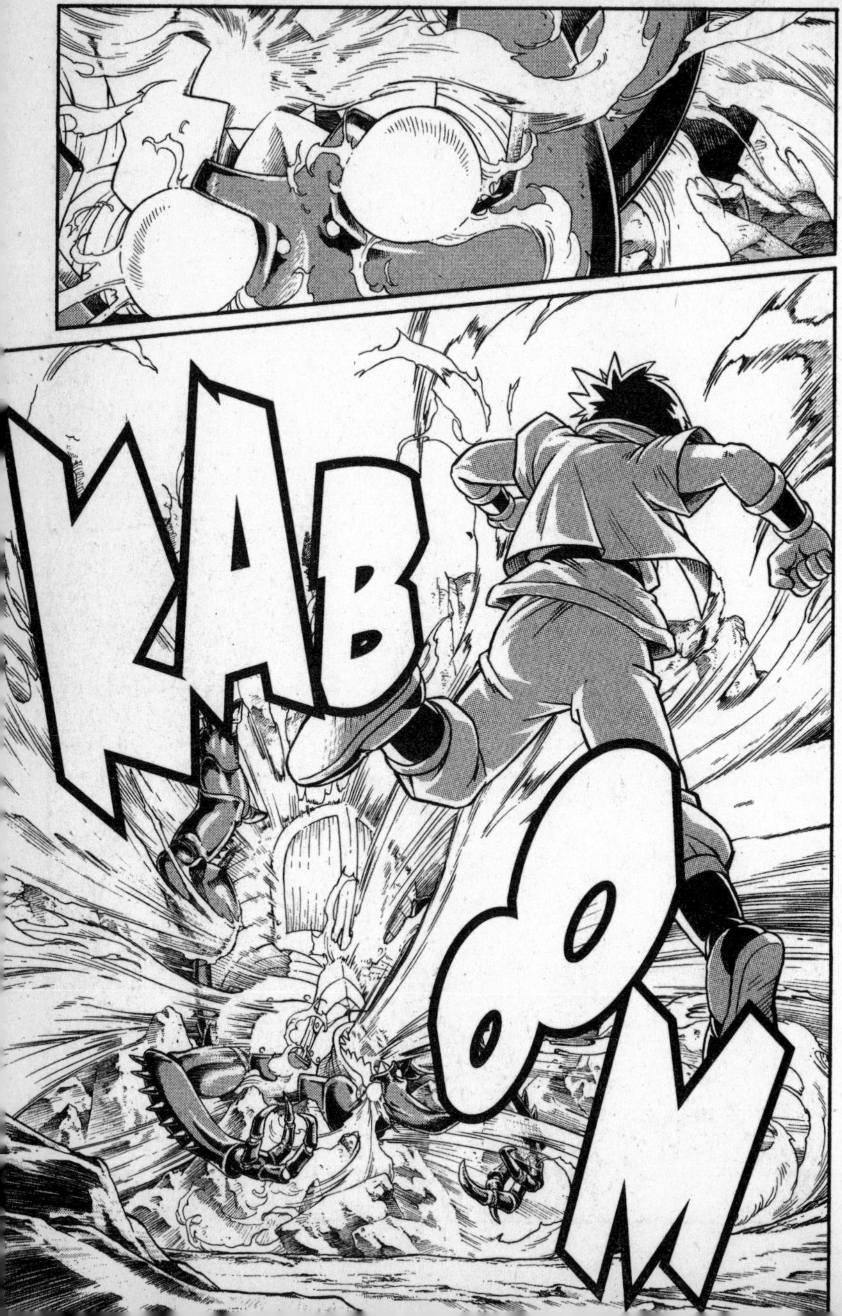
WABOOM

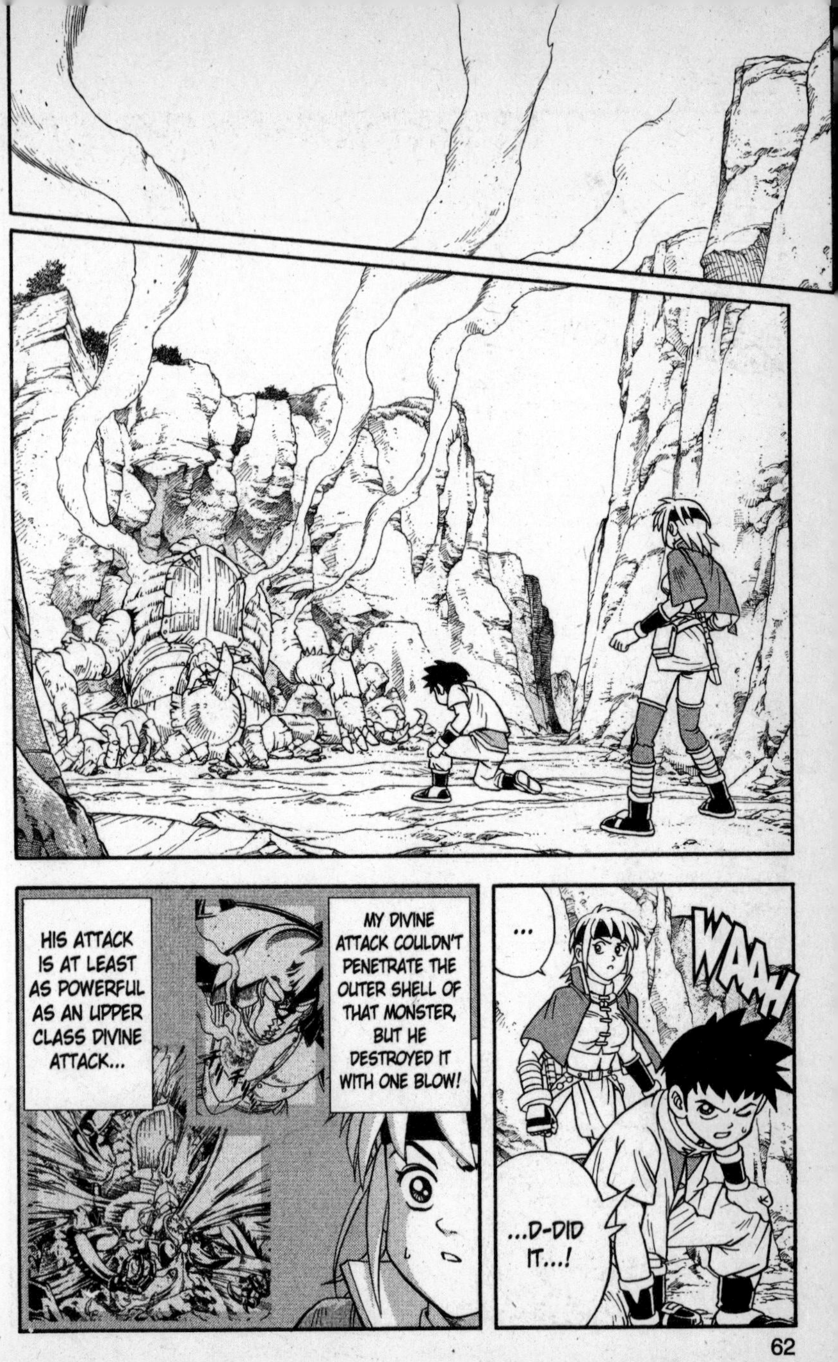
WAAH
...
...D-DID IT...!
MY DIVINE ATTACK COULDN'T PENETRATE THE OUTER SHELL OF THAT MONSTER, BUT HE DESTROYED IT WITH ONE BLOW!
HIS ATTACK IS AT LEAST AS POWERFUL AS AN UPPER CLASS DIVINE ATTACK...

READ THIS WAY

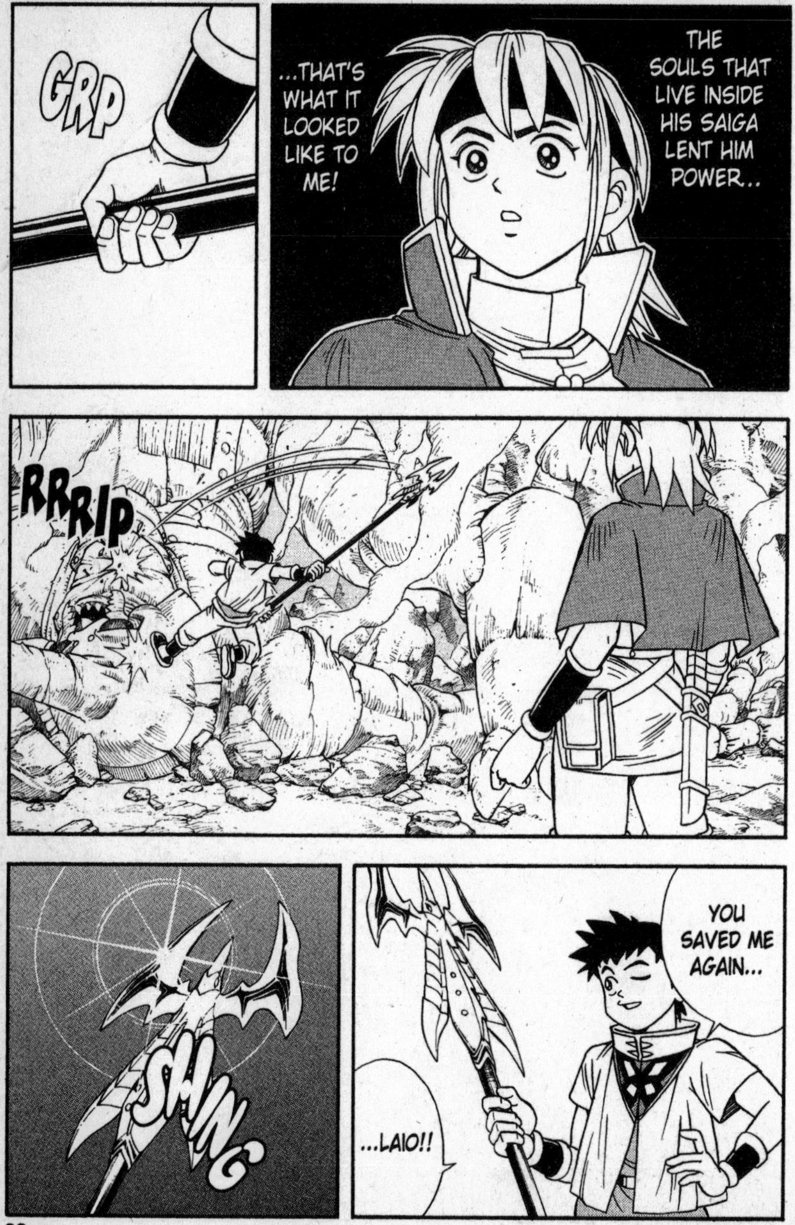
THE SOULS THAT LIVE INSIDE HIS SAIGA LENT HIM POWER...
...THAT'S WHAT IT LOOKED LIKE TO ME!
GRP
RRRIP
YOU SAVED ME AGAIN...
...LAIO!!
SHING

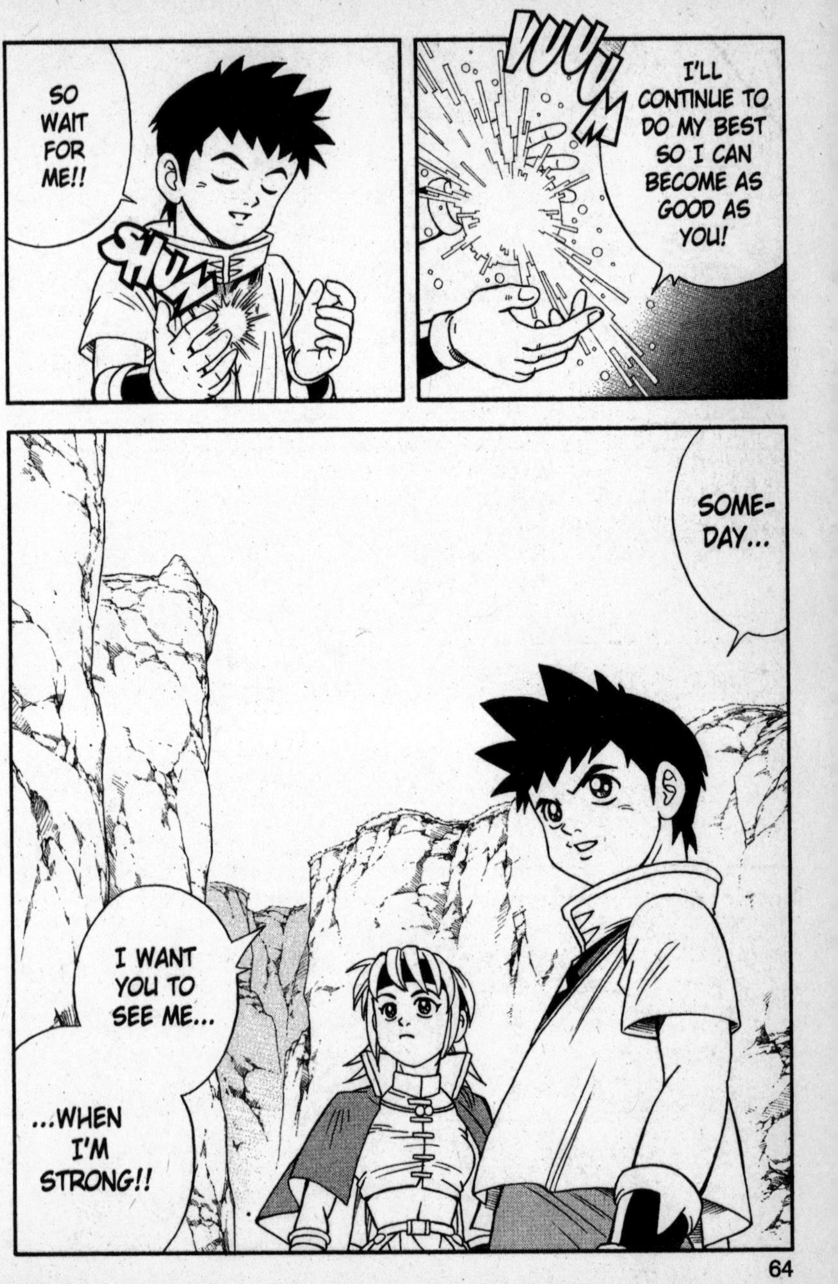
VUUUM
I'LL CONTINUE TO DO MY BEST SO I CAN BECOME AS GOOD AS YOU!
SO WAIT FOR ME!!
SHUN
SOME-DAY...
I WANT YOU TO SEE ME...
...WHEN I'M STRONG!!

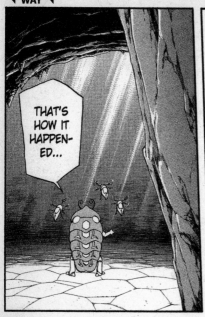

THAT'S HOW IT HAPPEN- ED...

SCRATCH SCRATCH

SKCH

SKCH

SKCH

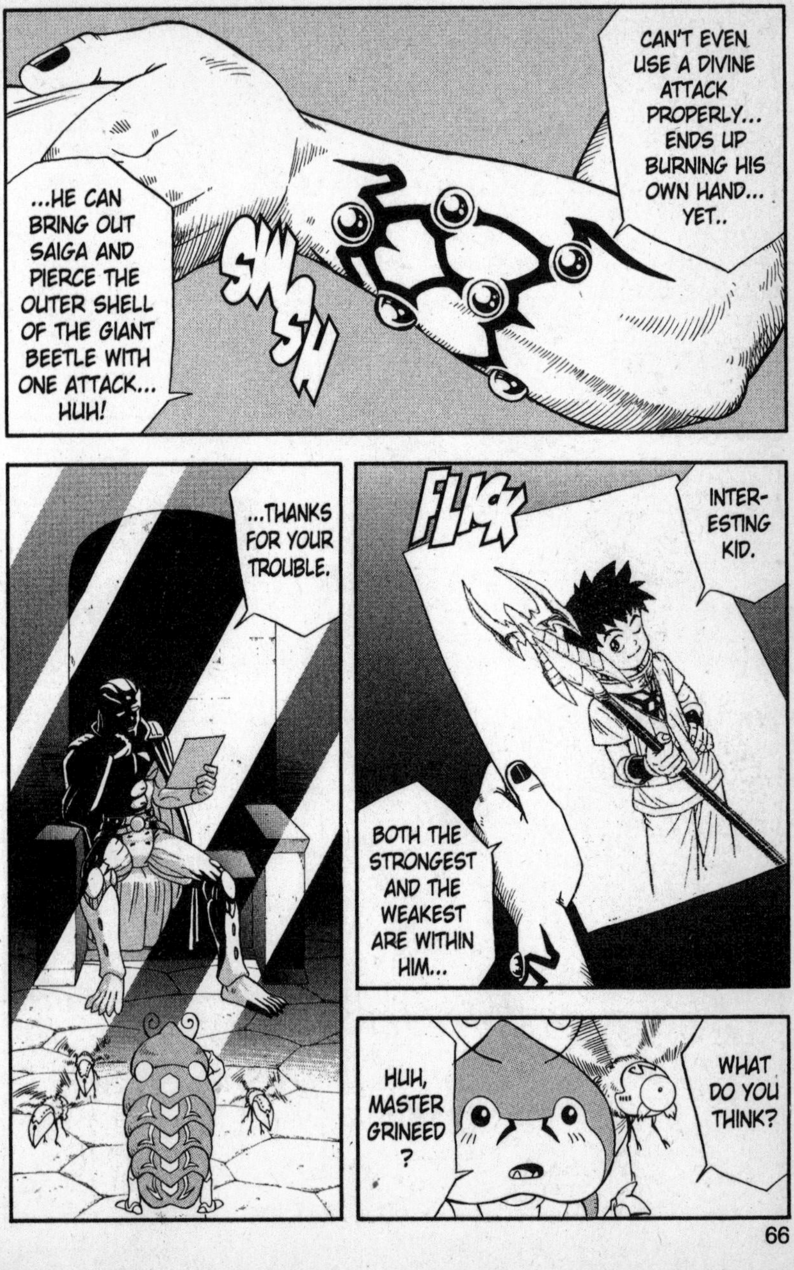
CAN'T EVEN USE A DIVINE ATTACK PROPERLY... ENDS UP BURNING HIS OWN HAND... YET..
SWISH
...HE CAN BRING OUT SAIGA AND PIERCE THE OUTER SHELL OF THE GIANT BEETLE WITH ONE ATTACK... HUH!
INTER-ESTING KID.
FLICK
BOTH THE STRONGEST AND THE WEAKEST ARE WITHIN HIM...
WHAT DO YOU THINK?
HUH, MASTER GRINEED ?
...THANKS FOR YOUR TROUBLE.

READ THIS WAY

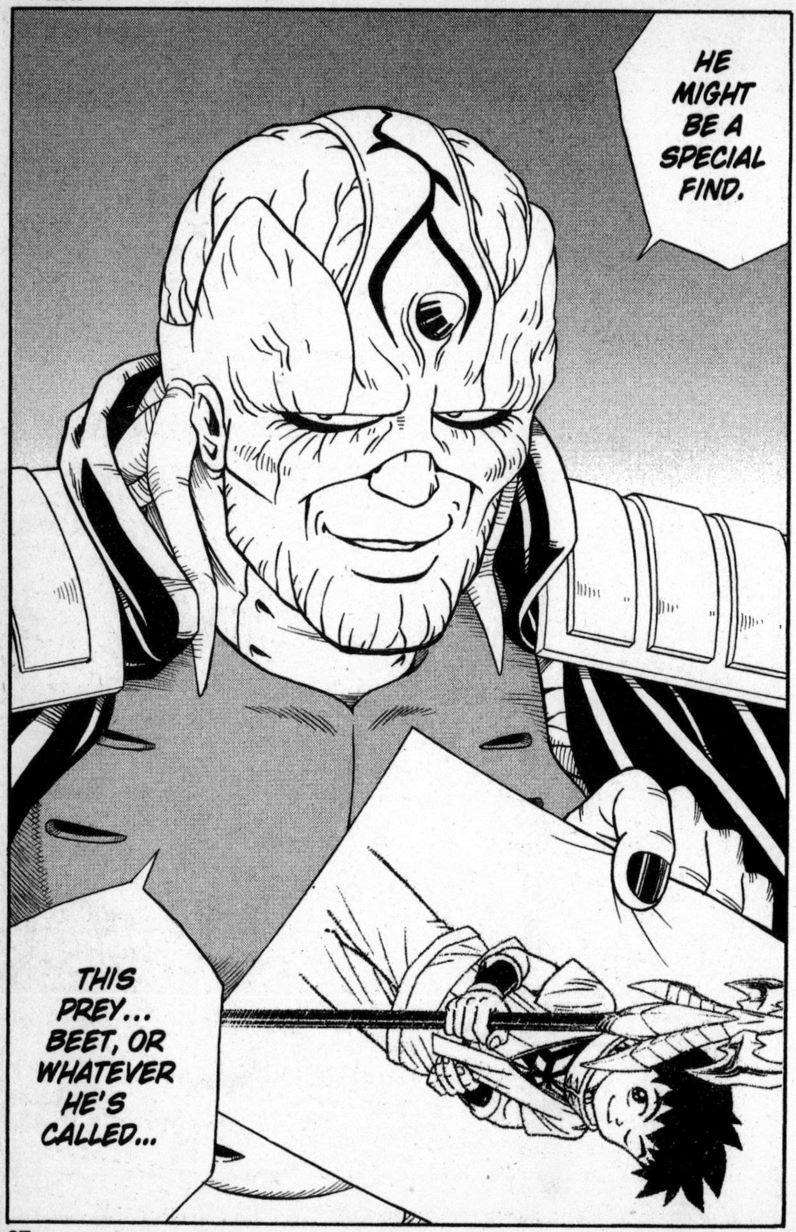
HE MIGHT BE A SPECIAL FIND.
THIS PREY... BEET, OR WHATEVER HE'S CALLED...

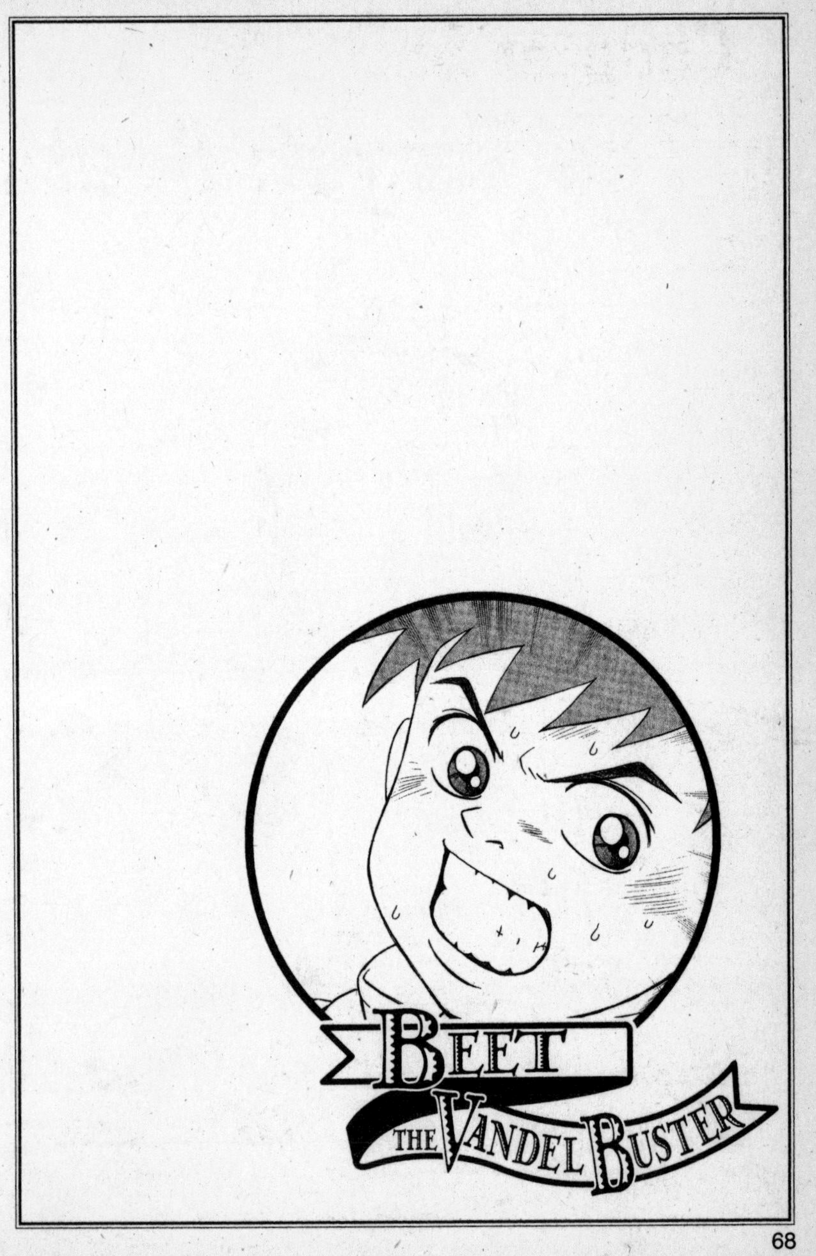
BEET
THE VANDEL BUSTER

Chapter 5:
The Target: Beet!

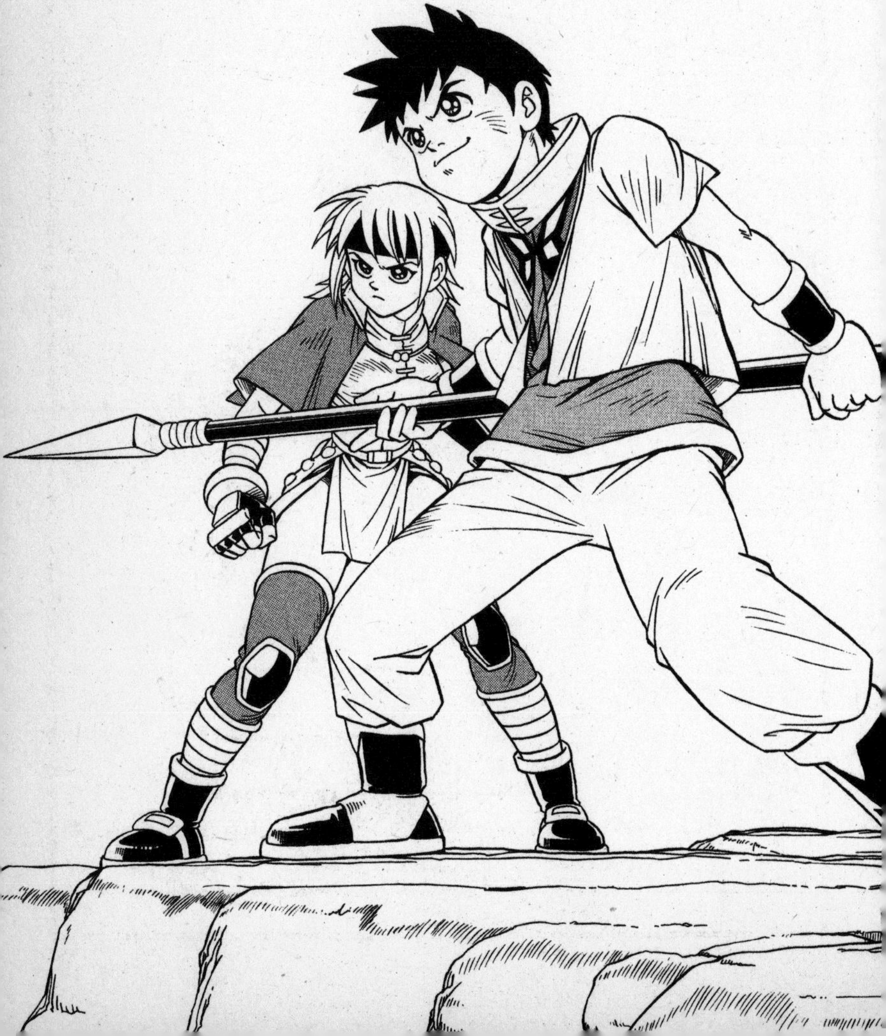

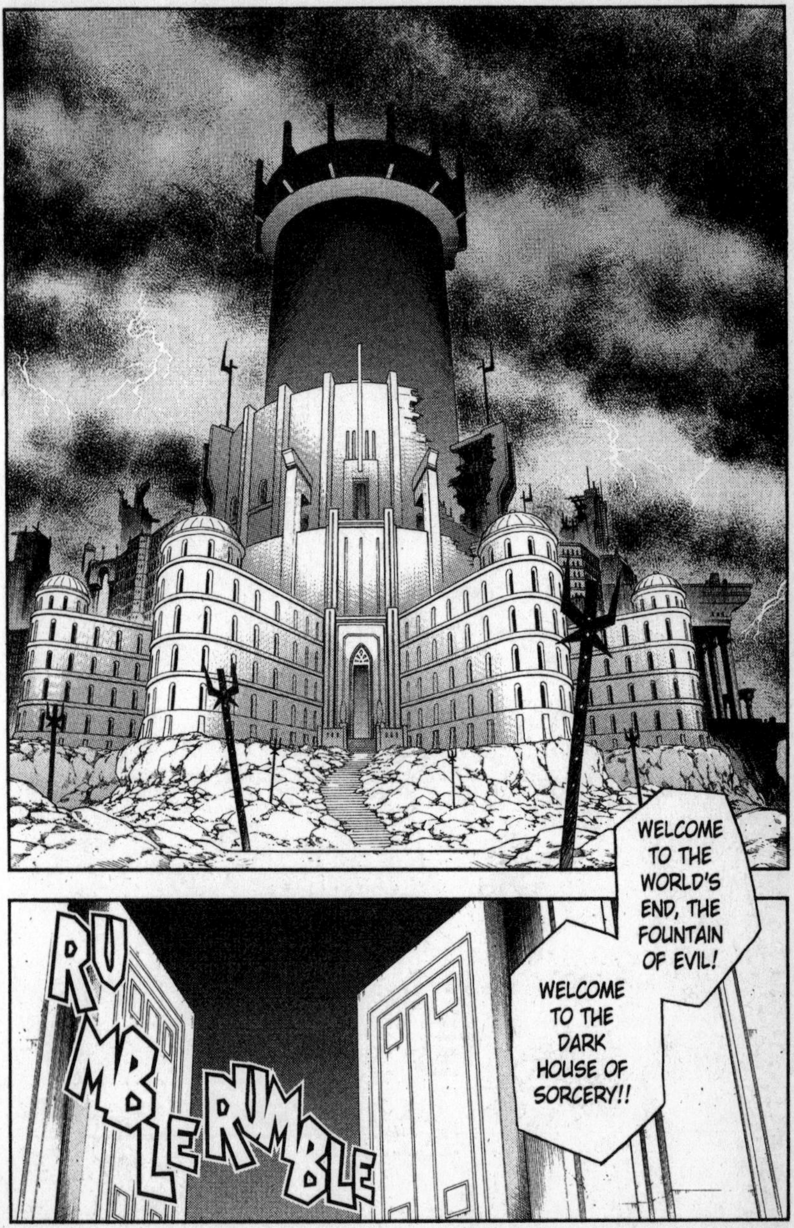
WELCOME TO THE WORLD'S END, THE FOUNTAIN OF EVIL!
WELCOME TO THE DARK HOUSE OF SORCERY!!
RUMBLE RUMBLE

READ THIS WAY

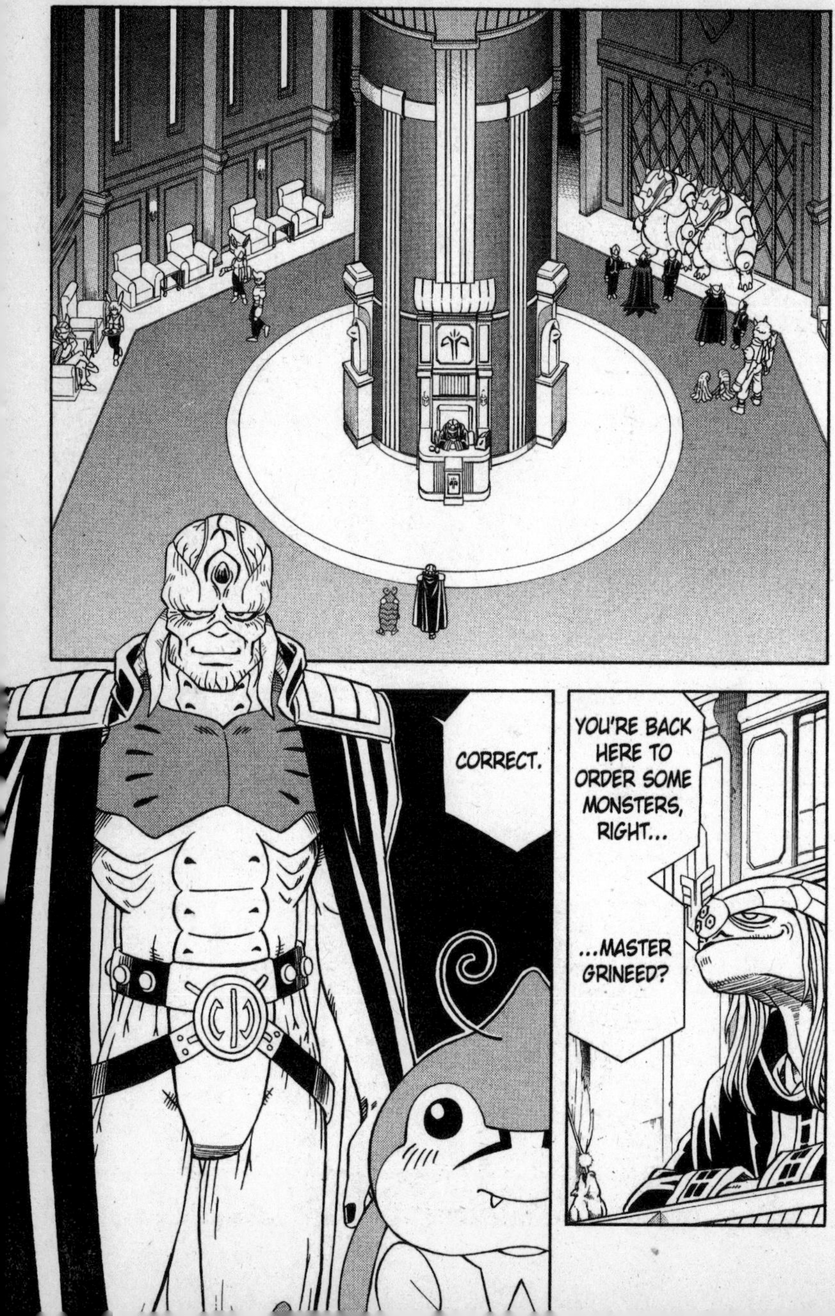
YOU'RE BACK HERE TO ORDER SOME MONSTERS, RIGHT...
...MASTER GRINEED?
CORRECT.

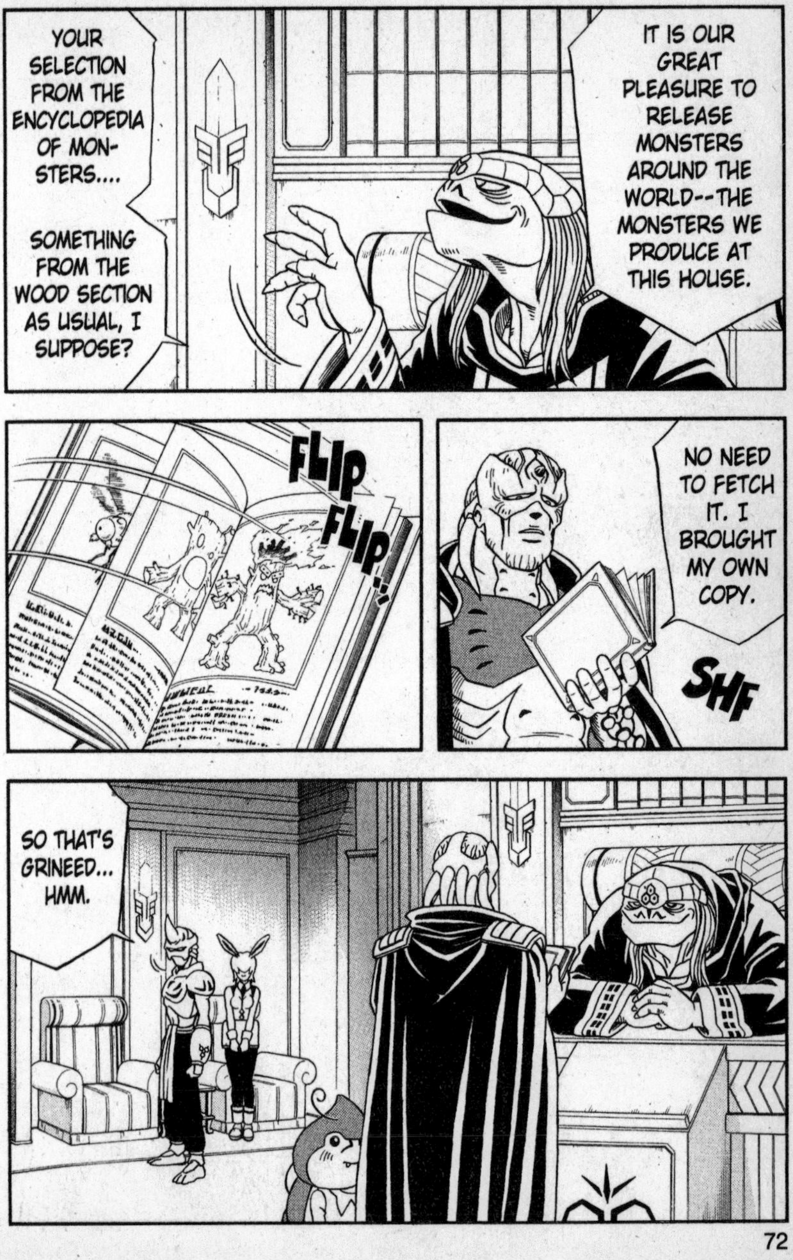
IT IS OUR GREAT PLEASURE TO RELEASE MONSTERS AROUND THE WORLD--THE MONSTERS WE PRODUCE AT THIS HOUSE.
YOUR SELECTION FROM THE ENCYCLOPEDIA OF MON-STERS....
SOMETHING FROM THE WOOD SECTION AS USUAL, I SUPPOSE?
NO NEED TO FETCH IT. I BROUGHT MY OWN COPY.
SHF
FLIP
FLIP..
SO THAT'S GRINEED... HMM.

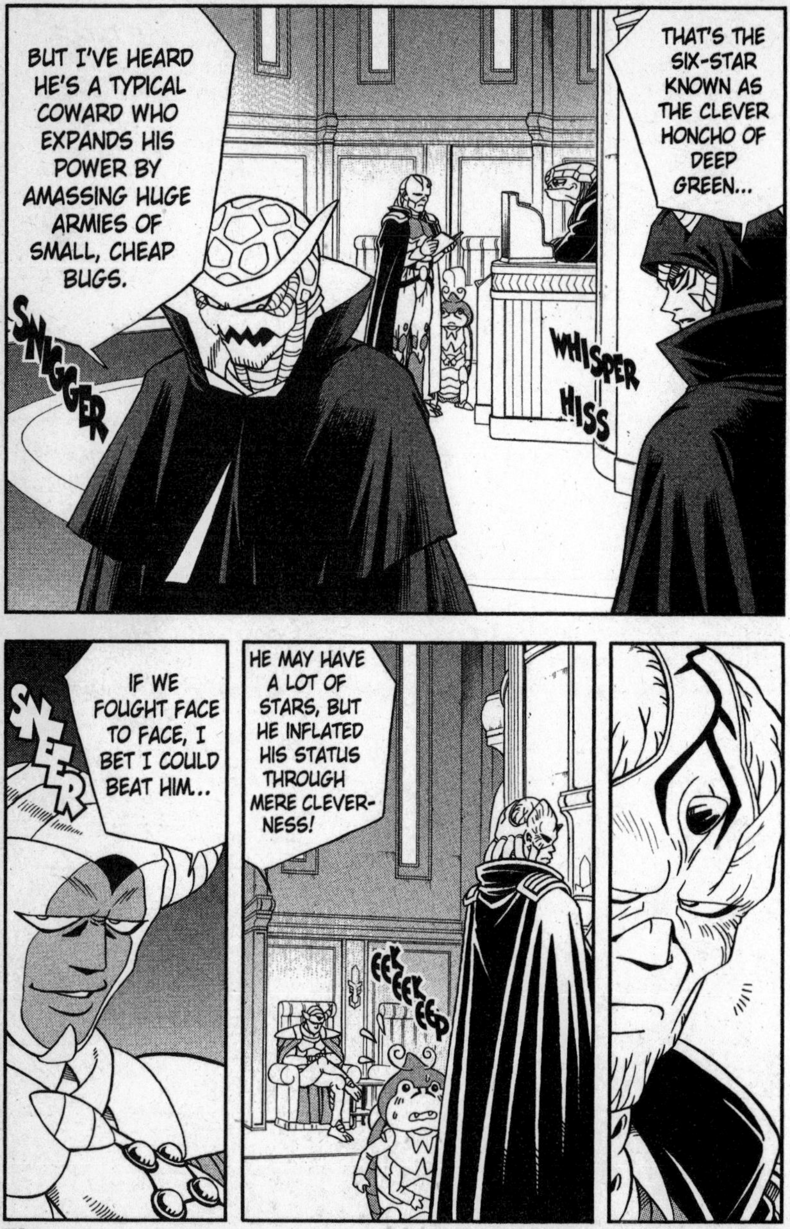
THAT'S THE SIX-STAR KNOWN AS THE CLEVER HONCHO OF DEEP GREEN...
WHISPER
HISS
BUT I'VE HEARD HE'S A TYPICAL COWARD WHO EXPANDS HIS POWER BY AMASSING HUGE ARMIES OF SMALL, CHEAP BUGS.
SNIGGER
HE MAY HAVE A LOT OF STARS, BUT HE INFLATED HIS STATUS THROUGH MERE CLEVER-NESS!
EEK EEK EEEP
IF WE FOUGHT FACE TO FACE, I BET I COULD BEAT HIM...
SNEER

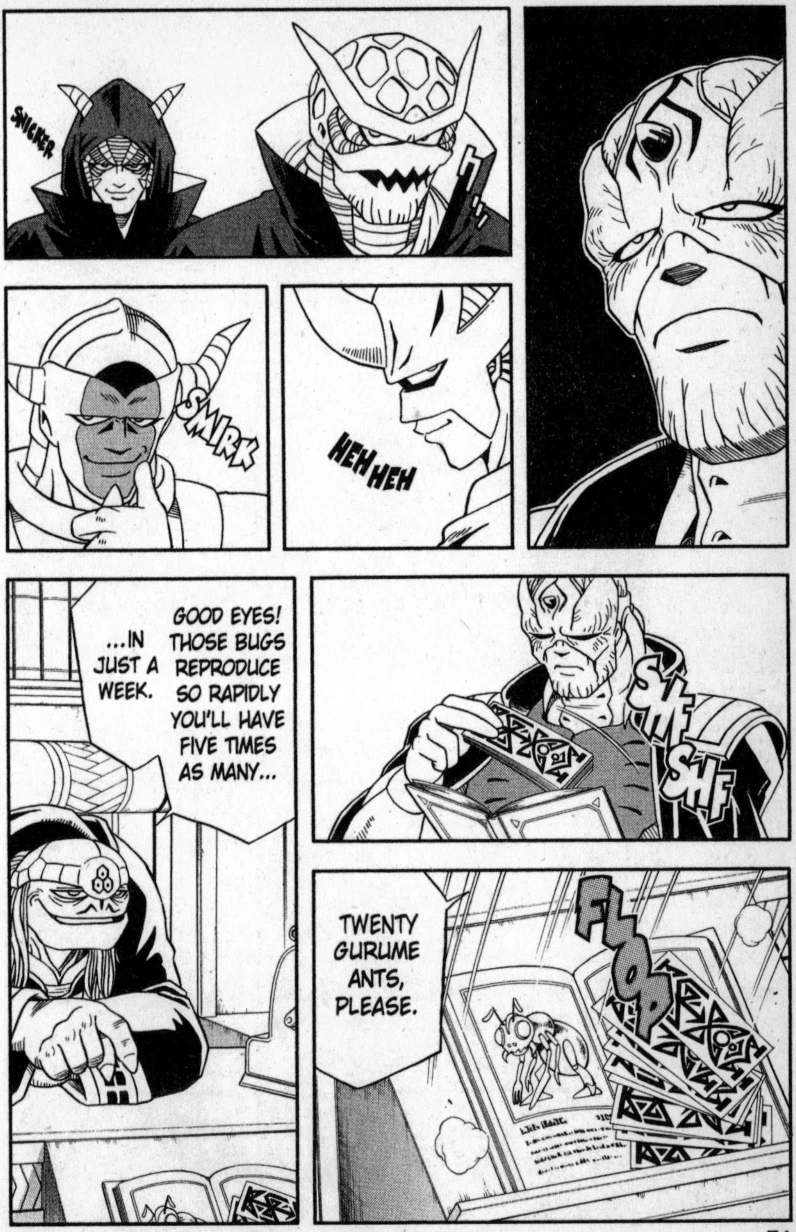
SNICKER
HEH HEH
SMIRK
SHF SHF
TWENTY GURUME ANTS, PLEASE.
FLOP
GOOD EYES! THOSE BUGS REPRODUCE SO RAPIDLY YOU'LL HAVE FIVE TIMES AS MANY...
...IN JUST A WEEK.

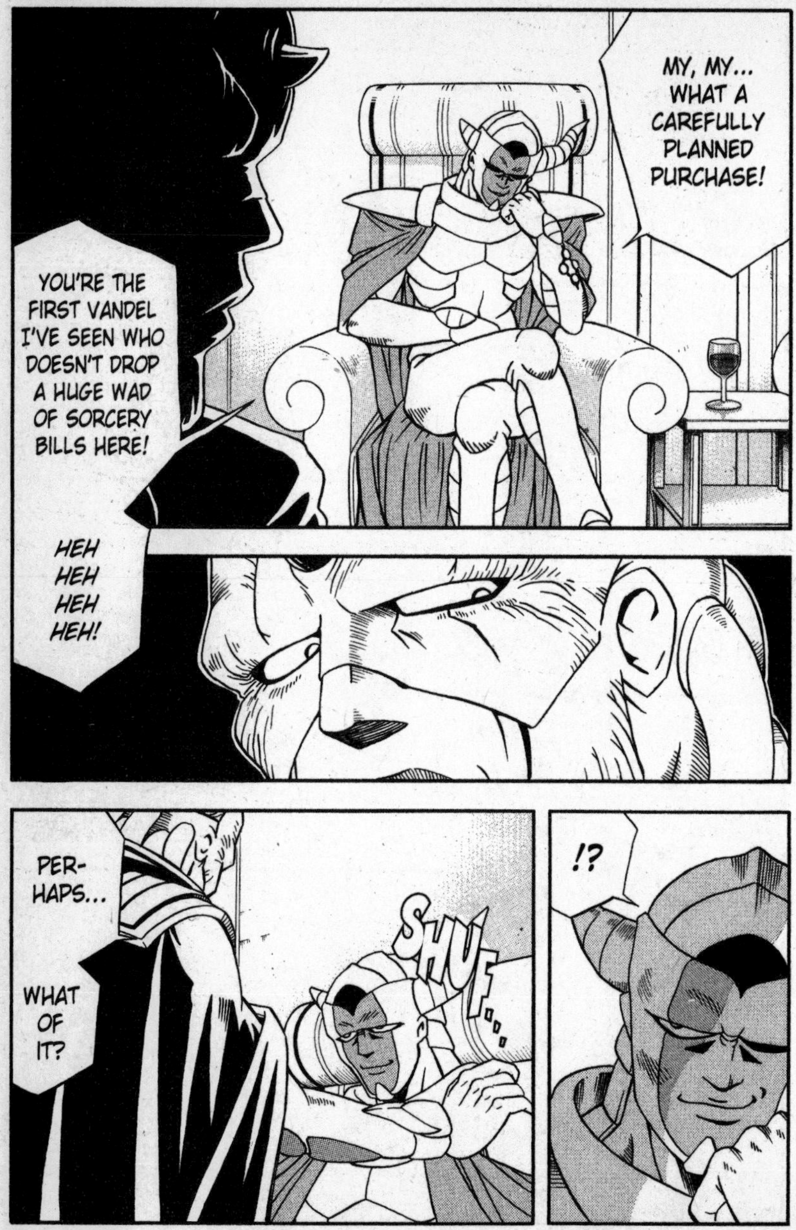
READ THIS WAY
MY, MY... WHAT A CAREFULLY PLANNED PURCHASE!
YOU'RE THE FIRST VANDEL I'VE SEEN WHO DOESN'T DROP A HUGE WAD OF SORCERY BILLS HERE!
HEH HEH HEH HEH!
!?
PER-HAPS...
SHUF...
WHAT OF IT?

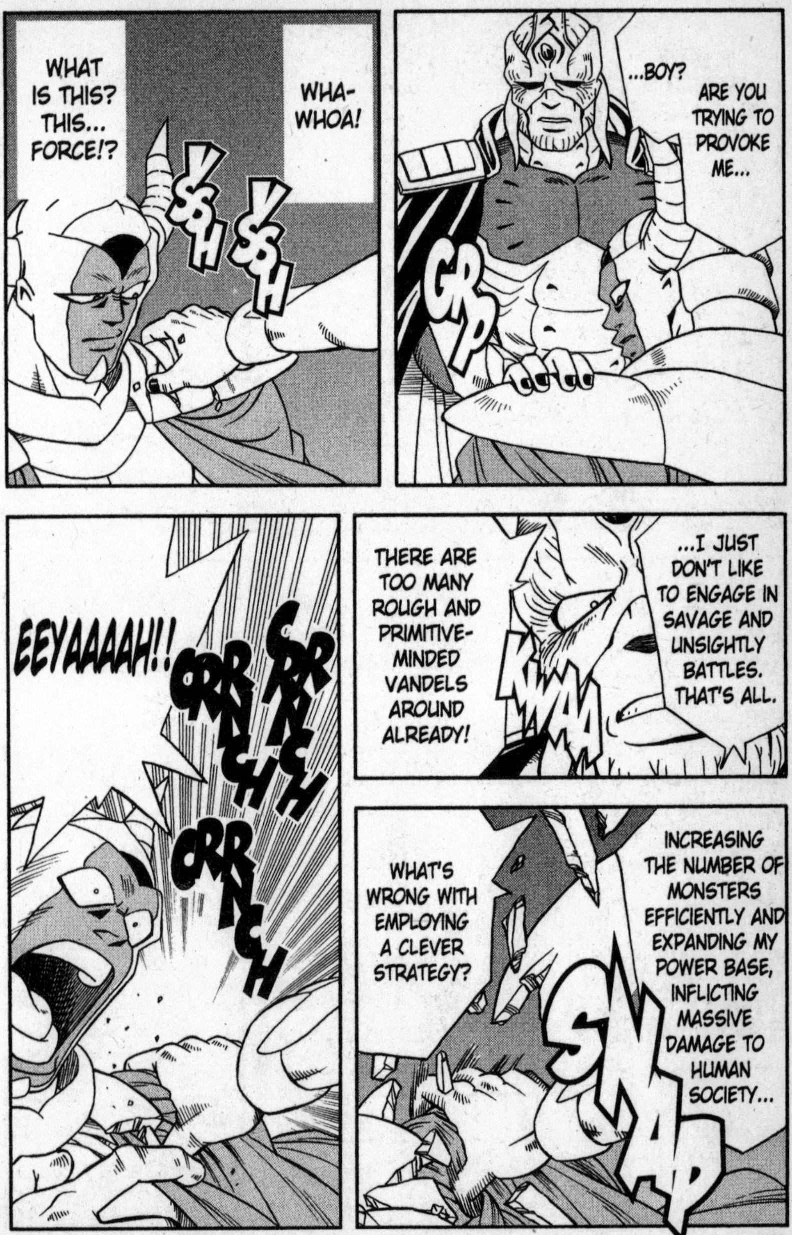
...BOY?
ARE YOU TRYING TO PROVOKE ME...
GRP
WHA-WHOA!
WHAT IS THIS? THIS... FORCE!?
YSSH
YSSH
...I JUST DON'T LIKE TO ENGAGE IN SAVAGE AND UNSIGHTLY BATTLES. THAT'S ALL.
KWAA
THERE ARE TOO MANY ROUGH AND PRIMITIVE-MINDED VANDELS AROUND ALREADY!
INCREASING THE NUMBER OF MONSTERS EFFICIENTLY AND EXPANDING MY POWER BASE, INFLICTING MASSIVE DAMAGE TO HUMAN SOCIETY...
SNAP
WHAT'S WRONG WITH EMPLOYING A CLEVER STRATEGY?
CRRNCH
CRRNCH
EEYAAAAH!!
CRRNCH

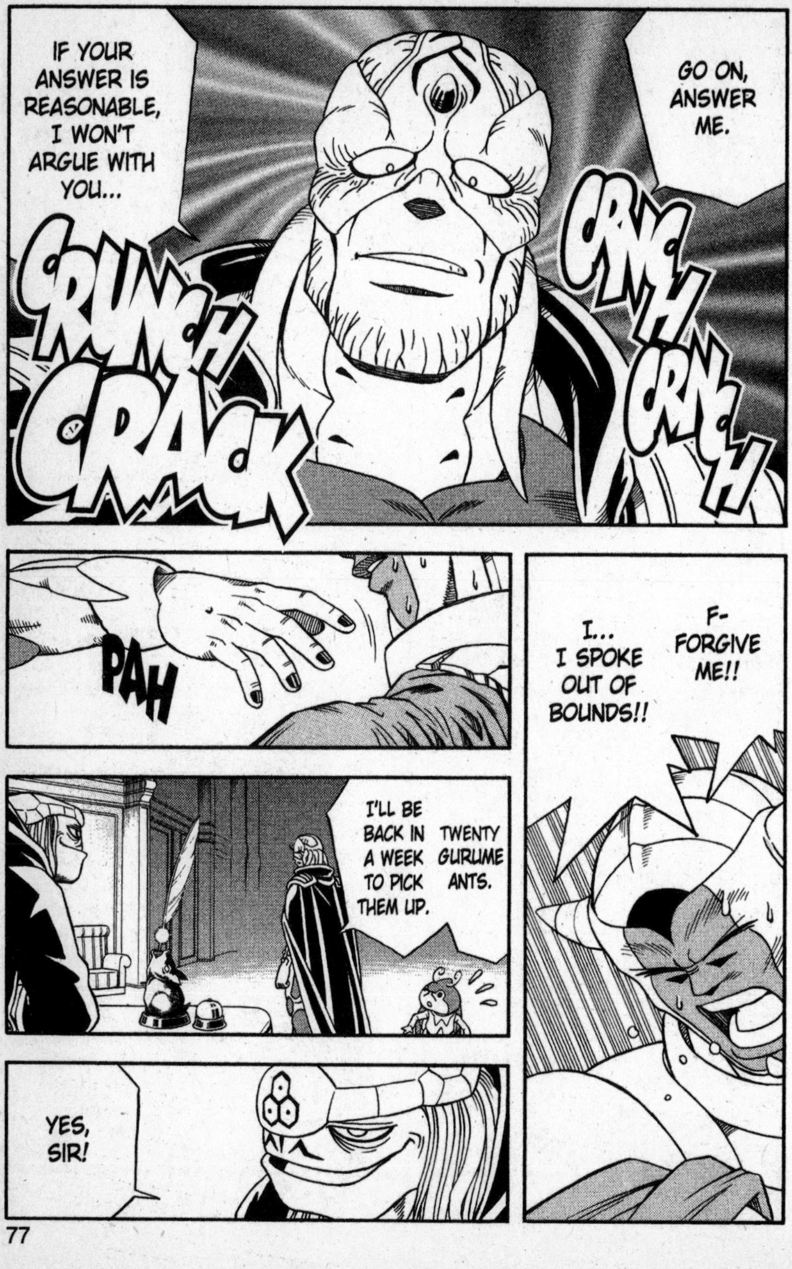
GO ON, ANSWER ME.
IF YOUR ANSWER IS REASONABLE, I WON'T ARGUE WITH YOU...
CRNCH CRNCH
CRUNCH CRACK
F- FORGIVE ME!!
I... I SPOKE OUT OF BOUNDS!!
PAH
TWENTY GURUME ANTS.
I'LL BE BACK IN A WEEK TO PICK THEM UP.
YES, SIR!

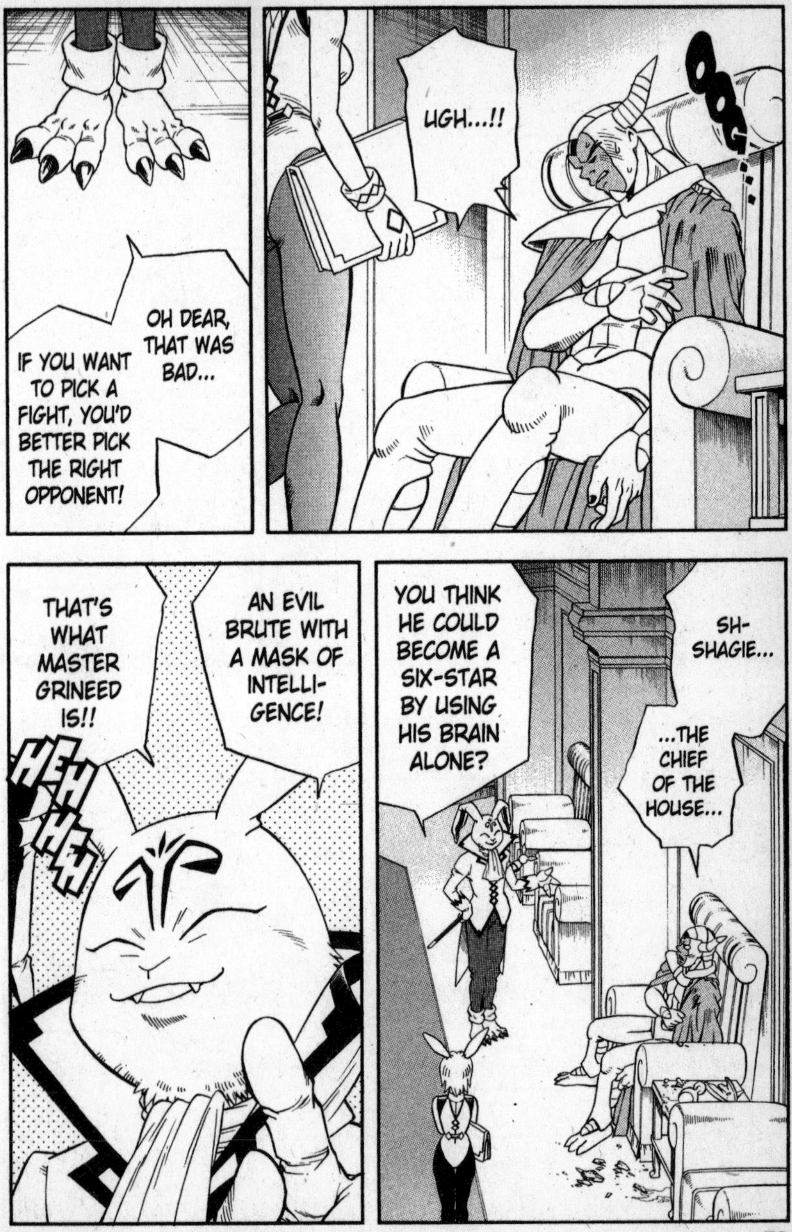
OOG...
UGH...!!
OH DEAR, THAT WAS BAD...
IF YOU WANT TO PICK A FIGHT, YOU'D BETTER PICK THE RIGHT OPPONENT!
SH-SHAGIE...
...THE CHIEF OF THE HOUSE...
YOU THINK HE COULD BECOME A SIX-STAR BY USING HIS BRAIN ALONE?
AN EVIL BRUTE WITH A MASK OF INTELLIGENCE!
THAT'S WHAT MASTER GRINEED IS!!
HEH HEH HEH

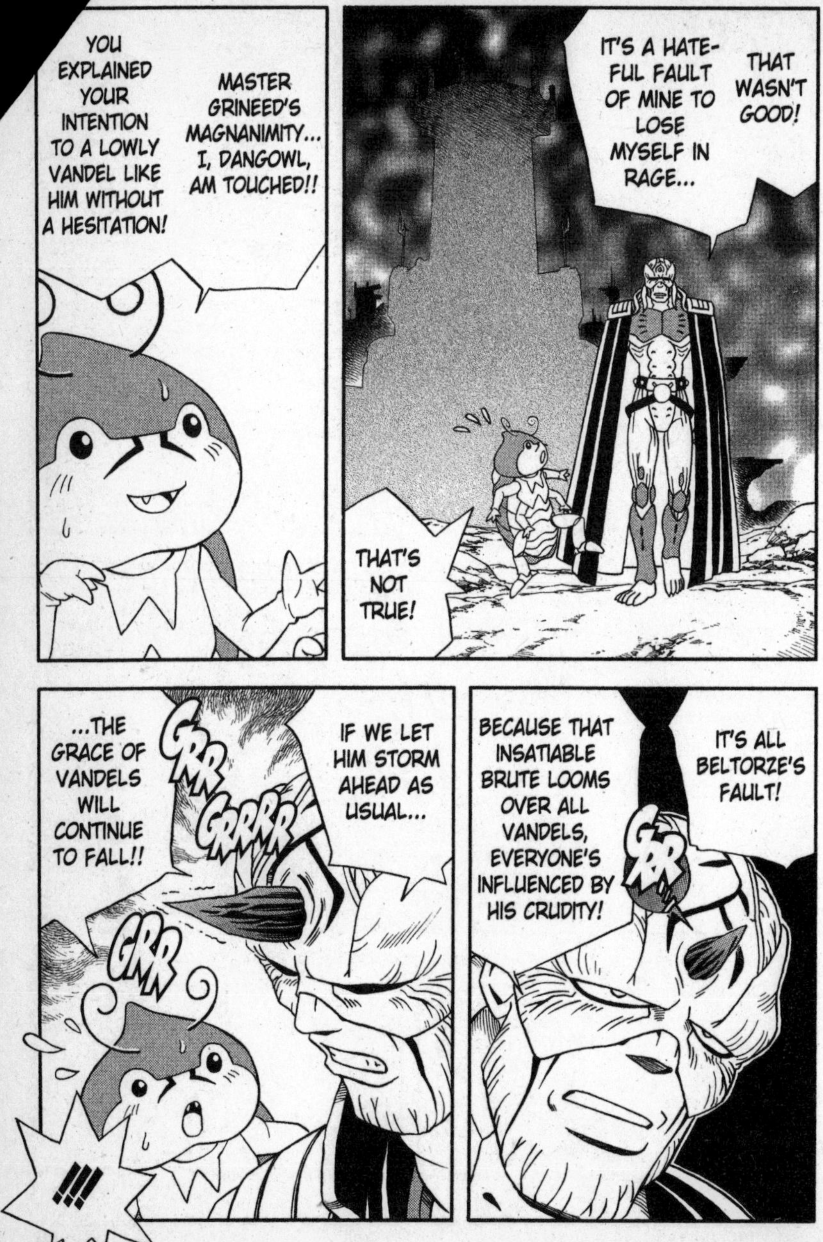
THAT WASN'T GOOD!
IT'S A HATE-FUL FAULT OF MINE TO LOSE MYSELF IN RAGE...
THAT'S NOT TRUE!
MASTER GRINEED'S MAGNANIMITY... I, DANGOWL, AM TOUCHED!!
YOU EXPLAINED YOUR INTENTION TO A LOWLY VANDEL LIKE HIM WITHOUT A HESITATION!
IT'S ALL BELTORZE'S FAULT!
BECAUSE THAT INSATIABLE BRUTE LOOMS OVER ALL VANDELS, EVERYONE'S INFLUENCED BY HIS CRUDITY!
GRR
IF WE LET HIM STORM AHEAD AS USUAL...
GRR
GRRRR
...THE GRACE OF VANDELS WILL CONTINUE TO FALL!!
GRR
!!!!

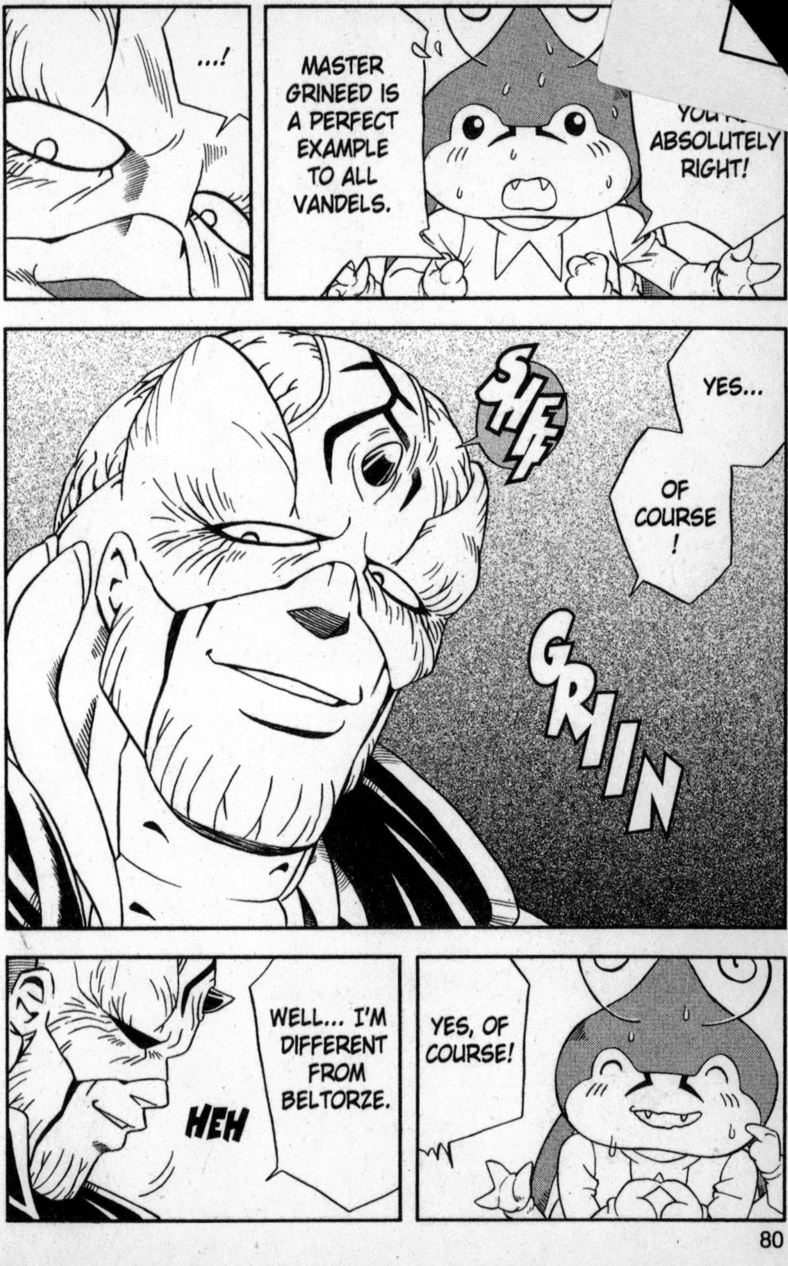
ABSOLUTELY RIGHT!
MASTER GRINEED IS A PERFECT EXAMPLE TO ALL VANDELS.
...!
YES...
OF COURSE!
GRIN
YES, OF COURSE!
WELL... I'M DIFFERENT FROM BELTORZE.
HEH

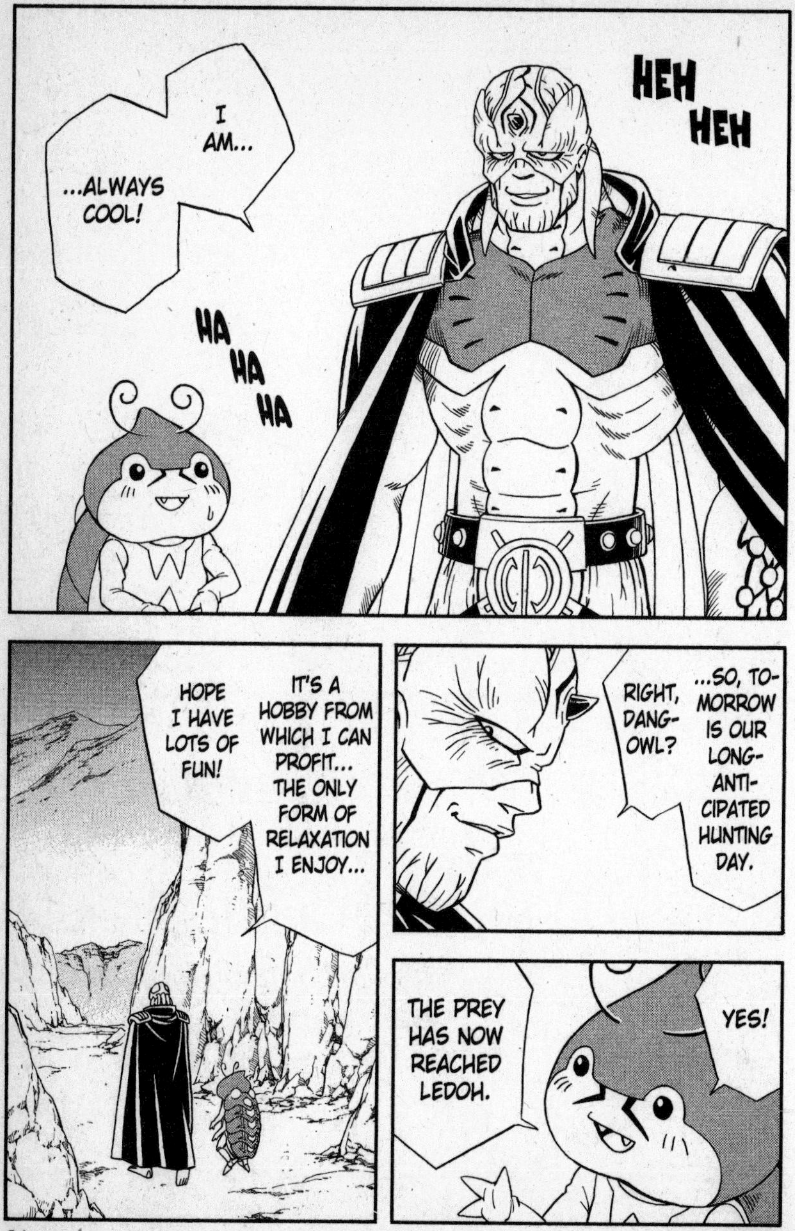

HEH HEH
I AM...
...ALWAYS COOL!
HA HA HA
...SO, TOMORROW IS OUR LONG-ANTICIPATED HUNTING DAY.
RIGHT, DANGOWL?
YES!
THE PREY HAS NOW REACHED LEDOH.
IT'S A HOBBY FROM WHICH I CAN PROFIT... THE ONLY FORM OF RELAXATION I ENJOY...
HOPE I HAVE LOTS OF FUN!

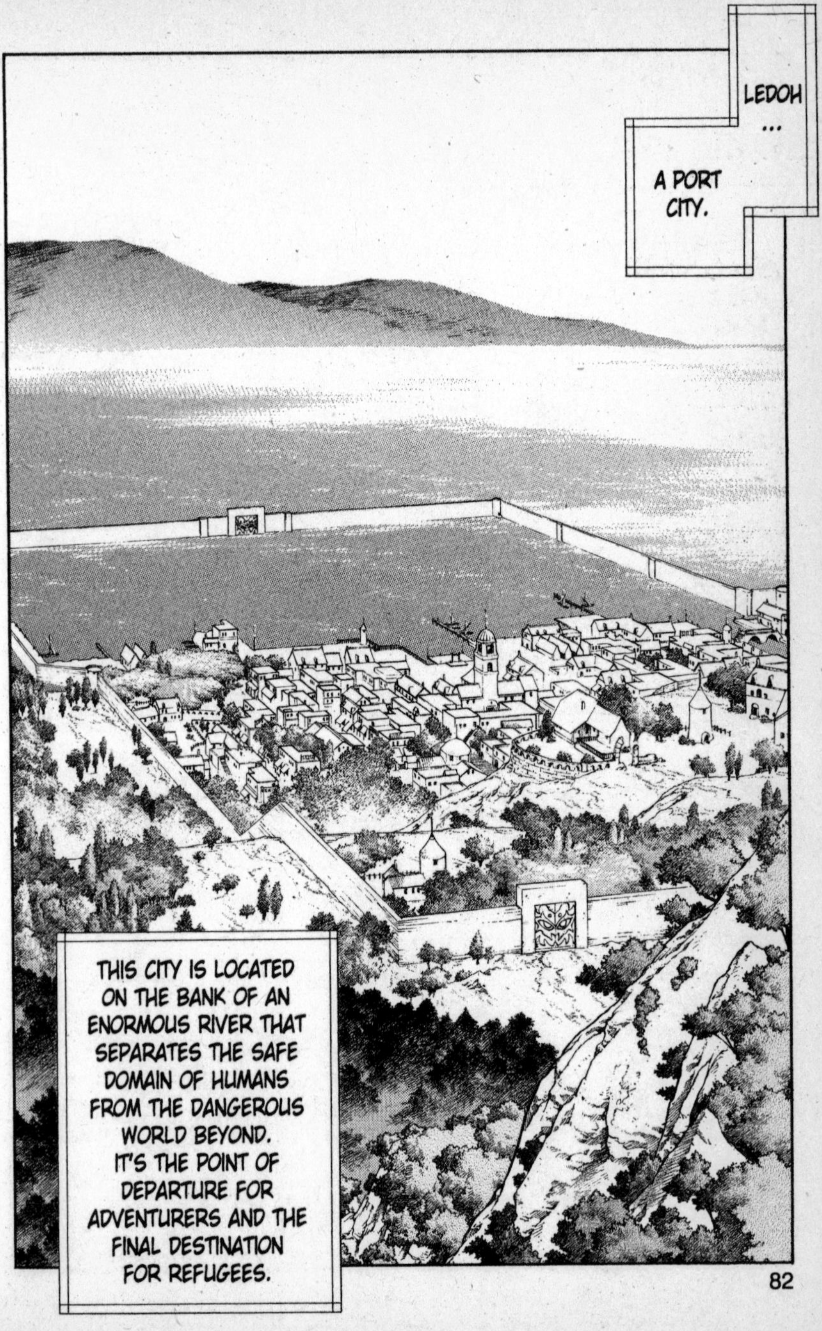
LEDOH ...
A PORT CITY.
THIS CITY IS LOCATED ON THE BANK OF AN ENORMOUS RIVER THAT SEPARATES THE SAFE DOMAIN OF HUMANS FROM THE DANGEROUS WORLD BEYOND. IT'S THE POINT OF DEPARTURE FOR ADVENTURERS AND THE FINAL DESTINATION FOR REFUGEES.

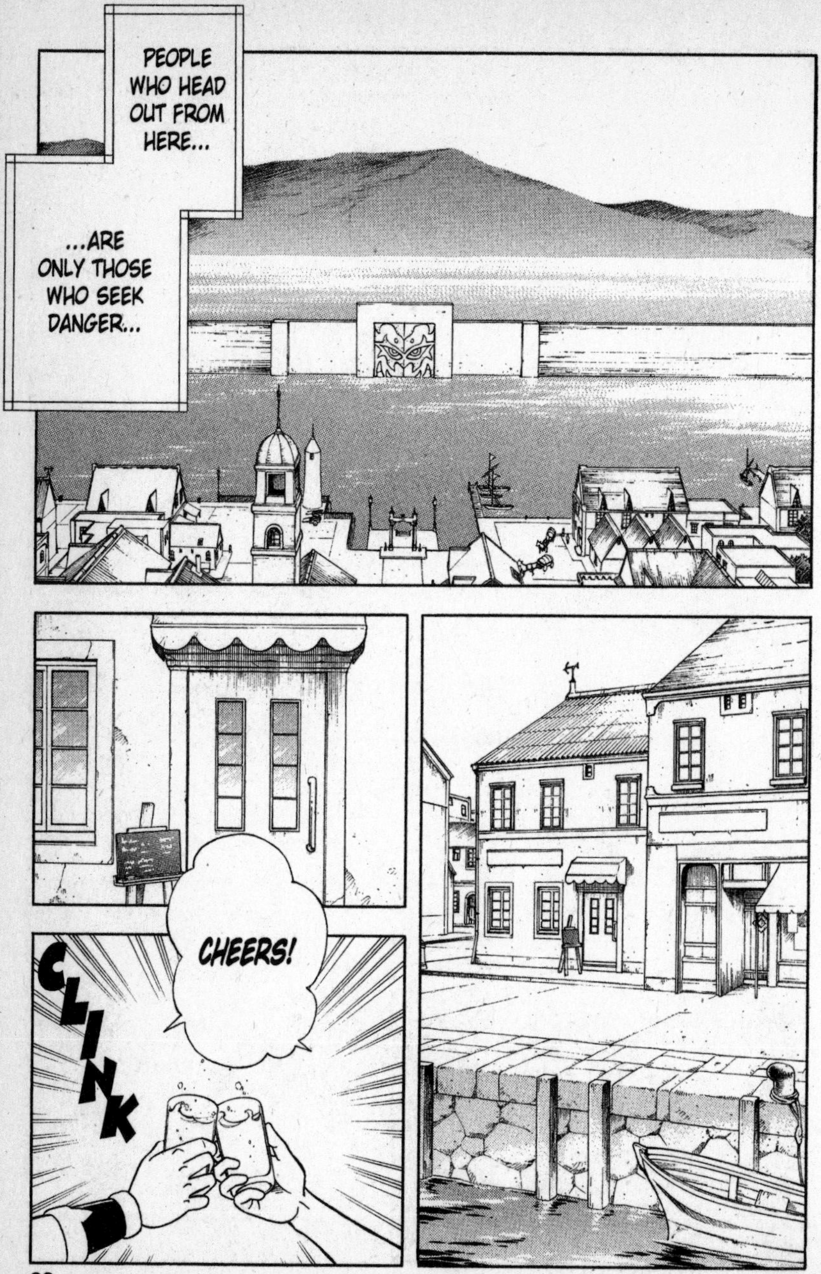
PEOPLE WHO HEAD OUT FROM HERE...
...ARE ONLY THOSE WHO SEEK DANGER...
CHEERS!
CLINK

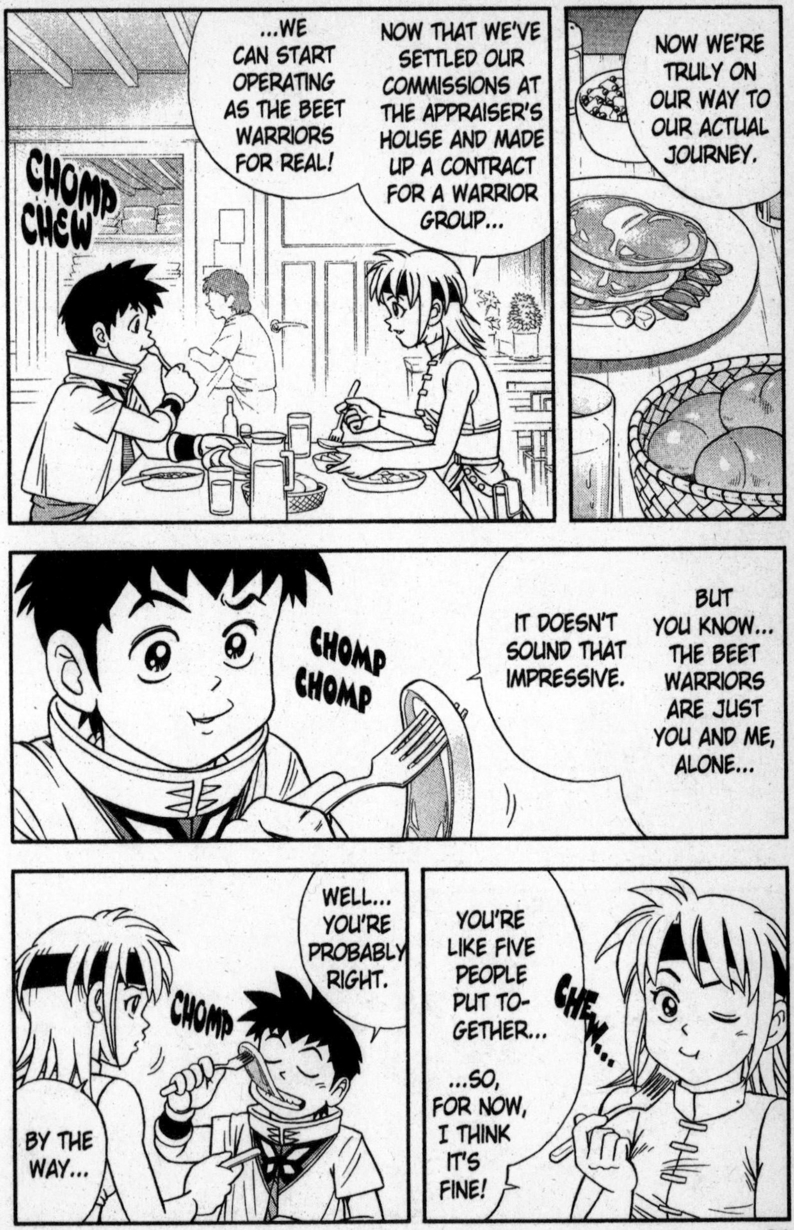
NOW WE'RE TRULY ON OUR WAY TO OUR ACTUAL JOURNEY.
NOW THAT WE'VE SETTLED OUR COMMISSIONS AT THE APPRAISER'S HOUSE AND MADE UP A CONTRACT FOR A WARRIOR GROUP...
...WE CAN START OPERATING AS THE BEET WARRIORS FOR REAL!
CHOMP CHEW
BUT YOU KNOW... THE BEET WARRIORS ARE JUST YOU AND ME, ALONE...
IT DOESN'T SOUND THAT IMPRESSIVE.
CHOMP CHOMP
YOU'RE LIKE FIVE PEOPLE PUT TO-GETHER...
...SO, FOR NOW, I THINK IT'S FINE!
CHEW...
WELL... YOU'RE PROBABLY RIGHT.
CHOMP
BY THE WAY...

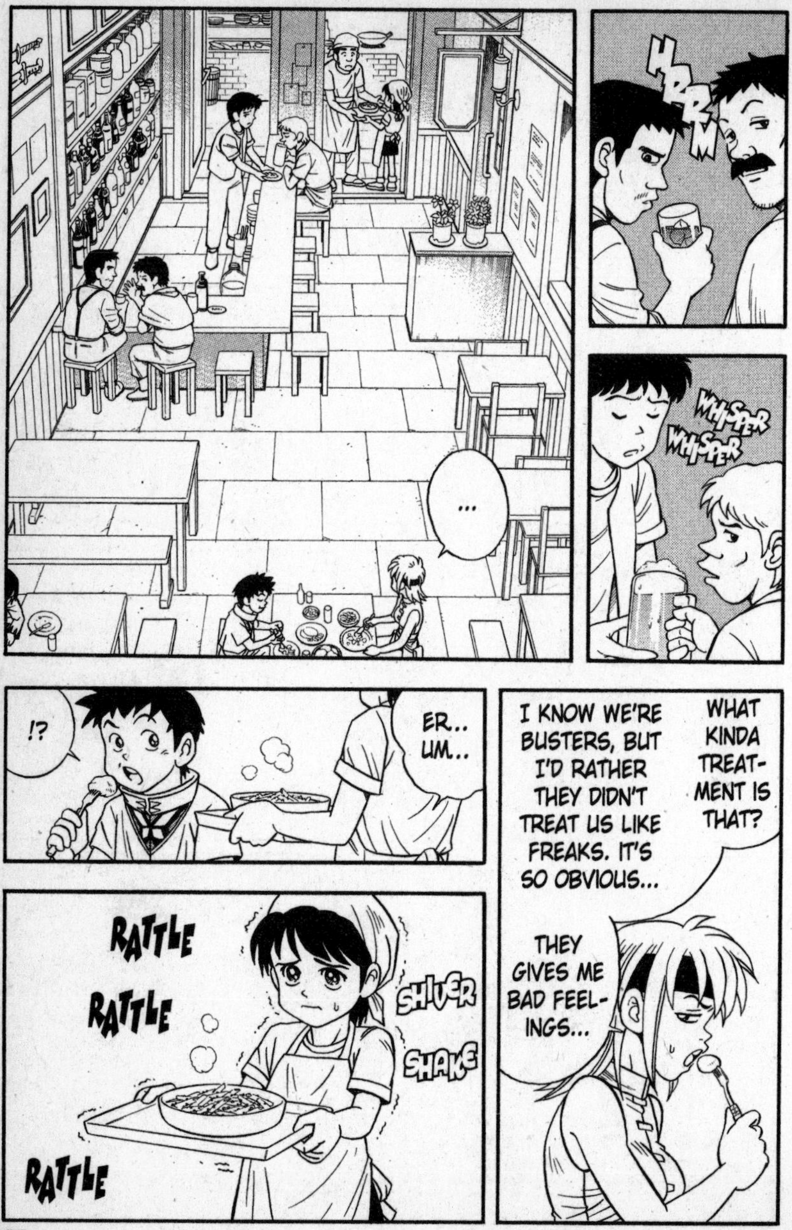
HRRM
WHISPER
WHISPER
...
WHAT KINDA TREATMENT IS THAT?
I KNOW WE'RE BUSTERS, BUT I'D RATHER THEY DIDN'T TREAT US LIKE FREAKS. IT'S SO OBVIOUS...
THEY GIVES ME BAD FEELINGS...
ER... UM...
!?
SHIVER
SHAKE
RATTLE
RATTLE
RATTLE

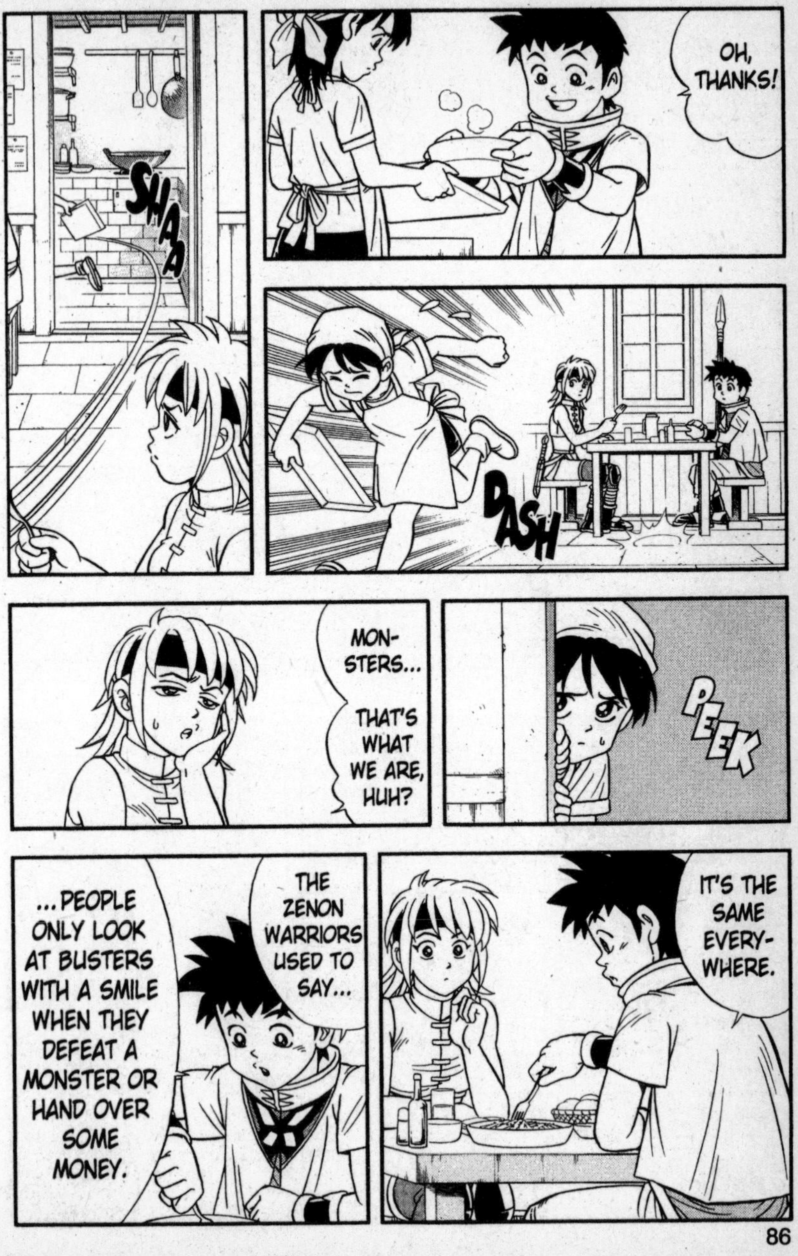

OH, THANKS!
DASH
SHAA
PEEK
MON-STERS...
THAT'S WHAT WE ARE, HUH?
IT'S THE SAME EVERY-WHERE.
THE ZENON WARRIORS USED TO SAY...
...PEOPLE ONLY LOOK AT BUSTERS WITH A SMILE WHEN THEY DEFEAT A MONSTER OR HAND OVER SOME MONEY.

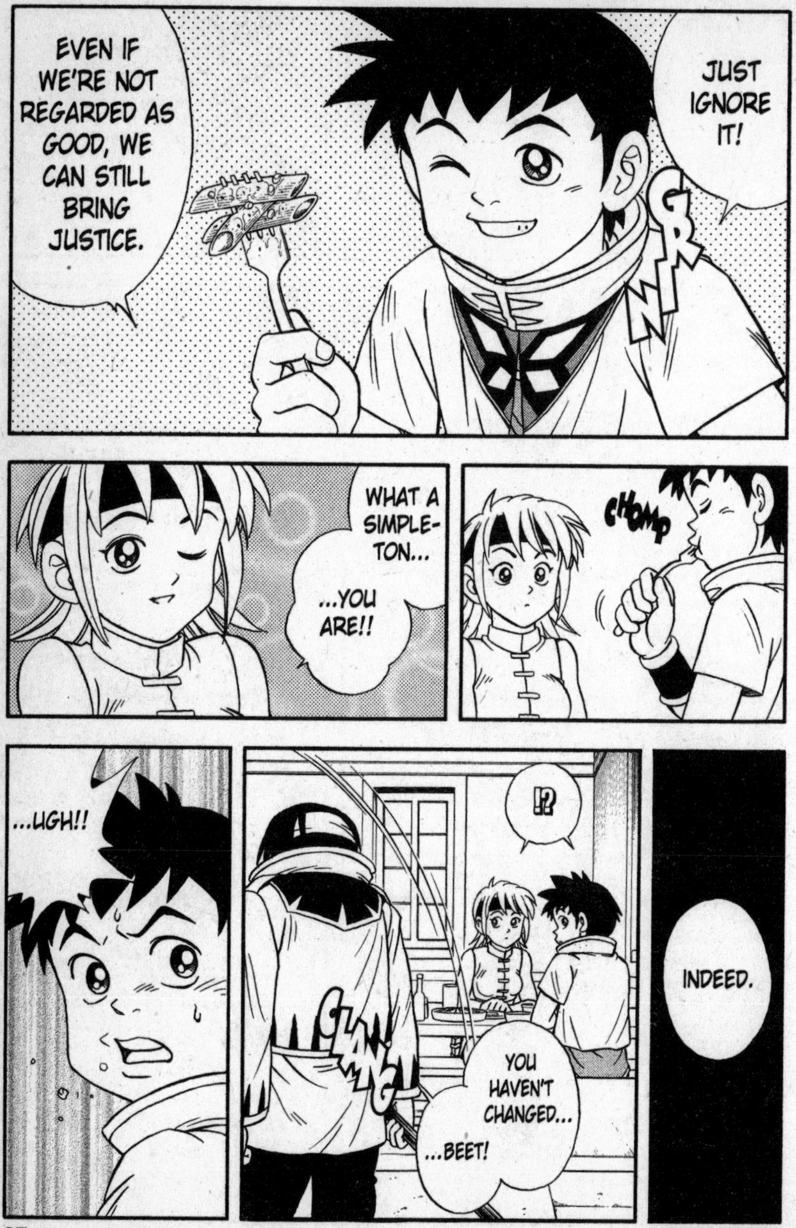
JUST IGNORE IT!
EVEN IF WE'RE NOT REGARDED AS GOOD, WE CAN STILL BRING JUSTICE.
CHOMP
WHAT A SIMPLE-TON...
...YOU ARE!!
INDEED.
!?
CLANG
YOU HAVEN'T CHANGED...
...BEET!
...UGH!!

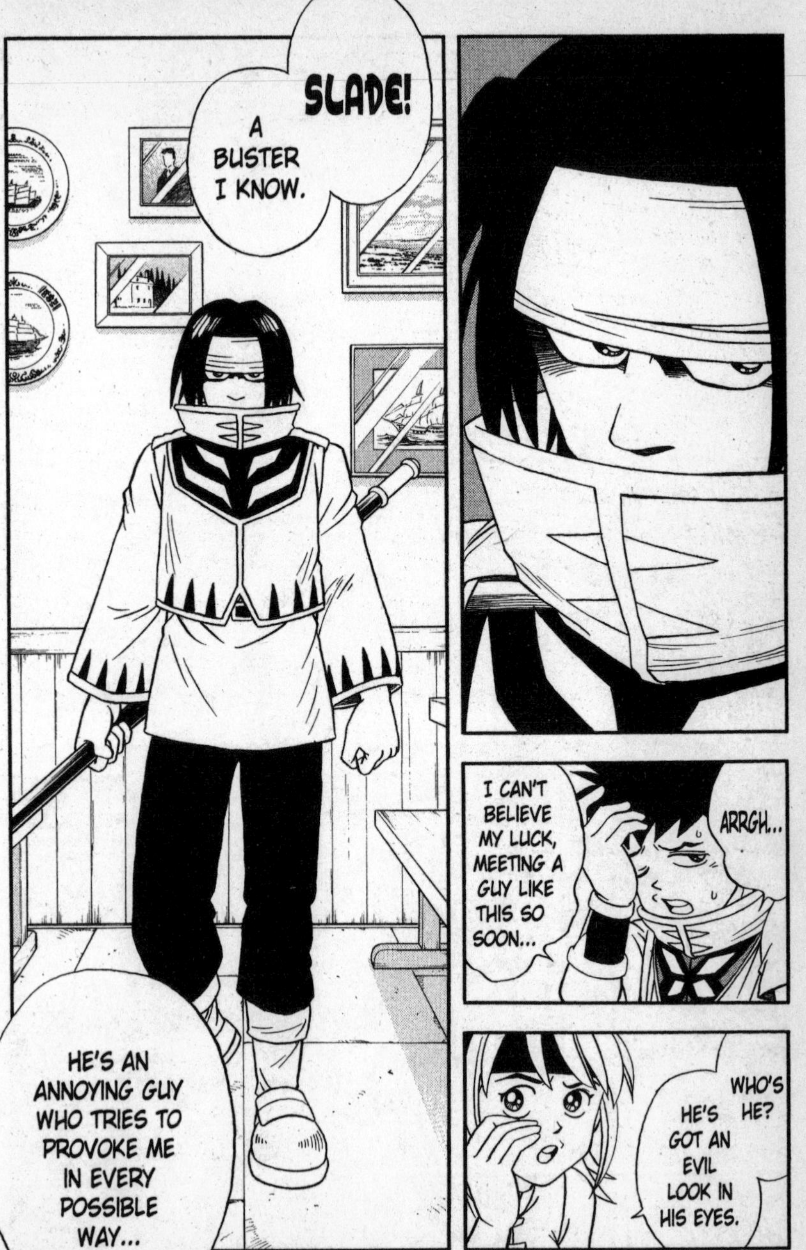
ARRGH...
I CAN'T BELIEVE MY LUCK, MEETING A GUY LIKE THIS SO SOON...
WHO'S HE?
HE'S GOT AN EVIL LOOK IN HIS EYES.
SLADE!
A BUSTER I KNOW.
HE'S AN ANNOYING GUY WHO TRIES TO PROVOKE ME IN EVERY POSSIBLE WAY...

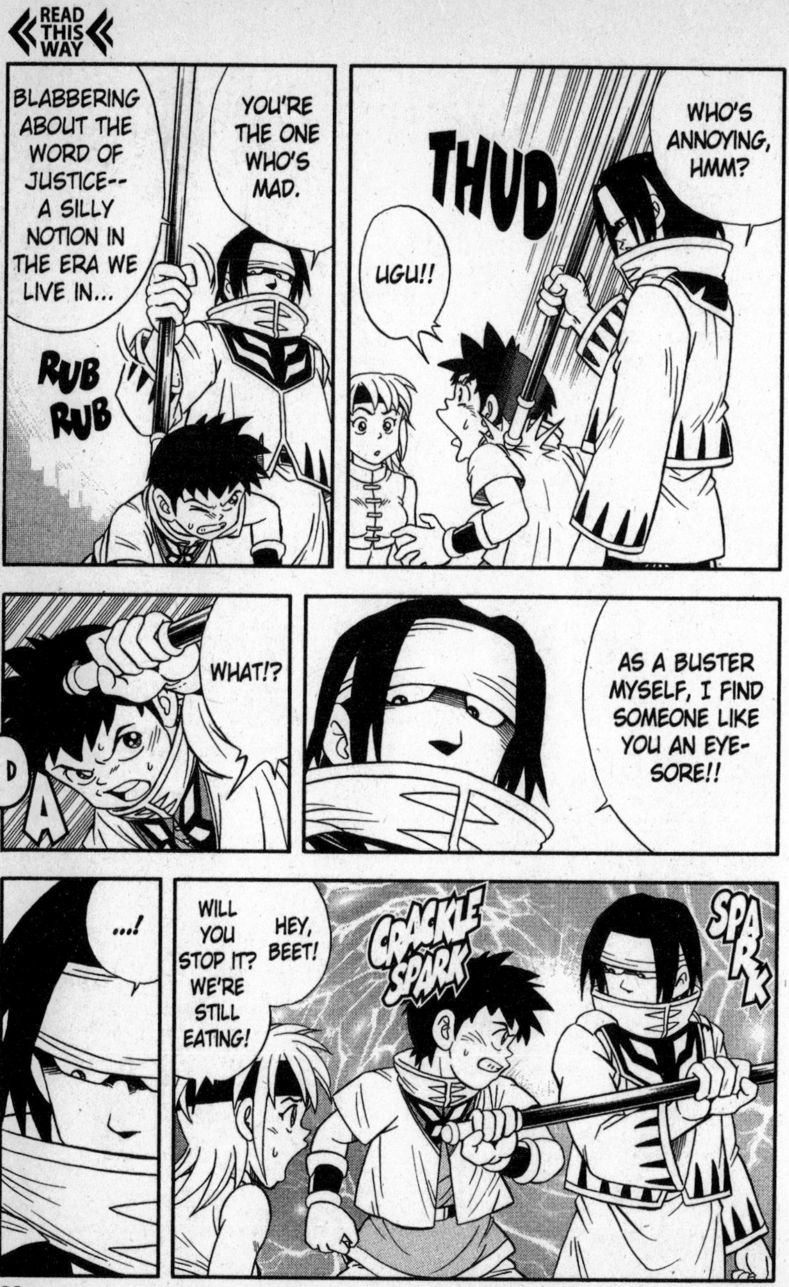
READ THIS WAY
WHO'S ANNOYING, HMM?
THUD
UGU!!
YOU'RE THE ONE WHO'S MAD.
BLABBERING ABOUT THE WORD OF JUSTICE-- A SILLY NOTION IN THE ERA WE LIVE IN...
RUB RUB
AS A BUSTER MYSELF, I FIND SOMEONE LIKE YOU AN EYE-SORE!!
WHAT!?
DA
SPARK
CRACKLE SPARK
HEY, BEET!
WILL YOU STOP IT? WE'RE STILL EATING!
...!

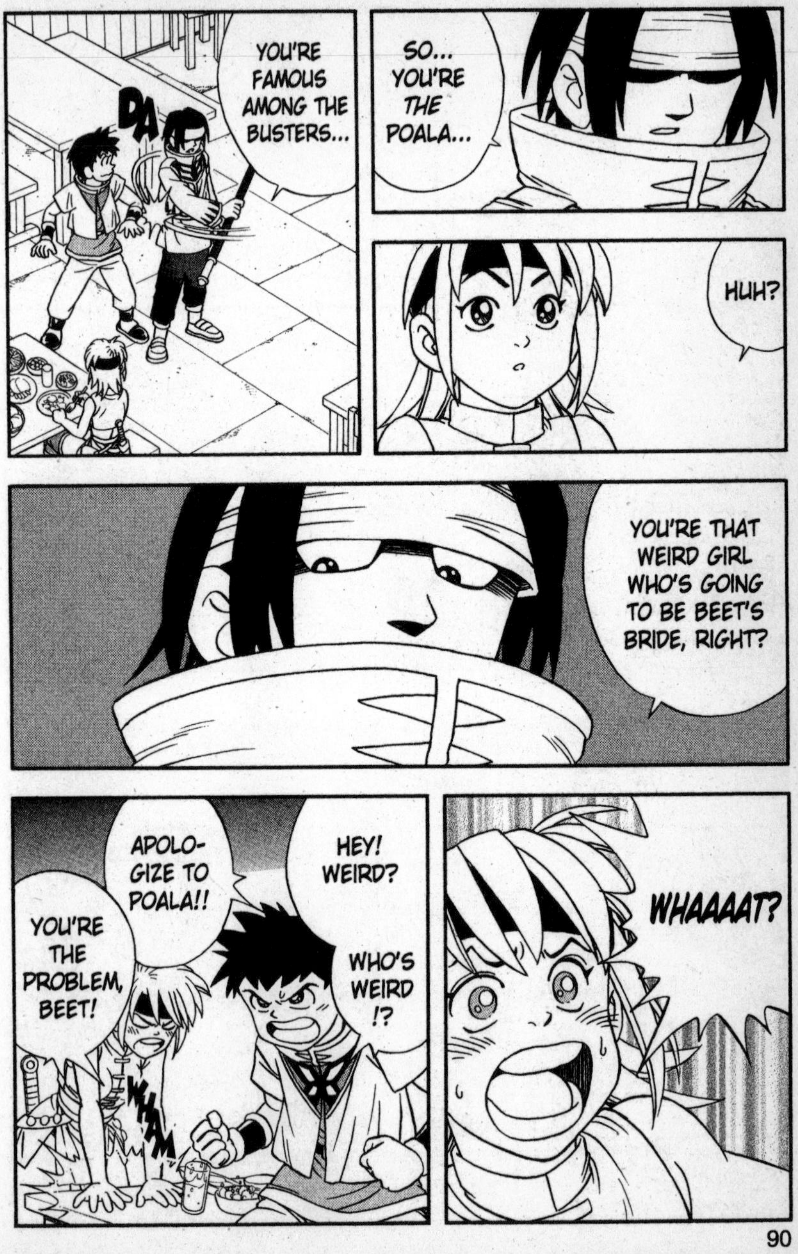
SO... YOU'RE THE POALA...
HUH?
YOU'RE FAMOUS AMONG THE BUSTERS...
DA
YOU'RE THAT WEIRD GIRL WHO'S GOING TO BE BEET'S BRIDE, RIGHT?
WHAAAAT?
HEY! WEIRD?
WHO'S WEIRD !?
APOLO-GIZE TO POALA!!
YOU'RE THE PROBLEM, BEET!
WHAM

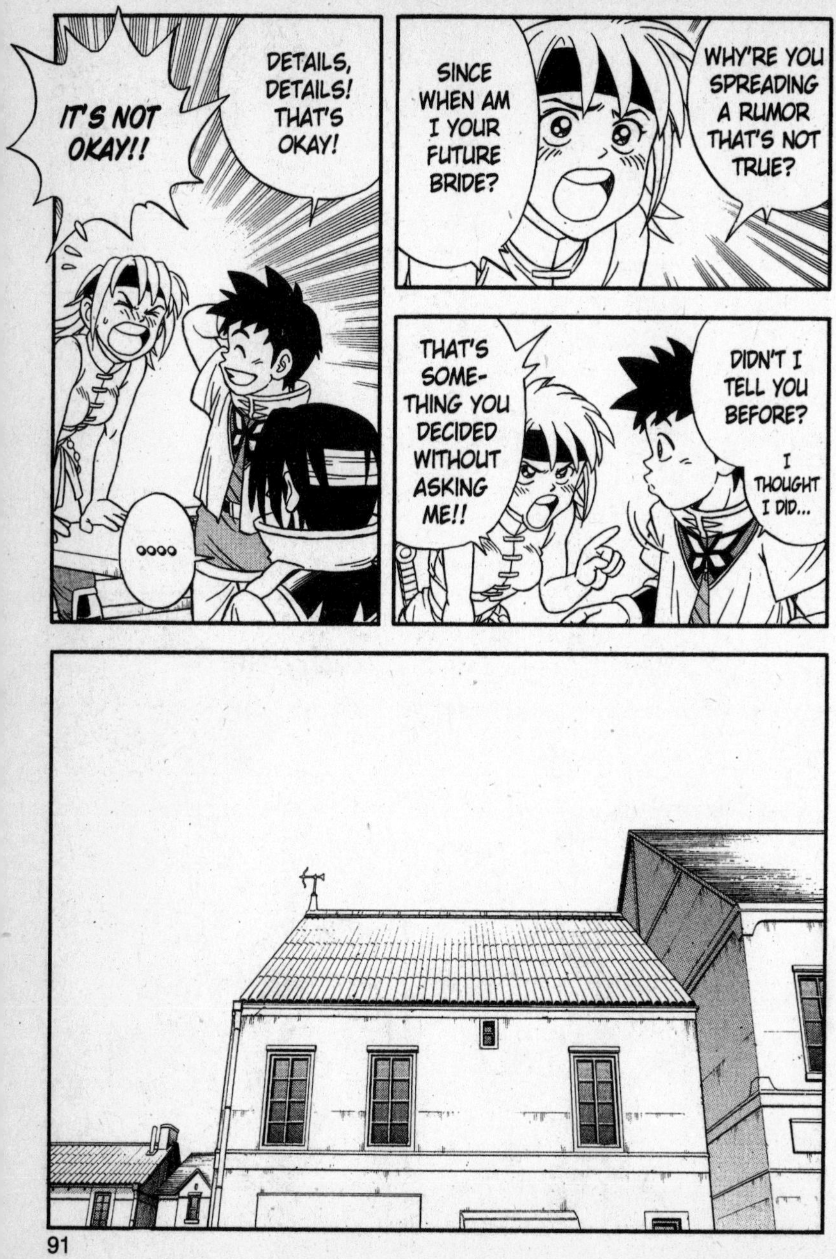
WHY'RE YOU SPREADING A RUMOR THAT'S NOT TRUE?
SINCE WHEN AM I YOUR FUTURE BRIDE?
DIDN'T I TELL YOU BEFORE?
I THOUGHT I DID...
THAT'S SOME-THING YOU DECIDED WITHOUT ASKING ME!!
DETAILS, DETAILS! THAT'S OKAY!
IT'S NOT OKAY!!
....

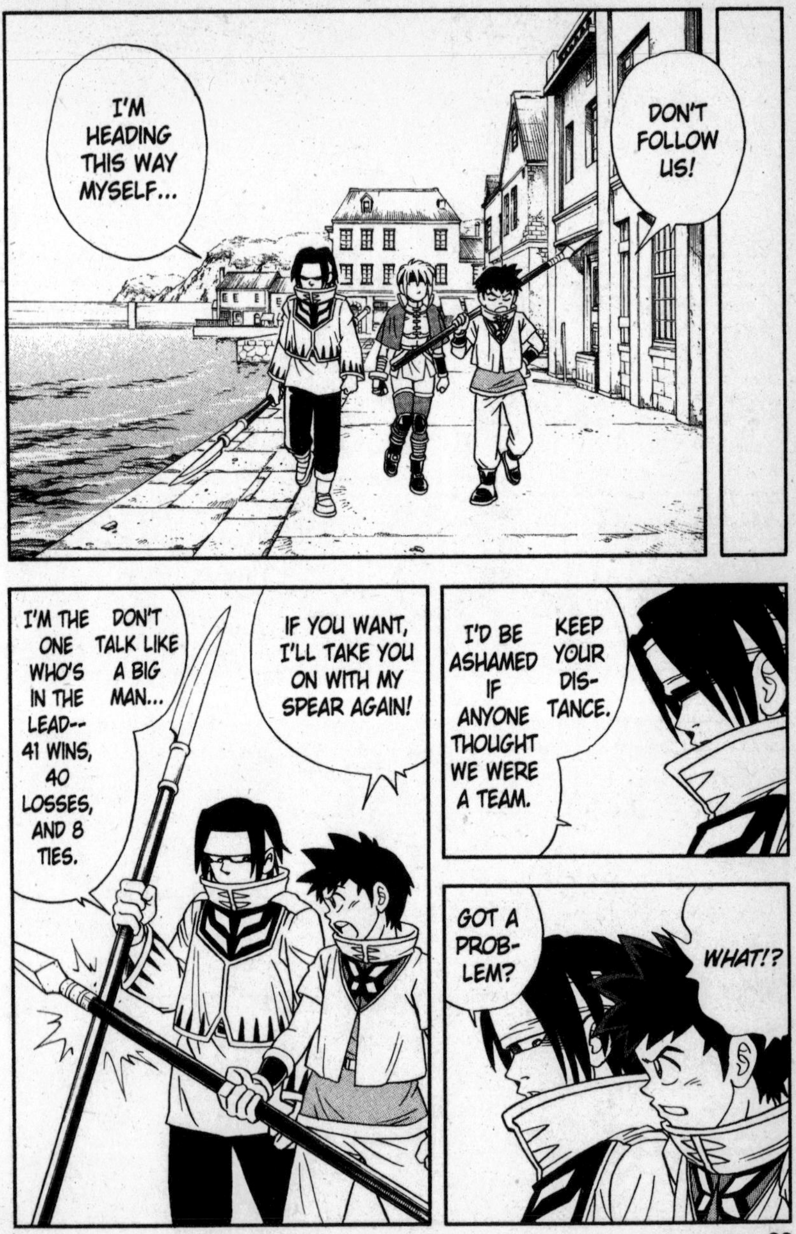
DON'T FOLLOW US!
I'M HEADING THIS WAY MYSELF...
KEEP YOUR DISTANCE.
I'D BE ASHAMED IF ANYONE THOUGHT WE WERE A TEAM.
WHAT!?
GOT A PROBLEM?
IF YOU WANT, I'LL TAKE YOU ON WITH MY SPEAR AGAIN!
DON'T TALK LIKE A BIG MAN...
I'M THE ONE WHO'S IN THE LEAD-- 41 WINS, 40 LOSSES, AND 8 TIES.

READ THIS WAY

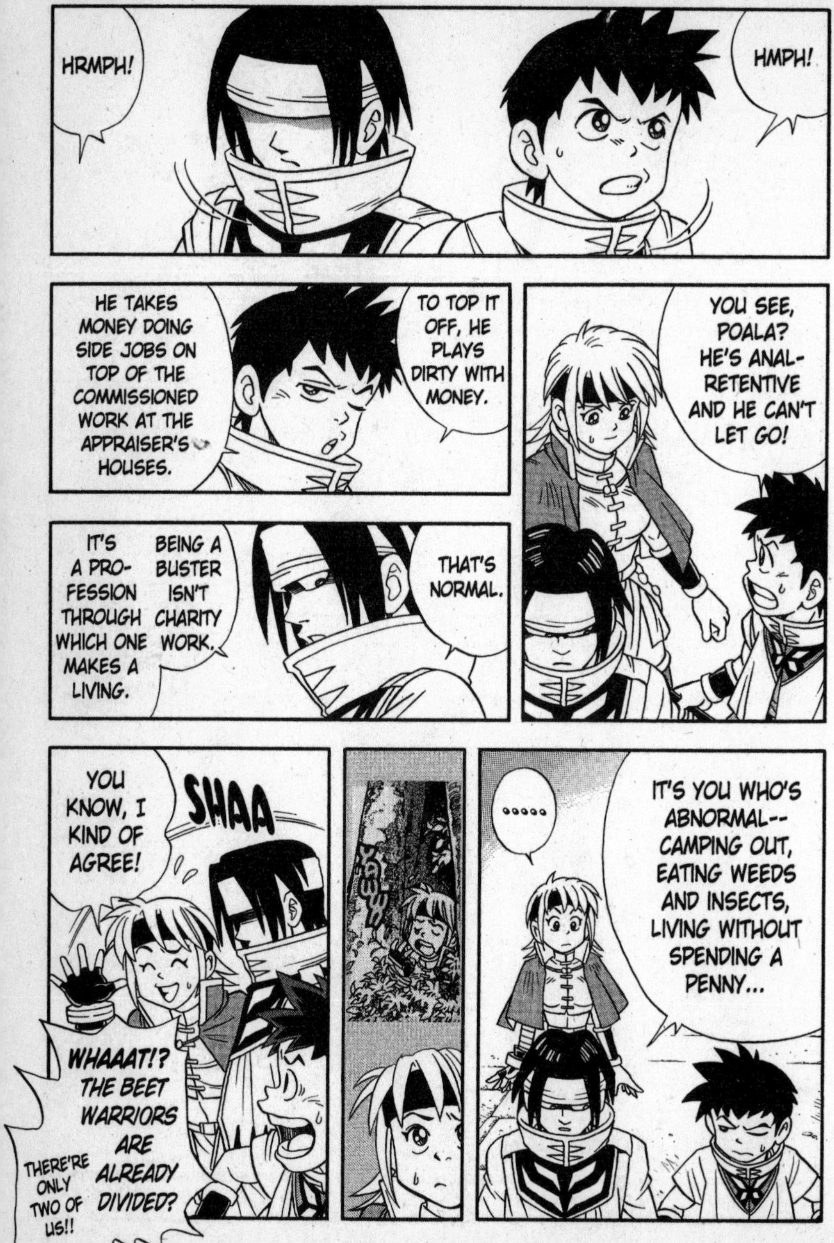
HMPH!
HRMPH!
YOU SEE, POALA? HE'S ANAL-RETENTIVE AND HE CAN'T LET GO!
TO TOP IT OFF, HE PLAYS DIRTY WITH MONEY.
HE TAKES MONEY DOING SIDE JOBS ON TOP OF THE COMMISSIONED WORK AT THE APPRAISER'S HOUSES.
THAT'S NORMAL.
BEING A BUSTER ISN'T CHARITY WORK.
IT'S A PROFESSION THROUGH WHICH ONE MAKES A LIVING.
.....
IT'S YOU WHO'S ABNORMAL-- CAMPING OUT, EATING WEEDS AND INSECTS, LIVING WITHOUT SPENDING A PENNY...
YOU KNOW, I KIND OF AGREE!
SHAA
WHAAAT!? THE BEET WARRIORS ARE ALREADY DIVIDED?
THERE'RE ONLY TWO OF US!!

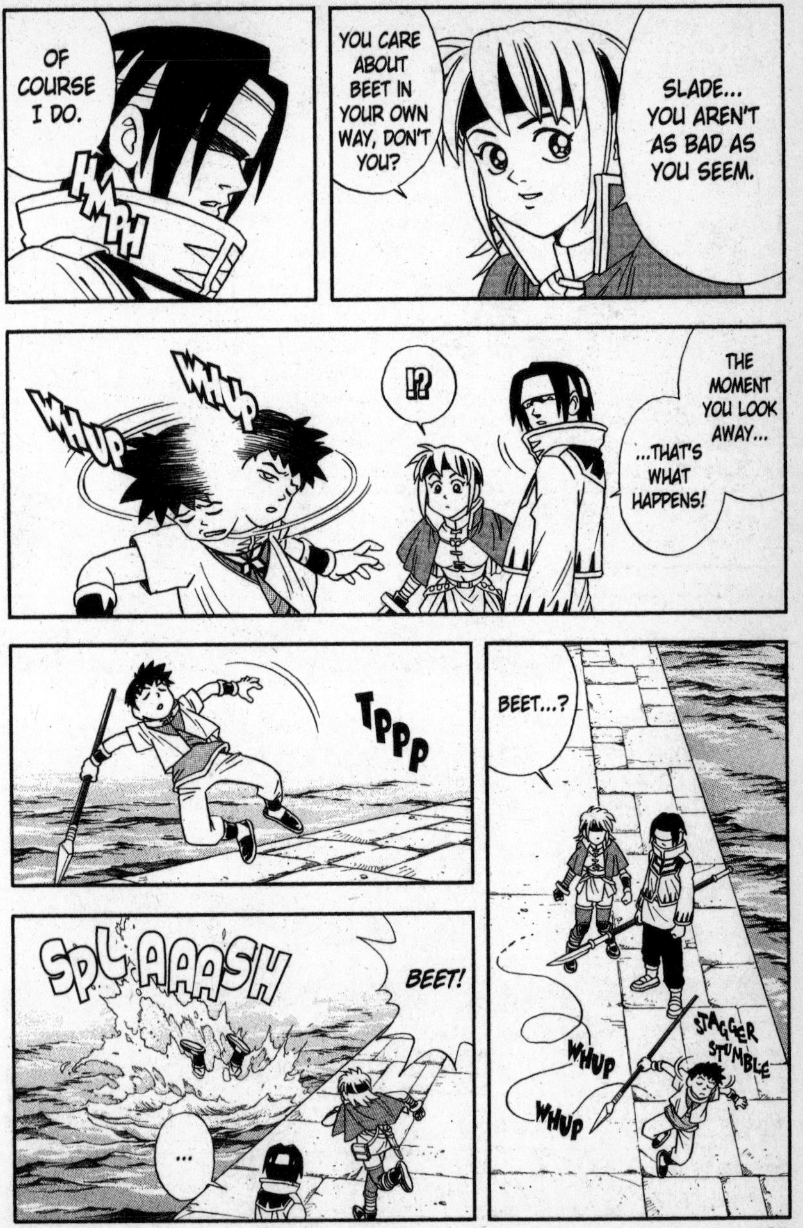
SLADE... YOU AREN'T AS BAD AS YOU SEEM.
YOU CARE ABOUT BEET IN YOUR OWN WAY, DON'T YOU?
OF COURSE I DO.
HMMPH
THE MOMENT YOU LOOK AWAY...
...THAT'S WHAT HAPPENS!
!?
WHUP
WHUP
BEET...?
STAGGER STUMBLE
WHUP
WHUP
TPPP
BEET!
SPLAAASH
...

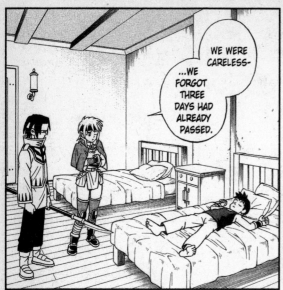

WE WERE CARELESS-
...WE FORGOT THREE DAYS HAD ALREADY PASSED.
NOW HE'S GOING TO SLEEP FOR A WHOLE DAY.
IT'S THE WAY HE IS.
WHEN BEET'S HEAD STARTS TO SWING, IT'S THE DANGER SIGNAL.
IF YOU'RE GONNA BE HIS BRIDE, YOU'D BETTER REMEMBER THAT.
LIKE I SAID, IT'S NOT LIKE THAT!!
GATCH
WHAT?
YOU'RE HEADING OUT ALREADY?

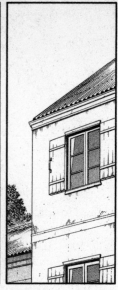

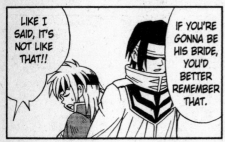

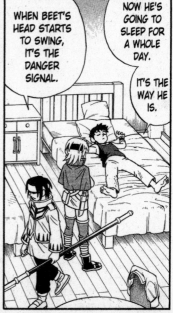

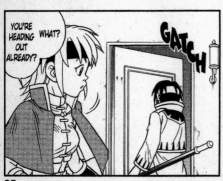

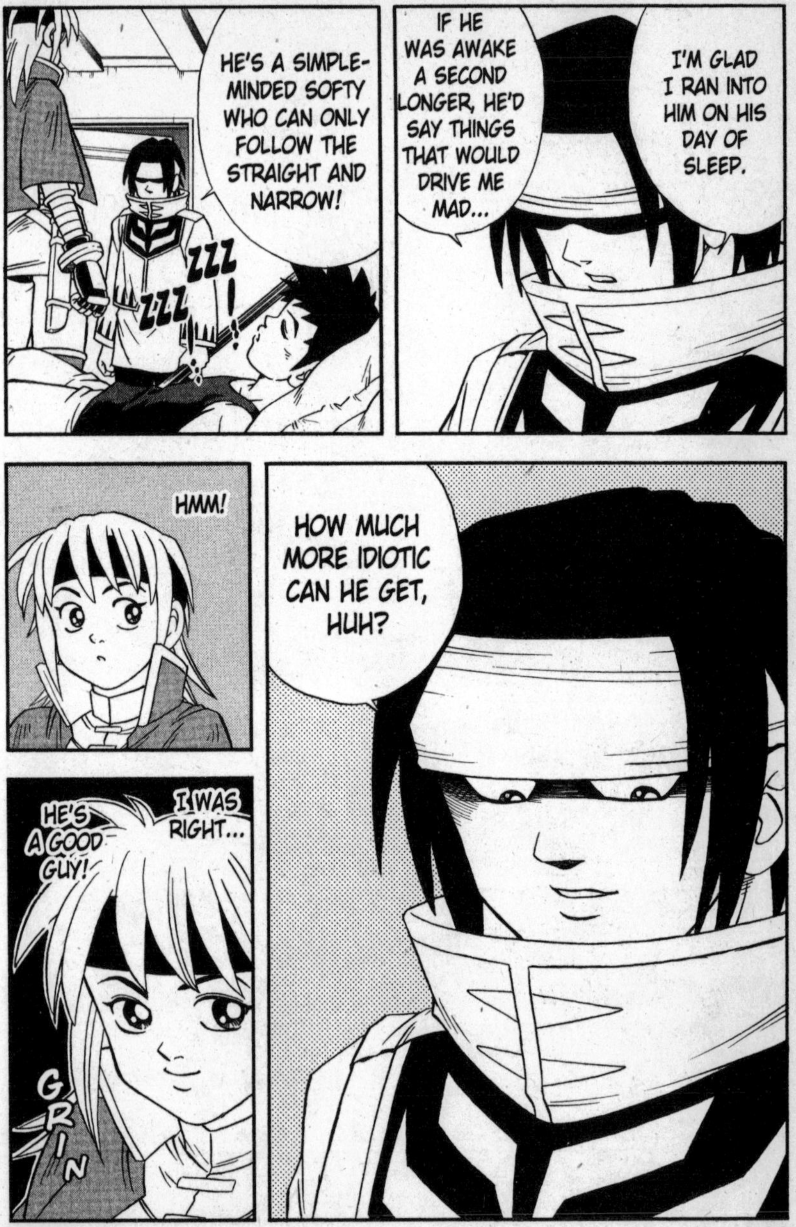
I'M GLAD I RAN INTO HIM ON HIS DAY OF SLEEP.
IF HE WAS AWAKE A SECOND LONGER, HE'D SAY THINGS THAT WOULD DRIVE ME MAD...
HE'S A SIMPLE-MINDED SOFTY WHO CAN ONLY FOLLOW THE STRAIGHT AND NARROW!
ZZZ
ZZZ
HOW MUCH MORE IDIOTIC CAN HE GET, HUH?
HMM!
I WAS RIGHT...
HE'S A GOOD GUY!
GRIN

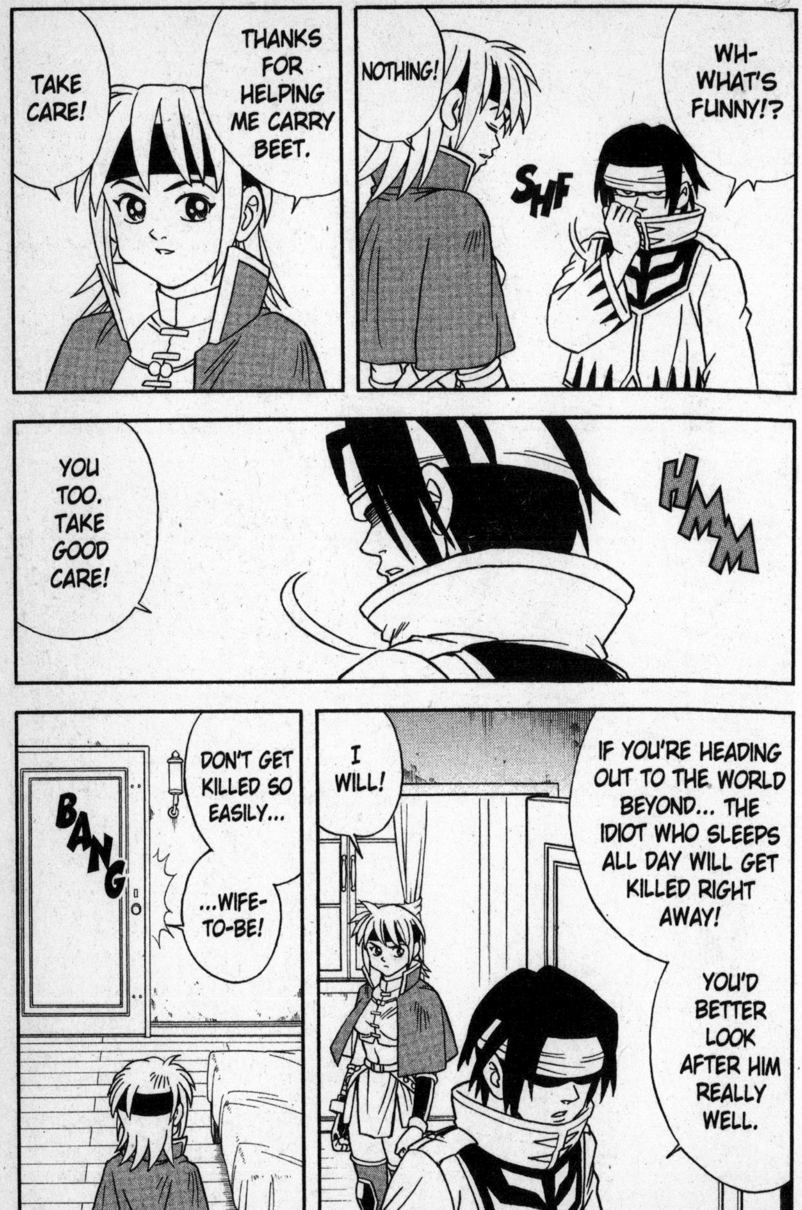
WH- WHAT'S FUNNY!?
SHF
NOTHING!
THANKS FOR HELPING ME CARRY BEET.
TAKE CARE!
HMMM
YOU TOO. TAKE GOOD CARE!
IF YOU'RE HEADING OUT TO THE WORLD BEYOND... THE IDIOT WHO SLEEPS ALL DAY WILL GET KILLED RIGHT AWAY!
YOU'D BETTER LOOK AFTER HIM REALLY WELL.
I WILL!
DON'T GET KILLED SO EASILY...
...WIFE-TO-BE!
BANG

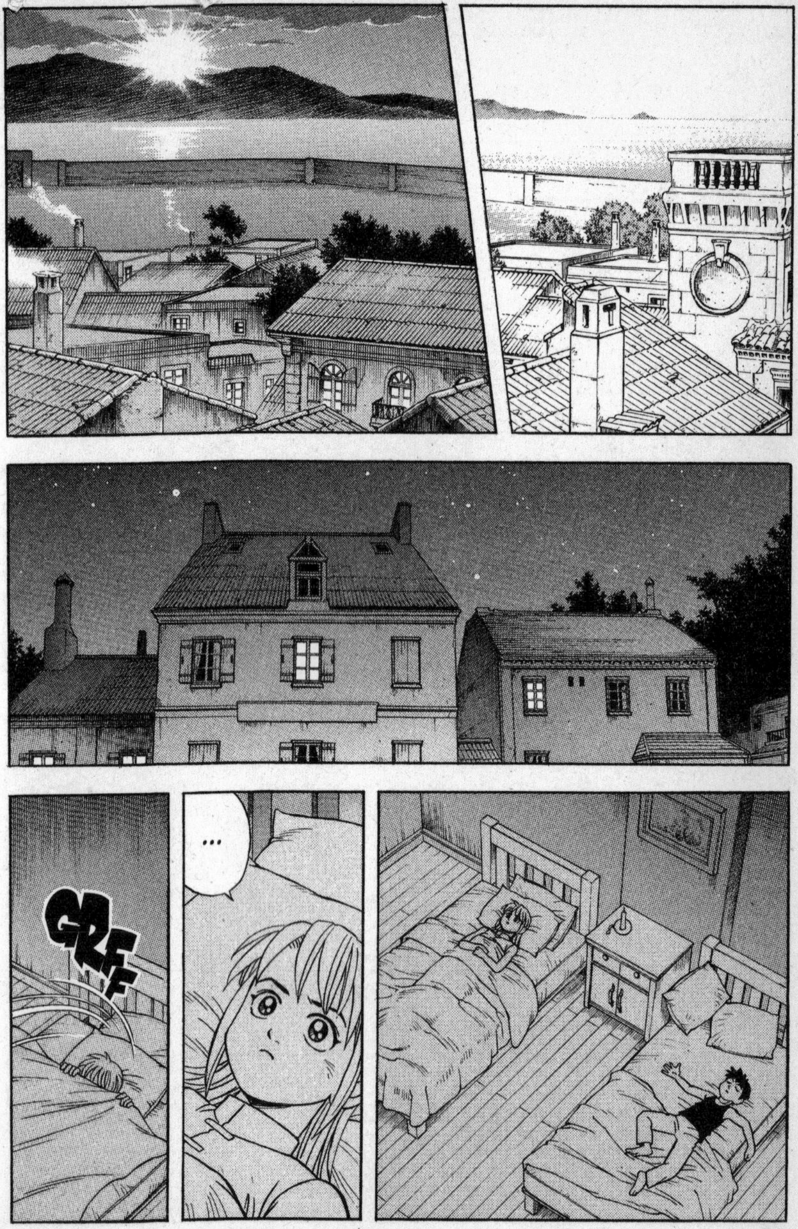
...
GRFF

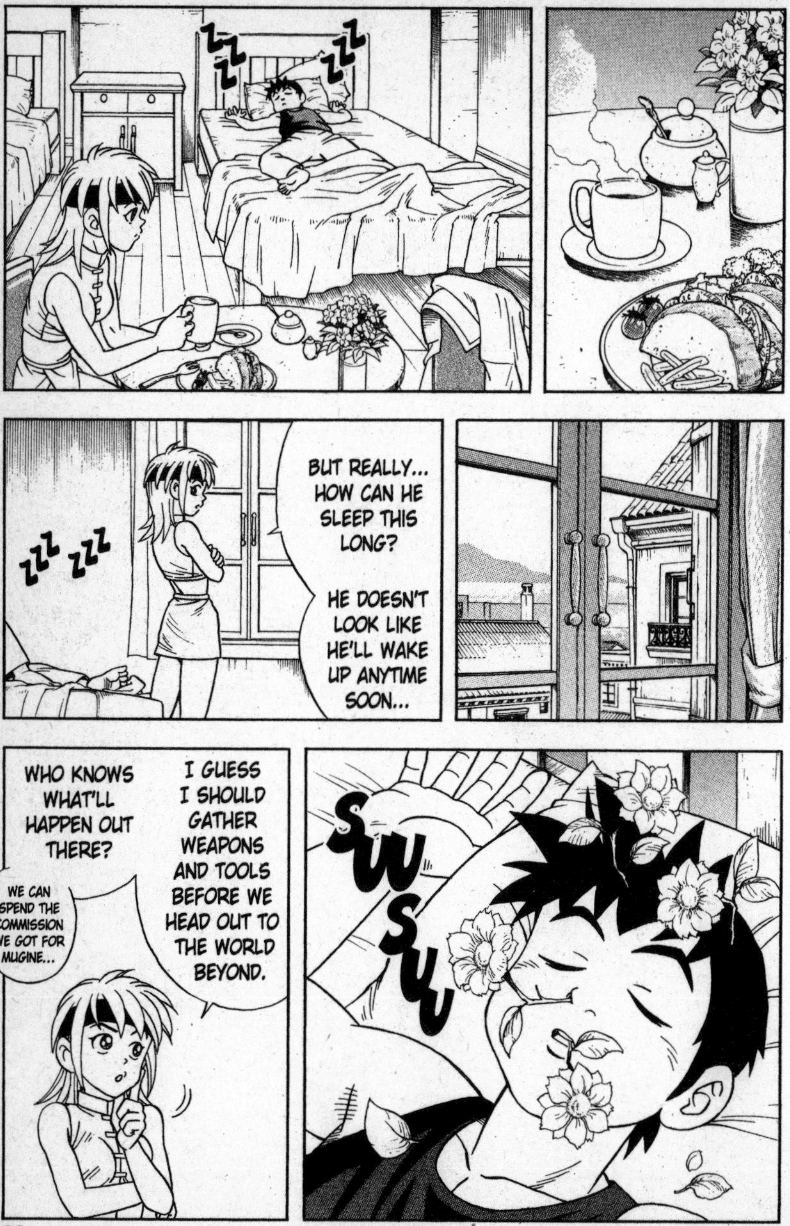
ZZZ ZZZ
BUT REALLY... HOW CAN HE SLEEP THIS LONG?
HE DOESN'T LOOK LIKE HE'LL WAKE UP ANYTIME SOON...
ZZZ ZZZ
SUU SUU
I GUESS I SHOULD GATHER WEAPONS AND TOOLS BEFORE WE HEAD OUT TO THE WORLD BEYOND.
WHO KNOWS WHAT'LL HAPPEN OUT THERE?
WE CAN SPEND THE COMMISSION WE GOT FOR MUGINE...

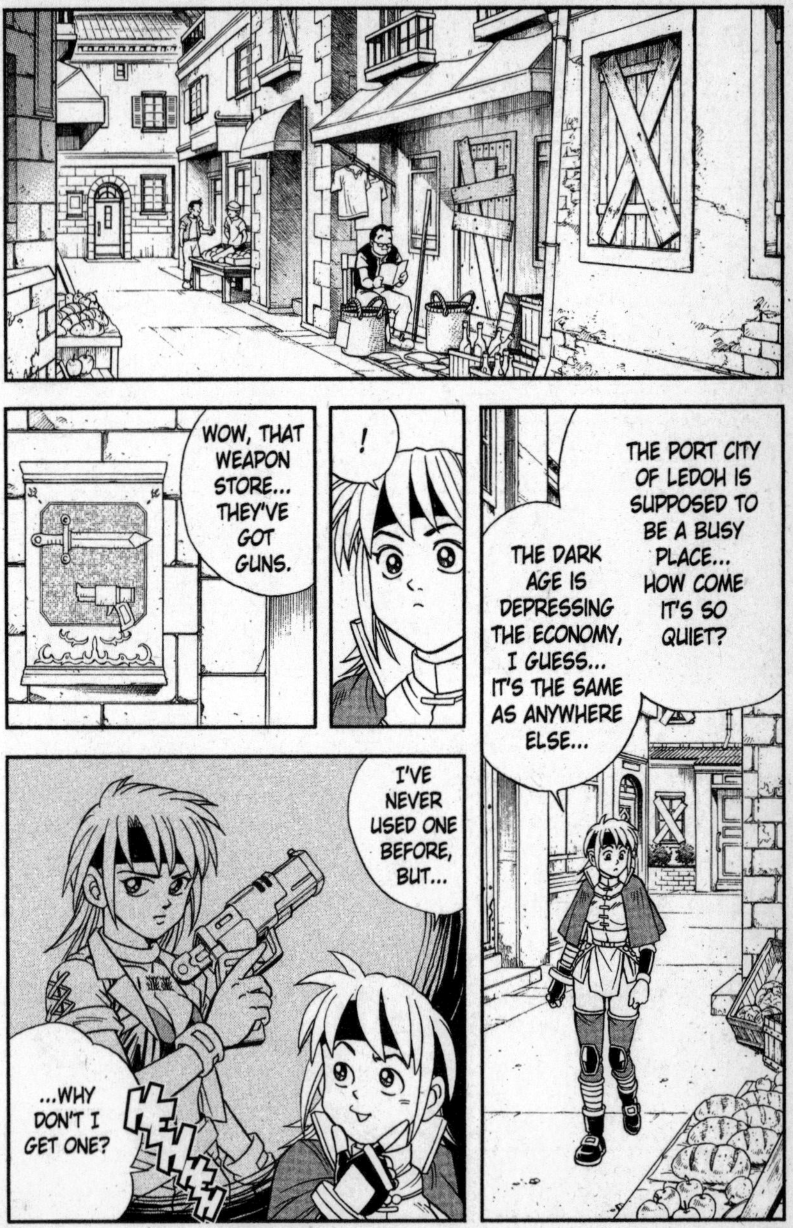
THE PORT CITY OF LEDOH IS SUPPOSED TO BE A BUSY PLACE... HOW COME IT'S SO QUIET?
THE DARK AGE IS DEPRESSING THE ECONOMY, I GUESS... IT'S THE SAME AS ANYWHERE ELSE...
!
WOW, THAT WEAPON STORE... THEY'VE GOT GUNS.
I'VE NEVER USED ONE BEFORE, BUT...
...WHY DON'T I GET ONE?

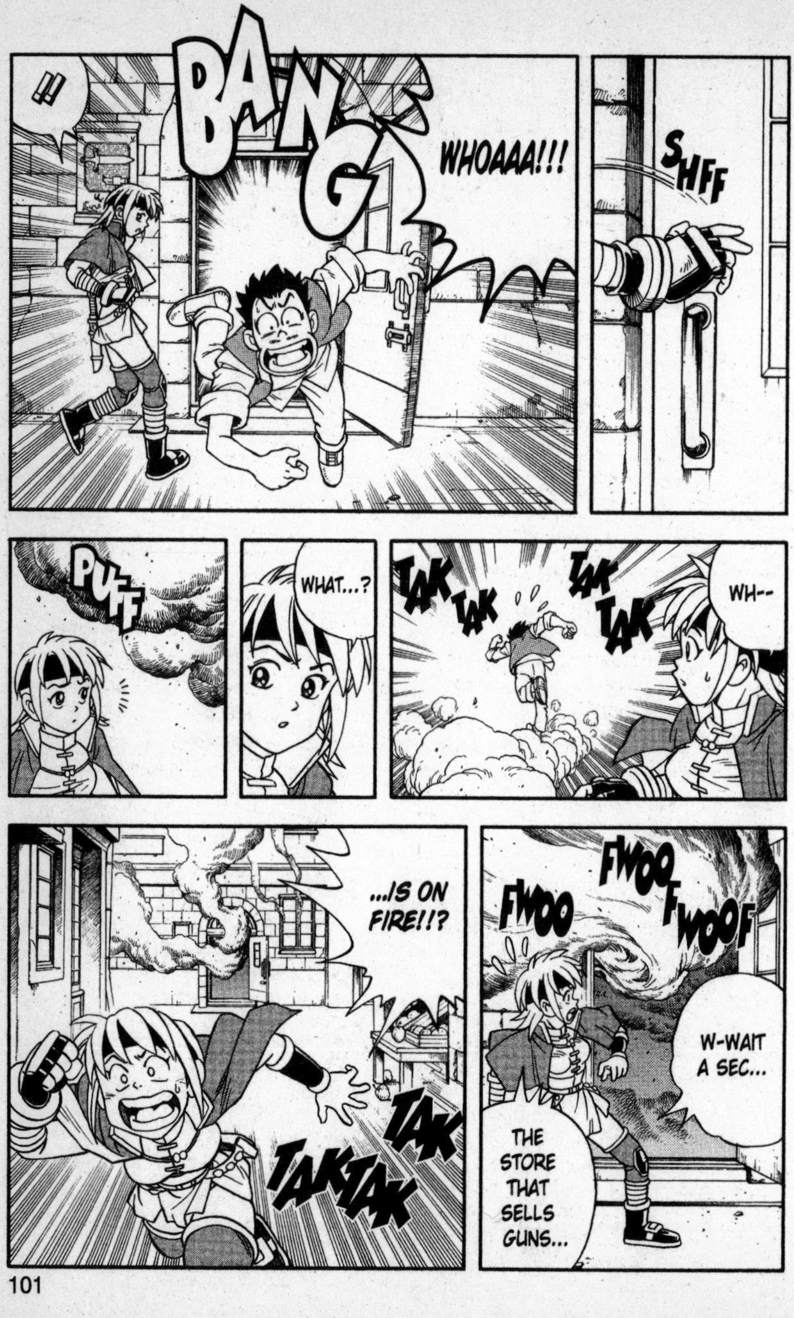
SHFF
WHOAAA!!!
BANG
!!
WH--
TAK TAK
TAK TAK
WHAT...?
PUFF
FWOOF WOOF
FWOO
W-WAIT A SEC...
THE STORE THAT SELLS GUNS...
...IS ON FIRE!!?
TAK TAKTAK

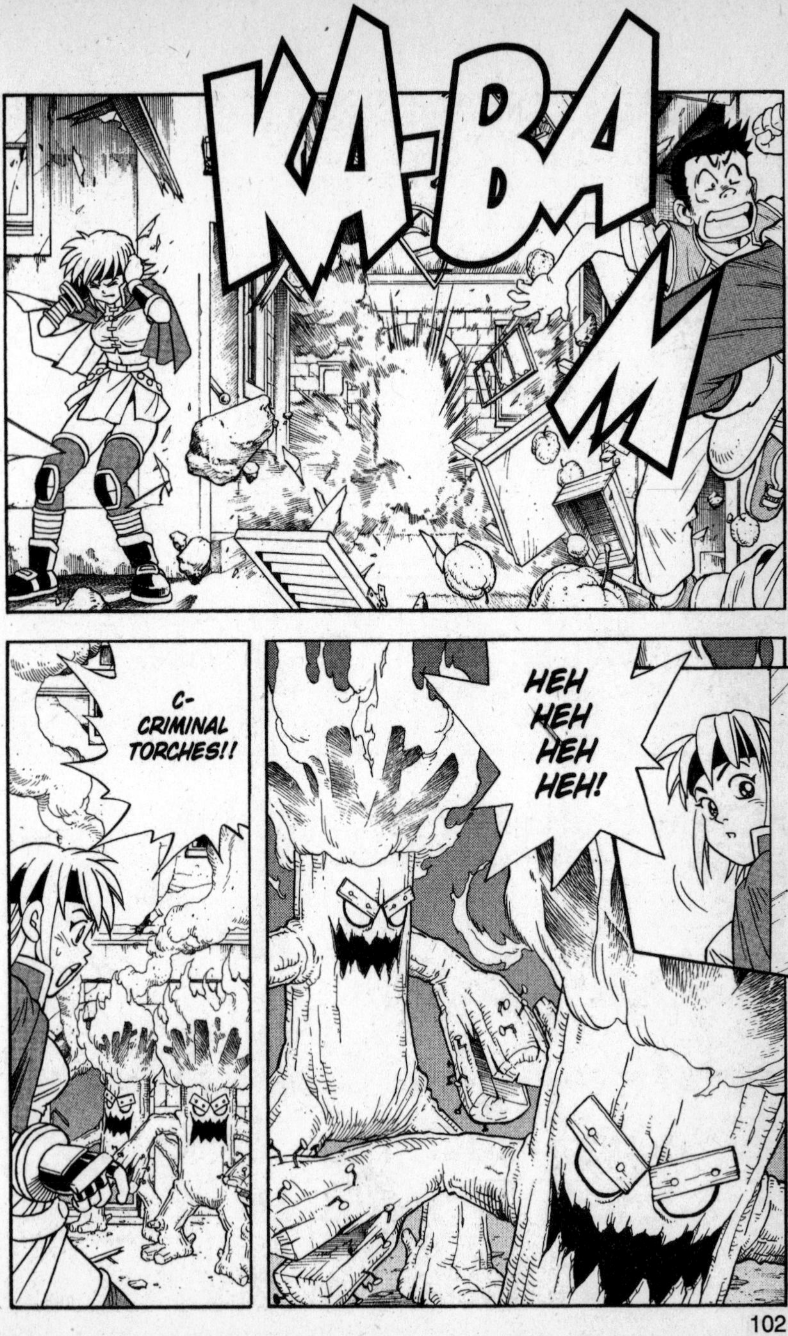
KA-BAM
HEH HEH HEH HEH!
C-CRIMINAL TORCHES!!

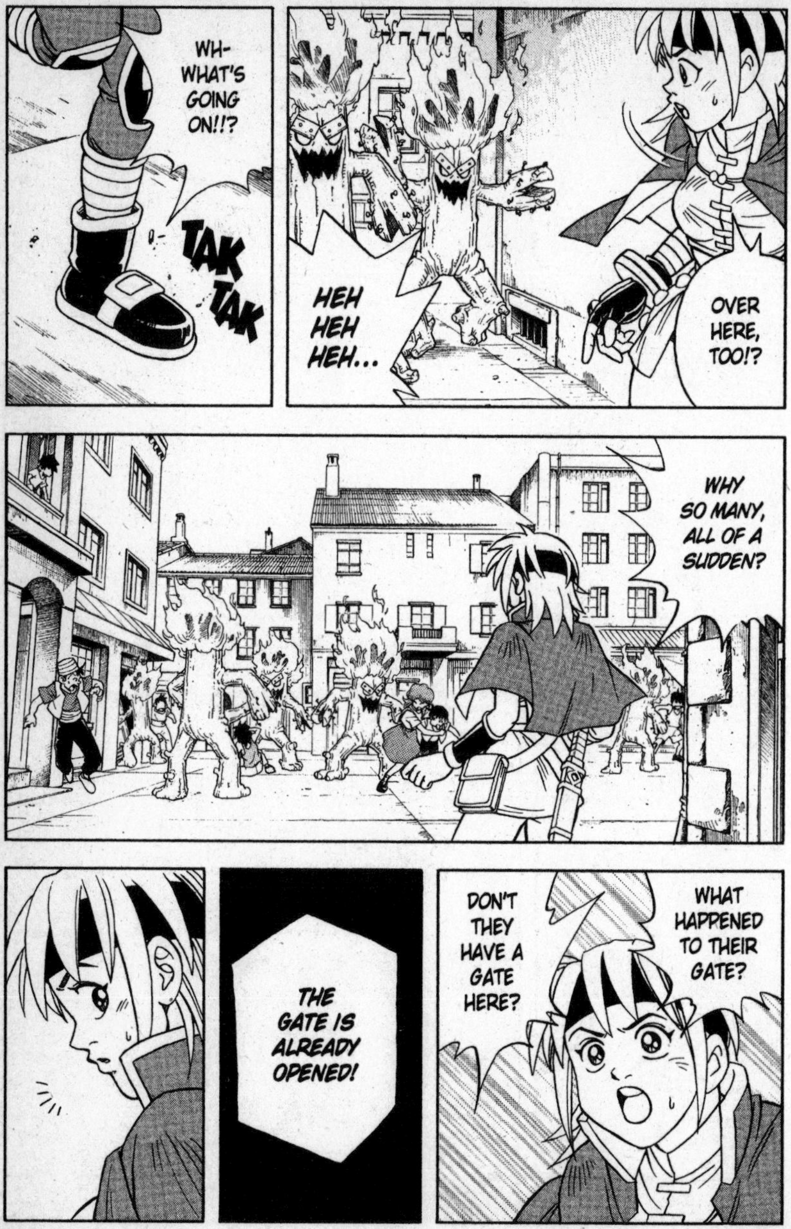
OVER HERE, TOO!?
HEH HEH HEH...
WH- WHAT'S GOING ON!!?
TAK TAK
WHY SO MANY, ALL OF A SUDDEN?
WHAT HAPPENED TO THEIR GATE?
DON'T THEY HAVE A GATE HERE?
THE GATE IS ALREADY OPENED!

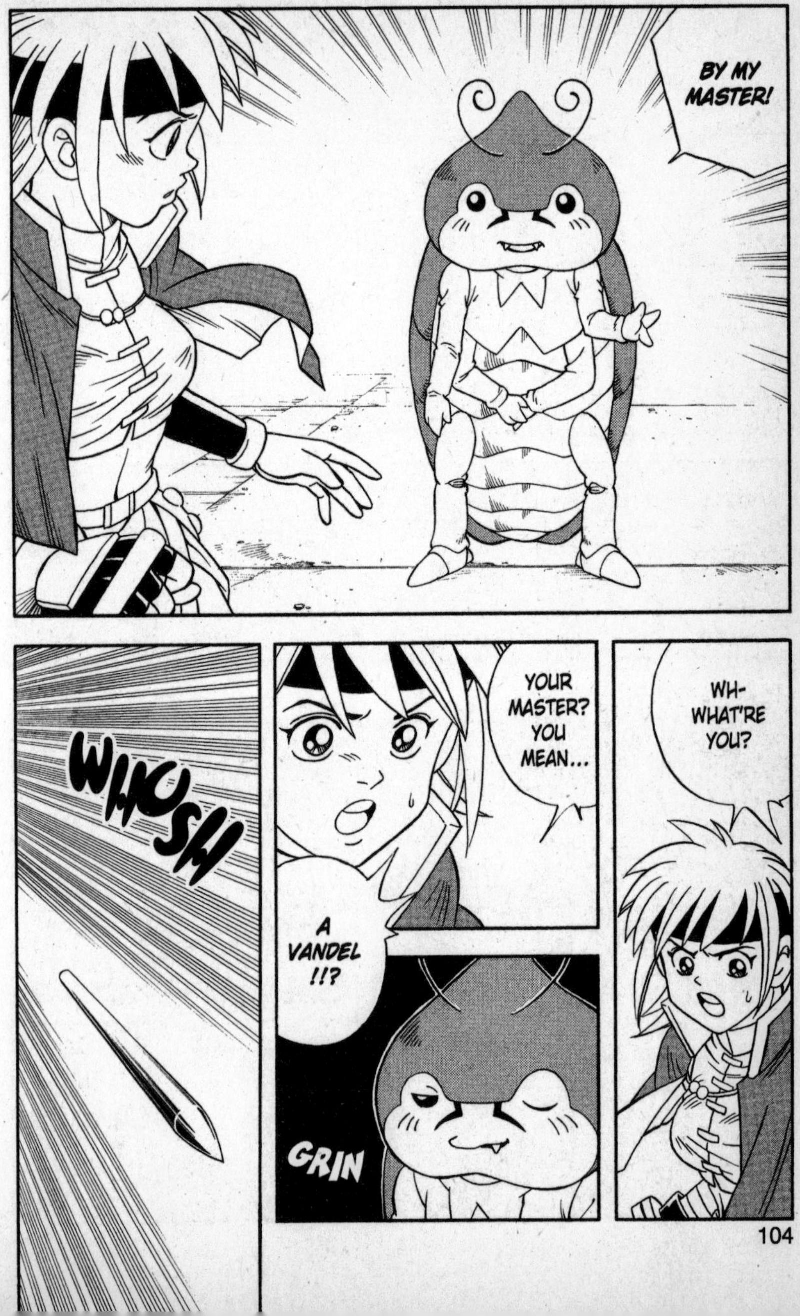
BY MY MASTER!
WH- WHAT'RE YOU?
YOUR MASTER? YOU MEAN...
A VANDEL !!?
GRIN
WHOSH

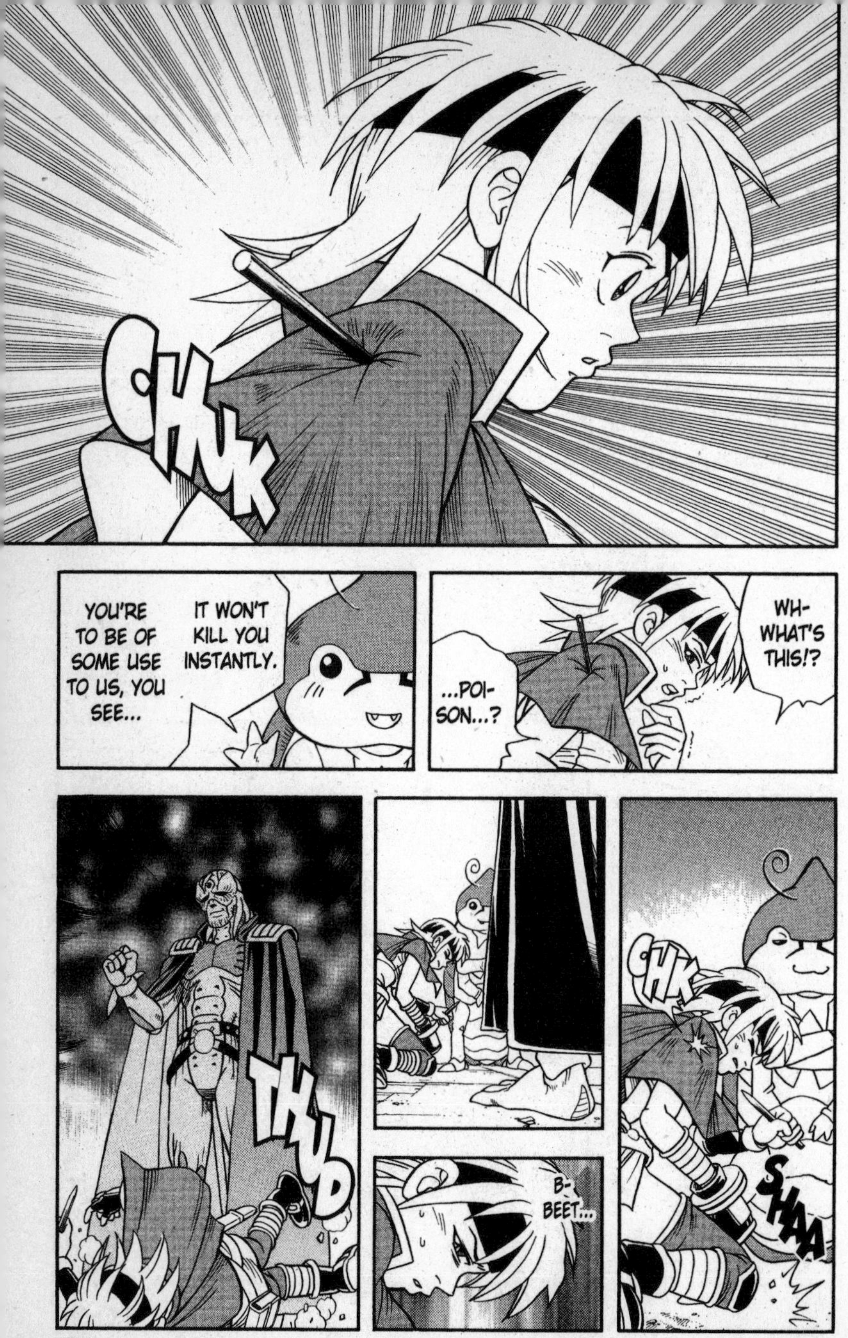
CHUK
WH- WHAT'S THIS!?
...POI- SON...?
IT WON'T KILL YOU INSTANTLY.
YOU'RE TO BE OF SOME USE TO US, YOU SEE...
CHK
SHAA
B- BEET...
THUD

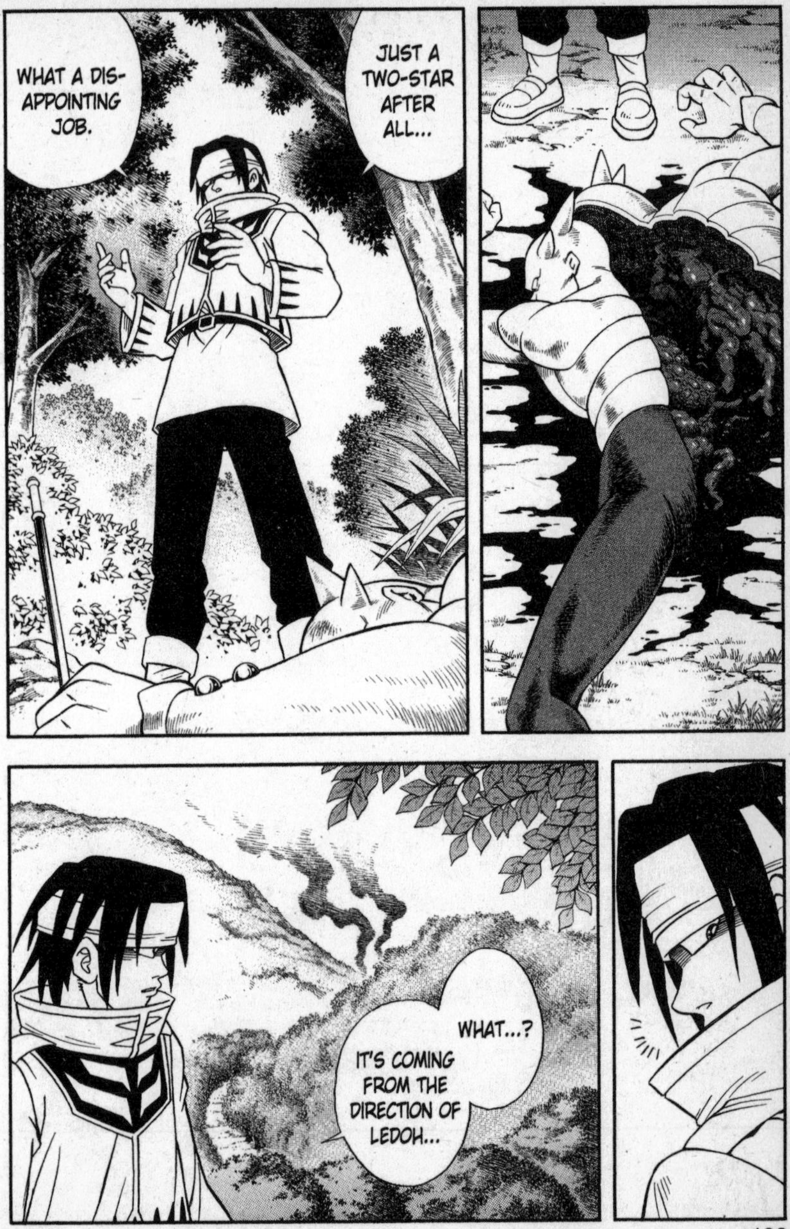
JUST A TWO-STAR AFTER ALL...
WHAT A DIS-APPOINTING JOB.
WHAT...?
IT'S COMING FROM THE DIRECTION OF LEDOH...

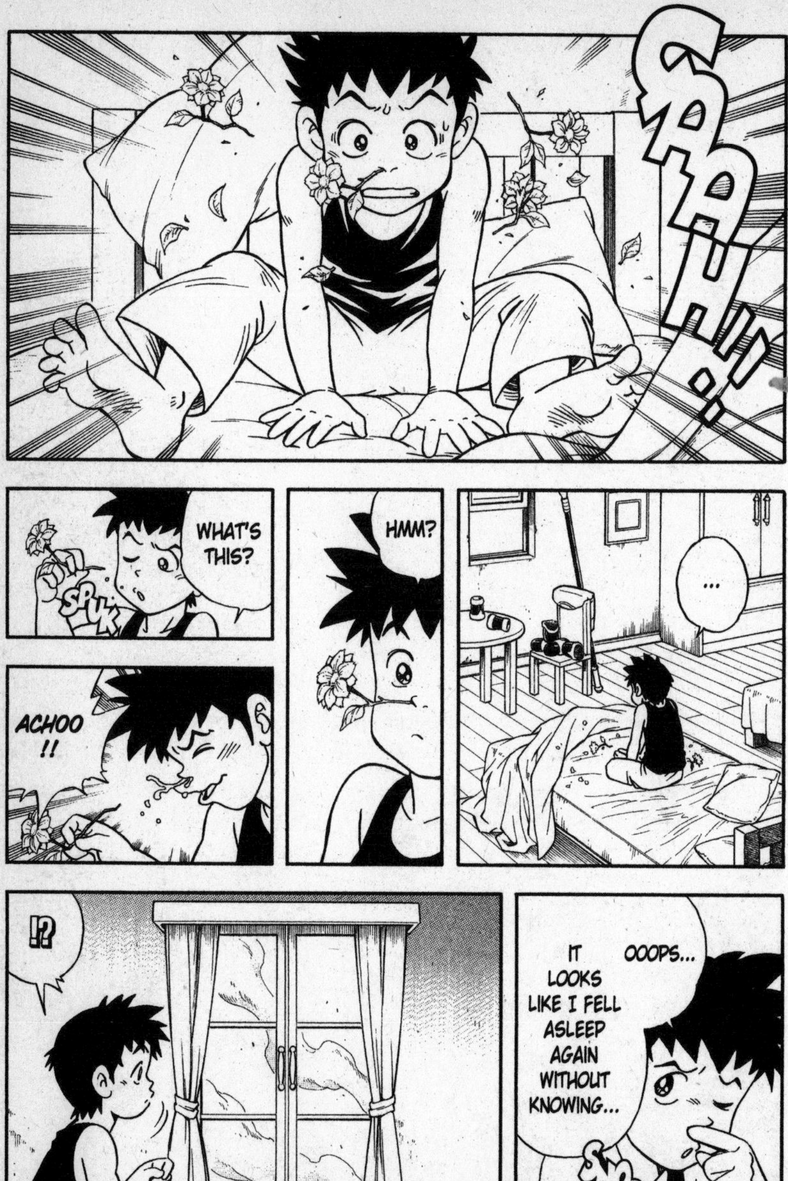
GAAUH!!
...
HMM?
WHAT'S THIS?
SPUK
ACHOO !!
OOOPS...
IT LOOKS LIKE I FELL ASLEEP AGAIN WITHOUT KNOWING...
SNORT
!?

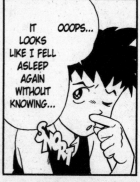

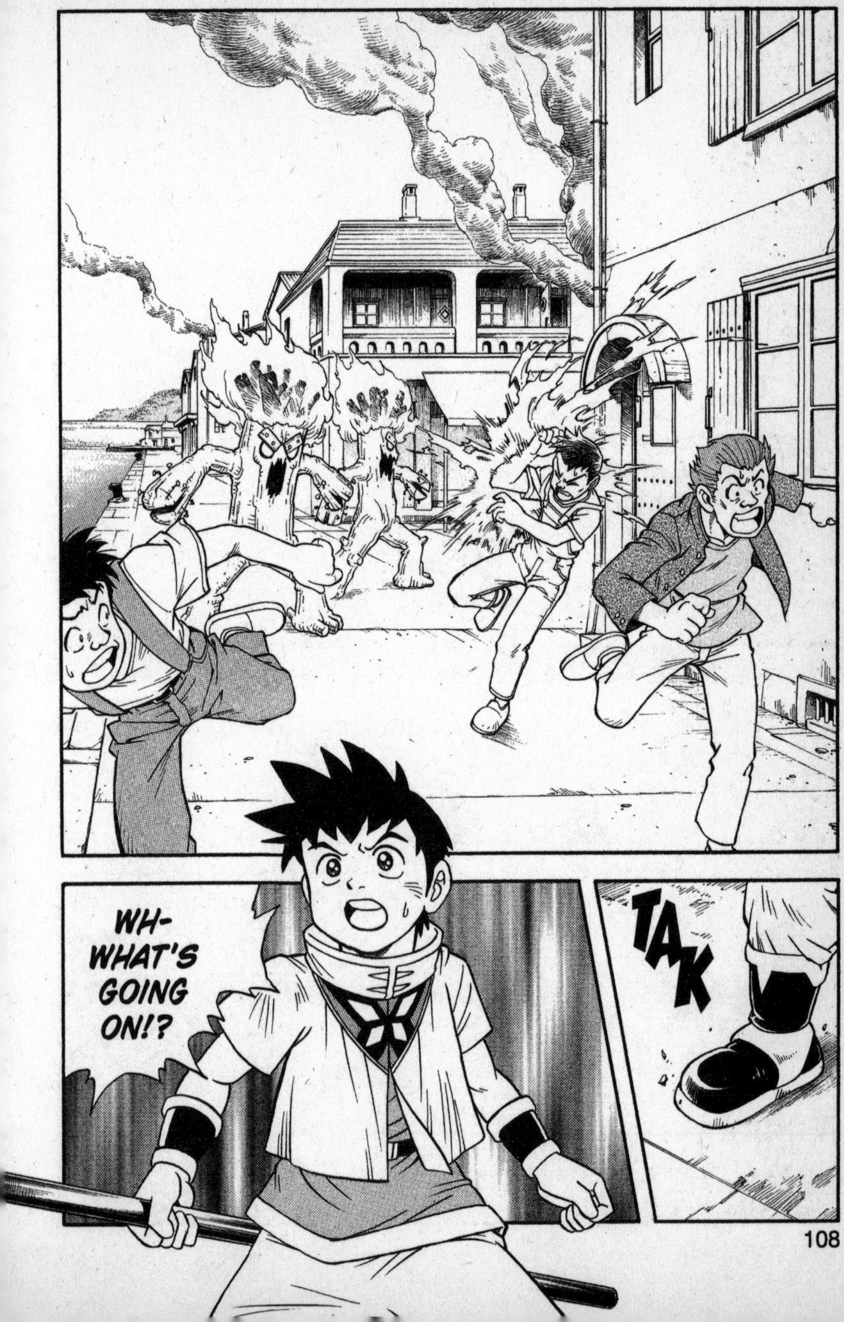
TAK
WH- WHAT'S GOING ON!?

READ THIS WAY

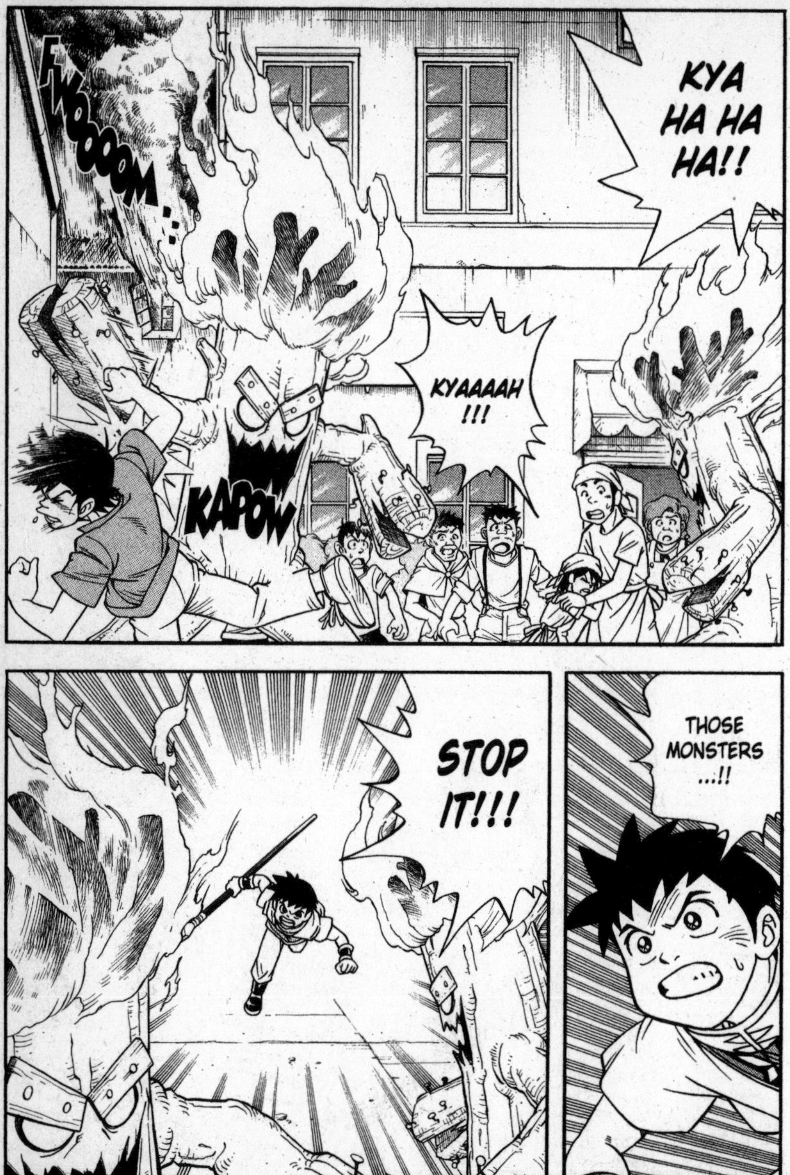
KYA HA HA HA!!
KYAAAAH !!!
FWOOOOOM...
KAPOW
THOSE MONSTERS ...!!
STOP IT!!!

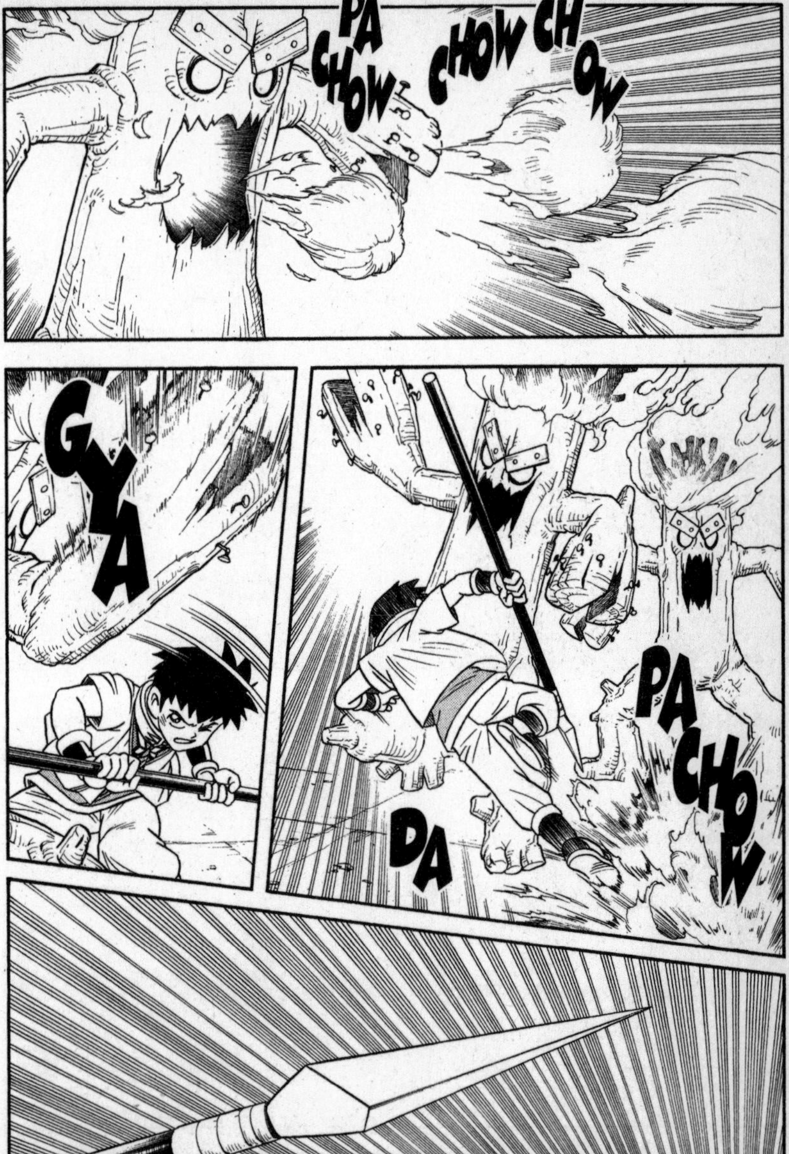
PA CHOW
CHOW CHOW
PA CHOW
DA
GYA

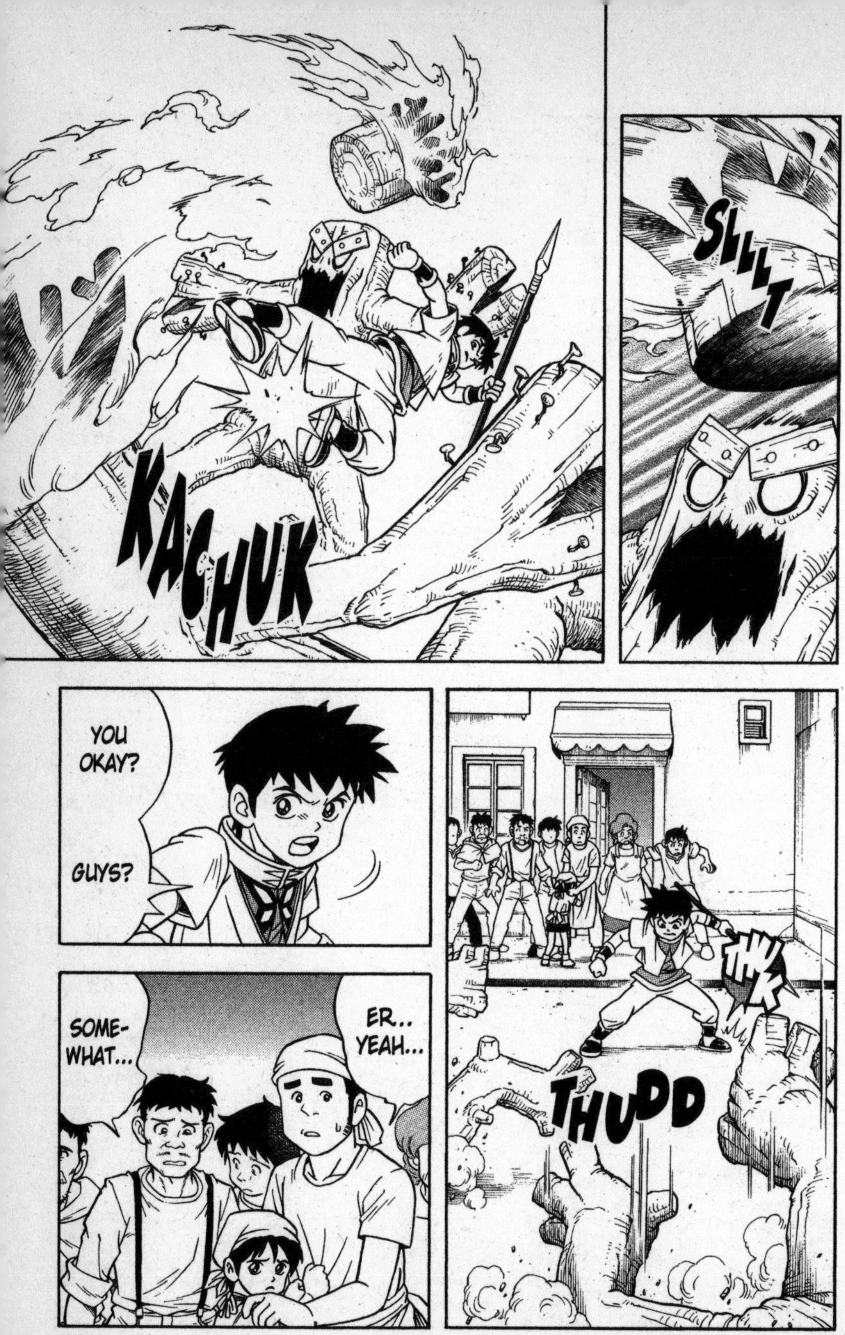
SLLLT
KACHUK
THUK
THUDD
YOU OKAY?
GUYS?
ER... YEAH...
SOME-WHAT...

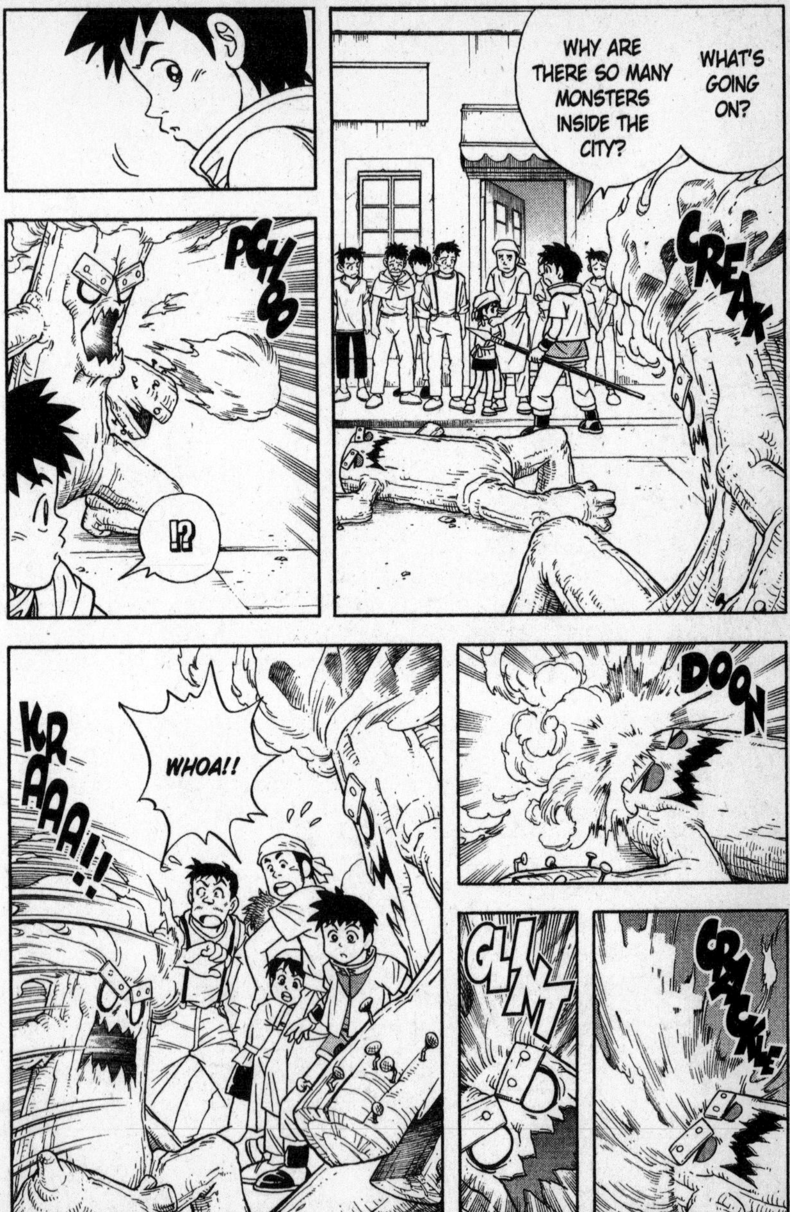
WHAT'S GOING ON?
WHY ARE THERE SO MANY MONSTERS INSIDE THE CITY?
CREAK
PCHOO
!?
DOON
CRACKLE
GLINT
WHOA!!
KRAAA!!

READ THIS WAY

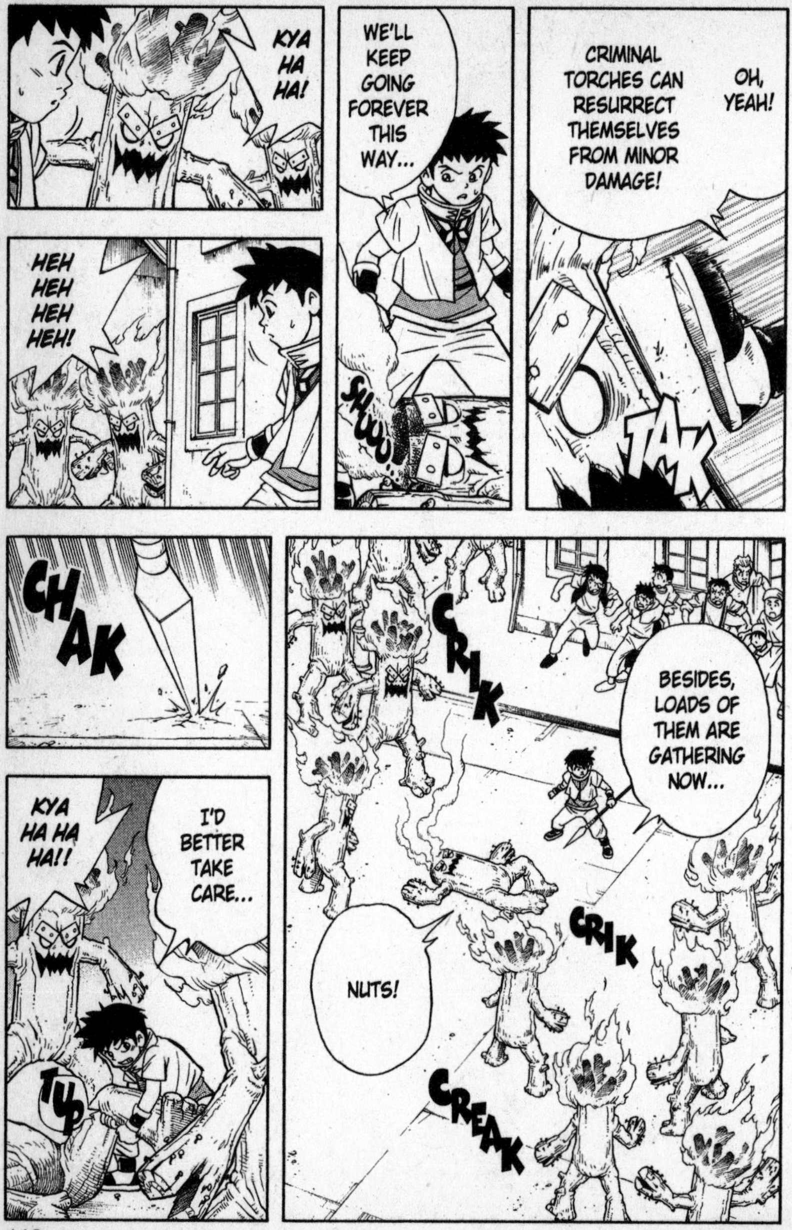
OH, YEAH!
CRIMINAL TORCHES CAN RESURRECT THEMSELVES FROM MINOR DAMAGE!
TAK
WE'LL KEEP GOING FOREVER THIS WAY...
SHUUU!
KYA HA HA!
HEH HEH HEH HEH!
BESIDES, LOADS OF THEM ARE GATHERING NOW...
CRIK
NUTS!
CRIK
CREAK
CHAK
I'D BETTER TAKE CARE...
KYA HA HA HA!!
TUP

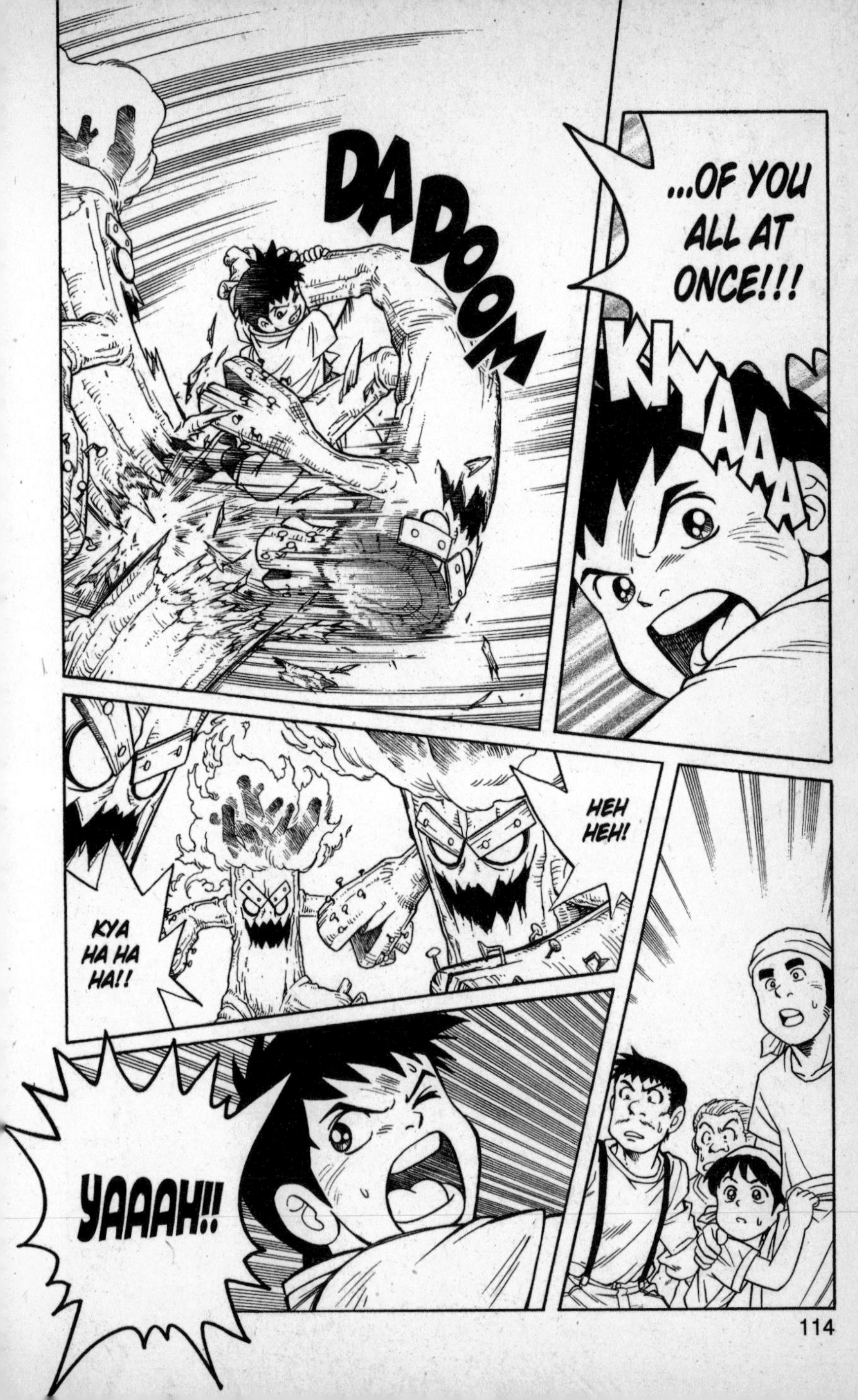
...OF YOU ALL AT ONCE!!!
KIYAAA
DADOOM
HEH HEH!
KYA HA HA HA!!
YAAAH!!

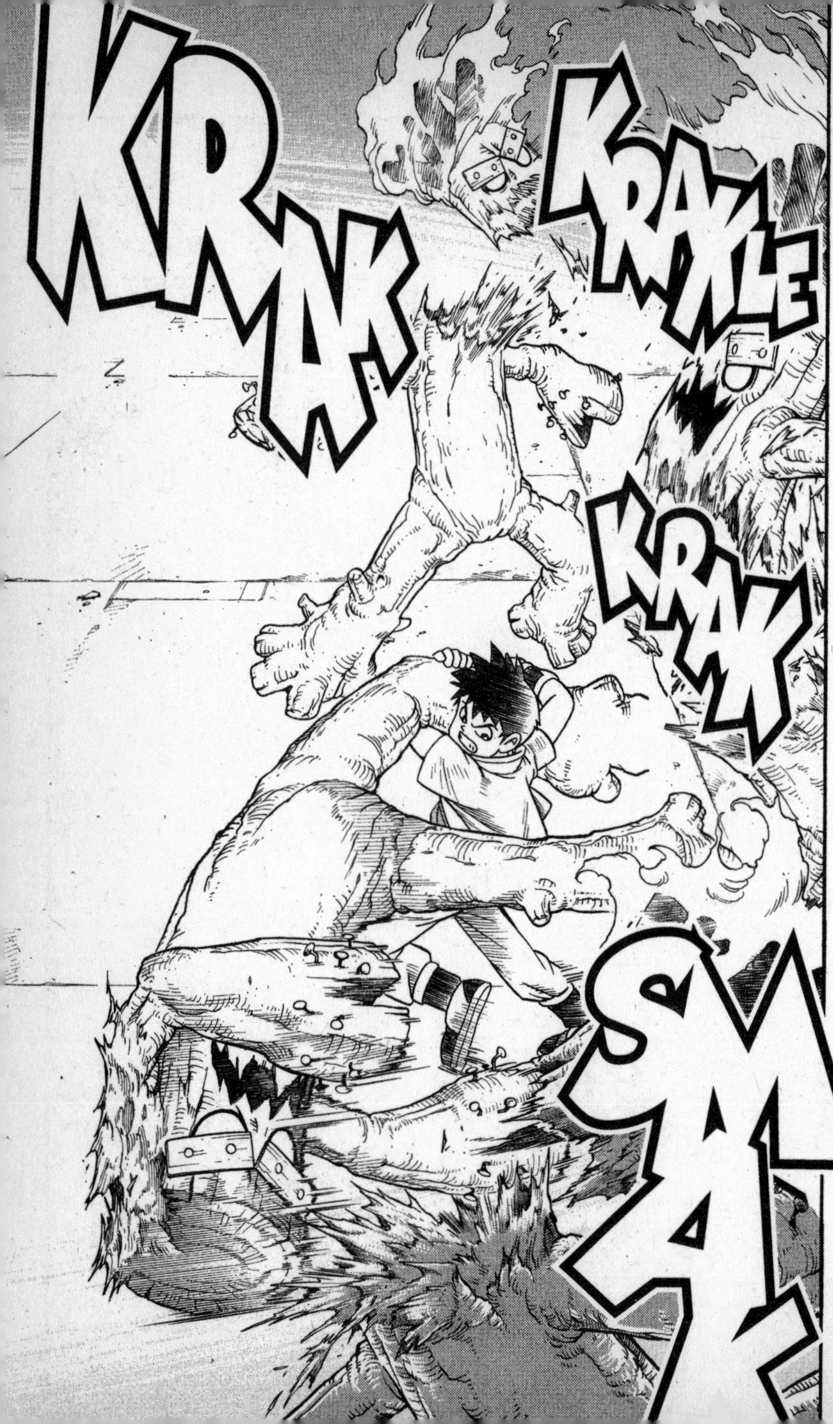
KRAKKLE
KRAK
KRAK
SMA

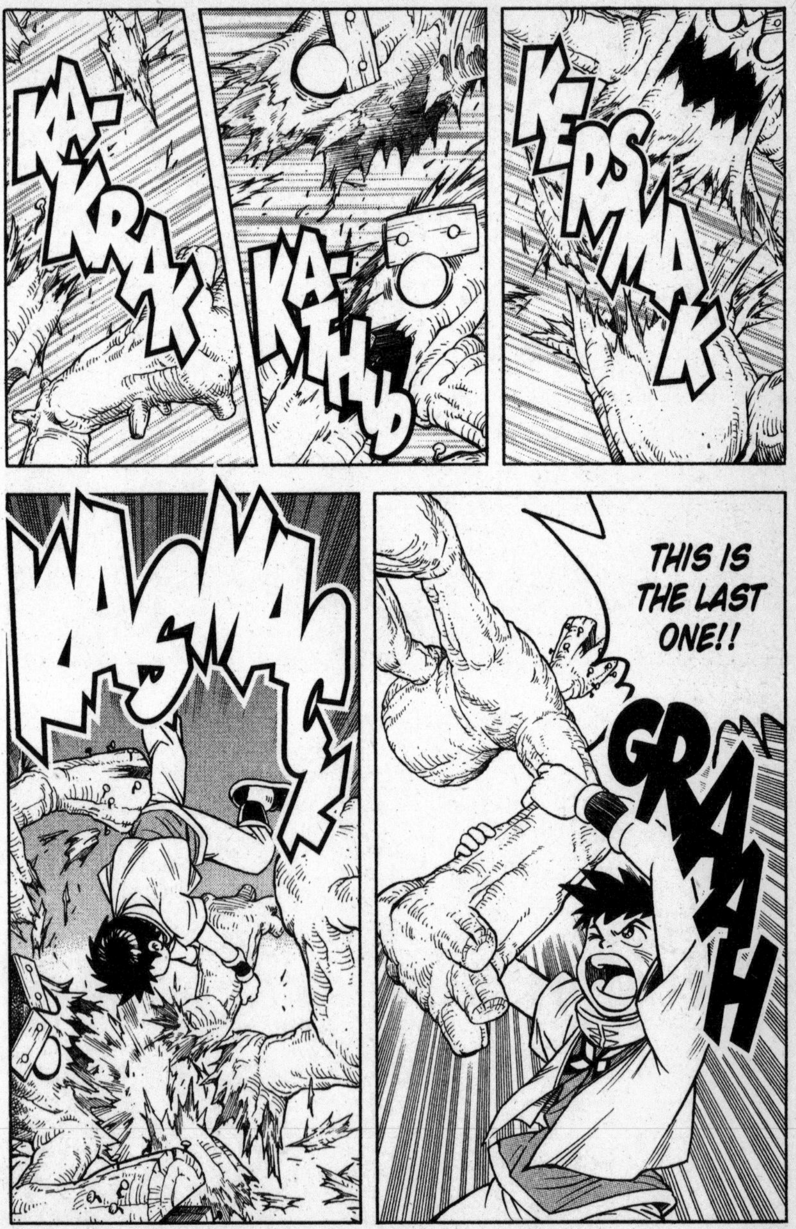
KERSMAK
KA-THUD
KA-KRAK
THIS IS THE LAST ONE!!
GRAAH
WASMACK

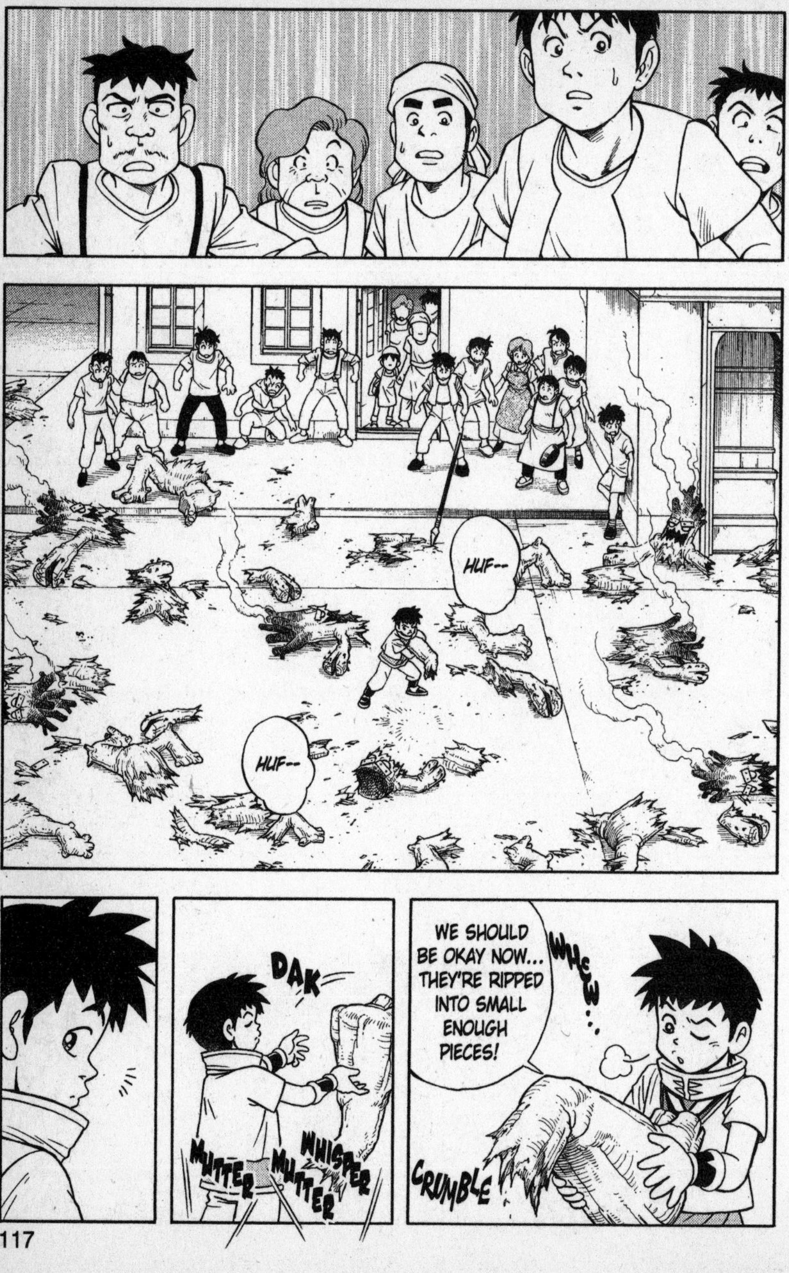
HUF--
HUF--
WE SHOULD BE OKAY NOW... THEY'RE RIPPED INTO SMALL ENOUGH PIECES!
WHEW...
CRUMBLE
DAK
WHISPER
MUTTER
MUTTER

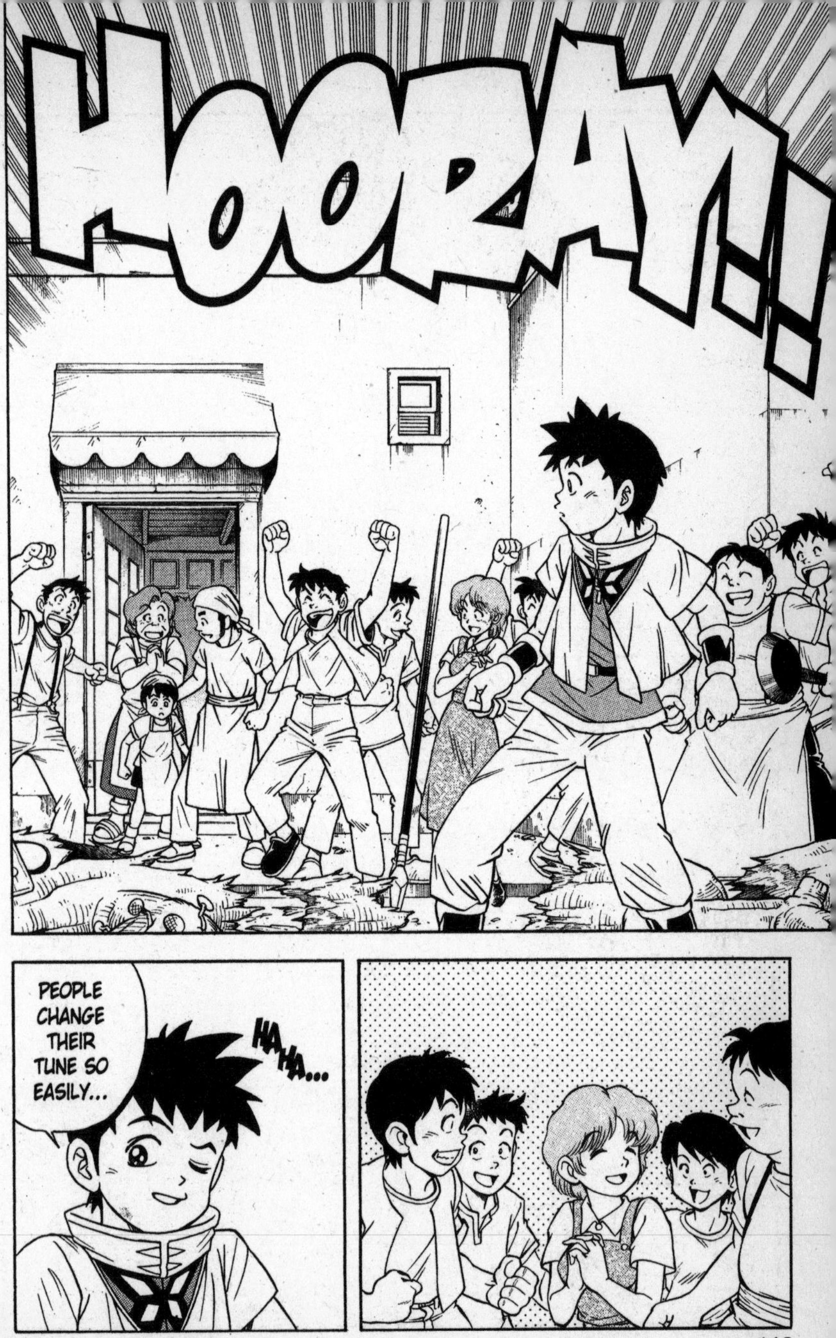
HOORAY!!
HAHA...
PEOPLE CHANGE THEIR TUNE SO EASILY...

READ THIS WAY

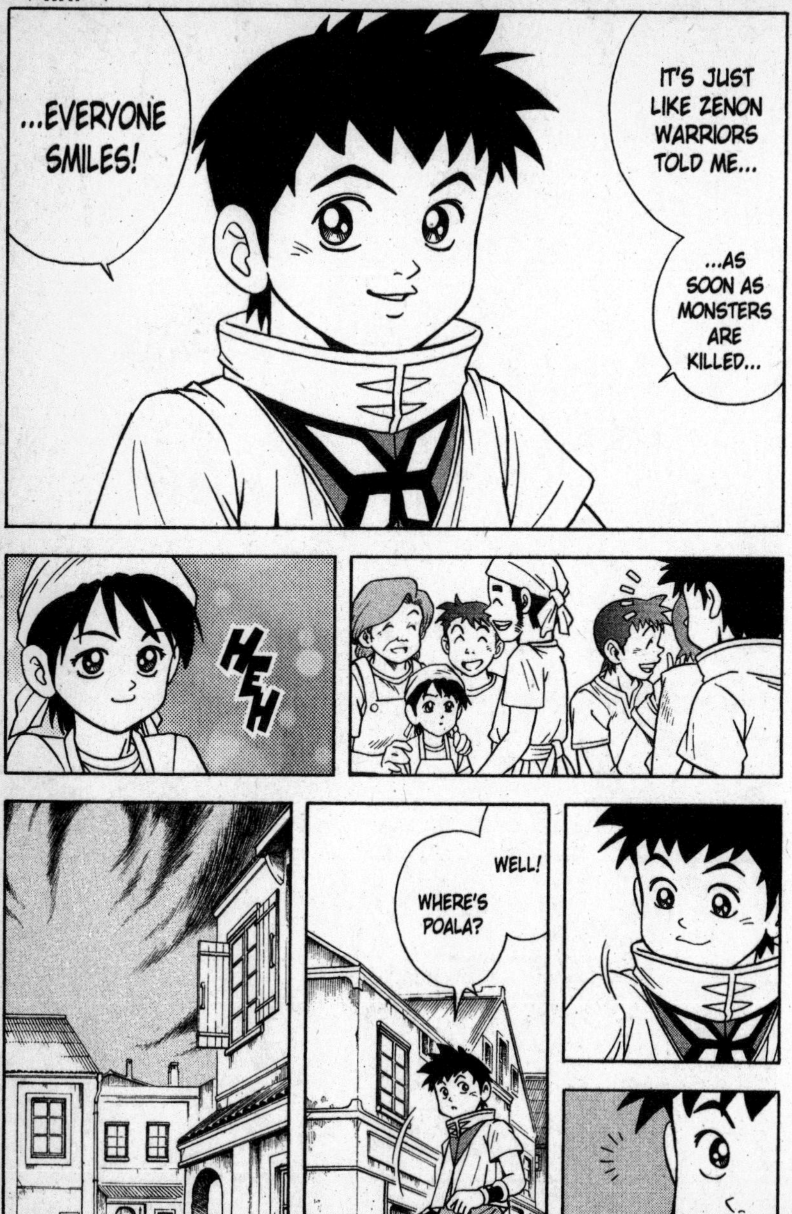
IT'S JUST LIKE ZENON WARRIORS TOLD ME...
...AS SOON AS MONSTERS ARE KILLED...
...EVERYONE SMILES!
HEH
WELL!
WHERE'S POALA?

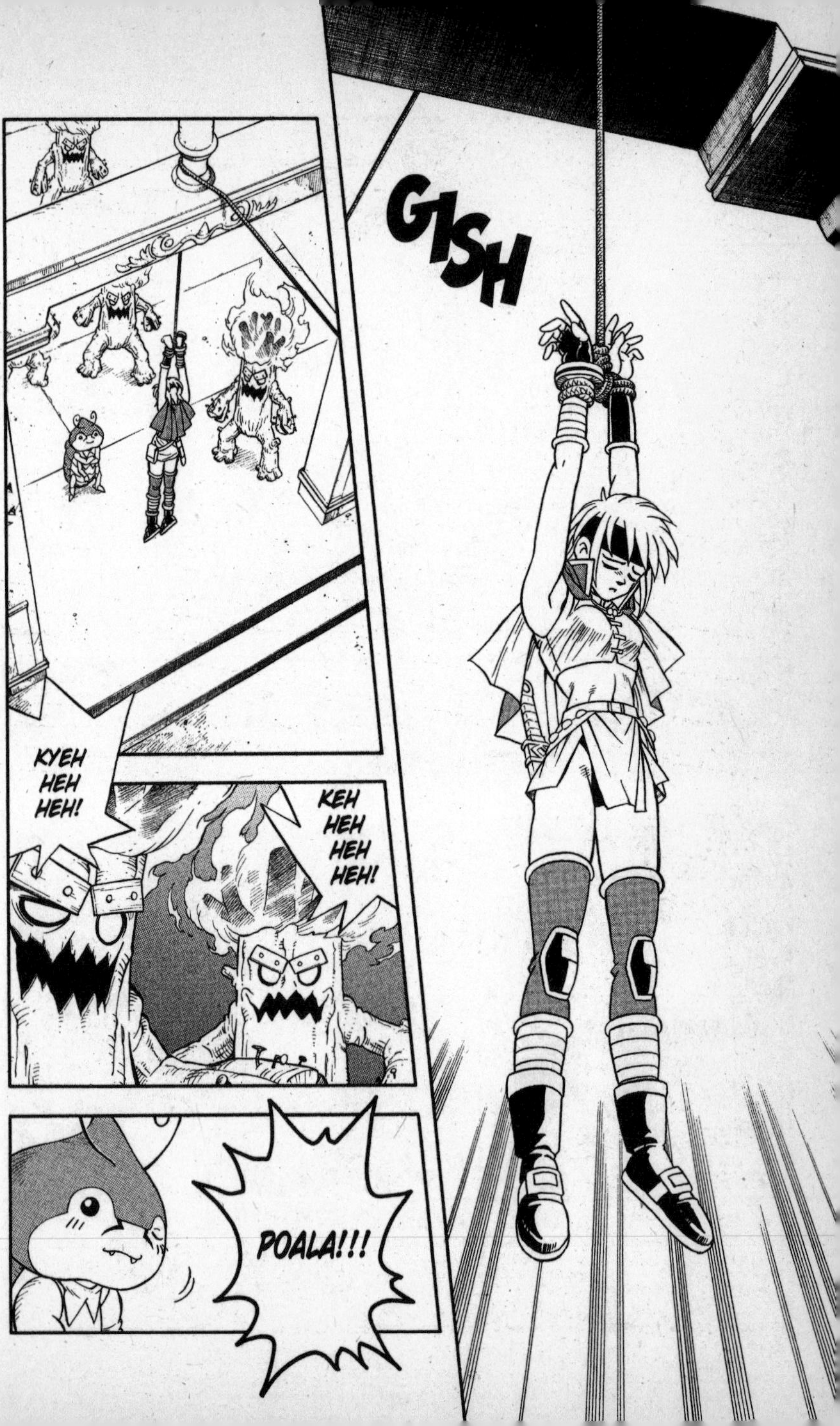
GISH
KYEH HEH HEH!
KEH HEH HEH HEH!
POALA!!!

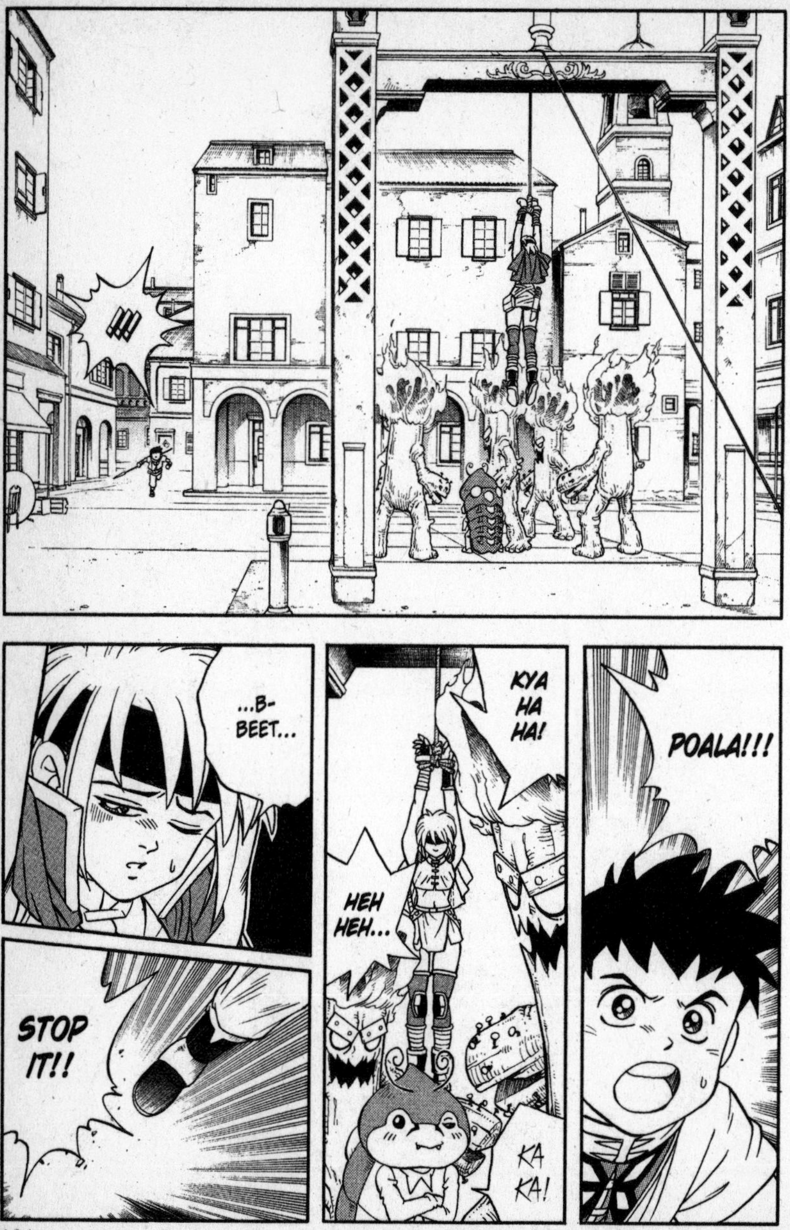
!!!
POALA!!!
KYA HA HA!
HEH HEH...
KA KA!
...B-BEET...
STOP IT!!

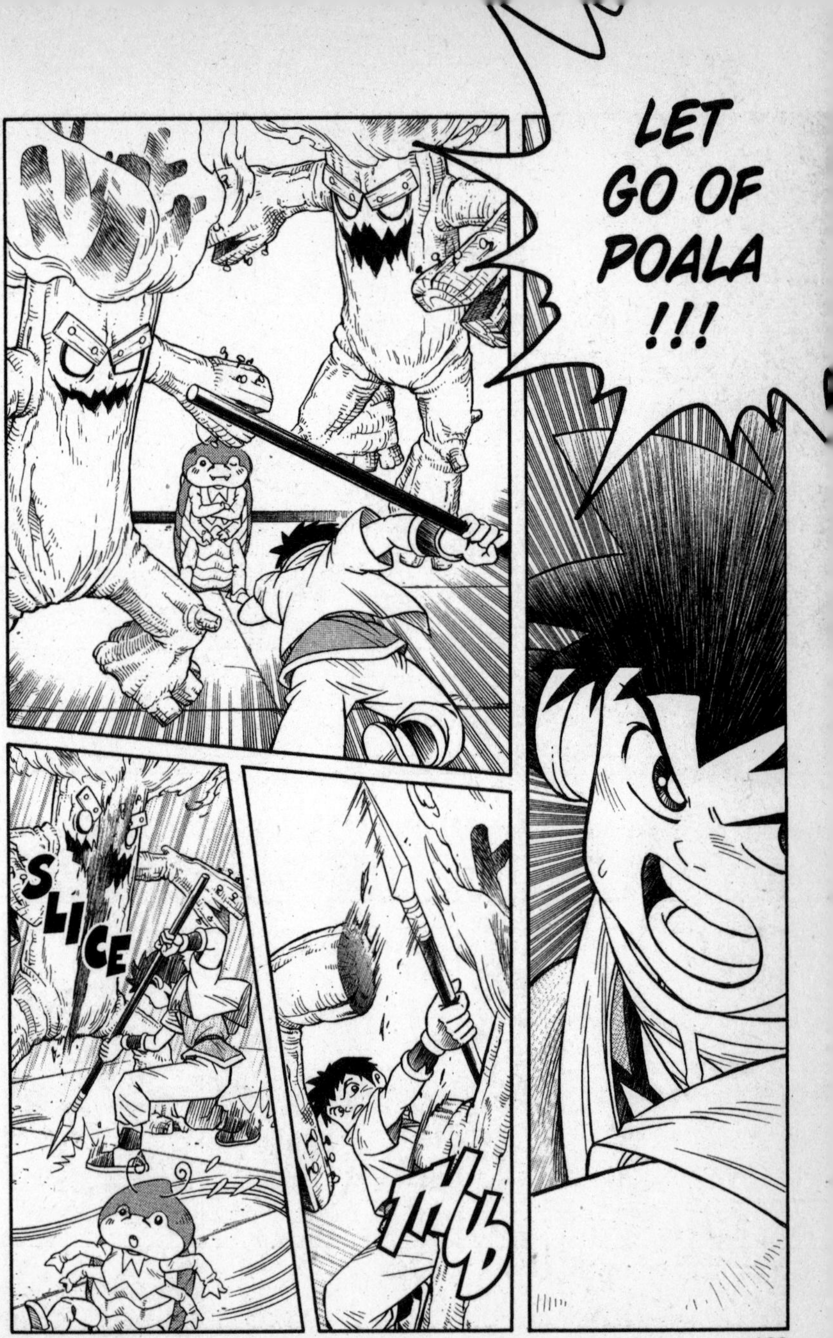
LET GO OF POALA !!!
SLICE
THUD

READ THIS WAY

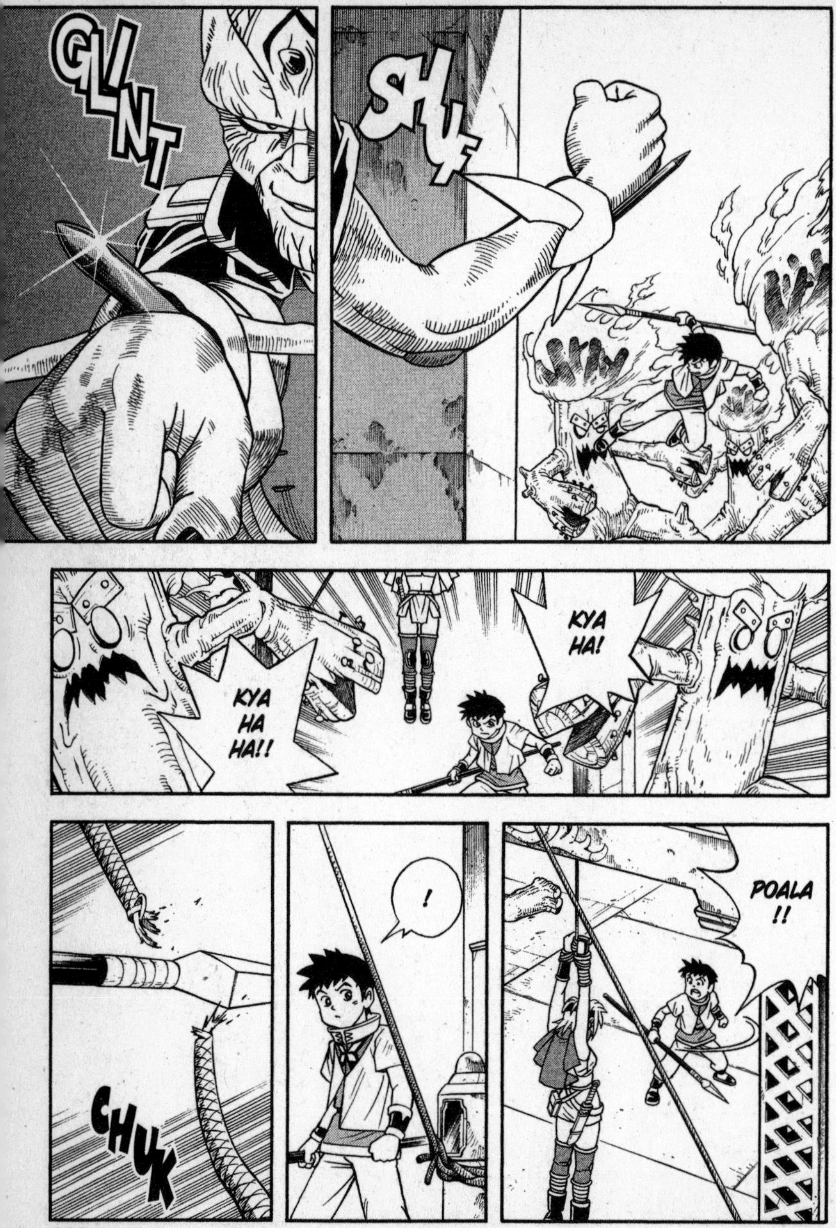
SHU
GLINT
KYA HA!
KYA HA HA!!
POALA !!
!
CHUK

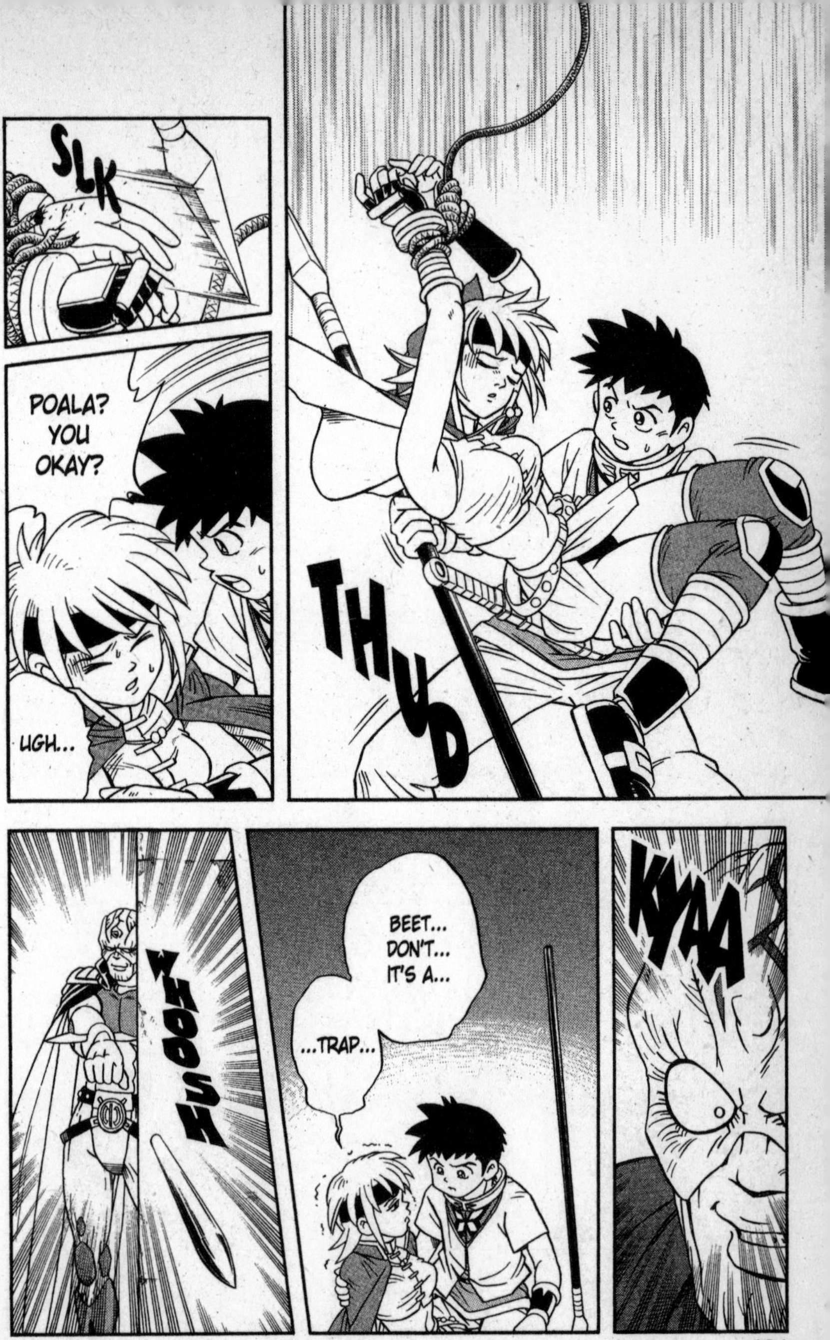
THUD
SLK
POALA? YOU OKAY?
UGH...
KYAA
BEET... DON'T... IT'S A...
...TRAP...
WHOOSH

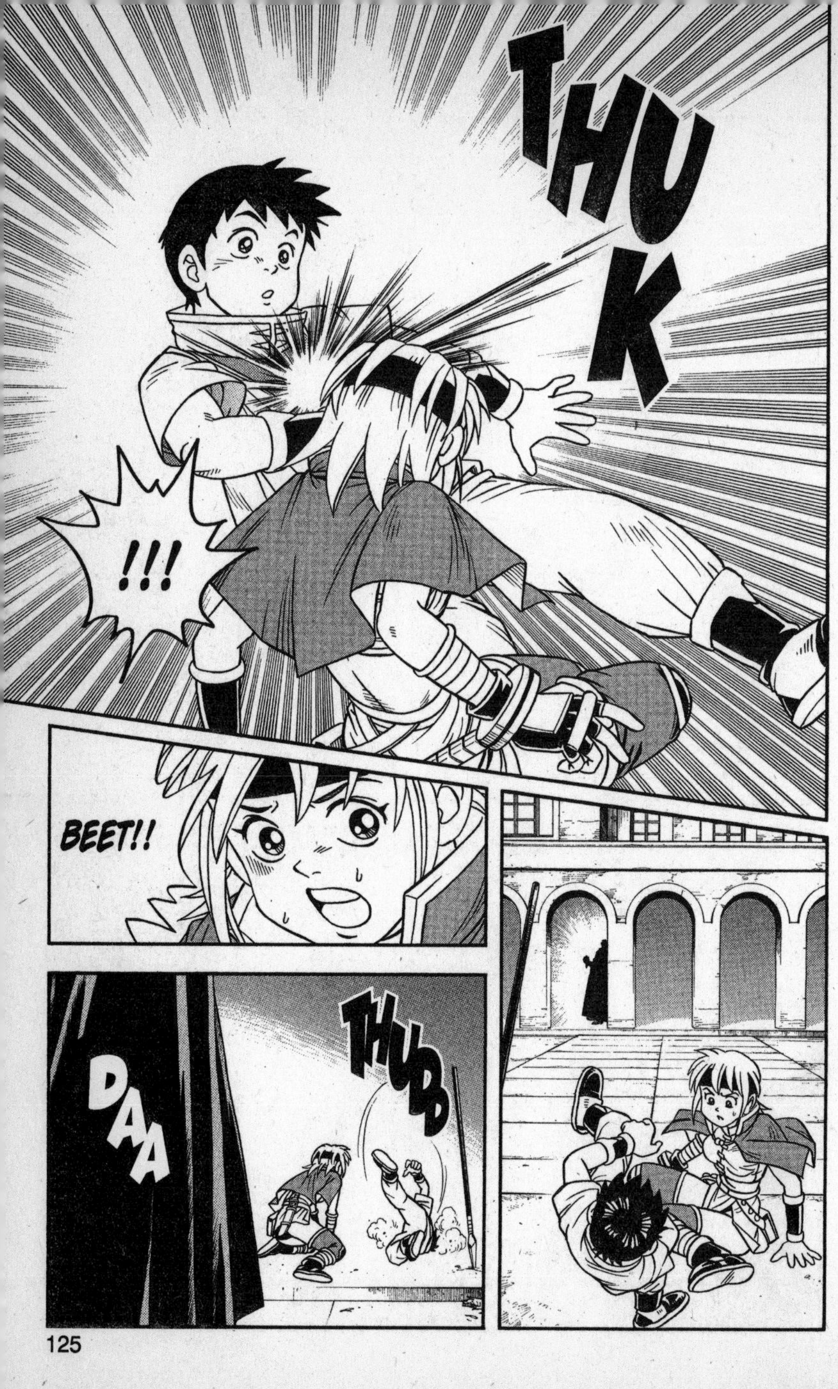
THUK
!!!
BEET!!
THUDD
DAA

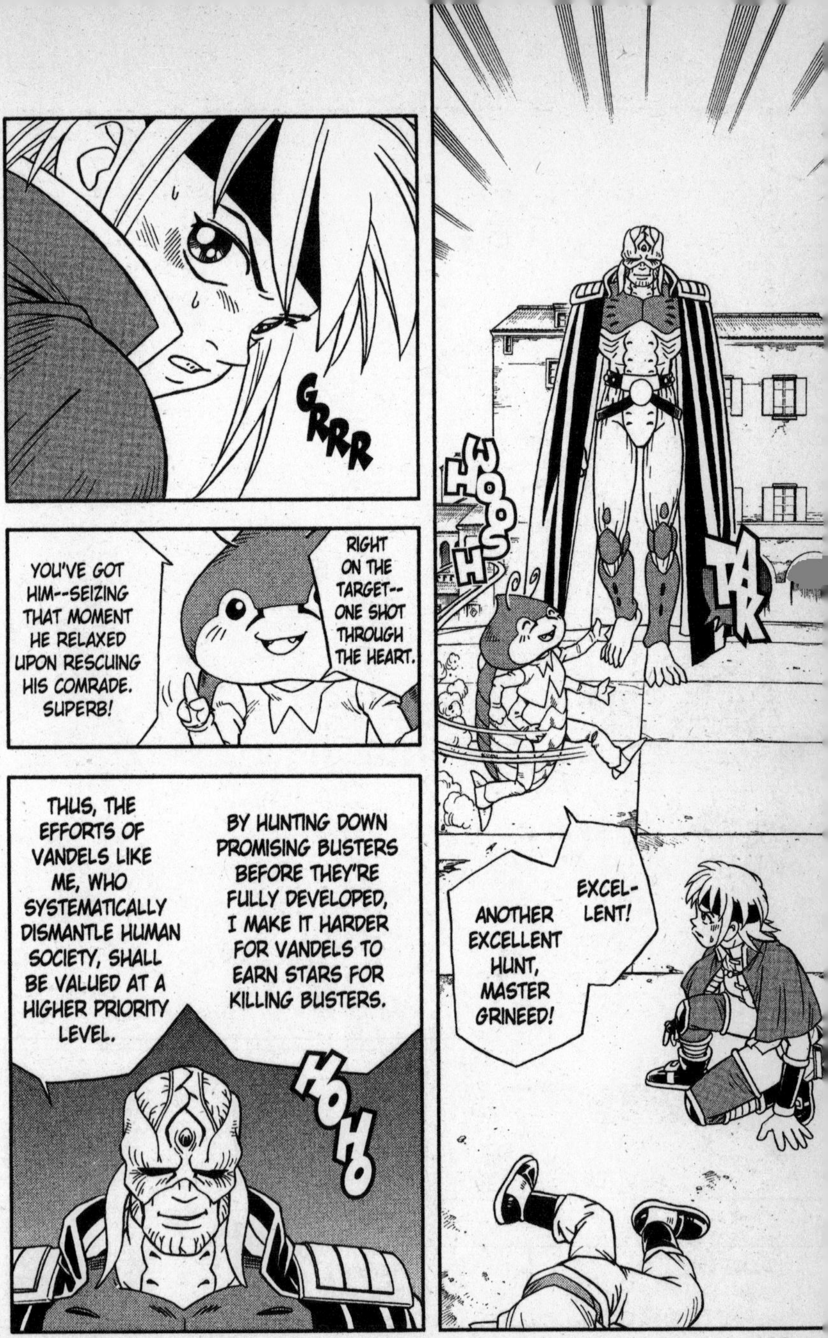
WHOOSH
TAK
EXCEL-LENT!
ANOTHER EXCELLENT HUNT, MASTER GRINEED!
GRRR
RIGHT ON THE TARGET-- ONE SHOT THROUGH THE HEART.
YOU'VE GOT HIM--SEIZING THAT MOMENT HE RELAXED UPON RESCUING HIS COMRADE. SUPERB!
BY HUNTING DOWN PROMISING BUSTERS BEFORE THEY'RE FULLY DEVELOPED, I MAKE IT HARDER FOR VANDELS TO EARN STARS FOR KILLING BUSTERS.
THUS, THE EFFORTS OF VANDELS LIKE ME, WHO SYSTEMATICALLY DISMANTLE HUMAN SOCIETY, SHALL BE VALUED AT A HIGHER PRIORITY LEVEL.
HO HO

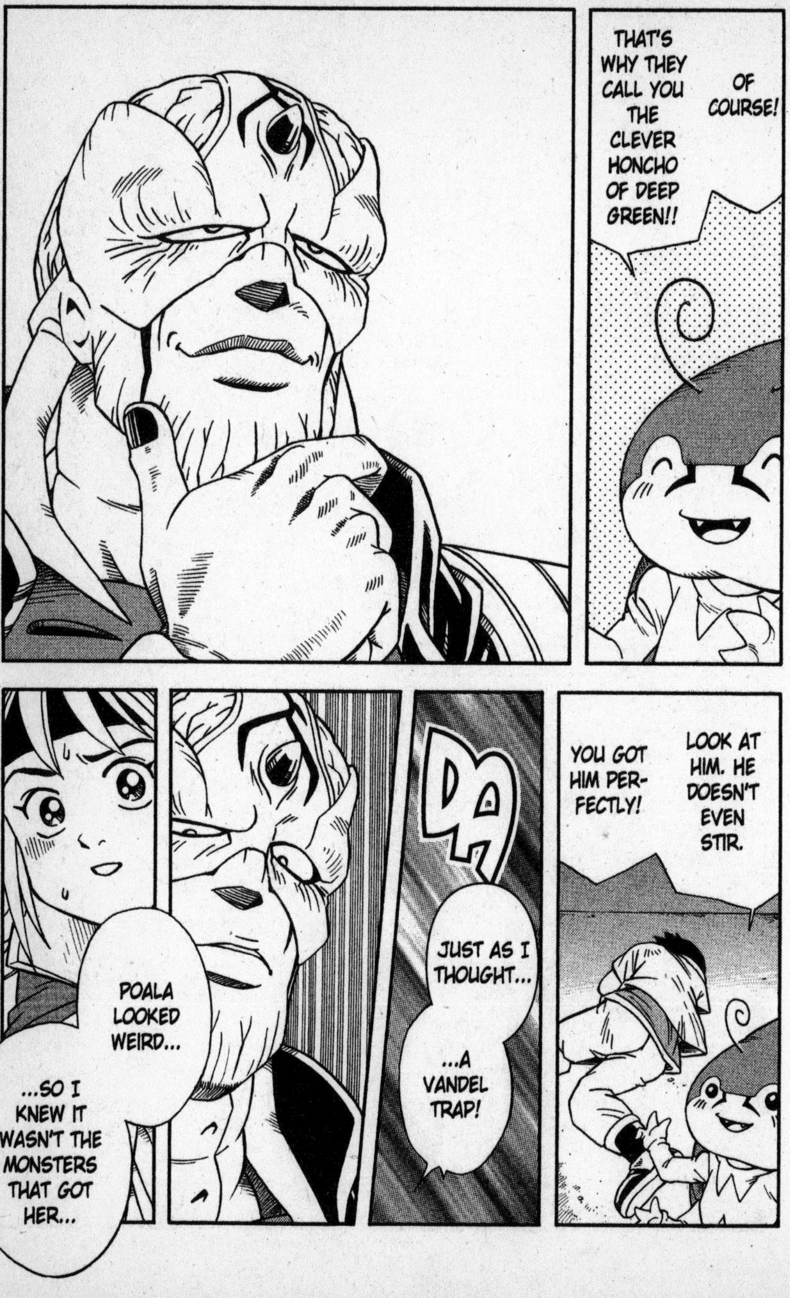

OF COURSE!
THAT'S WHY THEY CALL YOU THE CLEVER HONCHO OF DEEP GREEN!!
LOOK AT HIM. HE DOESN'T EVEN STIR.
YOU GOT HIM PER-FECTLY!
DA
JUST AS I THOUGHT...
...A VANDEL TRAP!
POALA LOOKED WEIRD...
...SO I KNEW IT WASN'T THE MONSTERS THAT GOT HER...

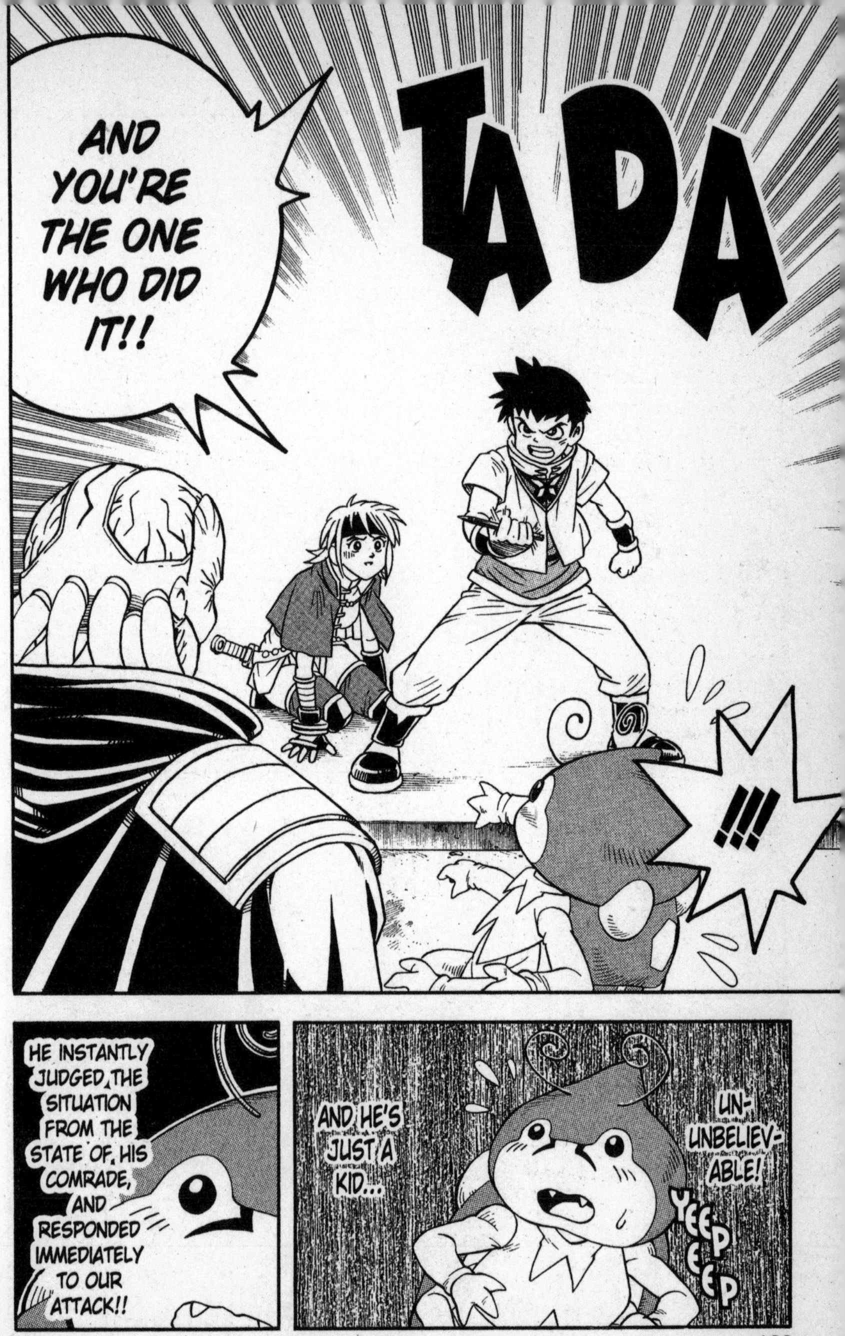
TADA
AND YOU'RE THE ONE WHO DID IT!!
!!!
UN-UNBELIEVABLE!
YEEP EEP
AND HE'S JUST A KID...
HE INSTANTLY JUDGED THE SITUATION FROM THE STATE OF HIS COMRADE, AND RESPONDED IMMEDIATELY TO OUR ATTACK!!

READ THIS WAY

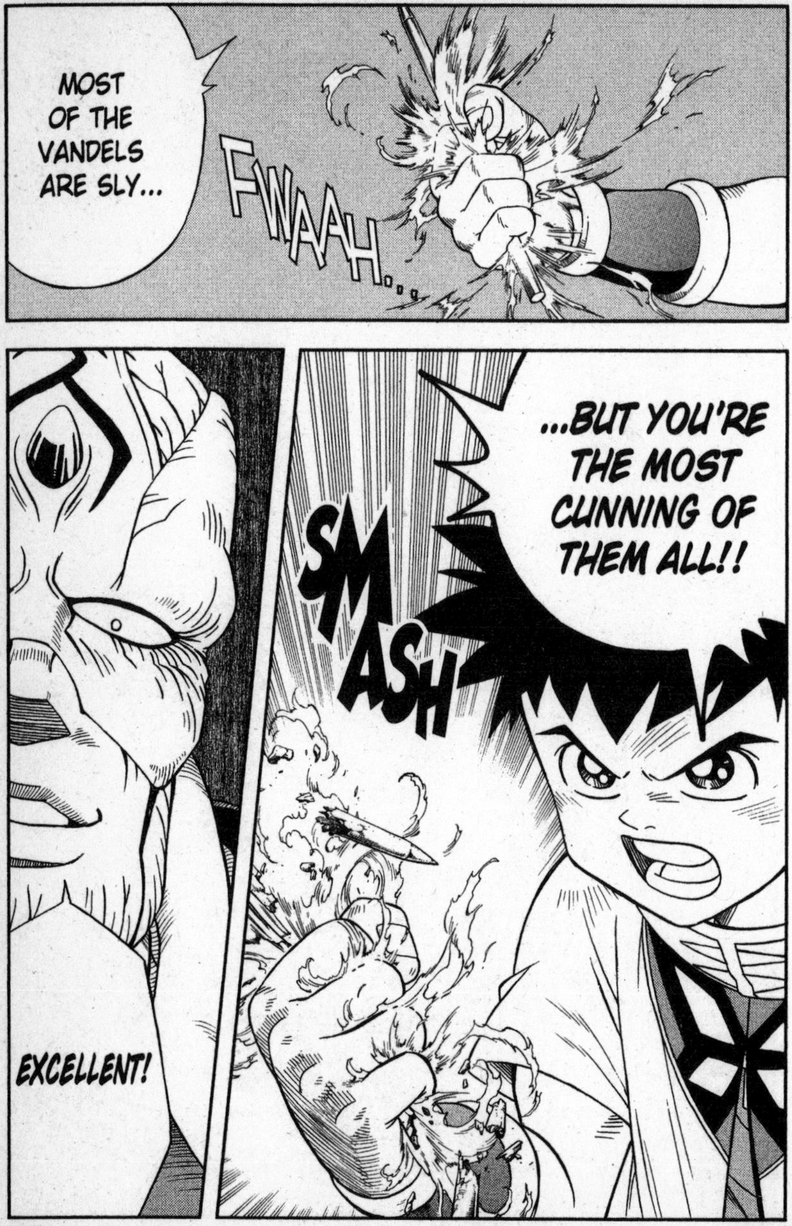

MOST OF THE VANDELS ARE SLY...
FWAAAH...
SMASH
...BUT YOU'RE THE MOST CUNNING OF THEM ALL!!
EXCELLENT!

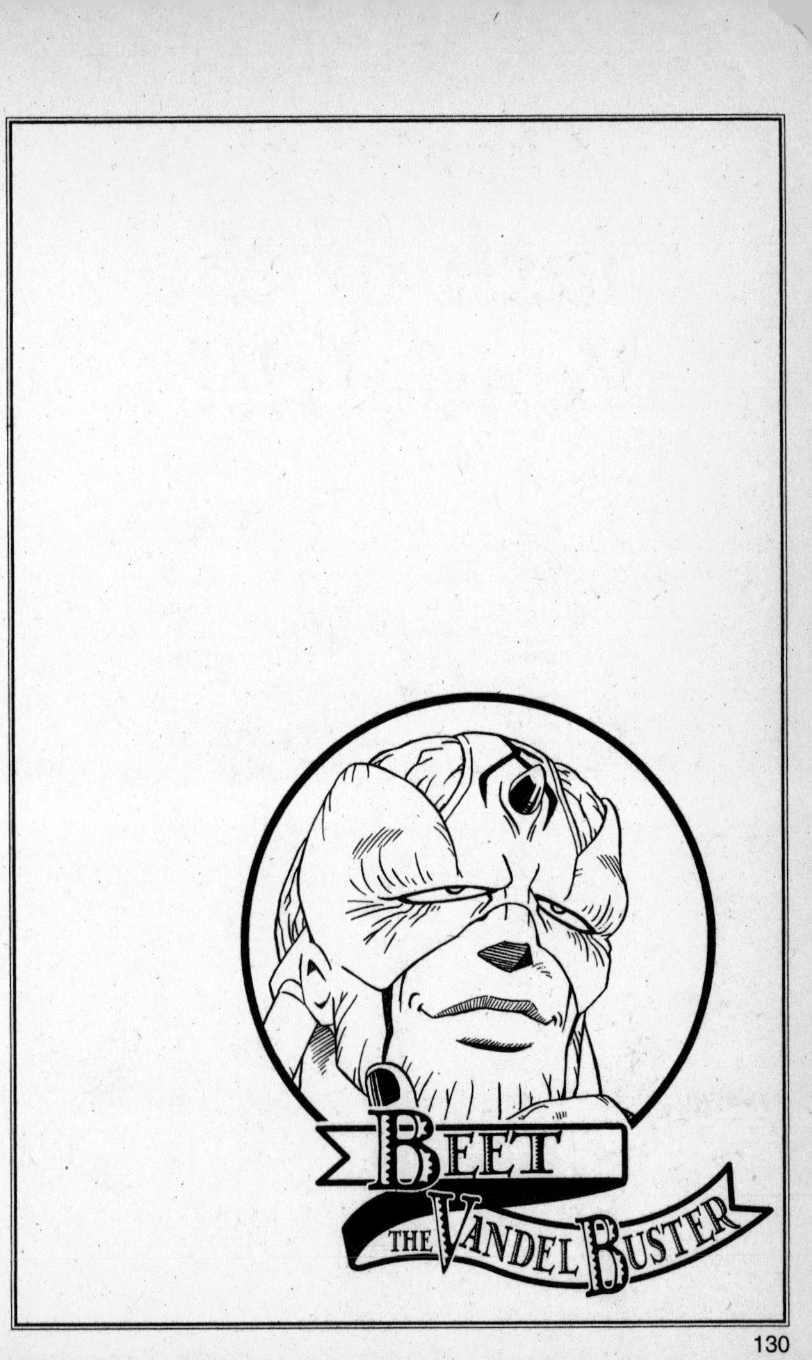
BEET
THE VANDEL BUSTER

Chapter 6:
Clash of the Vandels!!!

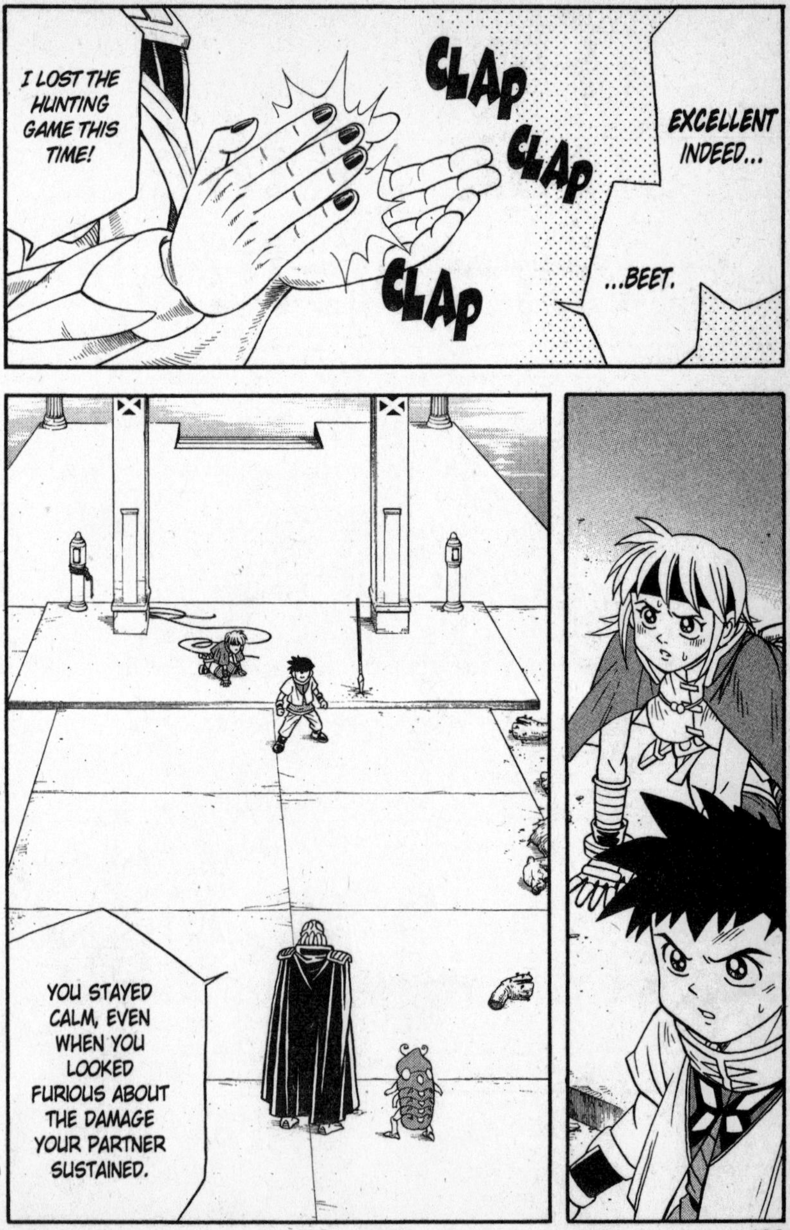
EXCELLENT INDEED...
...BEET.
CLAP
CLAP
CLAP
I LOST THE HUNTING GAME THIS TIME!
YOU STAYED CALM, EVEN WHEN YOU LOOKED FURIOUS ABOUT THE DAMAGE YOUR PARTNER SUSTAINED.

READ THIS WAY

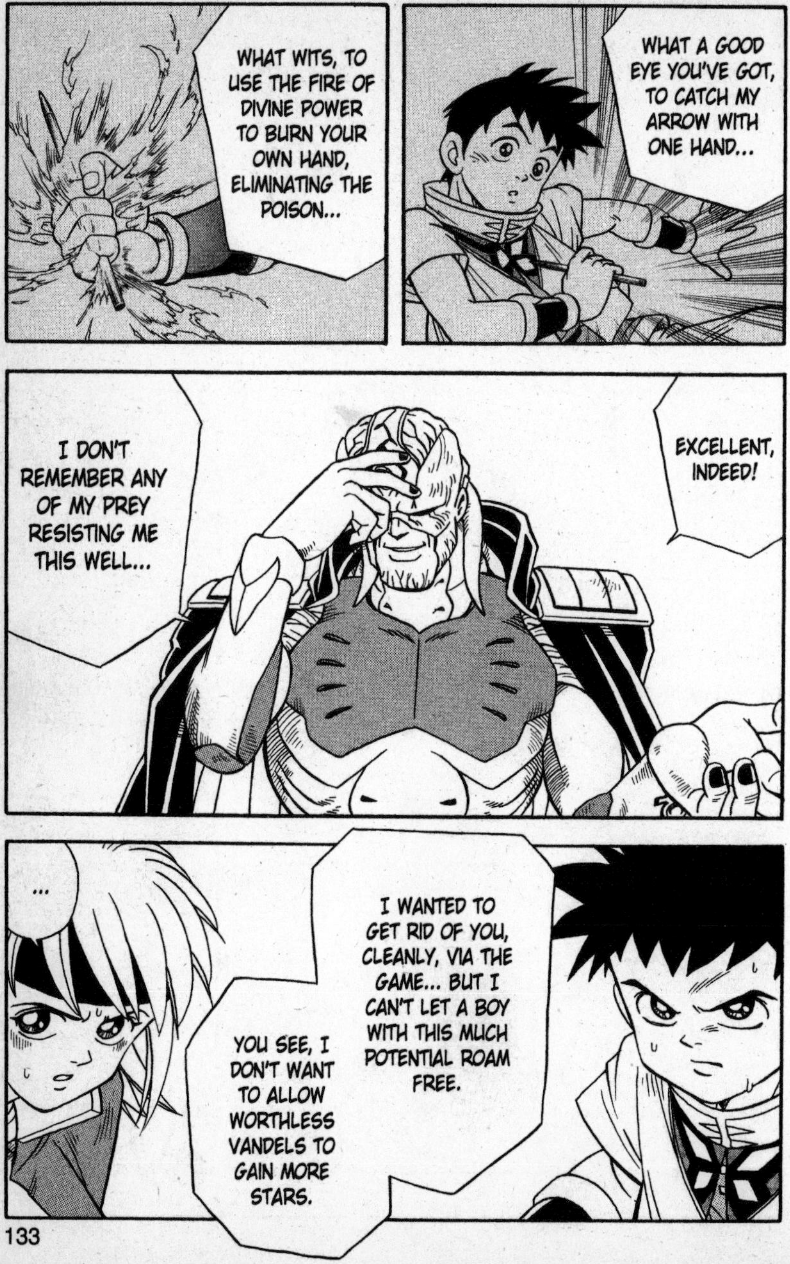

WHAT A GOOD EYE YOU'VE GOT, TO CATCH MY ARROW WITH ONE HAND...
WHAT WITS, TO USE THE FIRE OF DIVINE POWER TO BURN YOUR OWN HAND, ELIMINATING THE POISON...
EXCELLENT, INDEED!
I DON'T REMEMBER ANY OF MY PREY RESISTING ME THIS WELL...
I WANTED TO GET RID OF YOU, CLEANLY, VIA THE GAME... BUT I CAN'T LET A BOY WITH THIS MUCH POTENTIAL ROAM FREE.
YOU SEE, I DON'T WANT TO ALLOW WORTHLESS VANDELS TO GAIN MORE STARS.
...

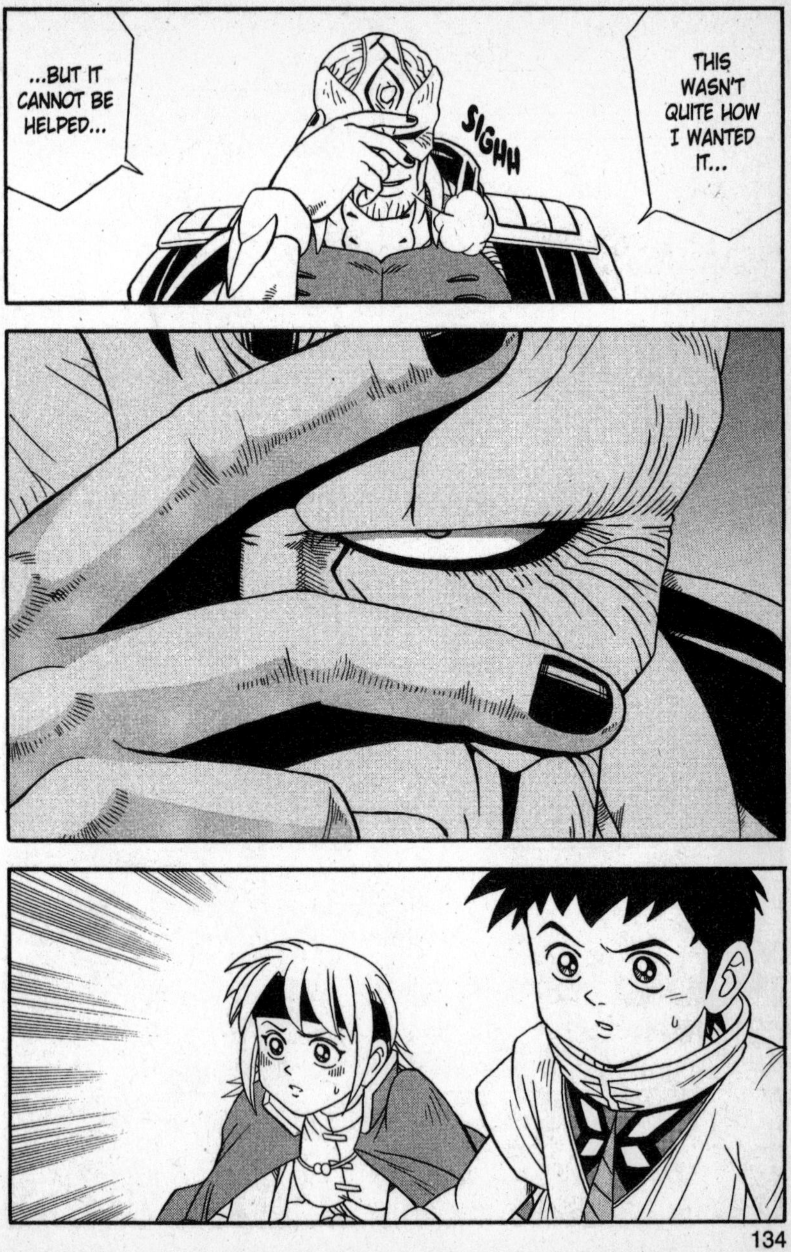
THIS WASN'T QUITE HOW I WANTED IT...
SIGHH
...BUT IT CANNOT BE HELPED...

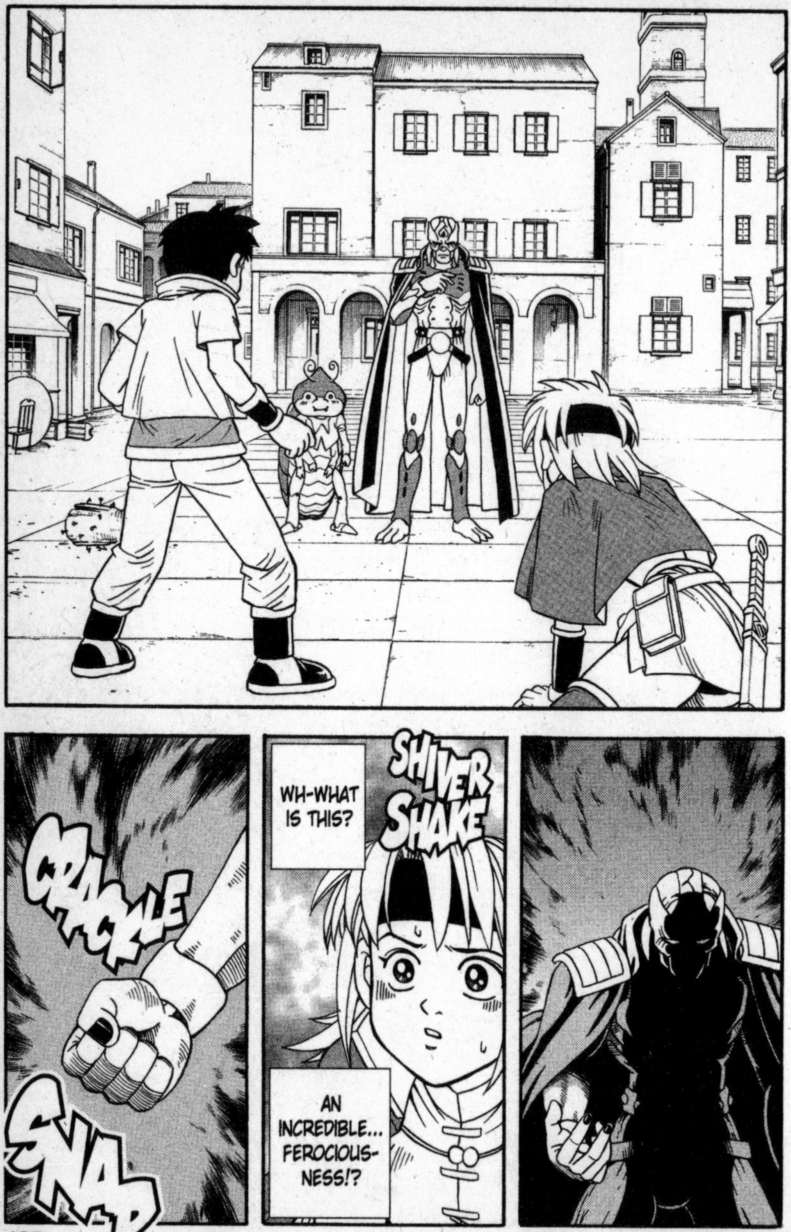
SHIVER
SHAKE
WH-WHAT IS THIS?
AN INCREDIBLE... FEROCIOUS-NESS!?
CRACKLE
SNAP

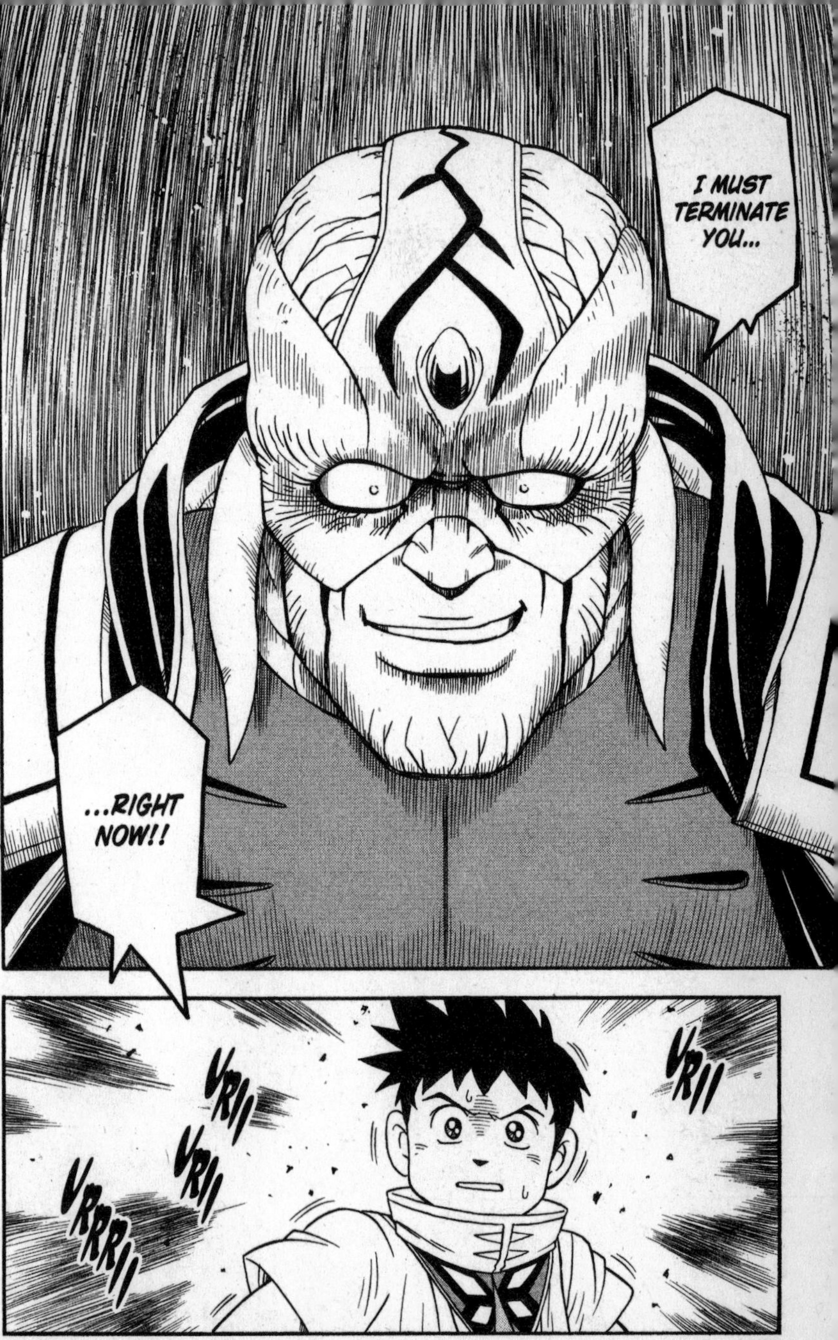
I MUST TERMINATE YOU...
...RIGHT NOW!!
URII
URII
URII
VRRRII

READ THIS WAY

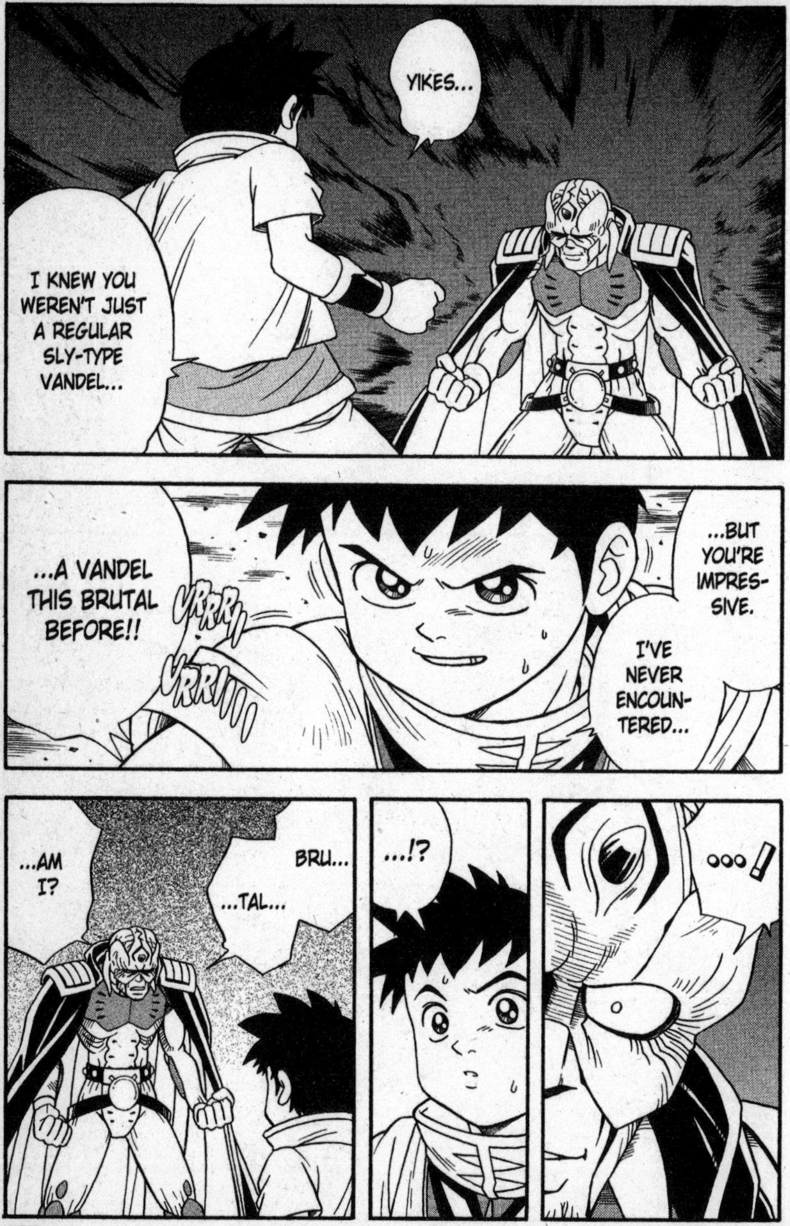
YIKES...
I KNEW YOU WEREN'T JUST A REGULAR SLY-TYPE VANDEL...
...BUT YOU'RE IMPRES-SIVE.
I'VE NEVER ENCOUN-TERED...
VRRRI
VRRIIII
...A VANDEL THIS BRUTAL BEFORE!!
ooo!
...!?
BRU...
...TAL...
...AM I?

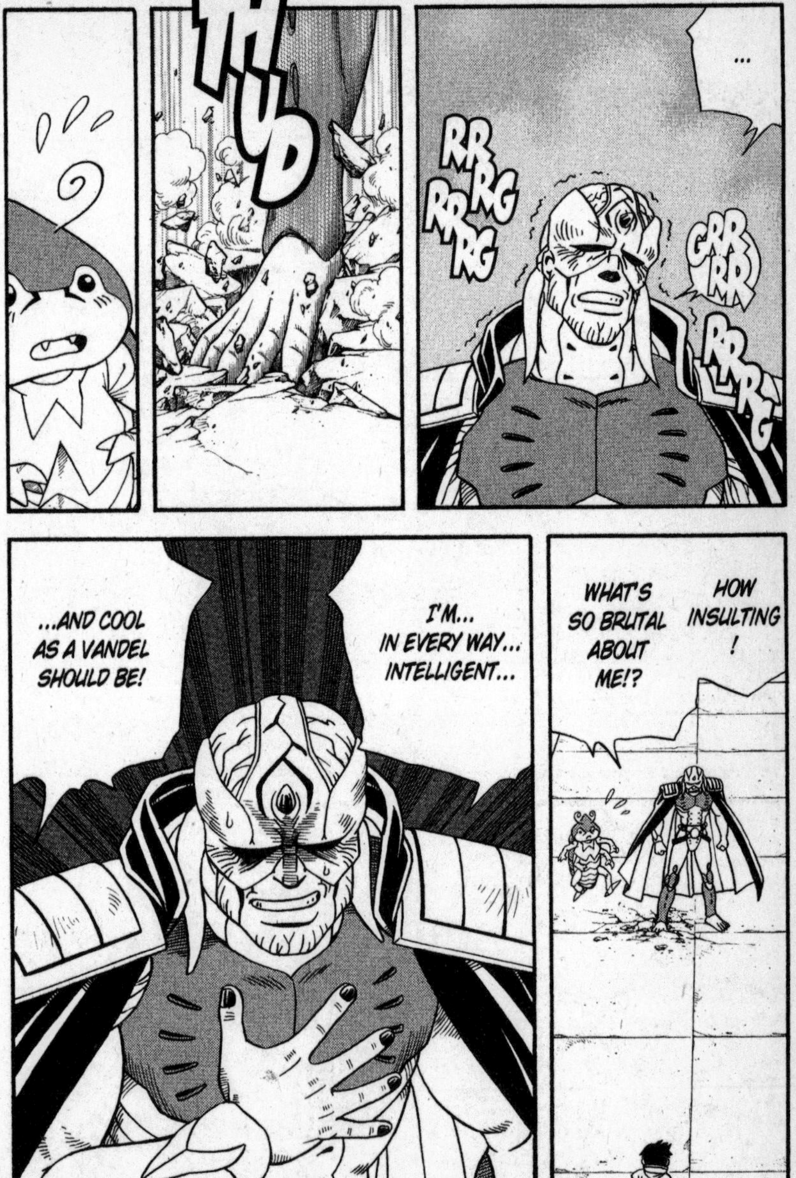

...
RRRG RRRG
GRRRR
RRRRG
THUD
HOW INSULTING!
WHAT'S SO BRUTAL ABOUT ME!?
I'M... IN EVERY WAY... INTELLIGENT...
...AND COOL AS A VANDEL SHOULD BE!

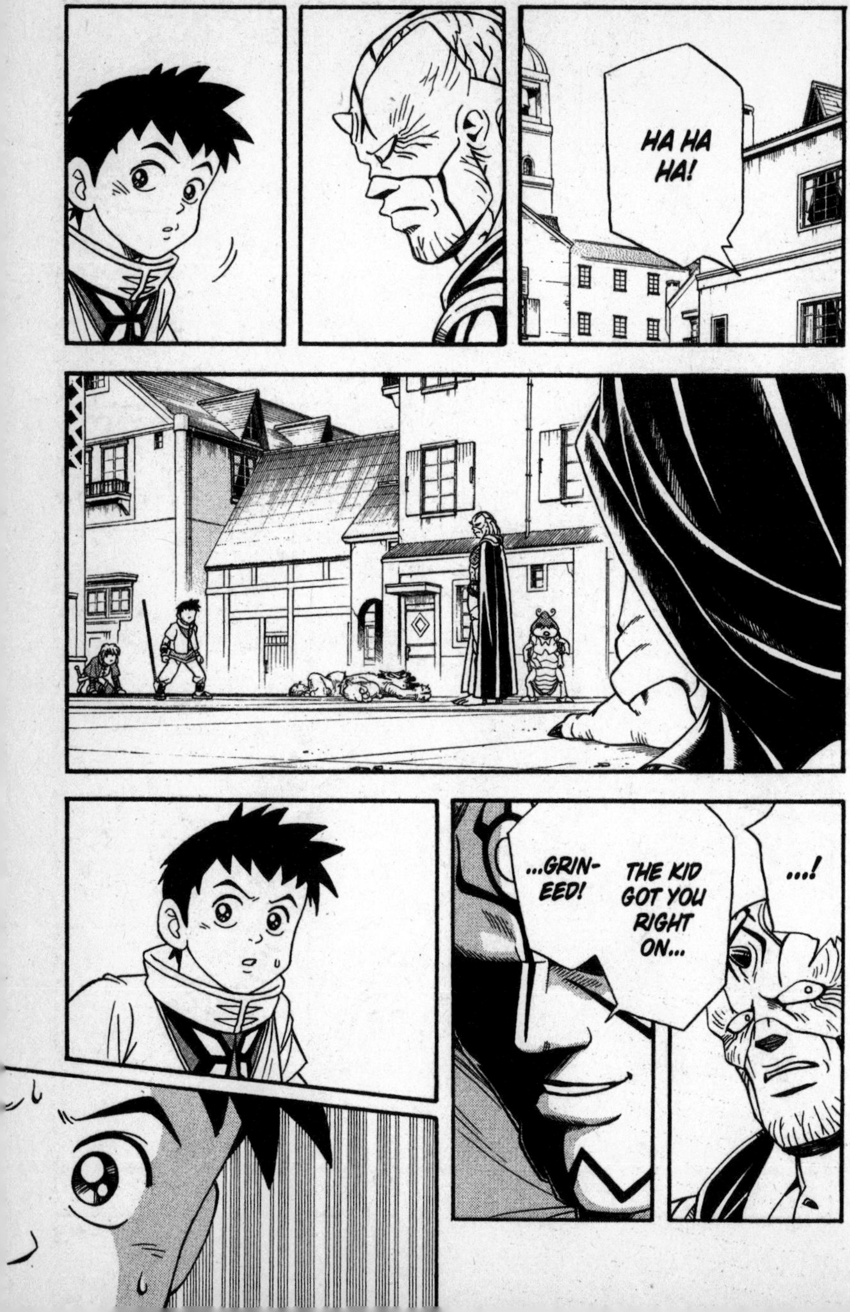
HA HA HA!
...!
...GRIN-EED! THE KID GOT YOU RIGHT ON...

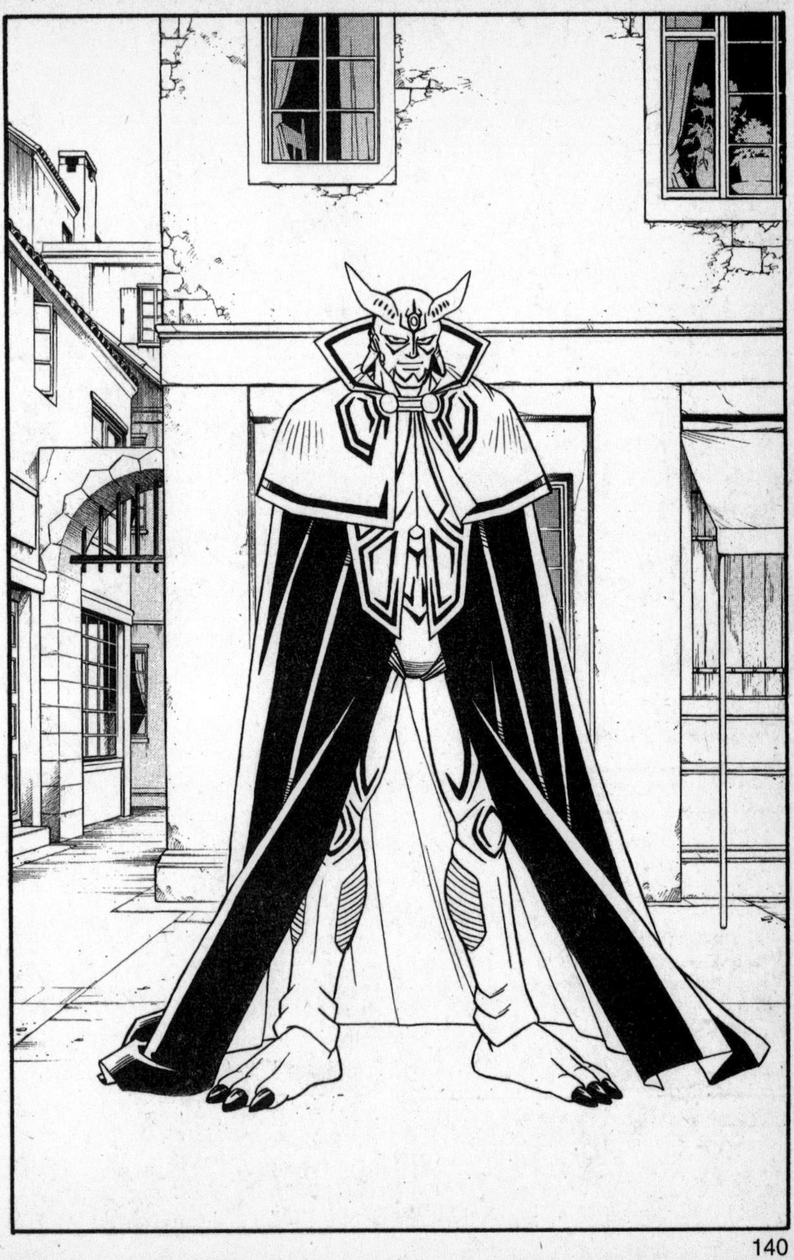

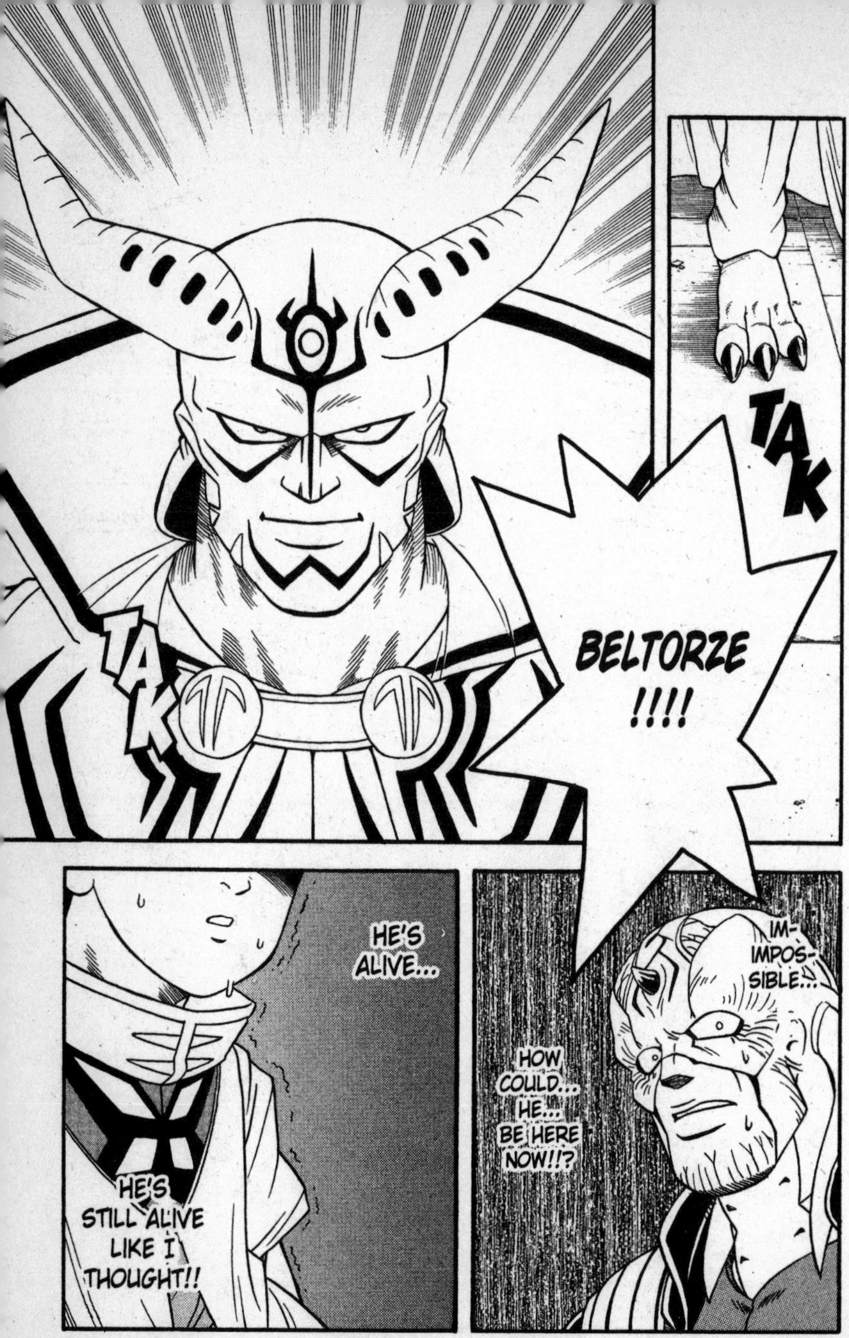
TAK
BELTORZE !!!!
TAK
IM- IMPOS- SIBLE...
HOW COULD... HE... BE HERE NOW!!?
HE'S ALIVE...
HE'S STILL ALIVE LIKE I THOUGHT!!

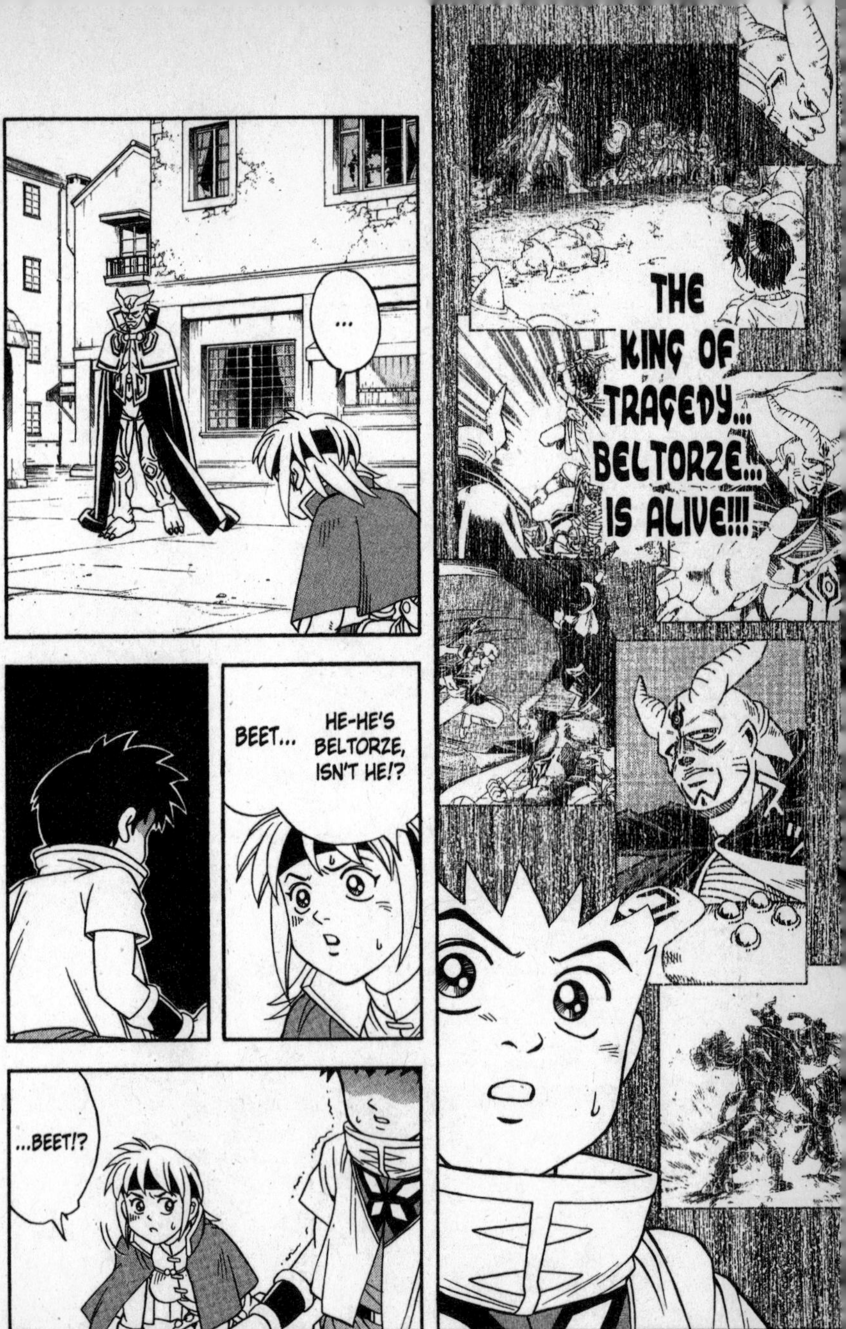
THE KING OF TRAGEDY... BELTORZE... IS ALIVE!!!
...
BEET... HE-HE'S BELTORZE, ISN'T HE!?
...BEET!?

READ THIS WAY

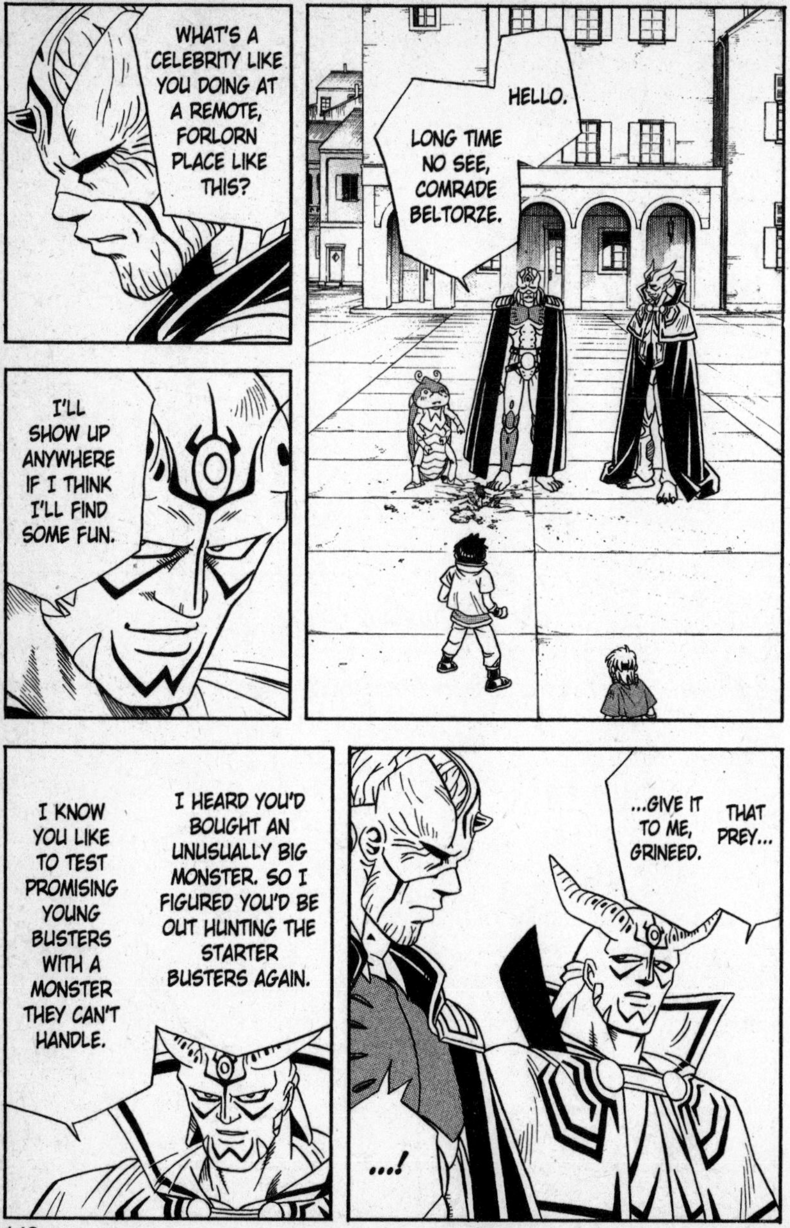
HELLO.
LONG TIME NO SEE, COMRADE BELTORZE.
WHAT'S A CELEBRITY LIKE YOU DOING AT A REMOTE, FORLORN PLACE LIKE THIS?
I'LL SHOW UP ANYWHERE IF I THINK I'LL FIND SOME FUN.
THAT PREY...
...GIVE IT TO ME, GRINEED.
...!
I HEARD YOU'D BOUGHT AN UNUSUALLY BIG MONSTER. SO I FIGURED YOU'D BE OUT HUNTING THE STARTER BUSTERS AGAIN.
I KNOW YOU LIKE TO TEST PROMISING YOUNG BUSTERS WITH A MONSTER THEY CAN'T HANDLE.

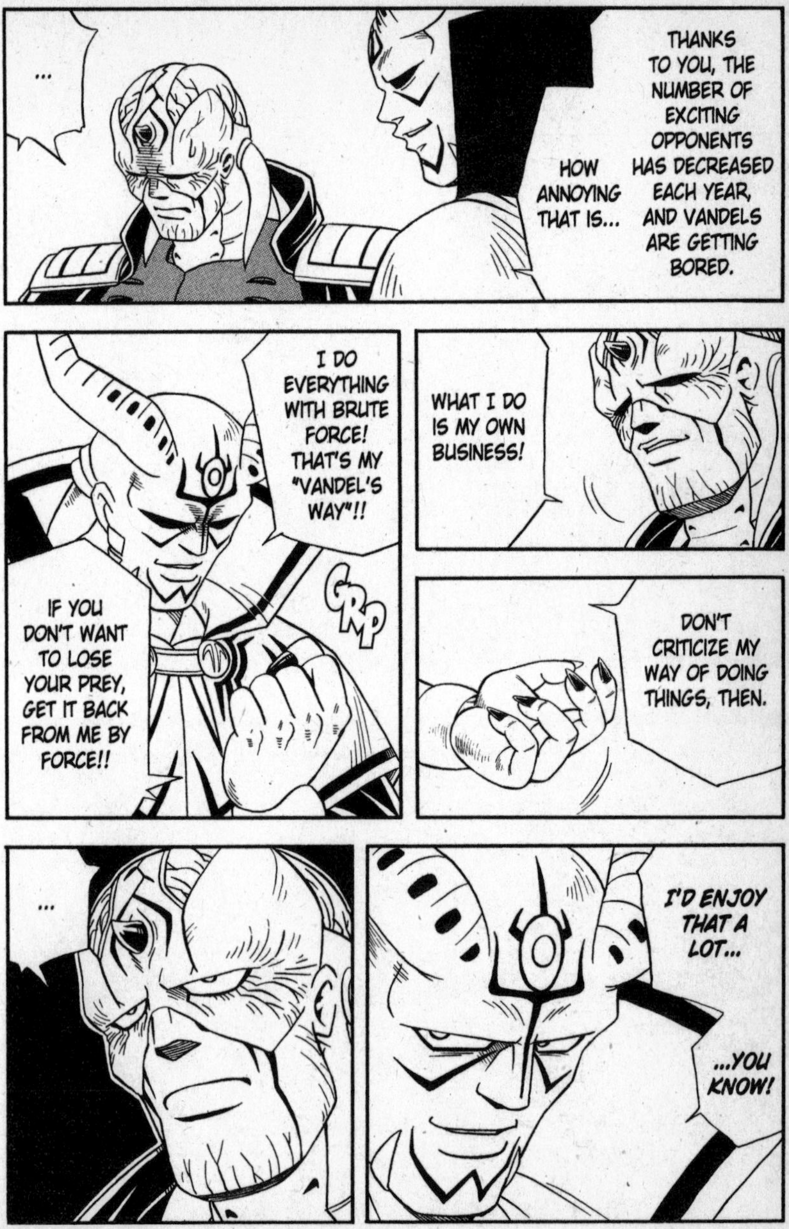
THANKS TO YOU, THE NUMBER OF EXCITING OPPONENTS HAS DECREASED EACH YEAR, AND VANDELS ARE GETTING BORED.
HOW ANNOYING THAT IS...
...
WHAT I DO IS MY OWN BUSINESS!
DON'T CRITICIZE MY WAY OF DOING THINGS, THEN.
I DO EVERYTHING WITH BRUTE FORCE! THAT'S MY "VANDEL'S WAY"!!
GRP
IF YOU DON'T WANT TO LOSE YOUR PREY, GET IT BACK FROM ME BY FORCE!!
I'D ENJOY THAT A LOT...
...YOU KNOW!
...

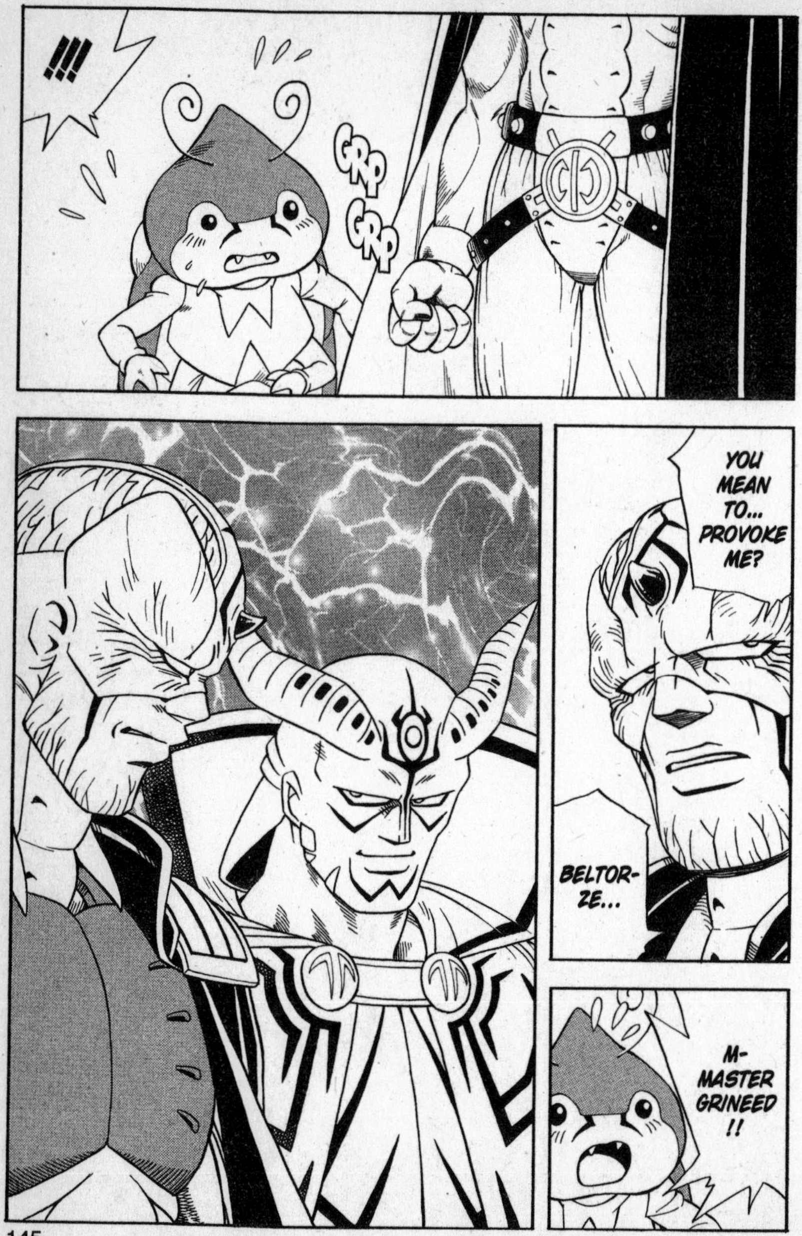
GRP GRP
!!!!
YOU MEAN TO... PROVOKE ME?
BELTOR-ZE...
M-MASTER GRINEED !!

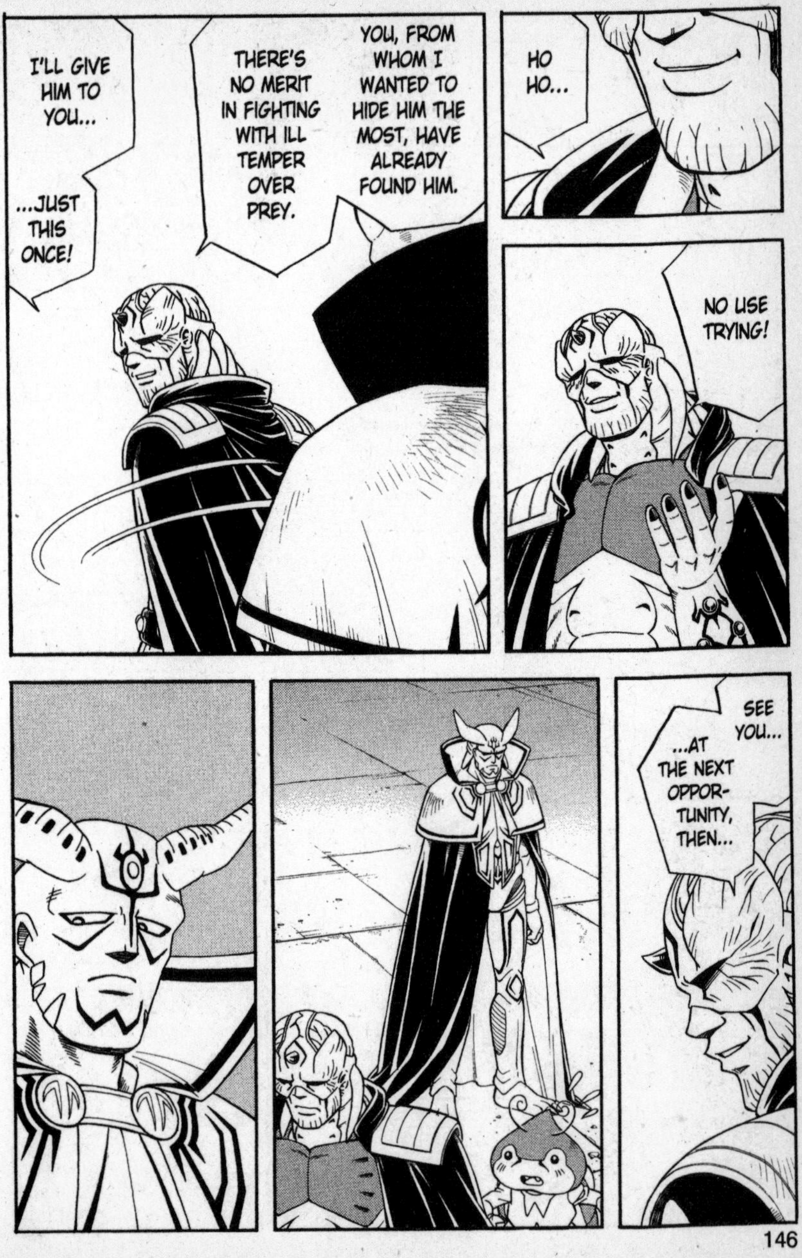
HO HO...
NO USE TRYING!
YOU, FROM WHOM I WANTED TO HIDE HIM THE MOST, HAVE ALREADY FOUND HIM.
THERE'S NO MERIT IN FIGHTING WITH ILL TEMPER OVER PREY.
I'LL GIVE HIM TO YOU...
...JUST THIS ONCE!
SEE YOU...
...AT THE NEXT OPPOR-TUNITY, THEN...

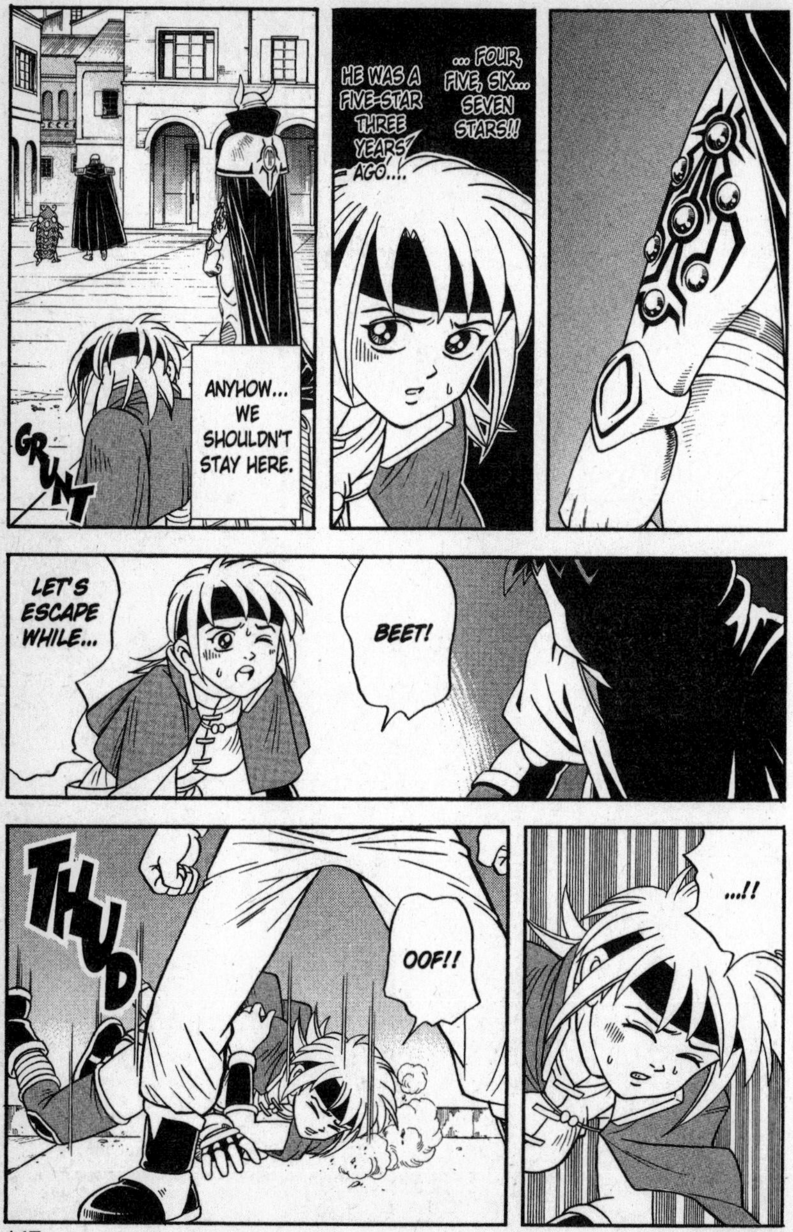
... FOUR, FIVE, SIX... SEVEN STARS!!
HE WAS A FIVE-STAR THREE YEARS AGO....
ANYHOW... WE SHOULDN'T STAY HERE.
GRUNT
BEET!
LET'S ESCAPE WHILE...
...!!
OOF!!
THUD

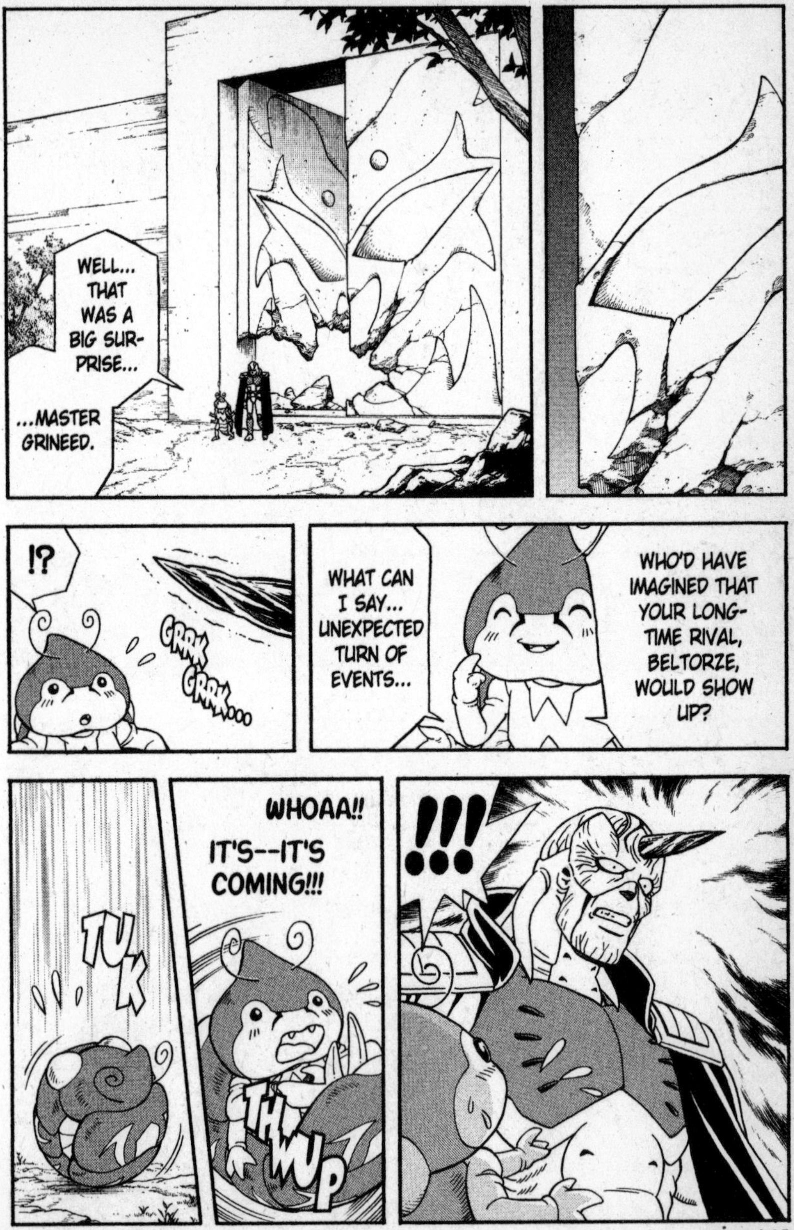
WELL... THAT WAS A BIG SURPRISE...
...MASTER GRINEED.
WHO'D HAVE IMAGINED THAT YOUR LONG-TIME RIVAL, BELTORZE, WOULD SHOW UP?
WHAT CAN I SAY... UNEXPECTED TURN OF EVENTS...
!?
GRRK GRRK...
!!!
WHOAA!!
IT'S--IT'S COMING!!!
THWUP
TUK

READ THIS WAY

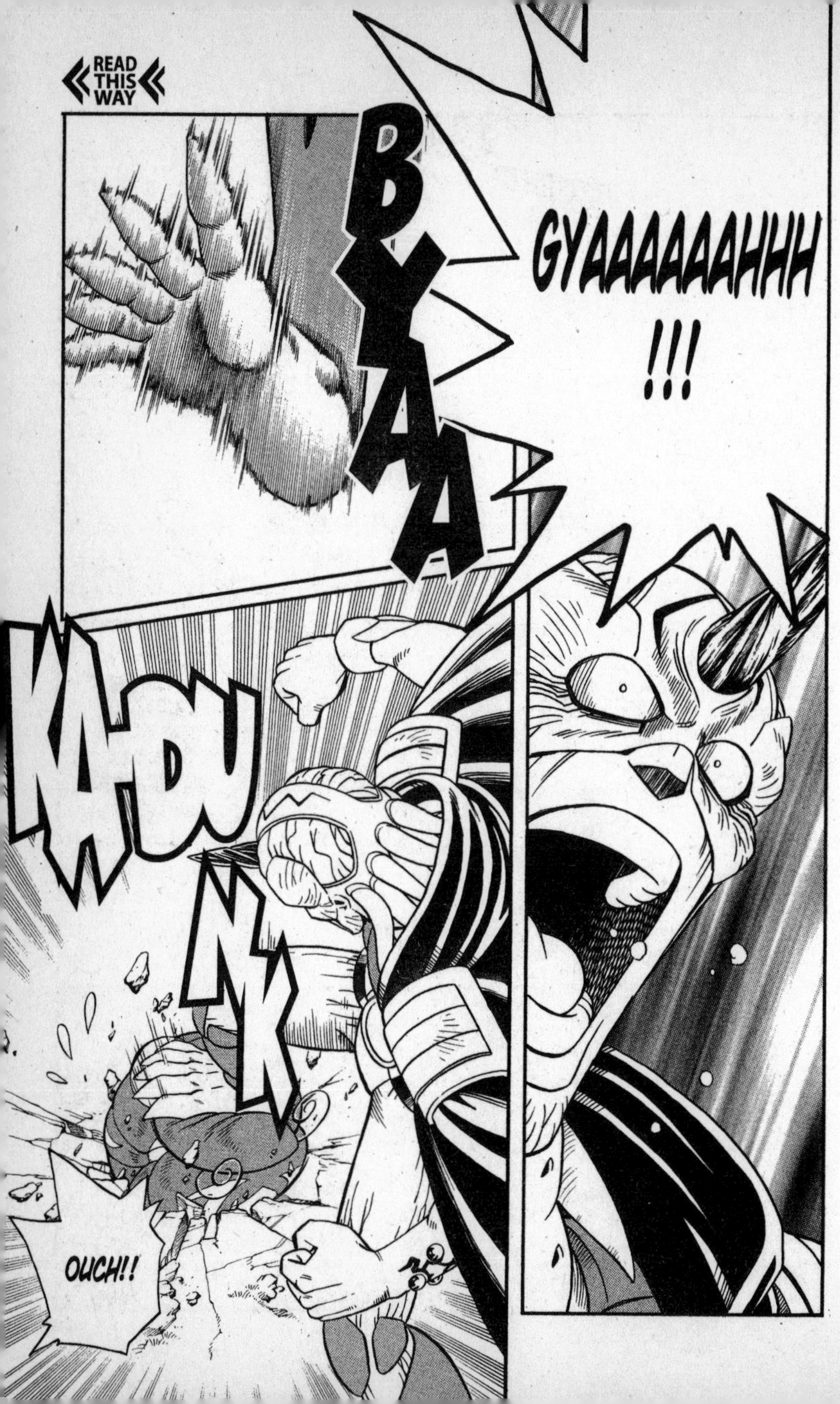
GYAAAAAAHHH
!!!
BYAA
KA-DUNK
OUCH!!

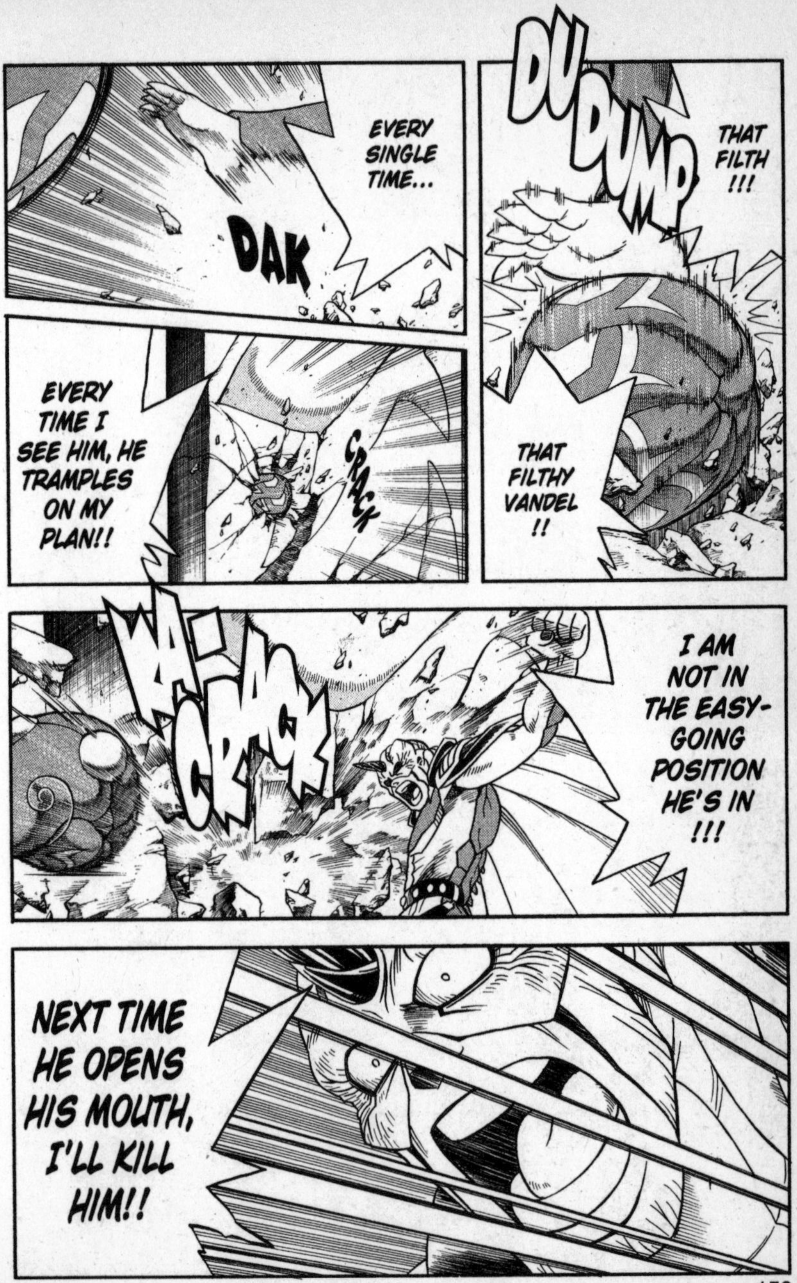
DU DUMP
THAT FILTH!!!
THAT FILTHY VANDEL!!
EVERY SINGLE TIME...
DAK
EVERY TIME I SEE HIM, HE TRAMPLES ON MY PLAN!!
CRACK
I AM NOT IN THE EASY-GOING POSITION HE'S IN!!!
NEXT TIME HE OPENS HIS MOUTH, I'LL KILL HIM!!

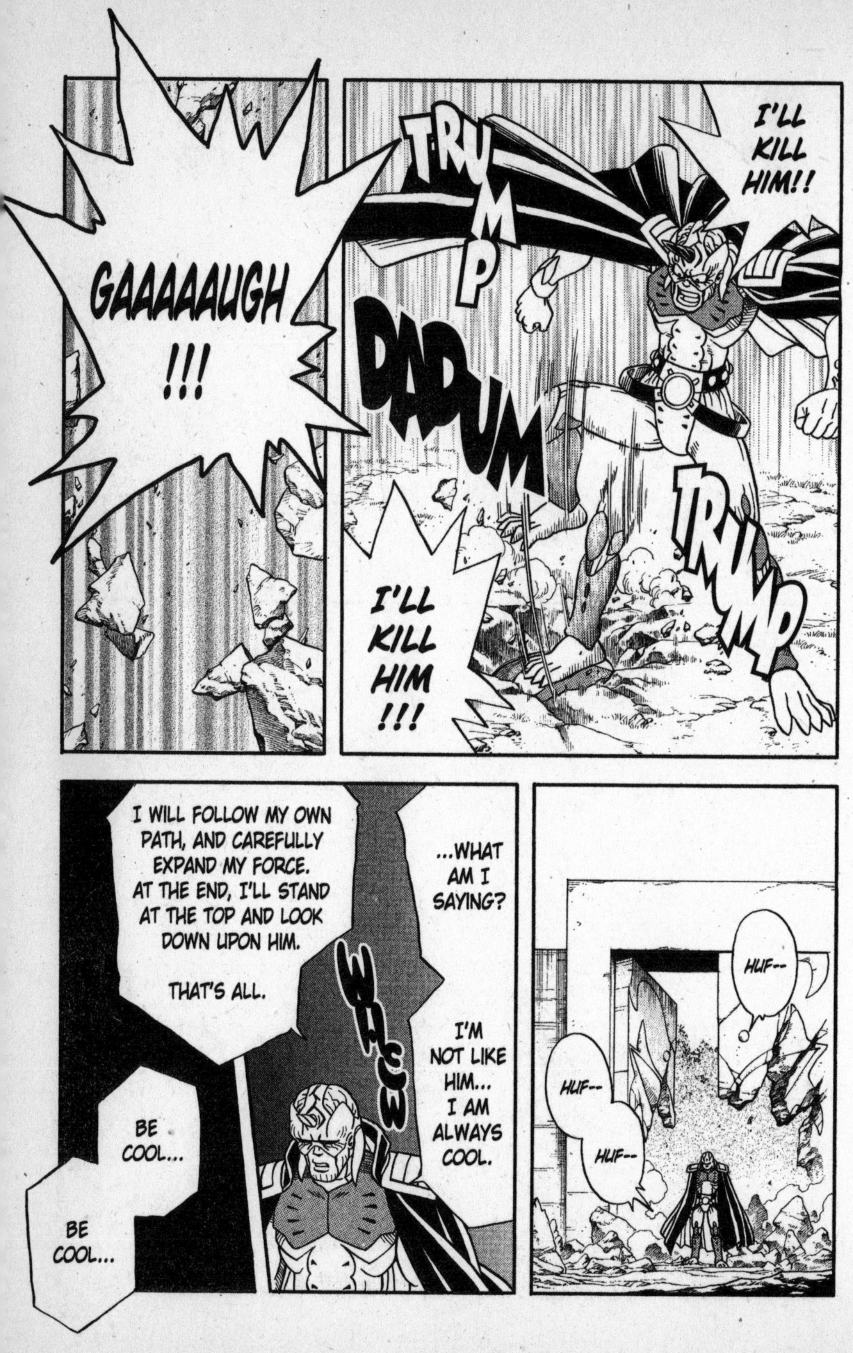
TRUMP
I'LL KILL HIM!!
DADUM
TRUMP
I'LL KILL HIM!!!
GAAAAAUGH!!!
HUF--
HUF--
HUF--
...WHAT AM I SAYING?
I'M NOT LIKE HIM... I AM ALWAYS COOL.
I WILL FOLLOW MY OWN PATH, AND CAREFULLY EXPAND MY FORCE. AT THE END, I'LL STAND AT THE TOP AND LOOK DOWN UPON HIM.
THAT'S ALL.
BE COOL...
BE COOL...

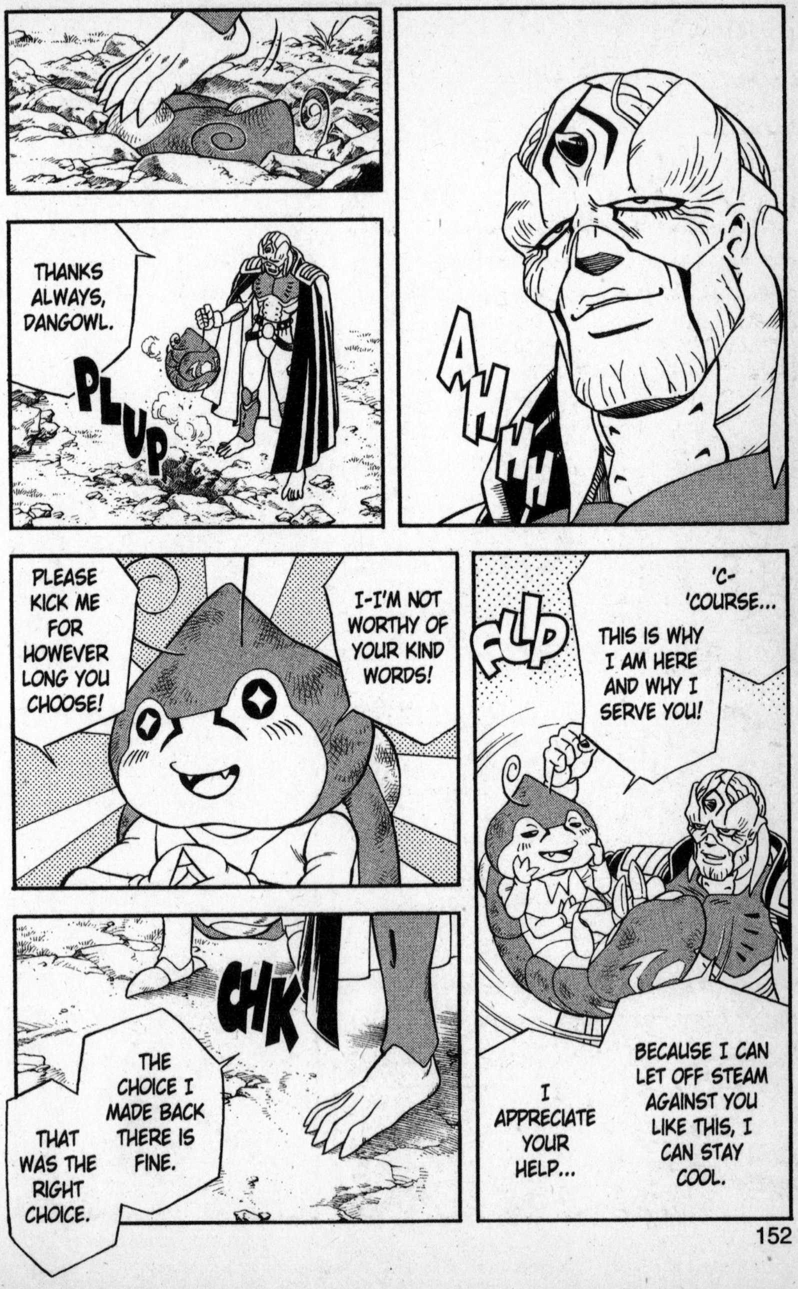
AHHHH
THANKS ALWAYS, DANGOWL.
PLUP
'C- 'COURSE...
THIS IS WHY I AM HERE AND WHY I SERVE YOU!
FLIP
BECAUSE I CAN LET OFF STEAM AGAINST YOU LIKE THIS, I CAN STAY COOL.
I APPRECIATE YOUR HELP...
I-I'M NOT WORTHY OF YOUR KIND WORDS!
PLEASE KICK ME FOR HOWEVER LONG YOU CHOOSE!
CHK
THE CHOICE I MADE BACK THERE IS FINE.
THAT WAS THE RIGHT CHOICE.

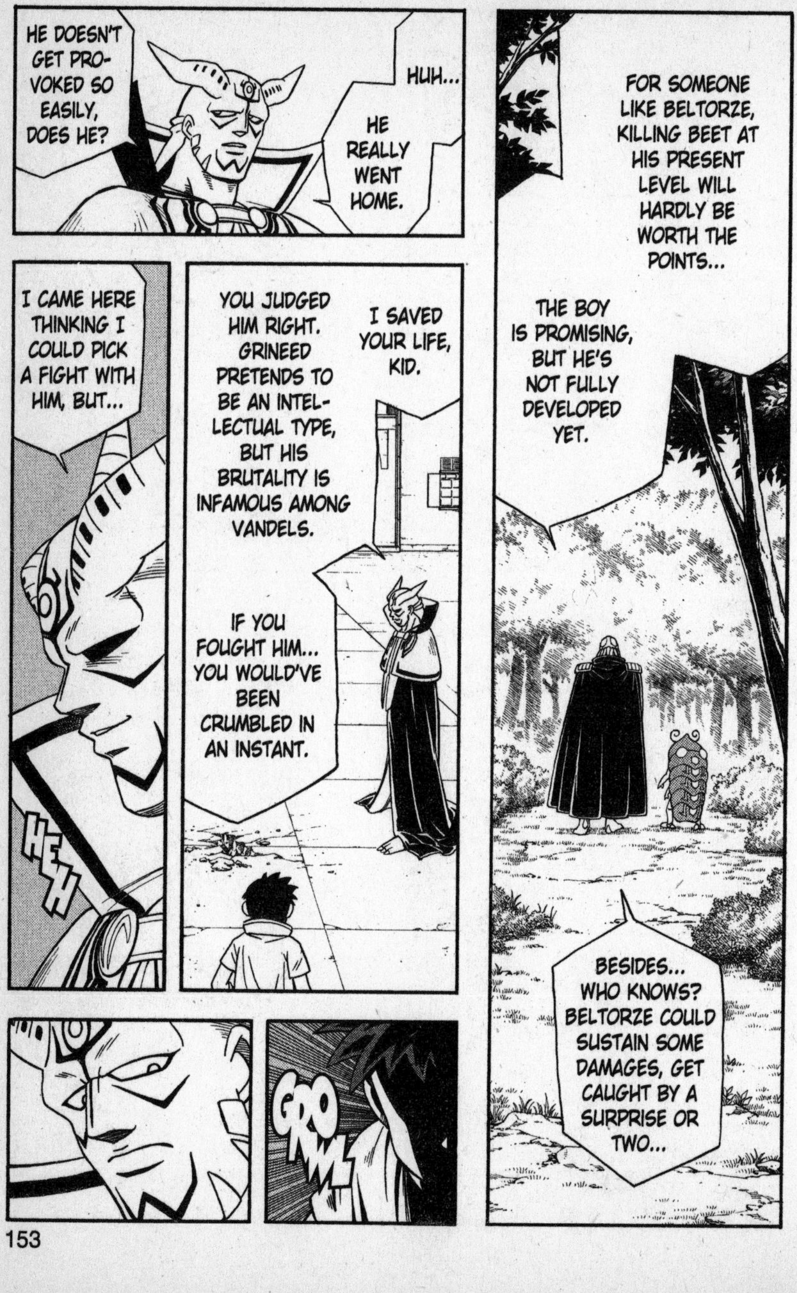
FOR SOMEONE LIKE BELTORZE, KILLING BEET AT HIS PRESENT LEVEL WILL HARDLY BE WORTH THE POINTS...
THE BOY IS PROMISING, BUT HE'S NOT FULLY DEVELOPED YET.
BESIDES... WHO KNOWS? BELTORZE COULD SUSTAIN SOME DAMAGES, GET CAUGHT BY A SURPRISE OR TWO...
HUH...
HE REALLY WENT HOME.
HE DOESN'T GET PRO-VOKED SO EASILY, DOES HE?
I SAVED YOUR LIFE, KID.
YOU JUDGED HIM RIGHT. GRINEED PRETENDS TO BE AN INTEL-LECTUAL TYPE, BUT HIS BRUTALITY IS INFAMOUS AMONG VANDELS.
IF YOU FOUGHT HIM... YOU WOULD'VE BEEN CRUMBLED IN AN INSTANT.
I CAME HERE THINKING I COULD PICK A FIGHT WITH HIM, BUT...
HEH
GRO GROWL

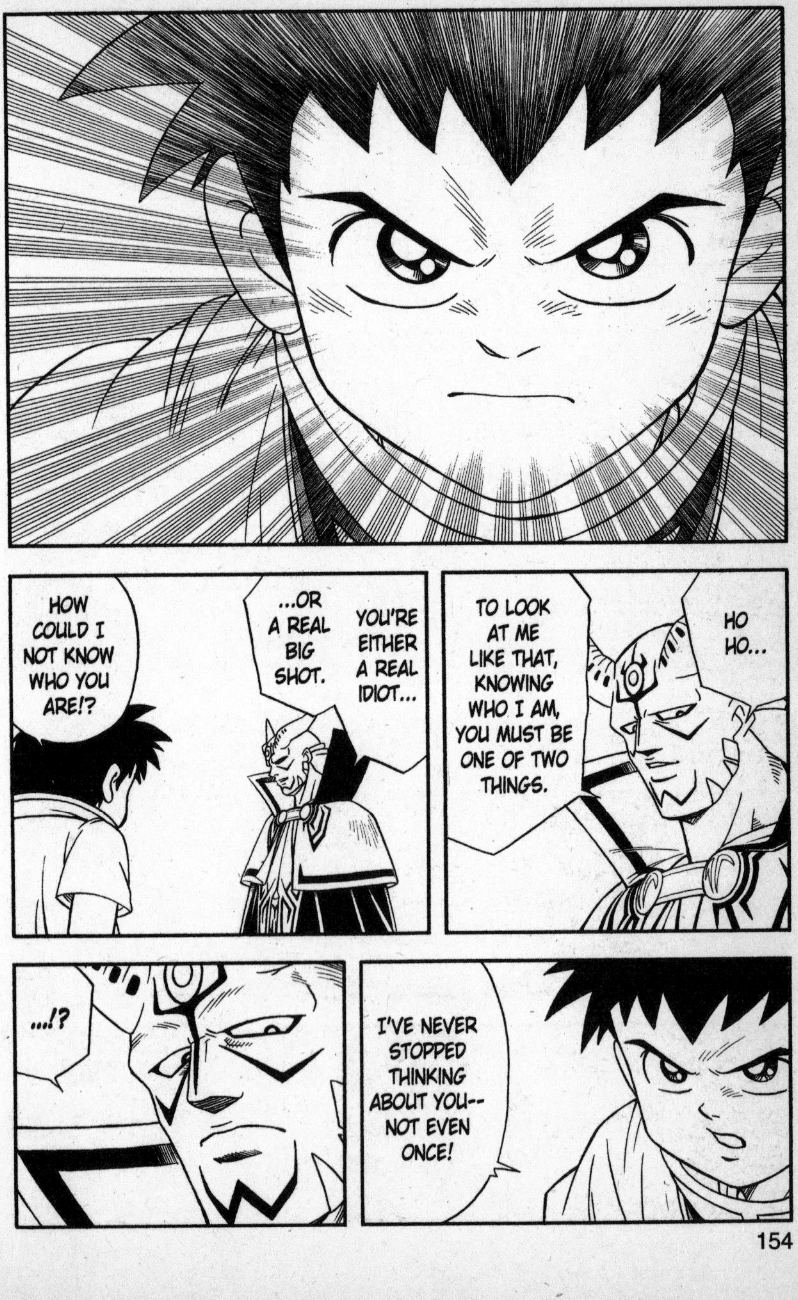
HO HO...
TO LOOK AT ME LIKE THAT, KNOWING WHO I AM, YOU MUST BE ONE OF TWO THINGS.
YOU'RE EITHER A REAL IDIOT...
...OR A REAL BIG SHOT.
HOW COULD I NOT KNOW WHO YOU ARE!?
I'VE NEVER STOPPED THINKING ABOUT YOU-- NOT EVEN ONCE!
...!?

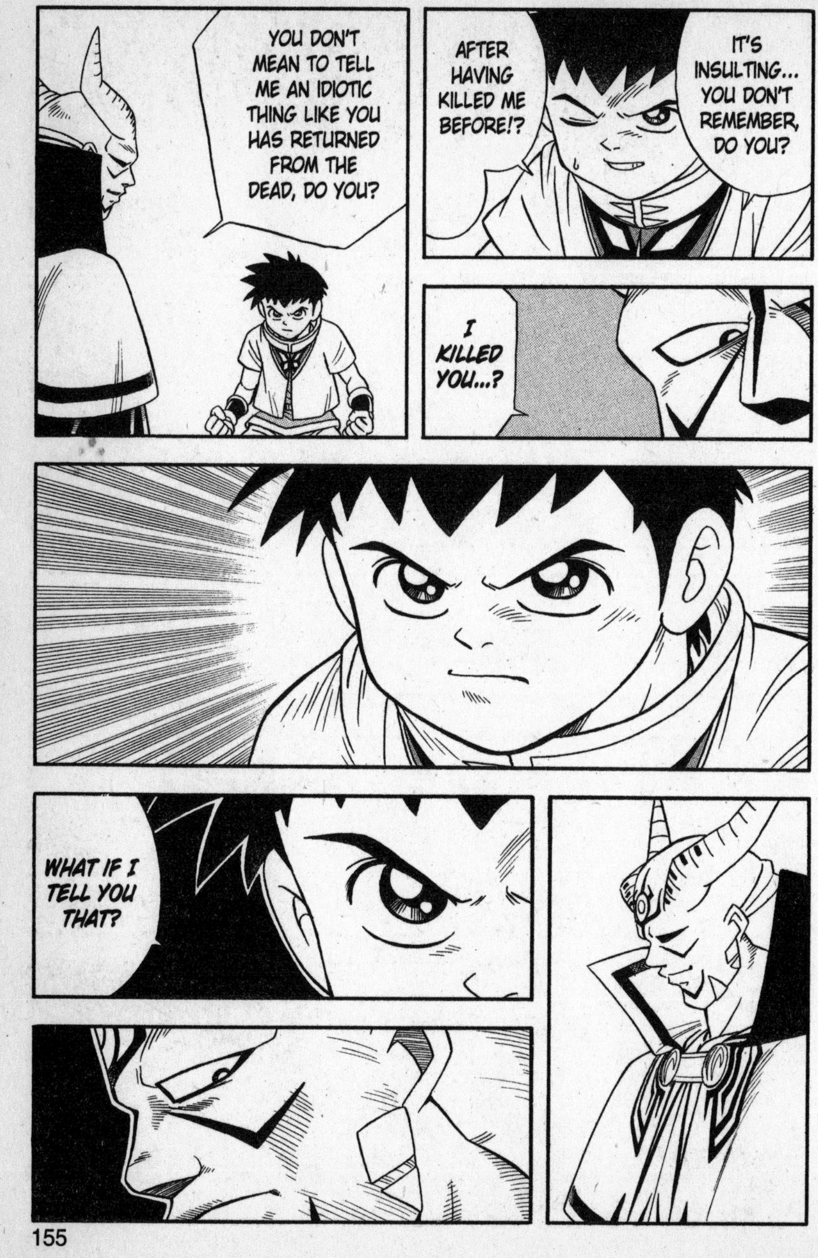
IT'S INSULTING... YOU DON'T REMEMBER, DO YOU?
AFTER HAVING KILLED ME BEFORE!?
I KILLED YOU...?
YOU DON'T MEAN TO TELL ME AN IDIOTIC THING LIKE YOU HAS RETURNED FROM THE DEAD, DO YOU?
WHAT IF I TELL YOU THAT?

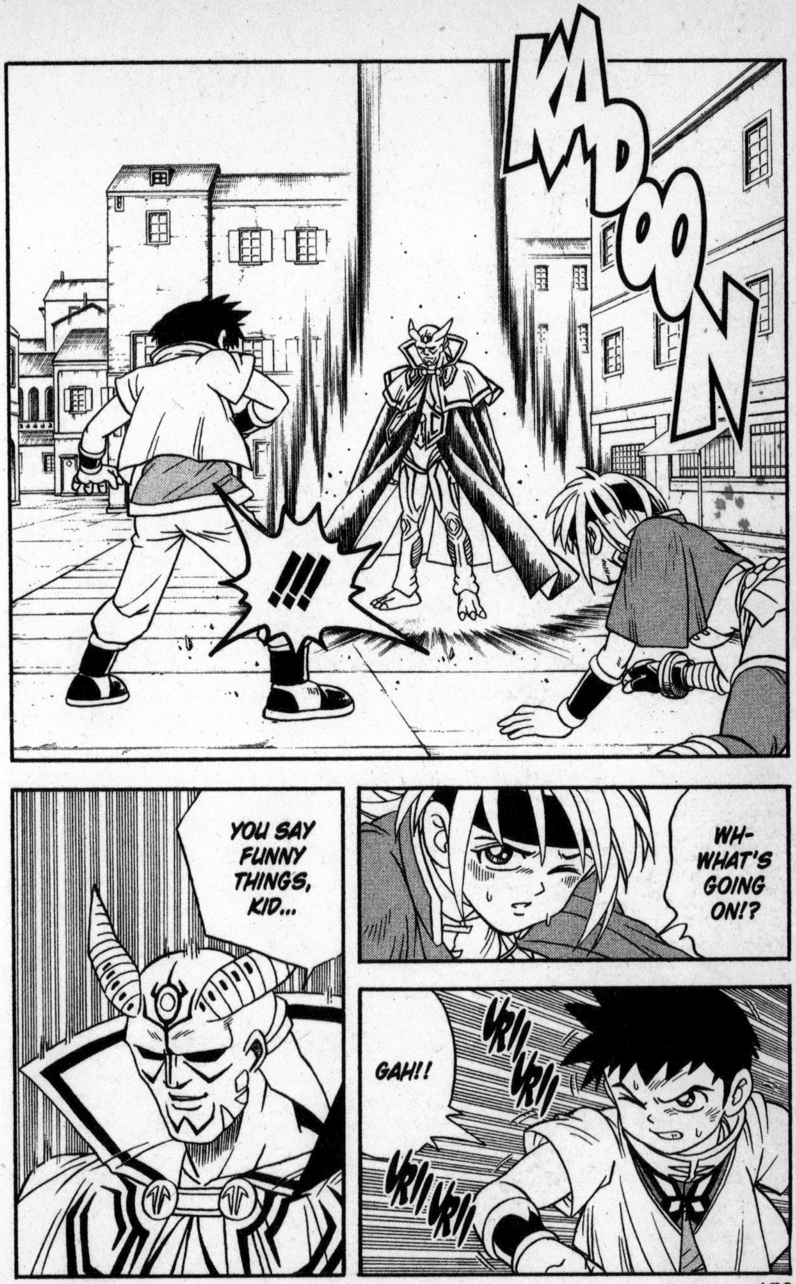
KADOOON
!!!!
WH- WHAT'S GOING ON!?
GAH!!
VRII VRII
VRII VRII
YOU SAY FUNNY THINGS, KID...

READ THIS WAY

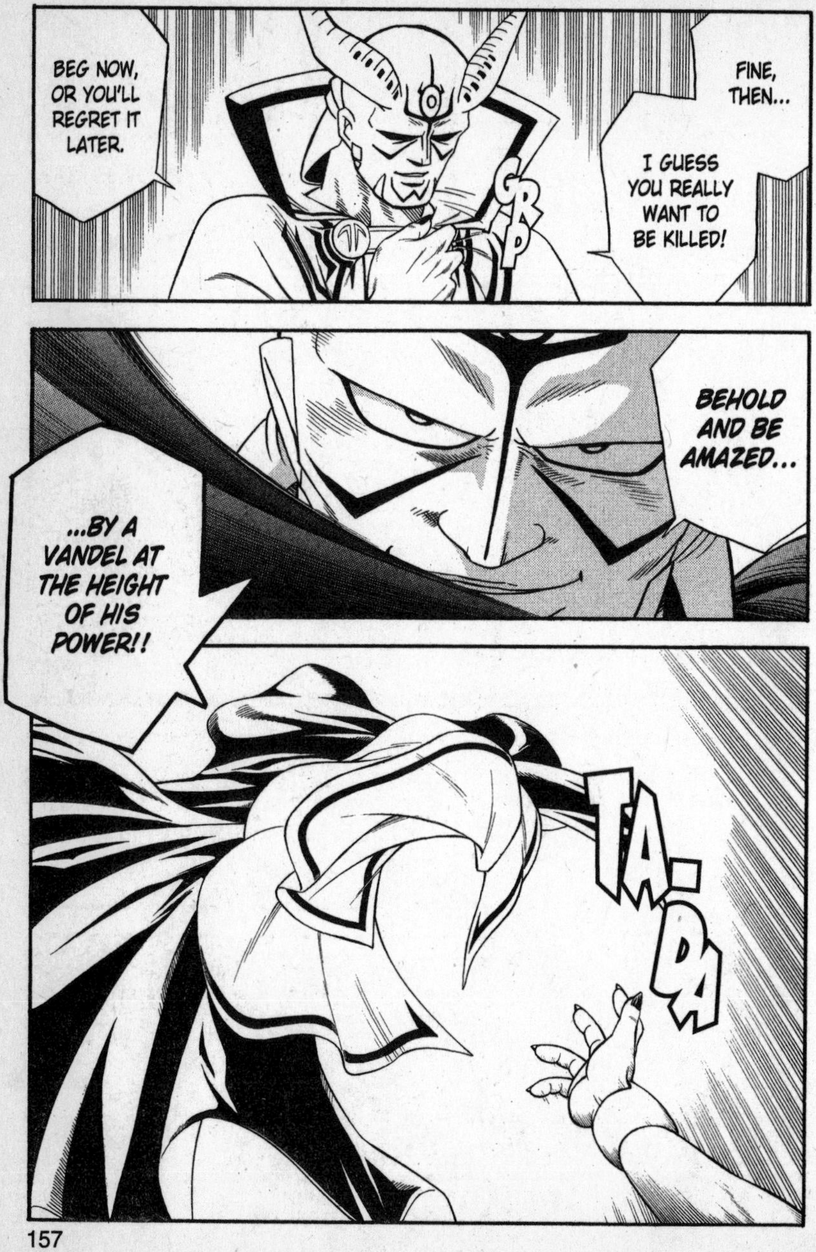
FINE, THEN...
I GUESS YOU REALLY WANT TO BE KILLED!
GRIP
BEG NOW, OR YOU'LL REGRET IT LATER.
BEHOLD AND BE AMAZED...
...BY A VANDEL AT THE HEIGHT OF HIS POWER!!
TA-DA

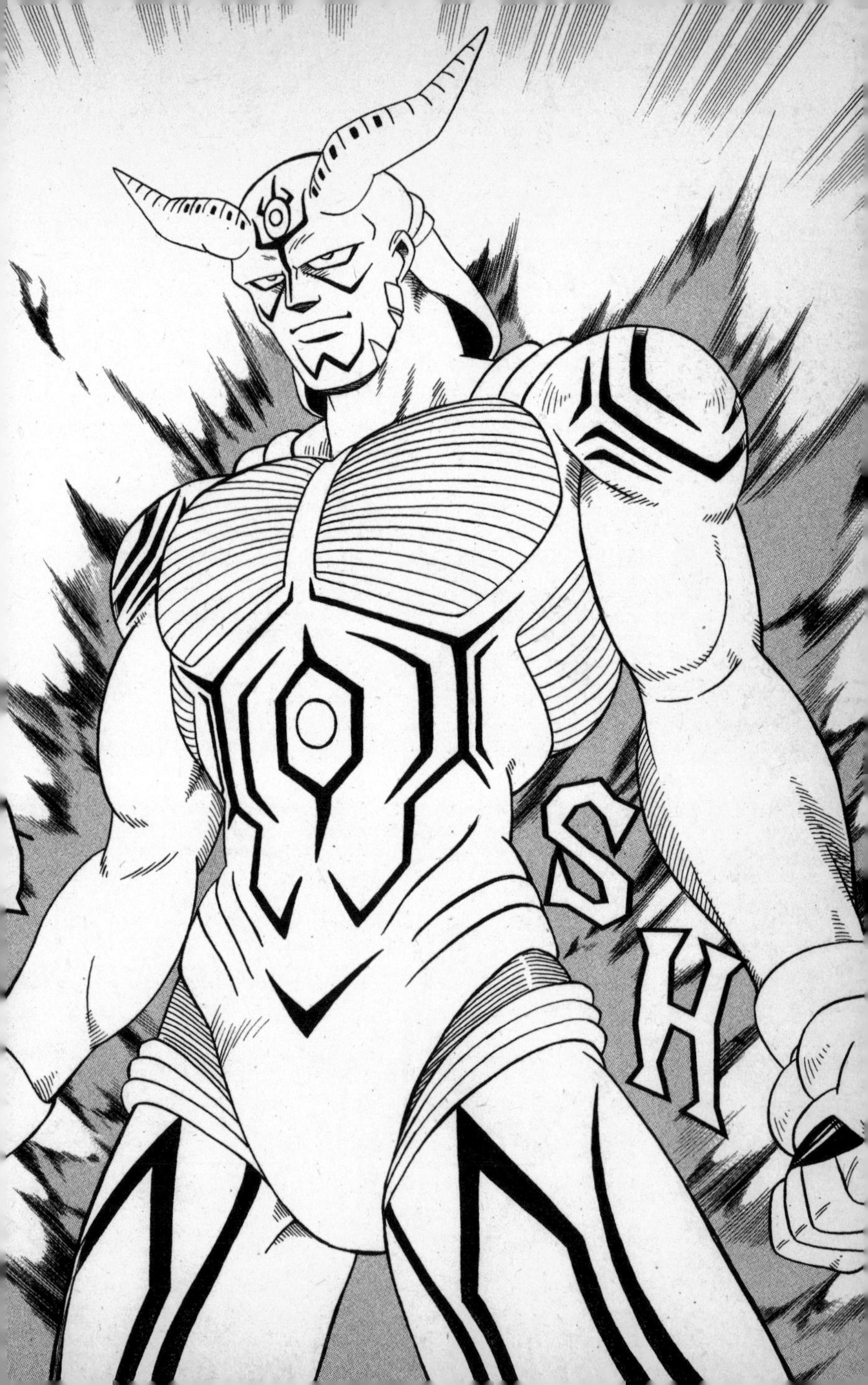
SH

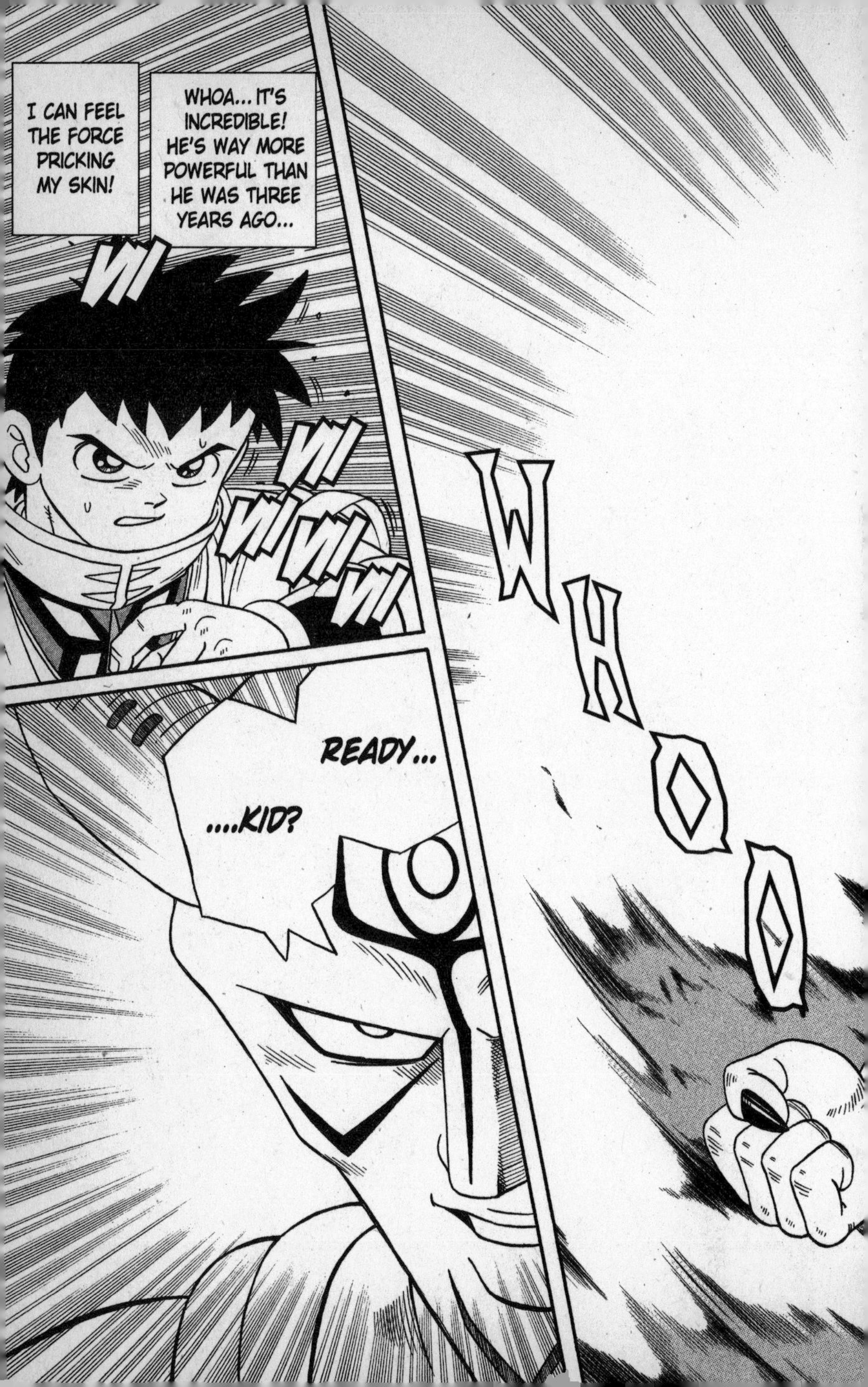
WHOO
WHOA... IT'S INCREDIBLE! HE'S WAY MORE POWERFUL THAN HE WAS THREE YEARS AGO...
I CAN FEEL THE FORCE PRICKING MY SKIN!
VN
VN VN VN VN
READY...
....KID?

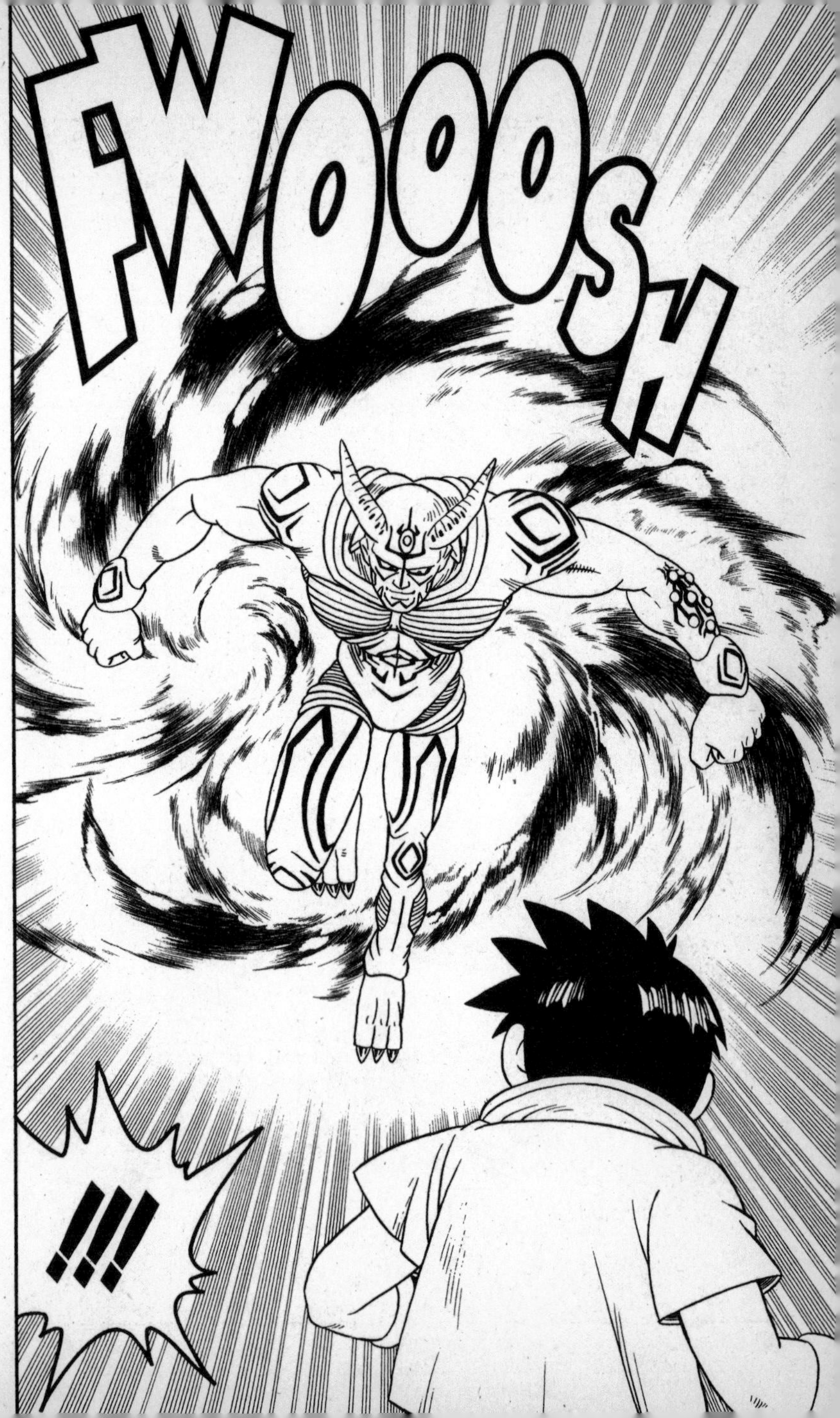
FWOOOSH
!!!

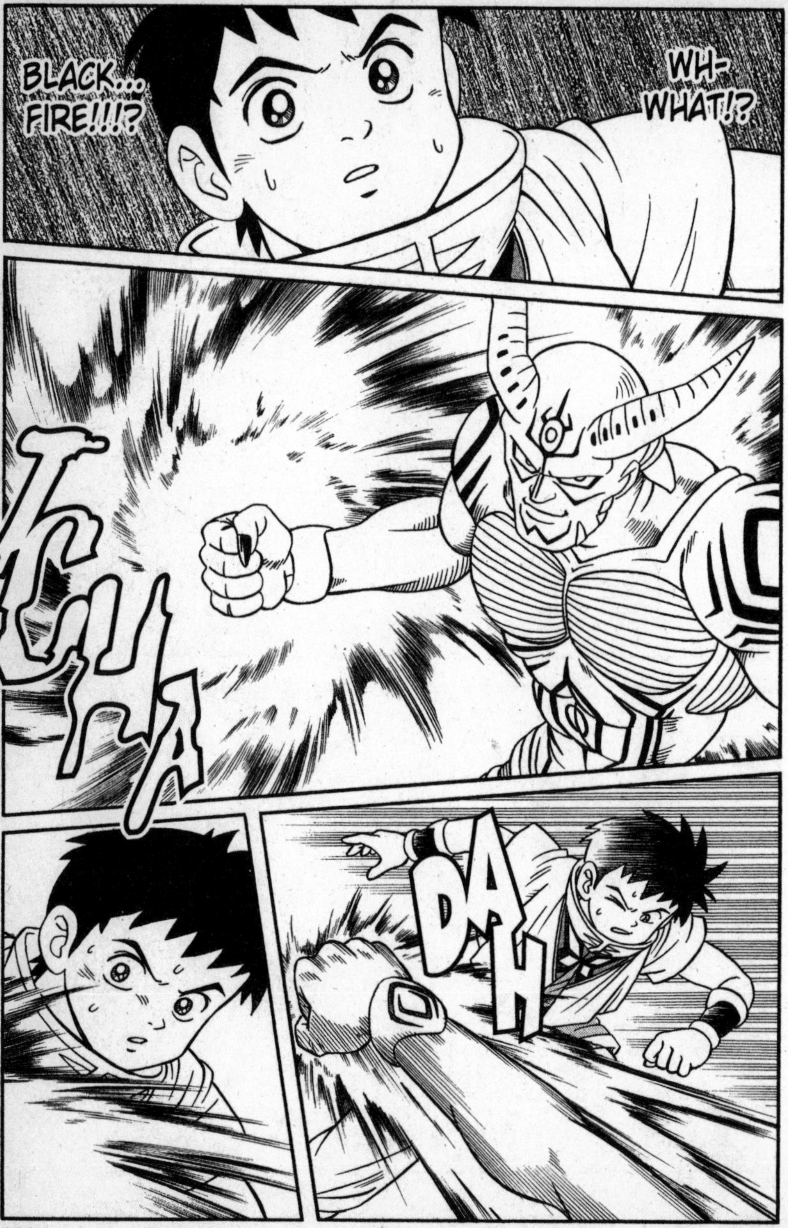
WH-WHAT!?
BLACK... FIRE!!!?
ICSHA
DAH

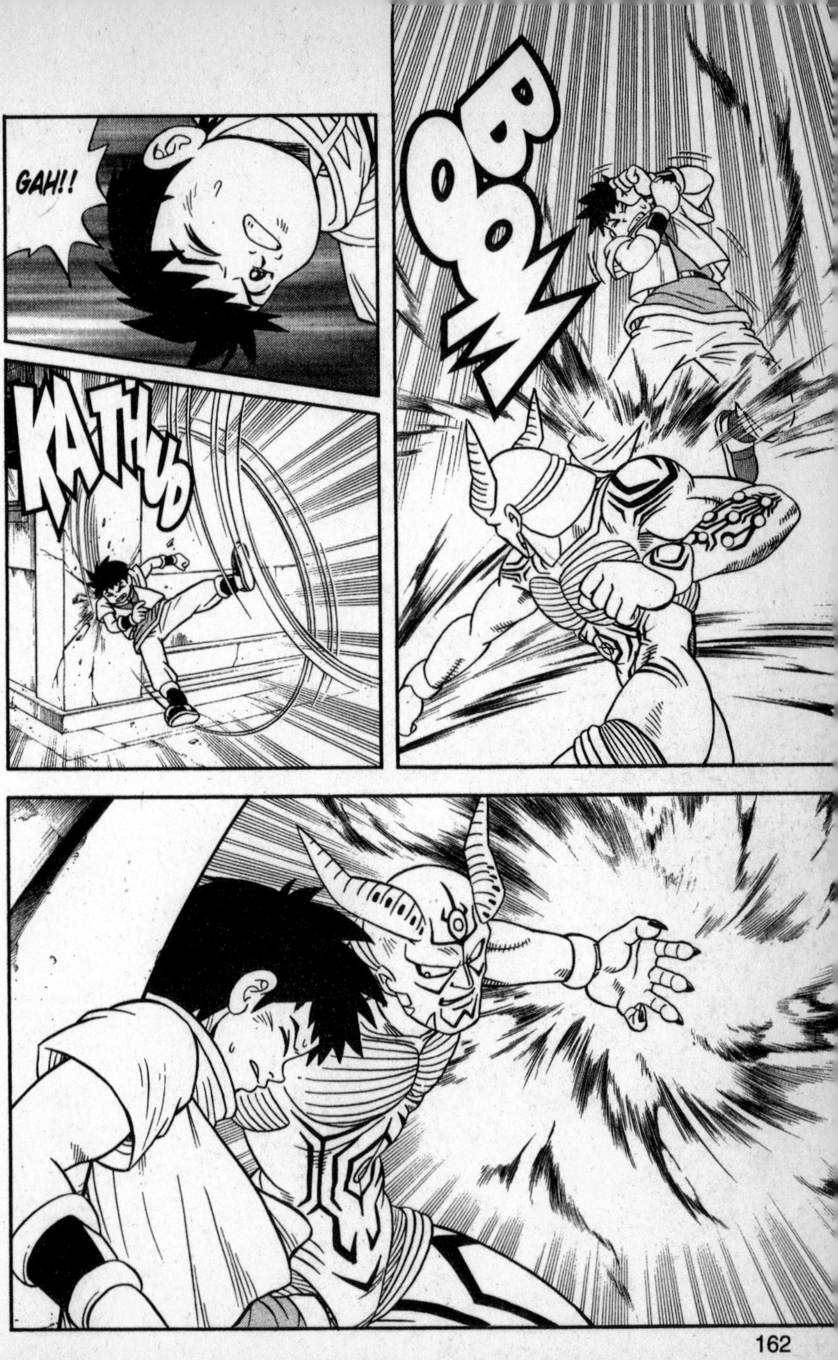
BOOM
GAH!!
KATHUD

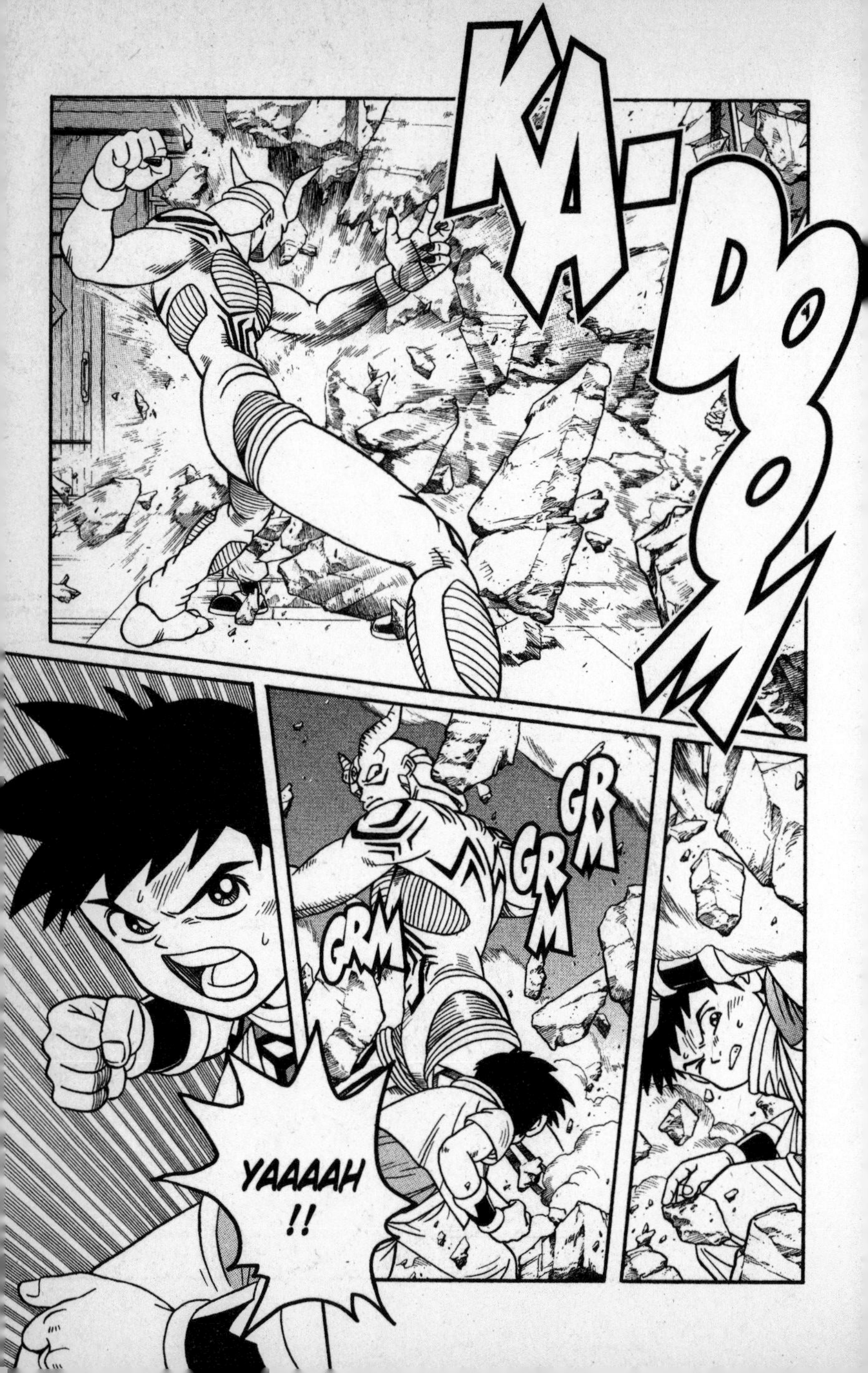
KA-DOOOM
GRM
GRM
GRM
YAAAAH !!

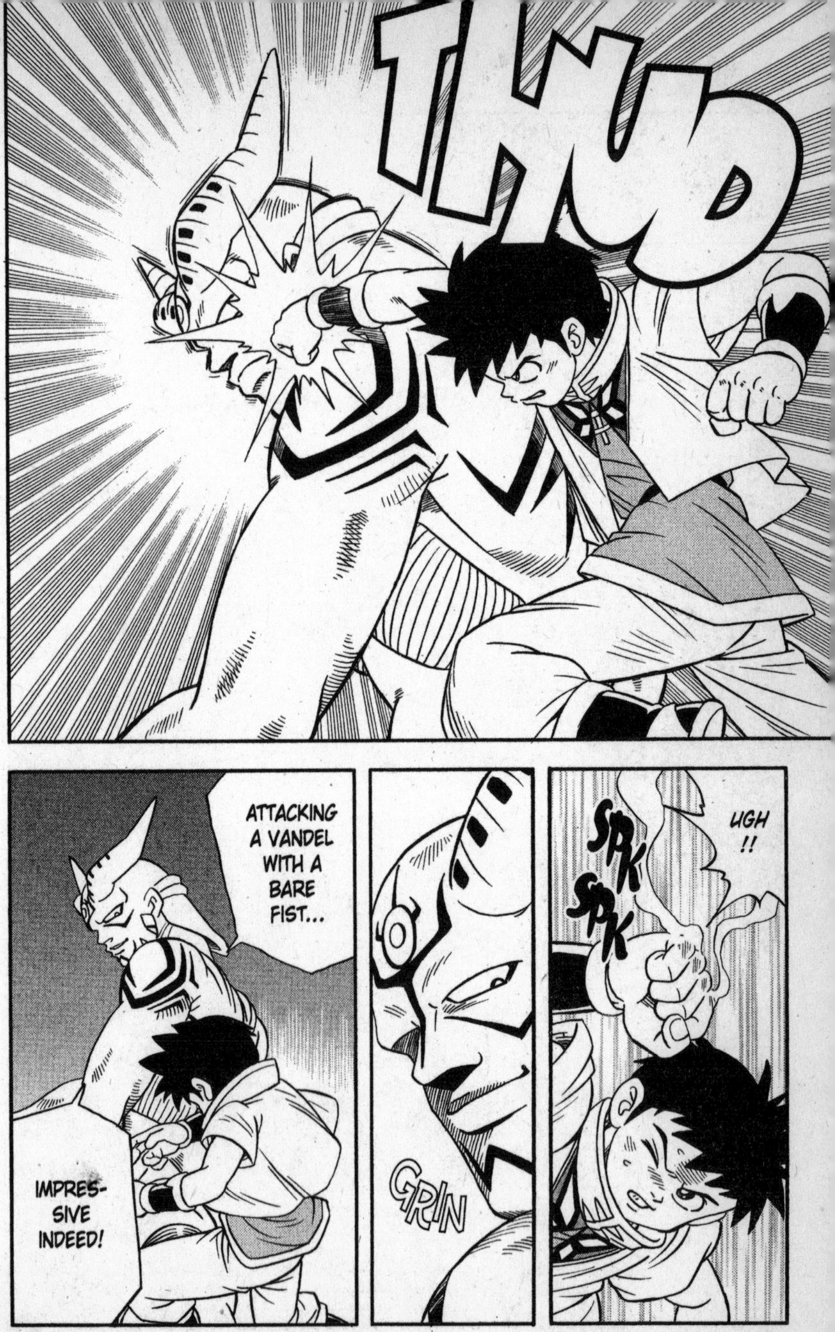
THUD
SPK
SPK
UGH !!
GRIN
ATTACKING A VANDEL WITH A BARE FIST...
IMPRES-SIVE INDEED!

READ THIS WAY

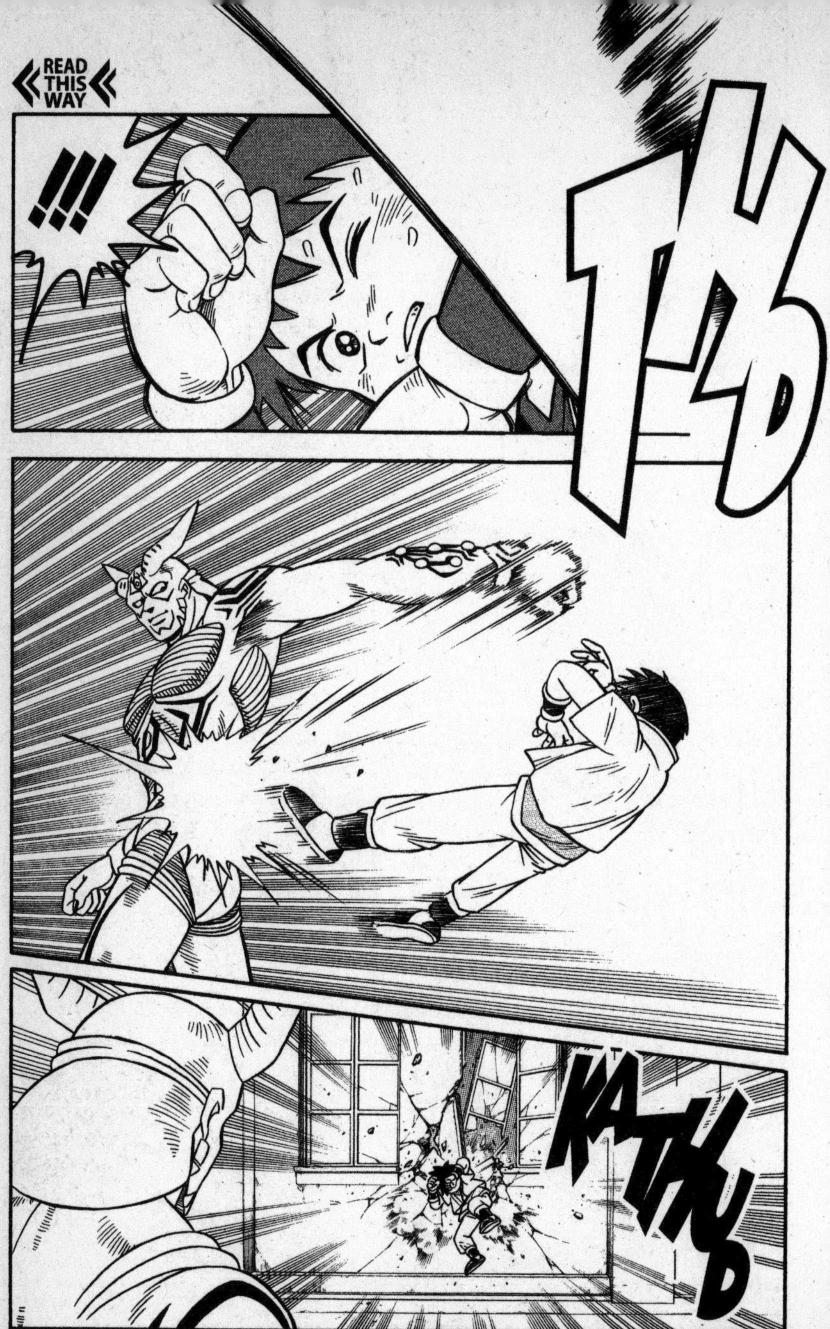
!!!
THUD
KATHUD

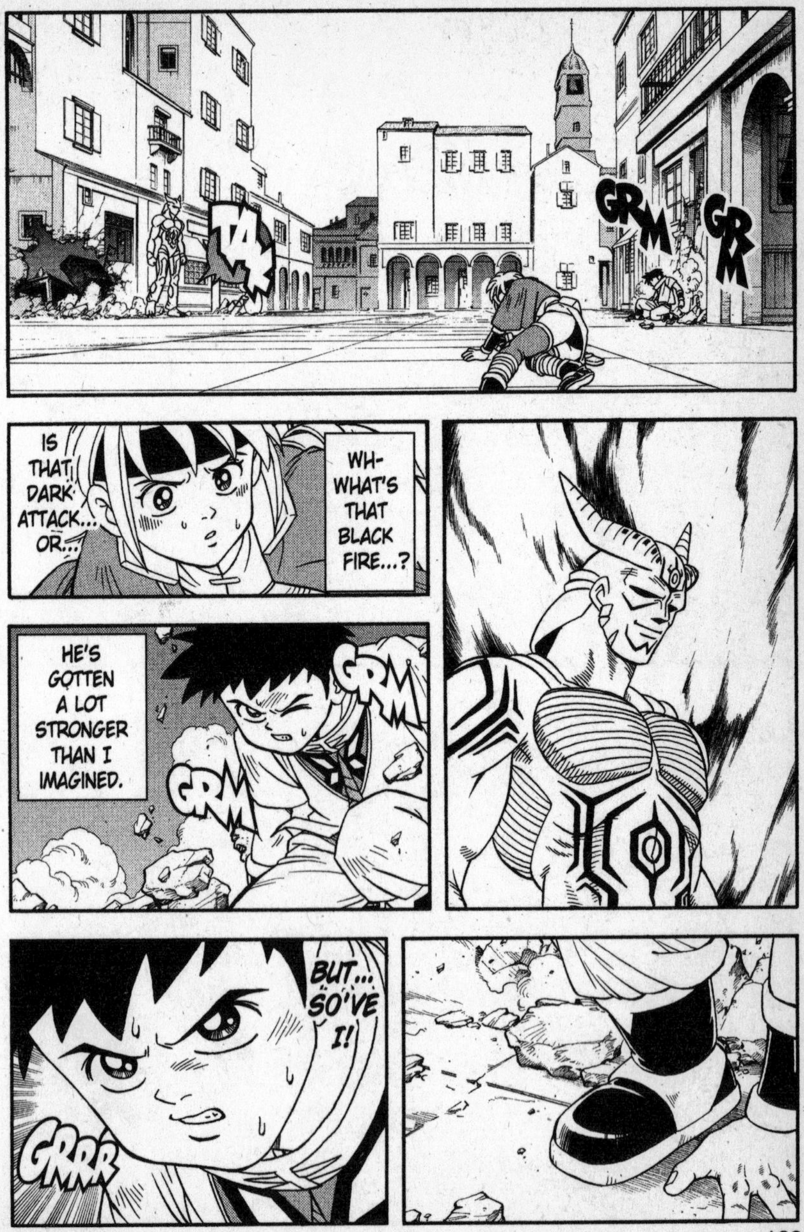
GRM GRM
TAK
WH- WHAT'S THAT BLACK FIRE...?
IS THAT DARK ATTACK... OR...
HE'S GOTTEN A LOT STRONGER THAN I IMAGINED.
GRM
GRM
BUT... SO'VE I!
GRRR

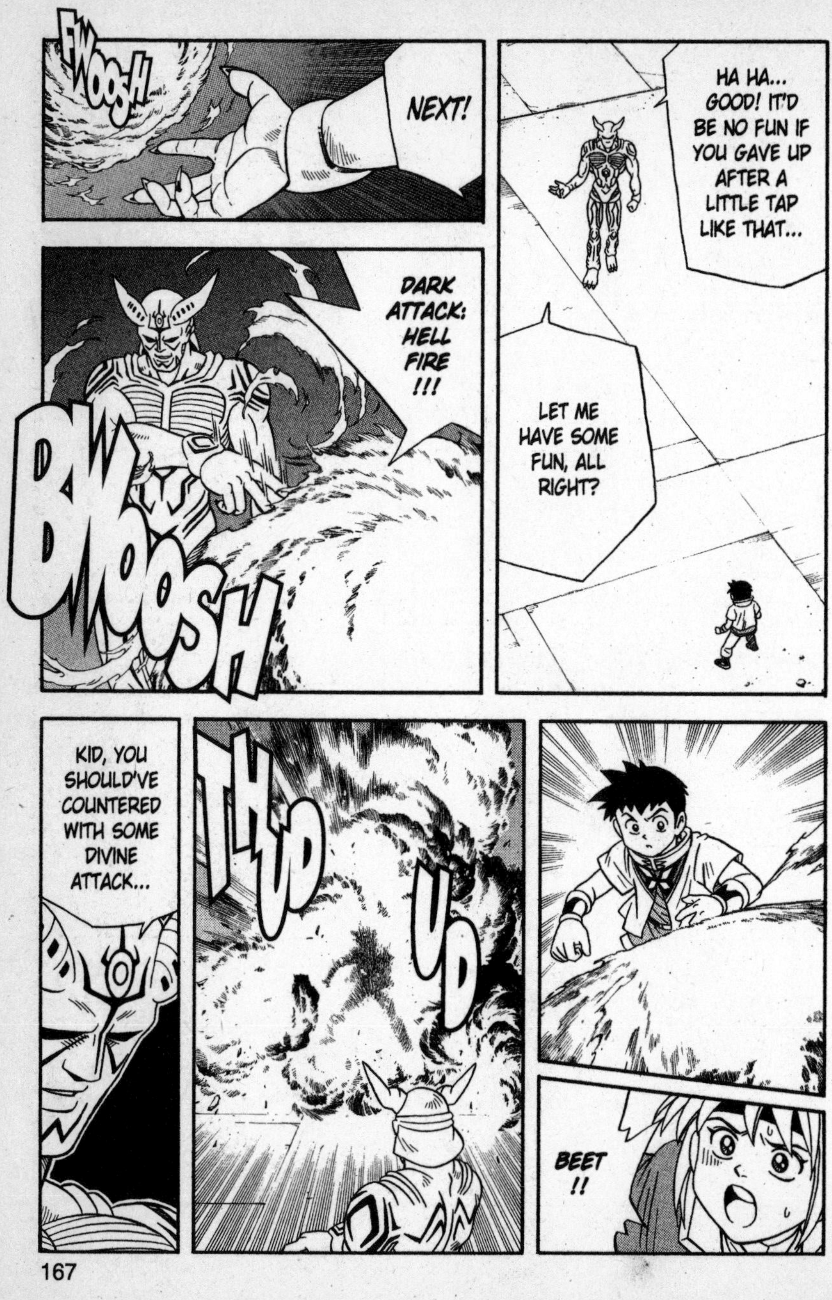

HA HA... GOOD! IT'D BE NO FUN IF YOU GAVE UP AFTER A LITTLE TAP LIKE THAT...
LET ME HAVE SOME FUN, ALL RIGHT?
NEXT!
FWOOSH
DARK ATTACK: HELL FIRE !!!
BWOOSH
BEET !!
THUD
UD
UD
KID, YOU SHOULD'VE COUNTERED WITH SOME DIVINE ATTACK...

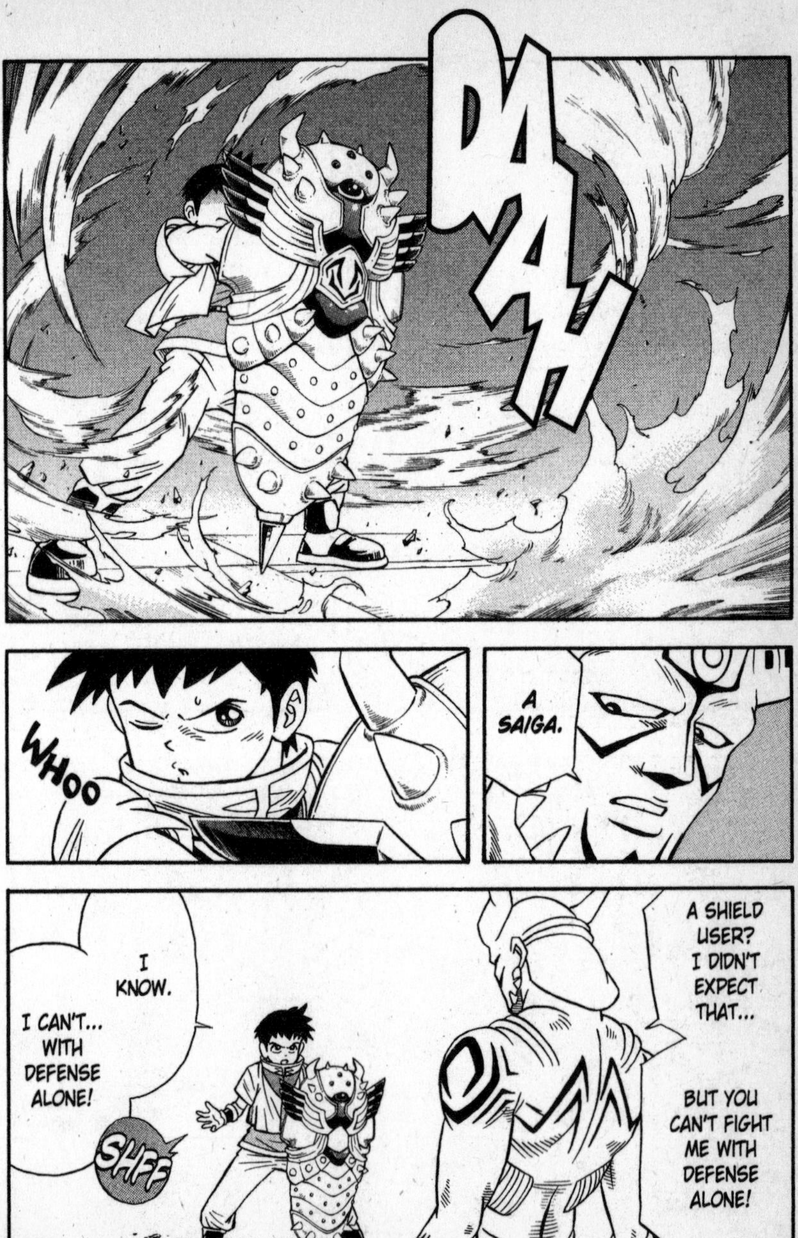
DAAH
A SAIGA.
WHOO
A SHIELD USER? I DIDN'T EXPECT THAT...
BUT YOU CAN'T FIGHT ME WITH DEFENSE ALONE!
I KNOW.
I CAN'T... WITH DEFENSE ALONE!
SHFF

READ THIS WAY

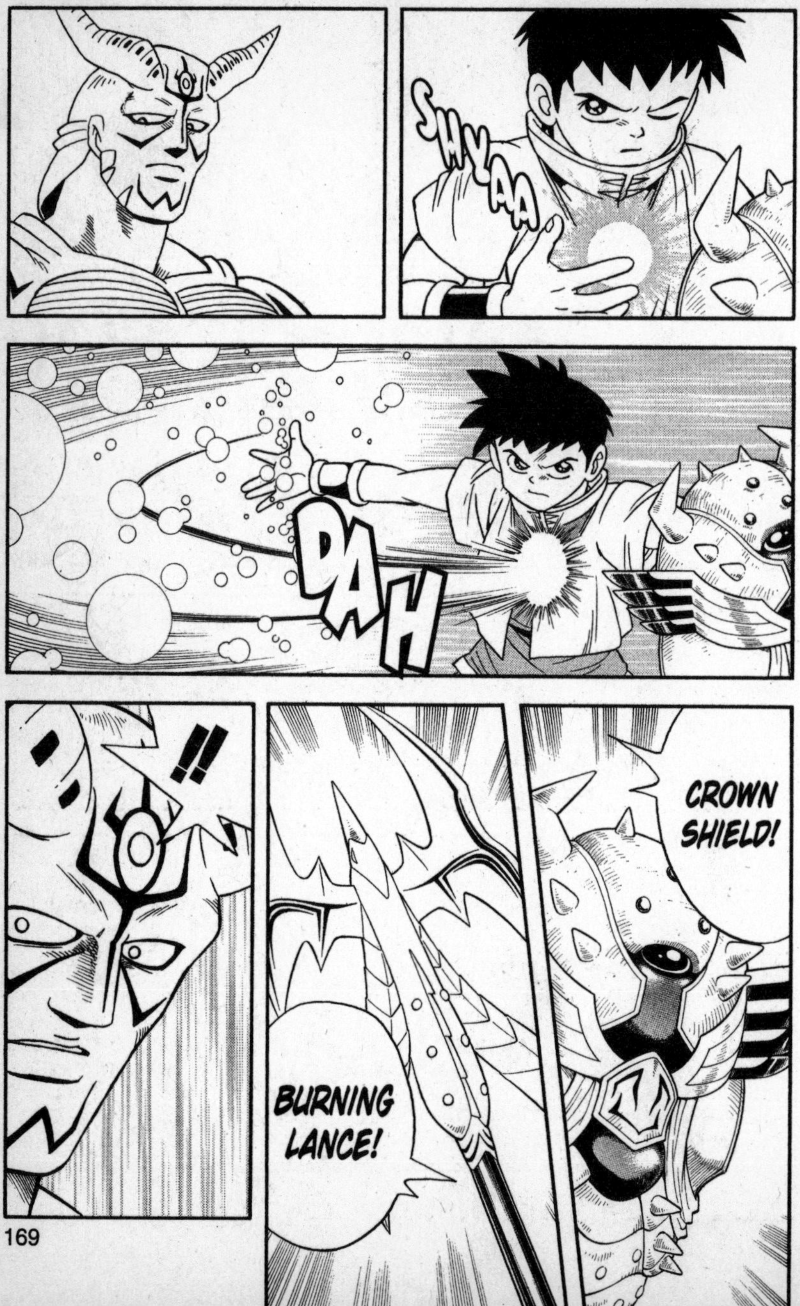
SHYAAA
DAH
CROWN SHIELD!
BURNING LANCE!
!!

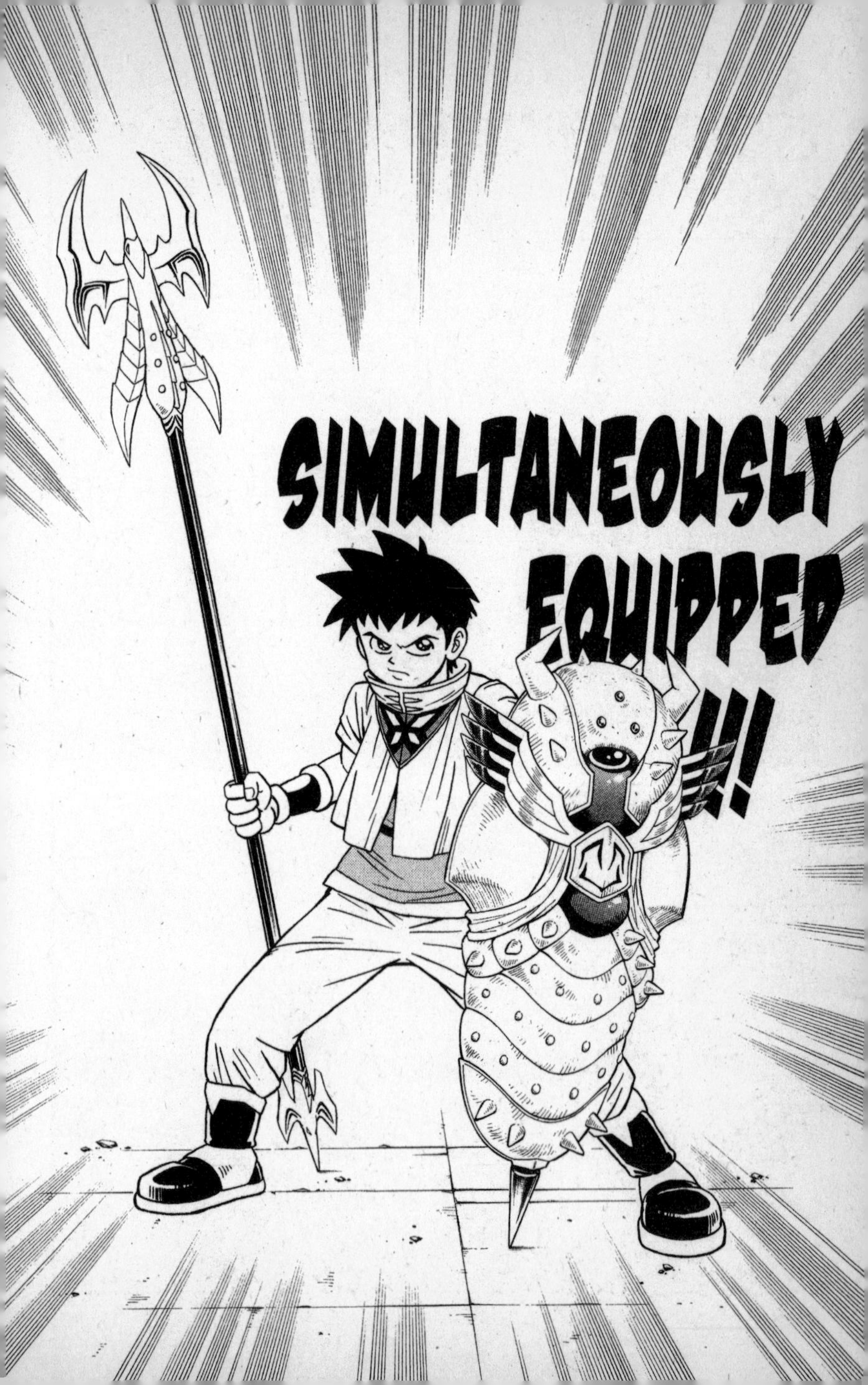
SIMULTANEOUSLY EQUIPPED!!

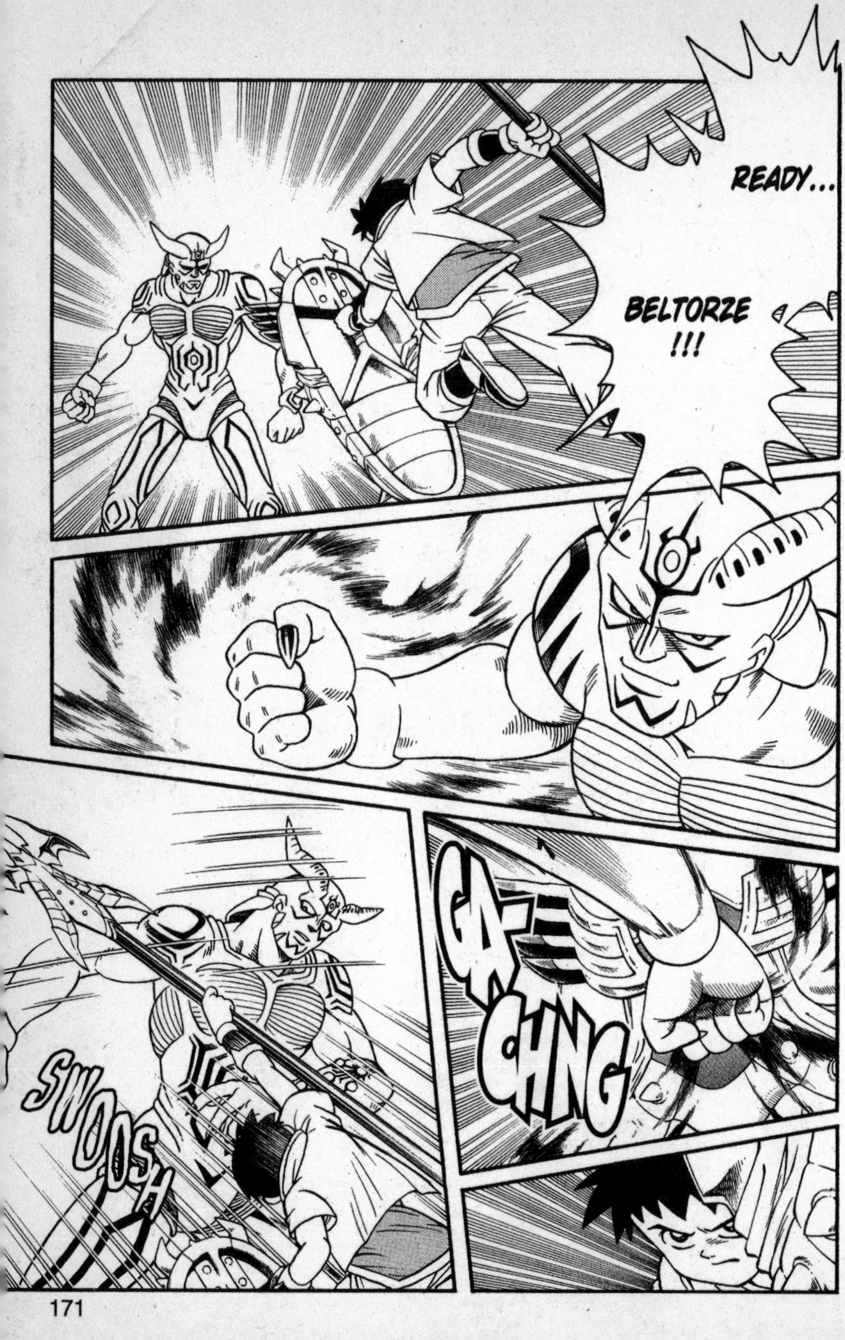
READY...
BELTORZE !!!
GA-CHING
SWOOSH

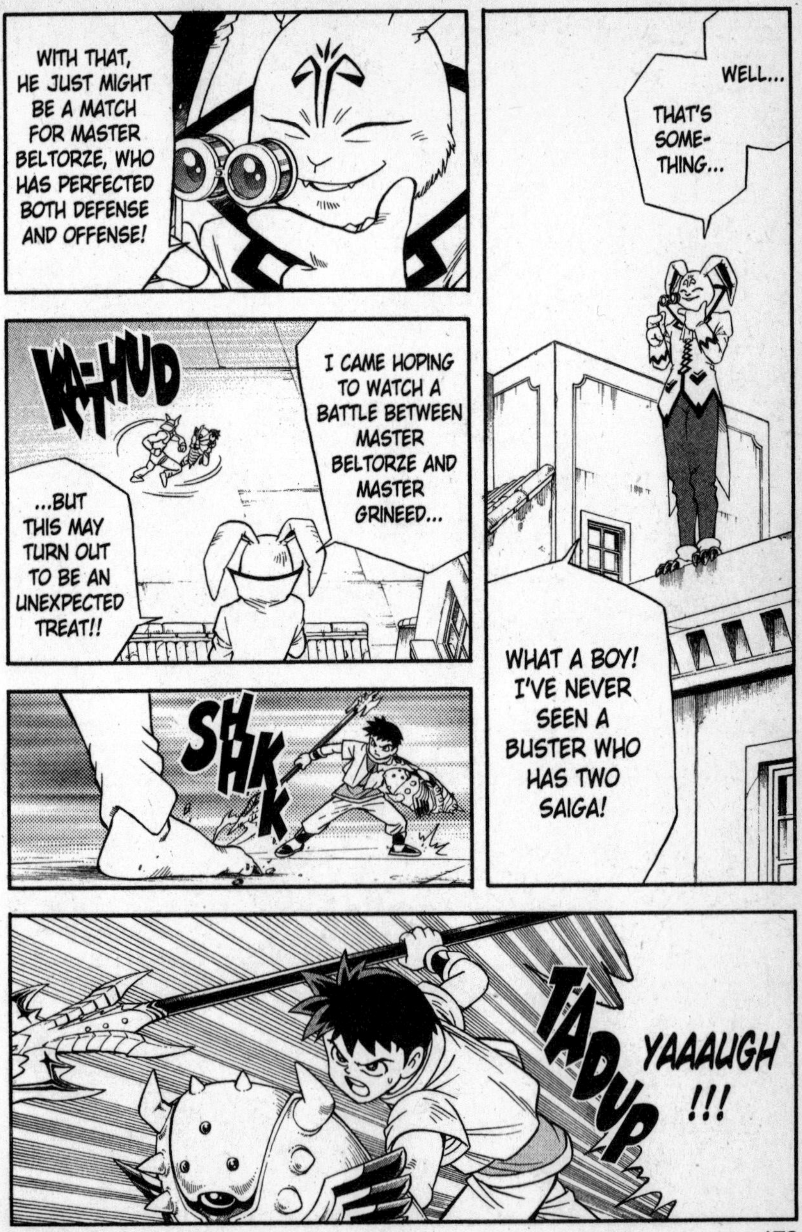

WELL...
THAT'S SOMETHING...
WHAT A BOY! I'VE NEVER SEEN A BUSTER WHO HAS TWO SAIGA!
WITH THAT, HE JUST MIGHT BE A MATCH FOR MASTER BELTORZE, WHO HAS PERFECTED BOTH DEFENSE AND OFFENSE!
I CAME HOPING TO WATCH A BATTLE BETWEEN MASTER BELTORZE AND MASTER GRINEED...
KA-THUD
...BUT THIS MAY TURN OUT TO BE AN UNEXPECTED TREAT!!
SHHKK
YAAAUGH !!!
TADUP

READ THIS WAY

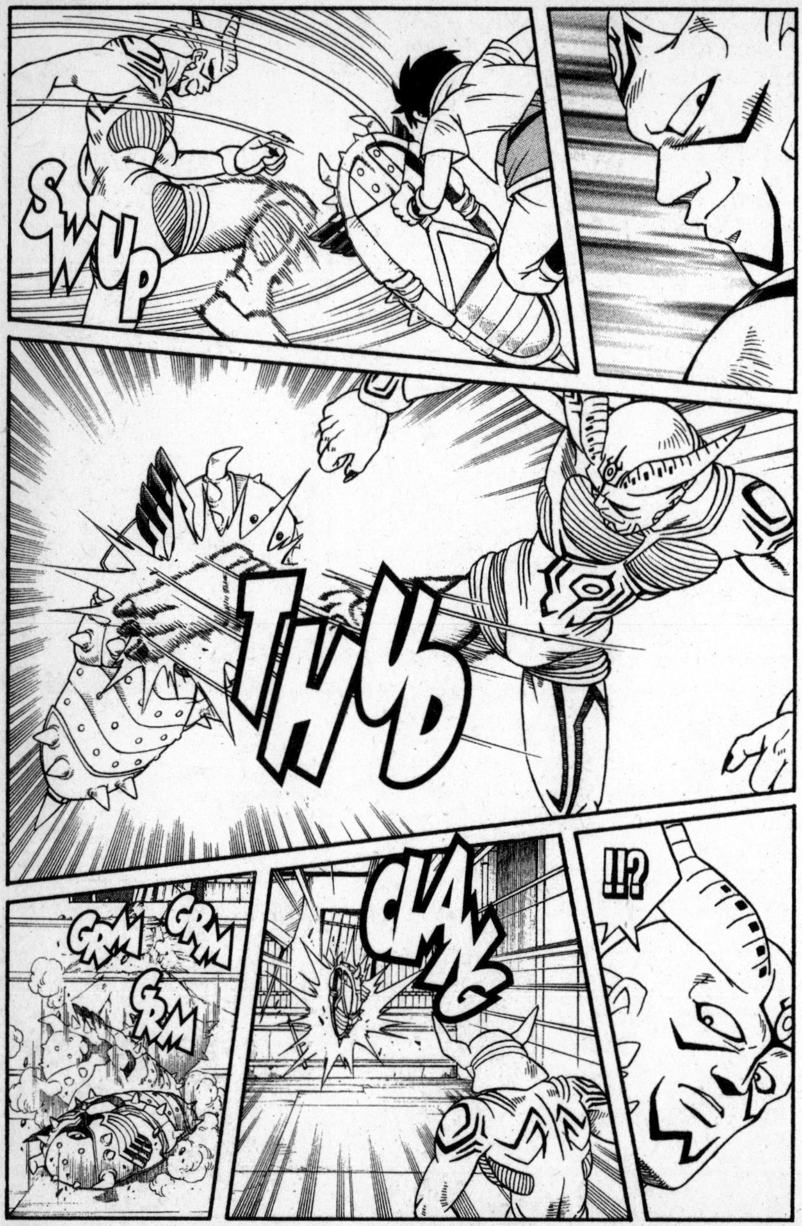
SWUP
THUD
!!?
CLANG
GRM GRM
GRM

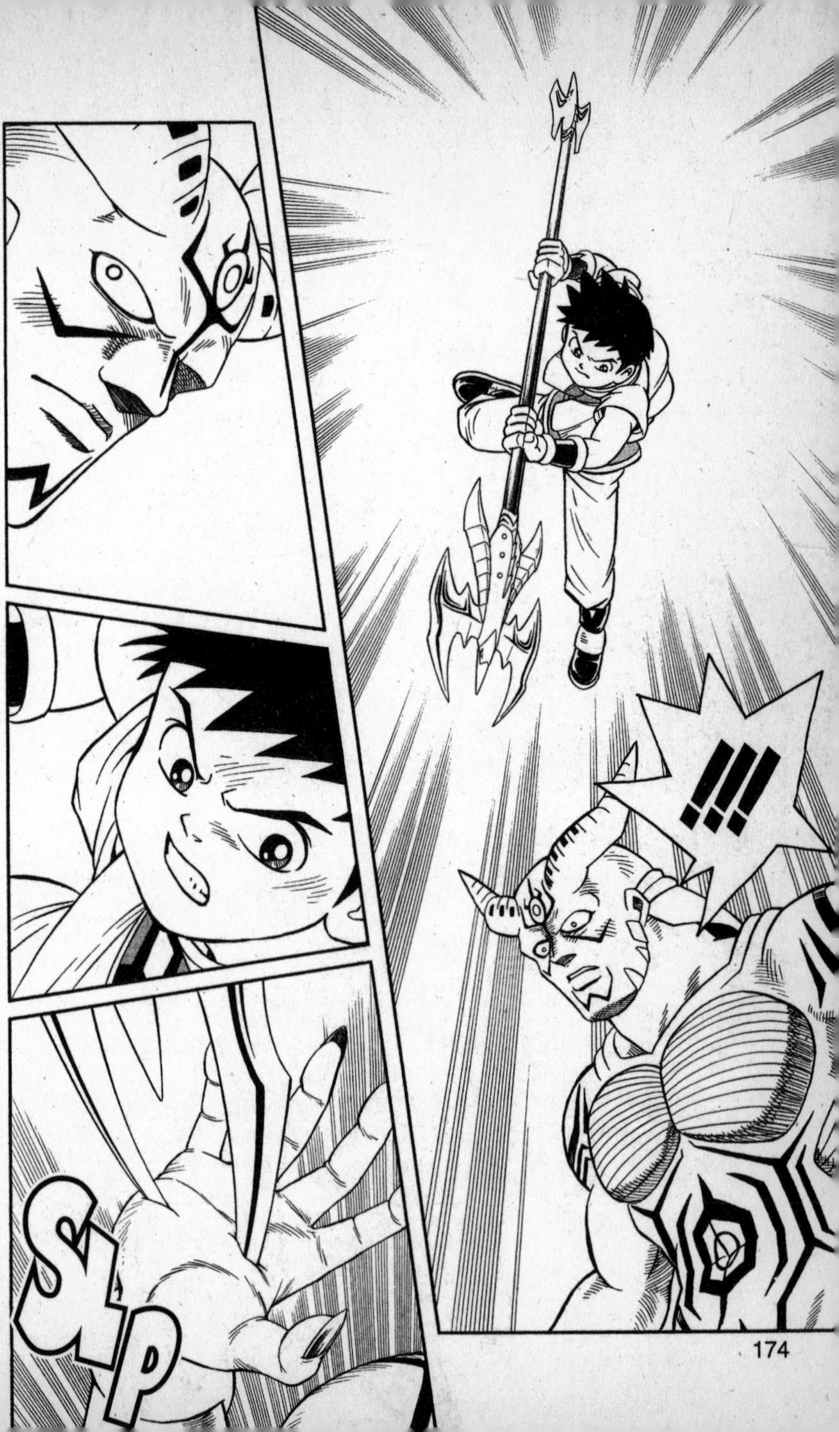
!!!!
Stp

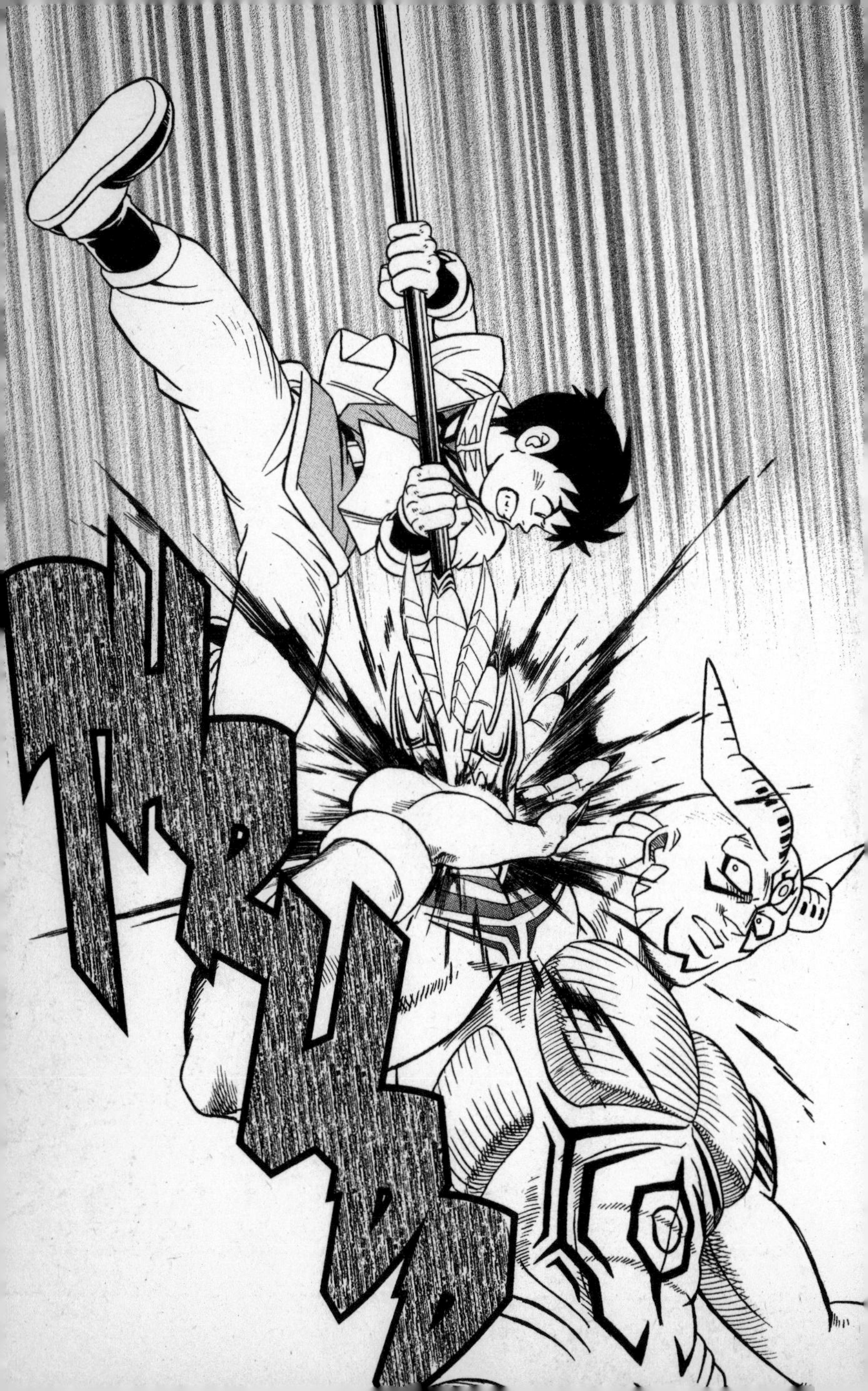

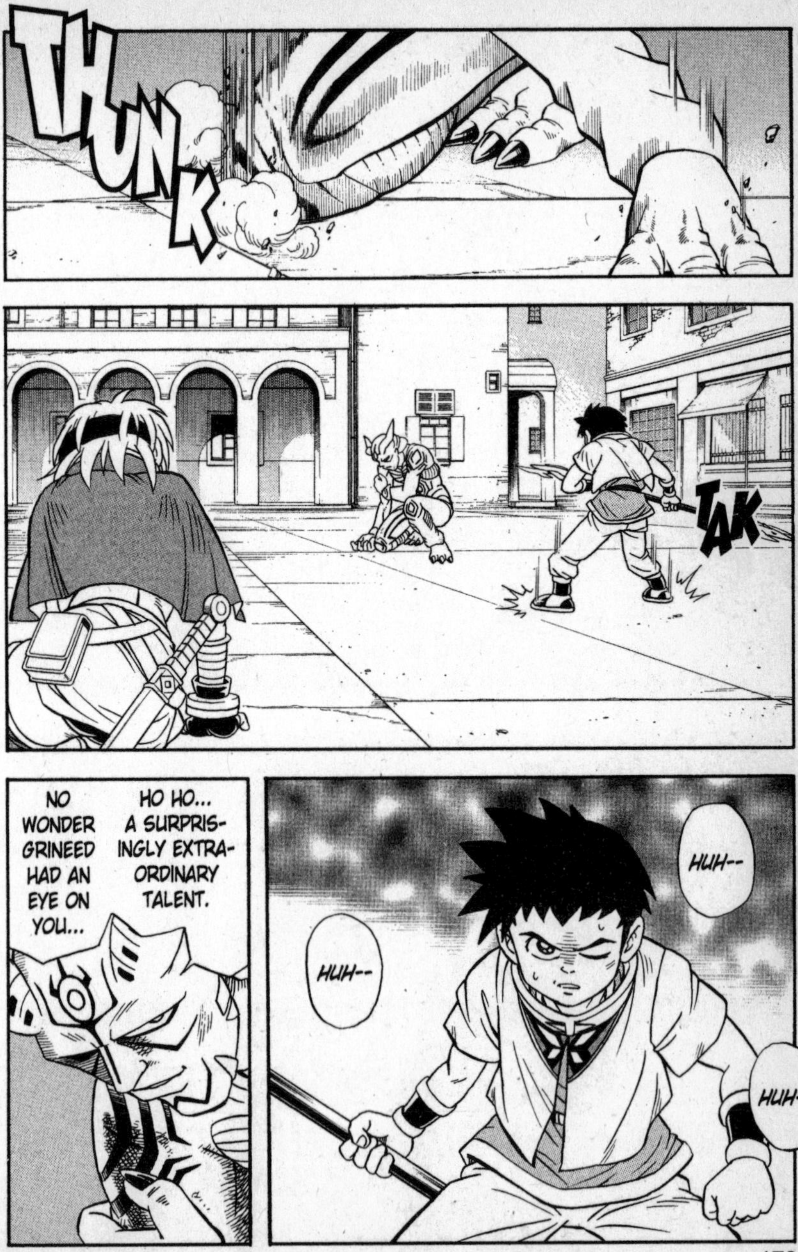
THUNK
TAK
HUH--
HUH--
HUH--
HO HO... A SURPRISINGLY EXTRAORDINARY TALENT.
NO WONDER GRINEED HAD AN EYE ON YOU...

READ THIS WAY

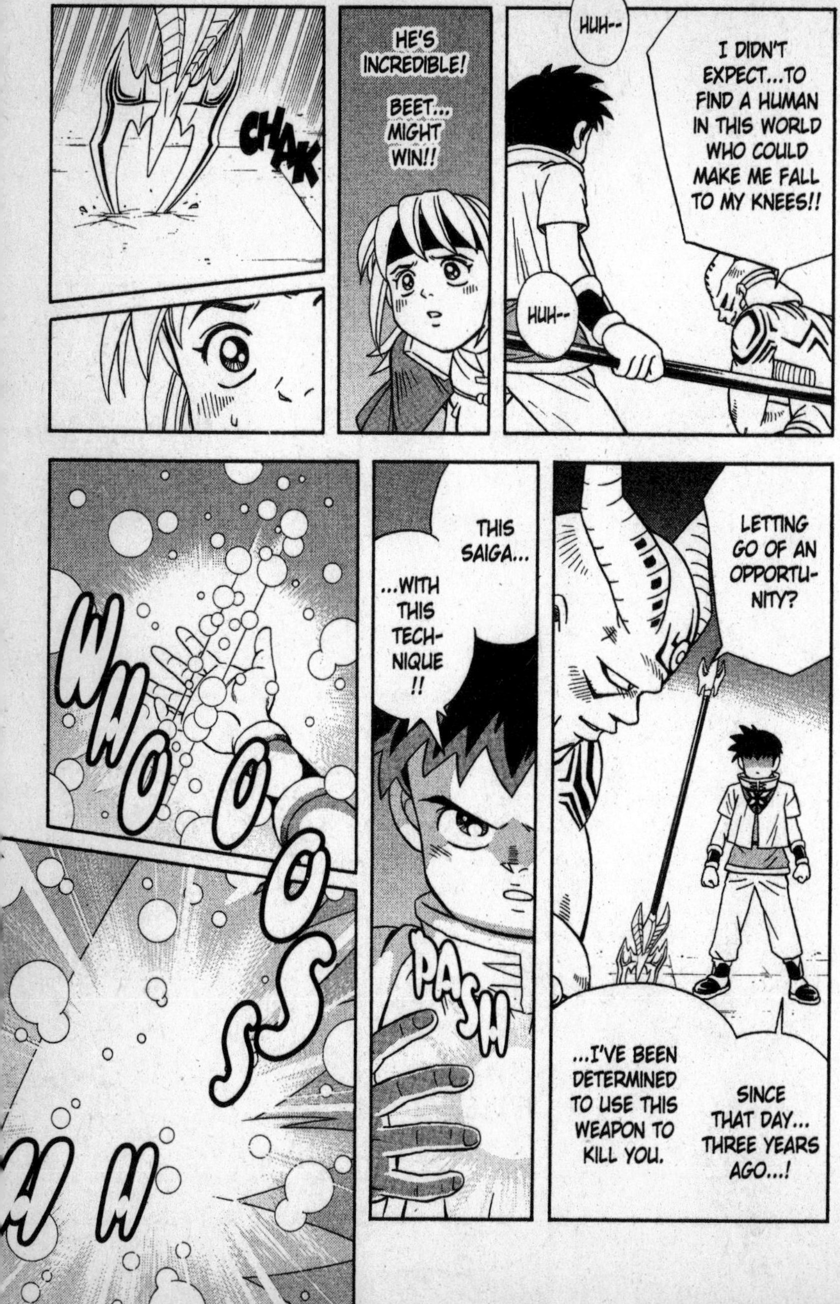
I DIDN'T EXPECT...TO FIND A HUMAN IN THIS WORLD WHO COULD MAKE ME FALL TO MY KNEES!!
HUH--
HUH--
HE'S INCREDIBLE!
BEET... MIGHT WIN!!
CHAK
LETTING GO OF AN OPPORTU-NITY?
SINCE THAT DAY... THREE YEARS AGO...!
...I'VE BEEN DETERMINED TO USE THIS WEAPON TO KILL YOU.
THIS SAIGA...
...WITH THIS TECH-NIQUE!!
PASH
WHOOOOSSHH

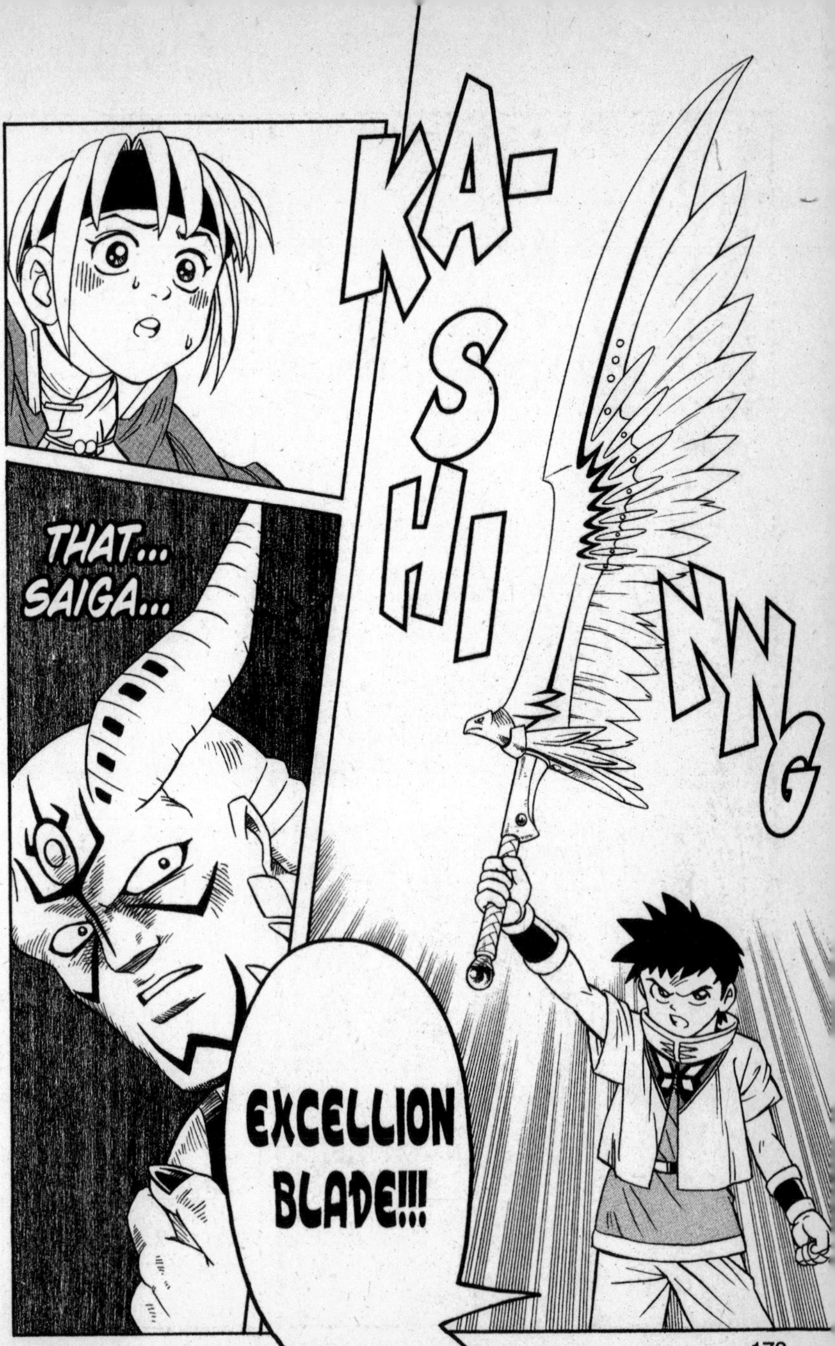
KA-SHI-NNG
EXCELLION BLADE!!!
THAT... SAIGA...

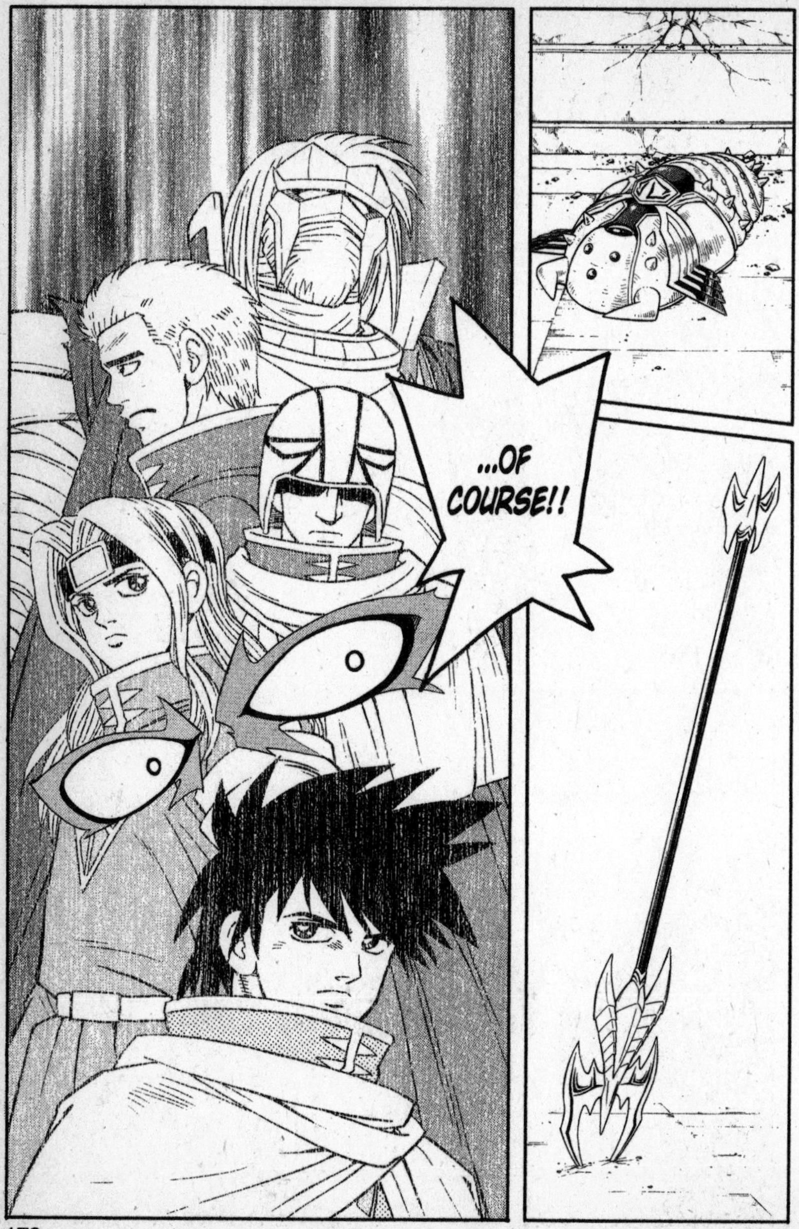
...OF COURSE!!

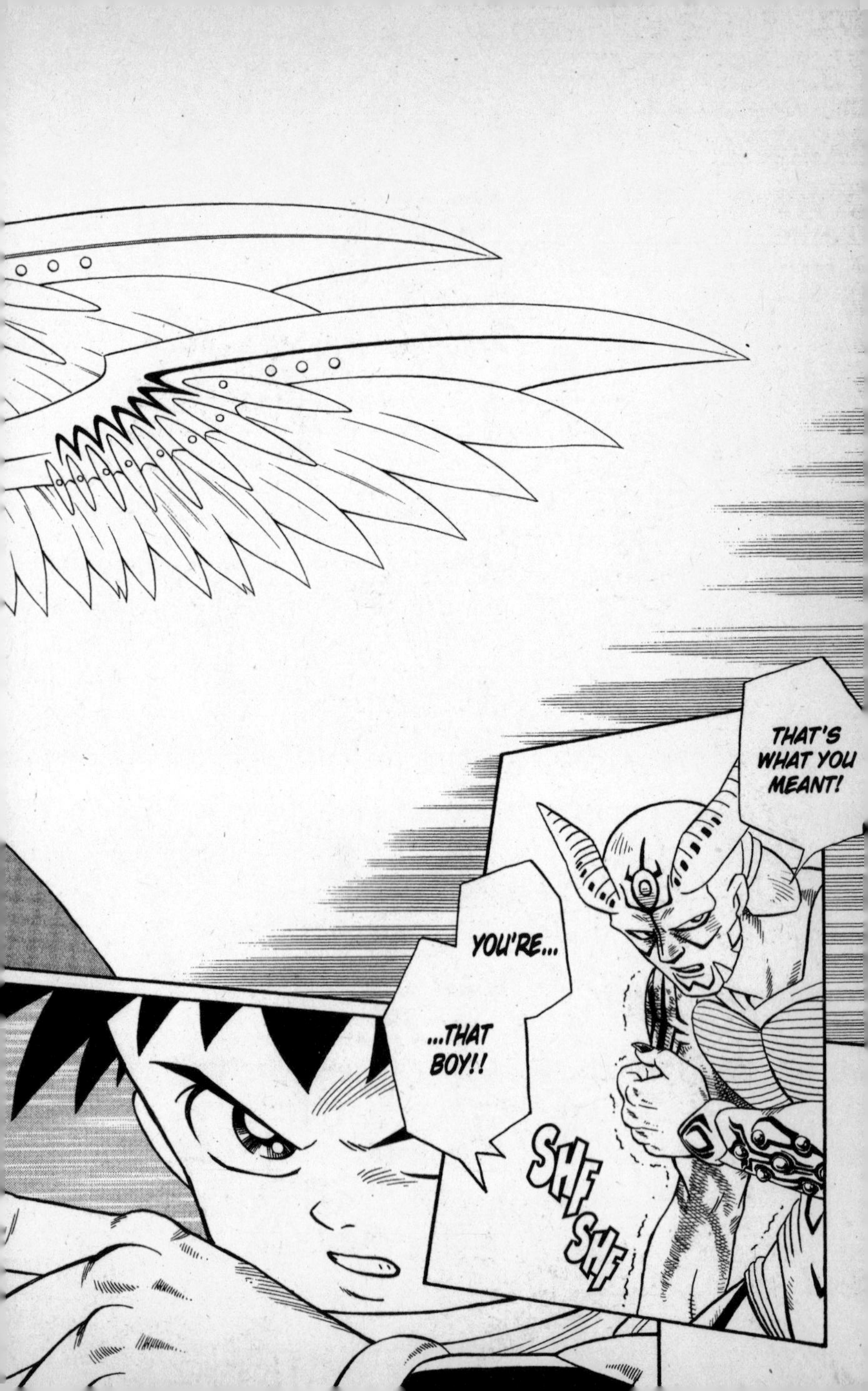
THAT'S WHAT YOU MEANT!
YOU'RE...
...THAT BOY!!
SHF SHF

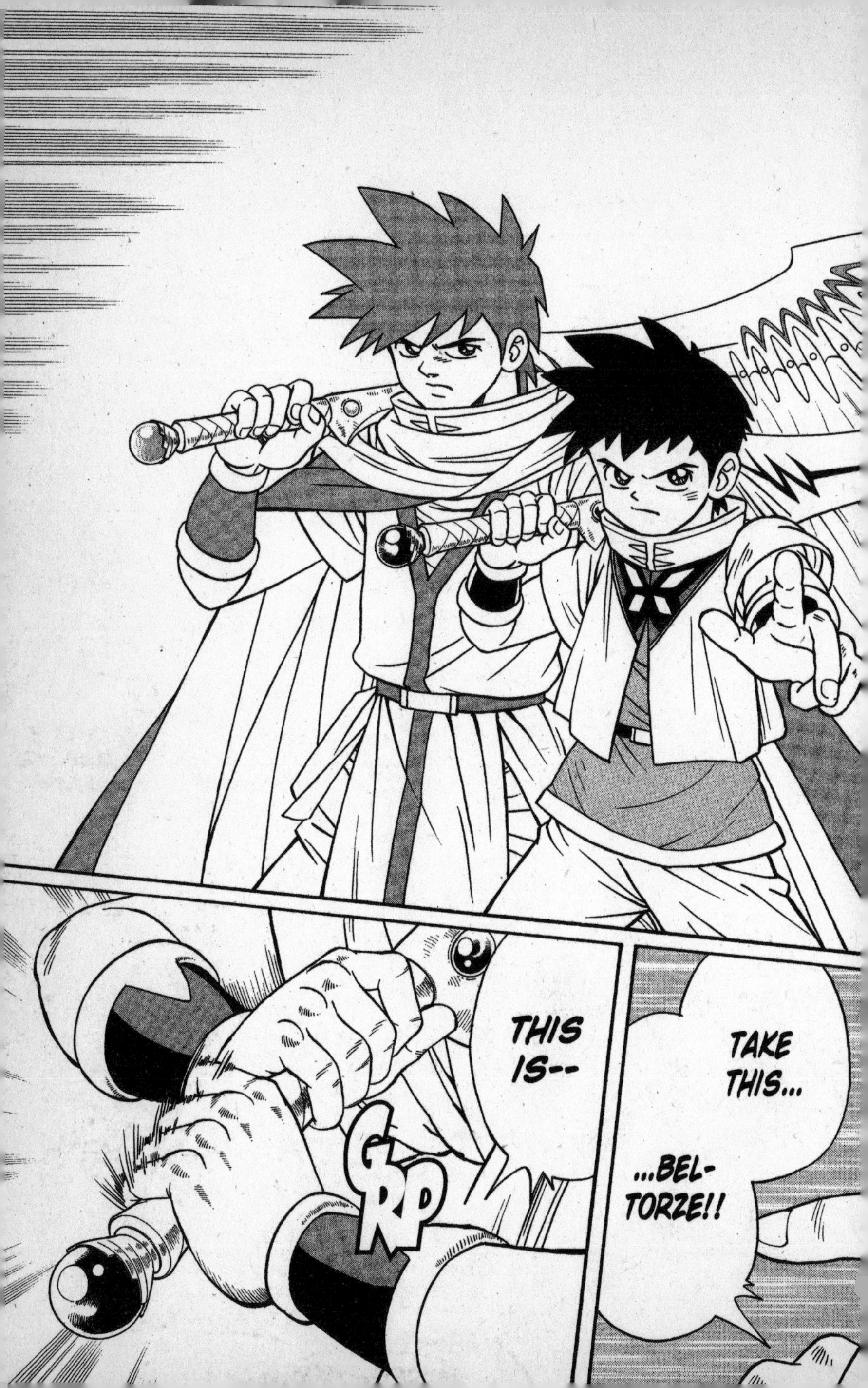
TAKE THIS...
...BEL-TORZE!!
THIS IS--
GRIP

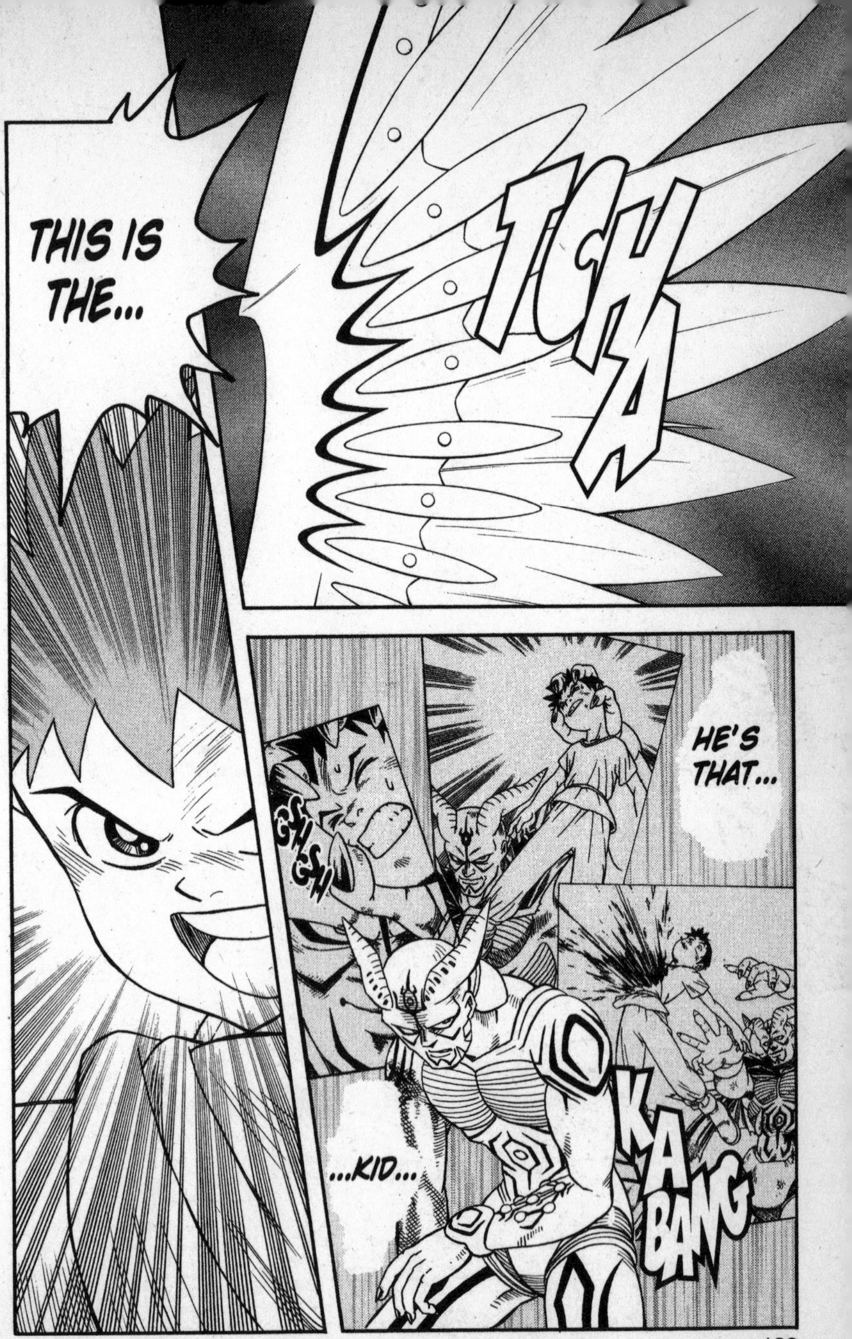
TCHA
HE'S THAT...
GSH GSH
...KID...
KA BANG
THIS IS THE...

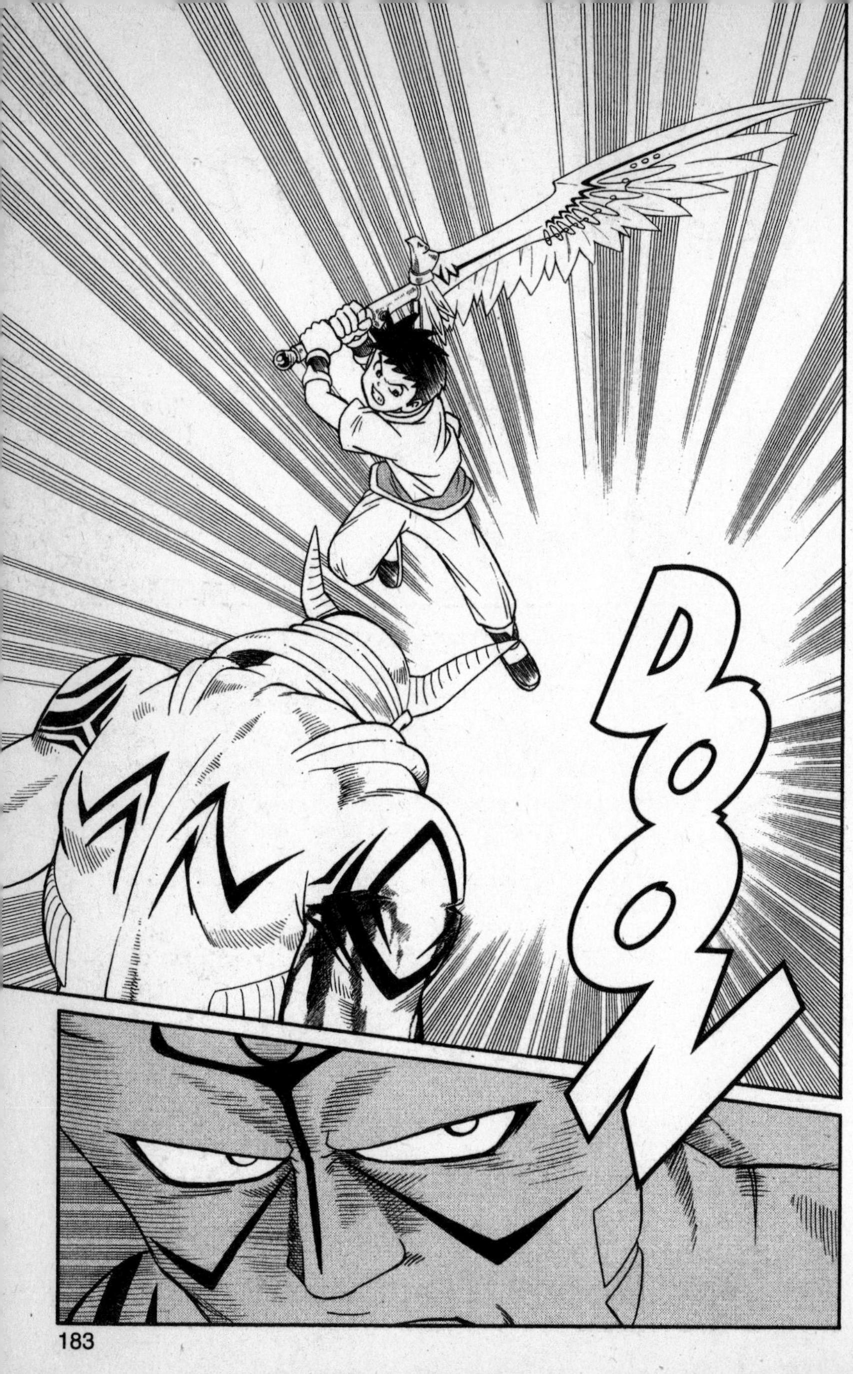
DOOON

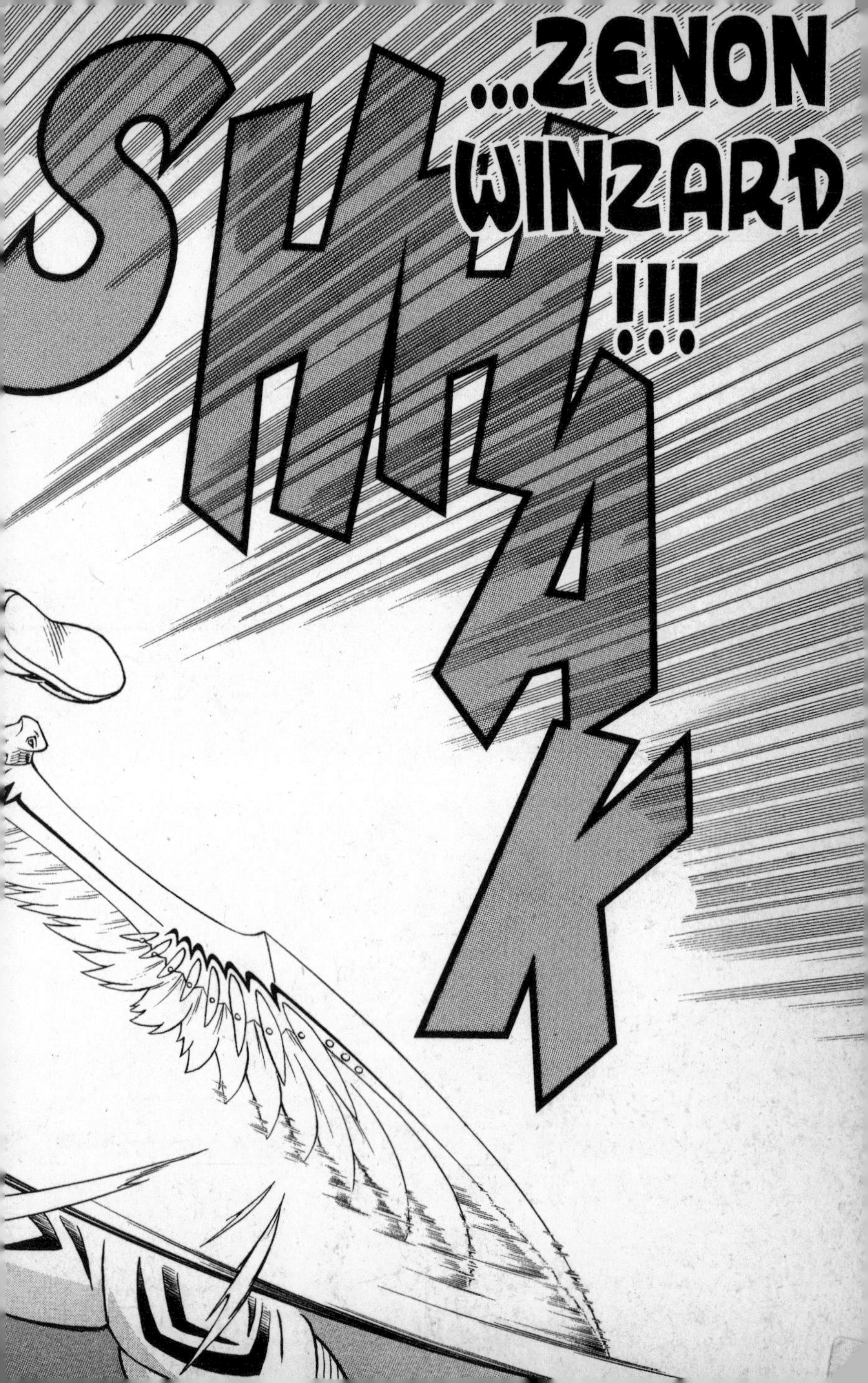
...ZENON WINZARD !!!
SHHAK

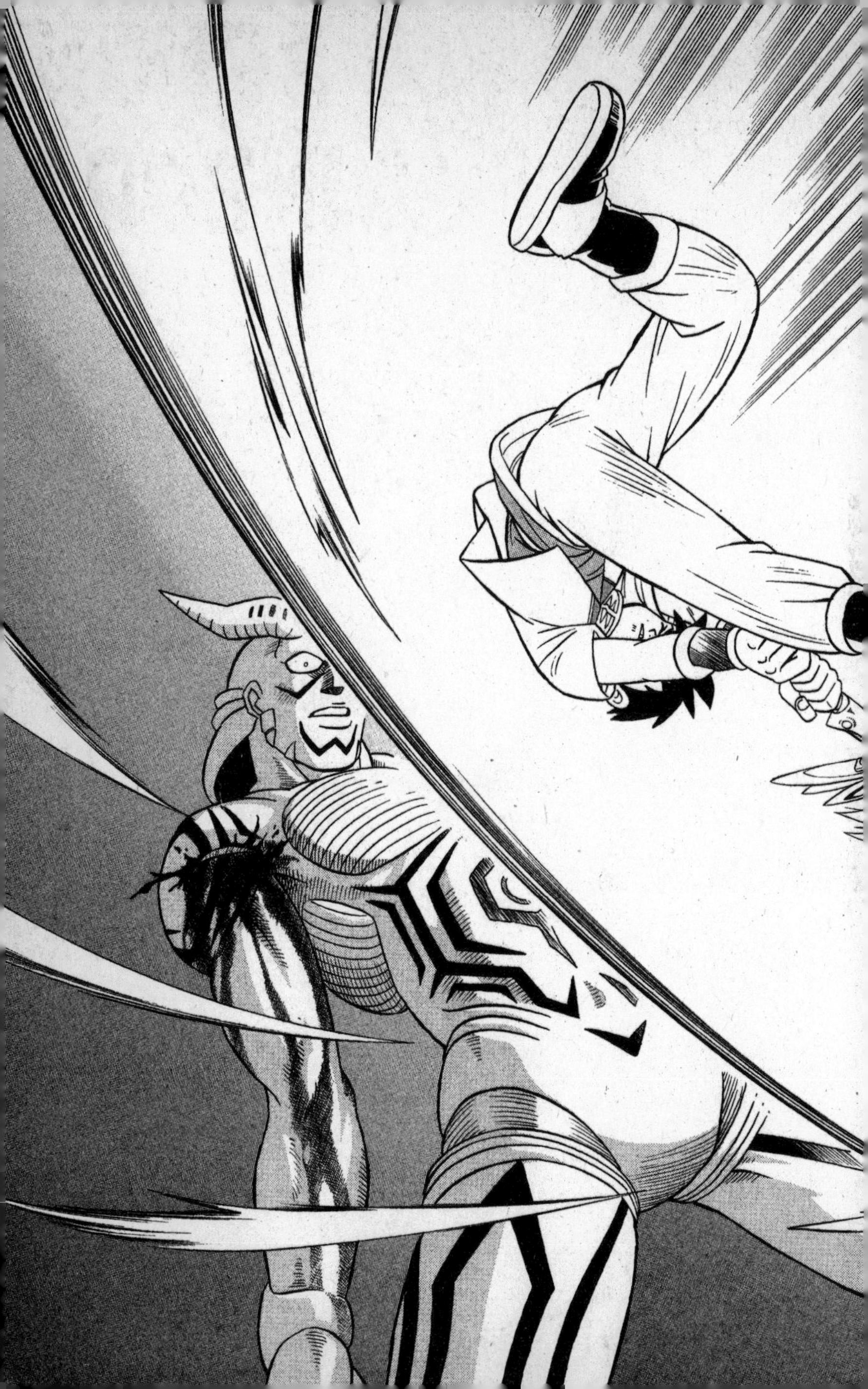

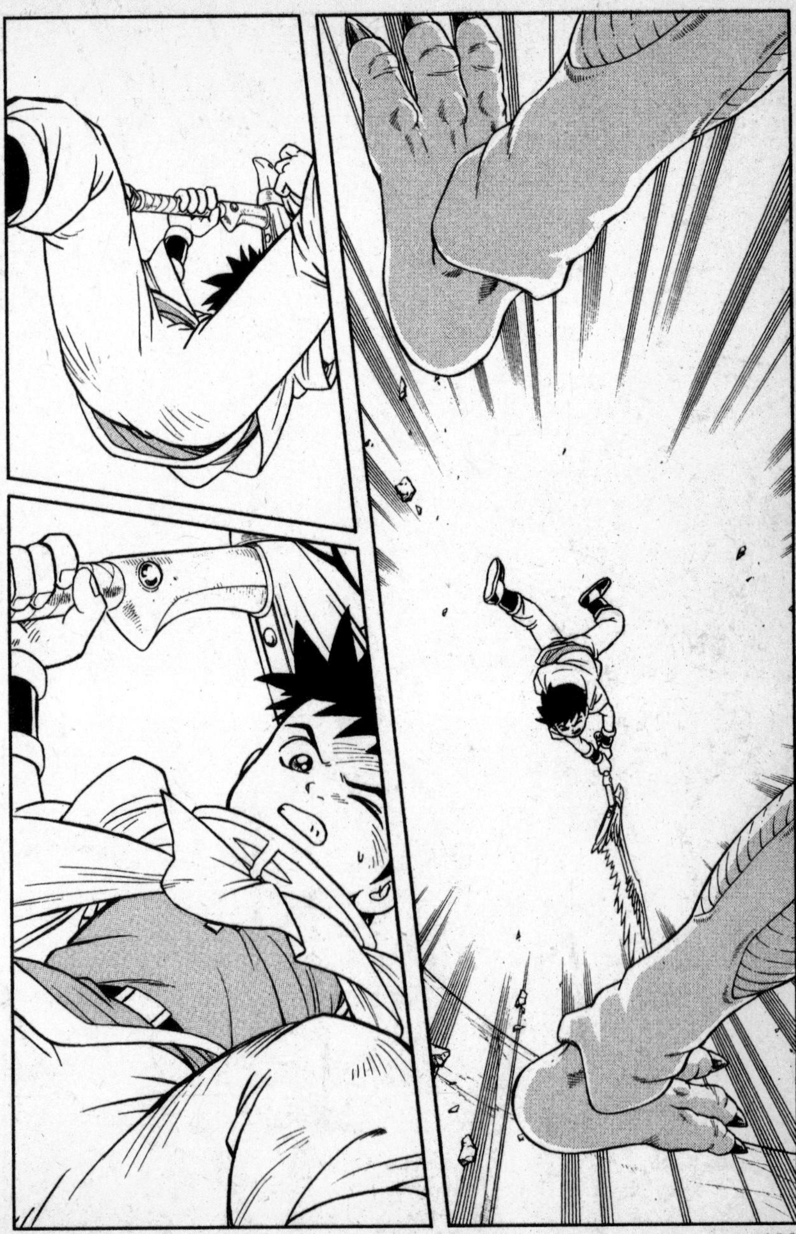

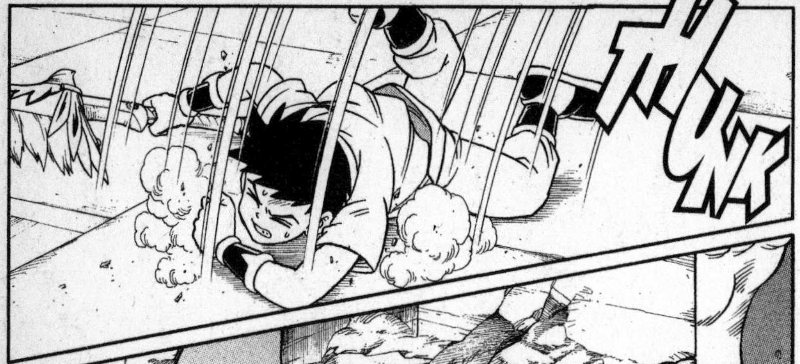
THUNK
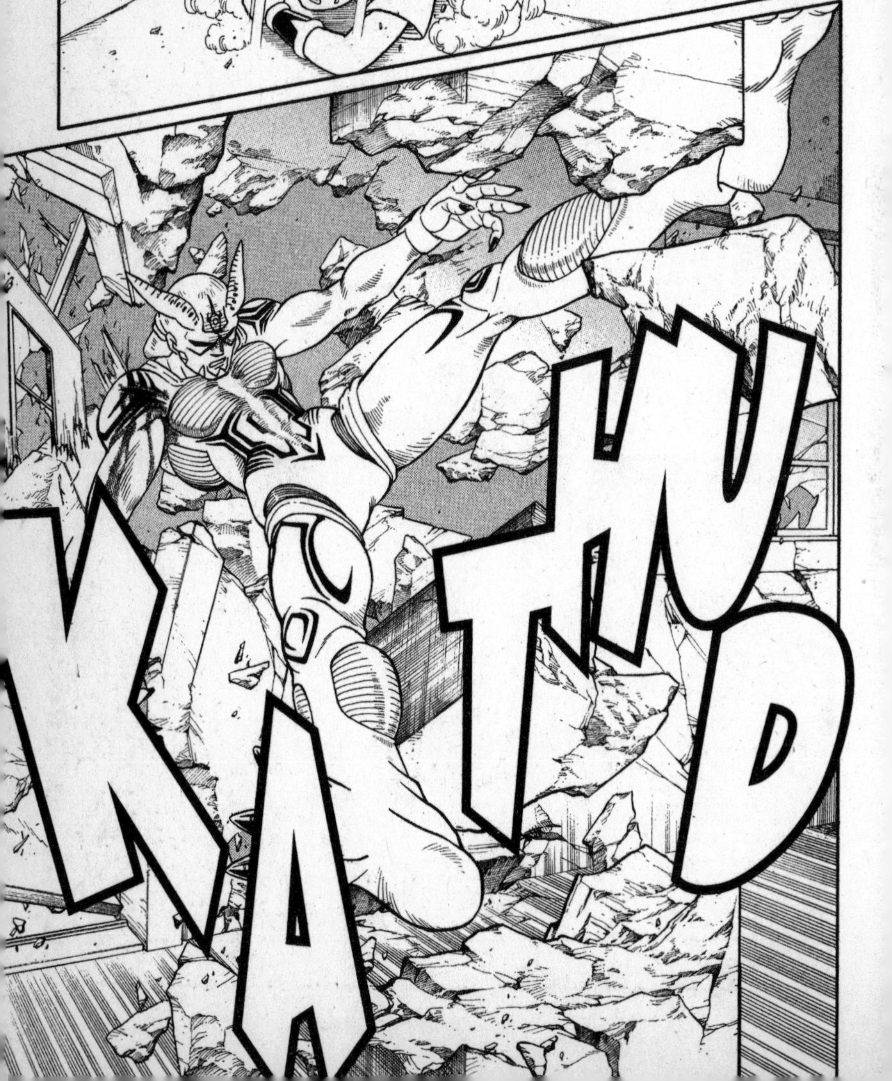
KA-THUD

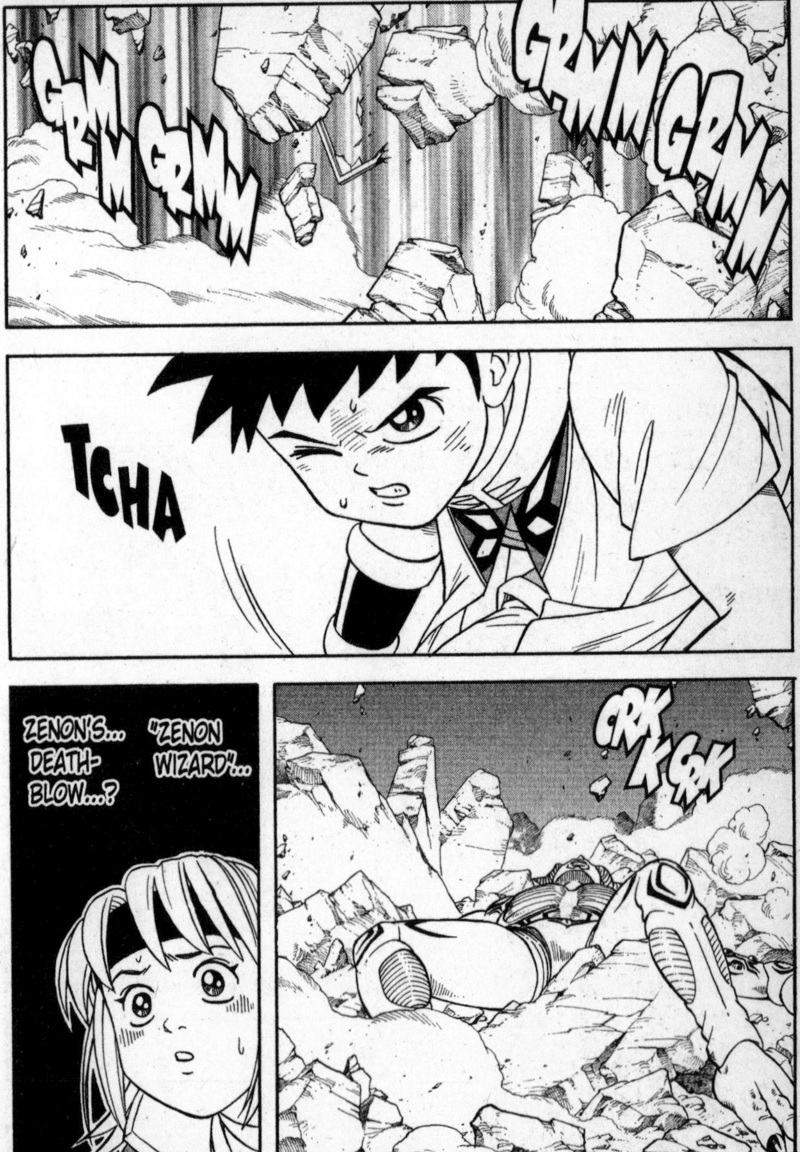
GRMM GRMM
GRM GRM GRMM
TCHA
GRK K GRK
"ZENON WIZARD"...
ZENON'S... DEATH-BLOW...?

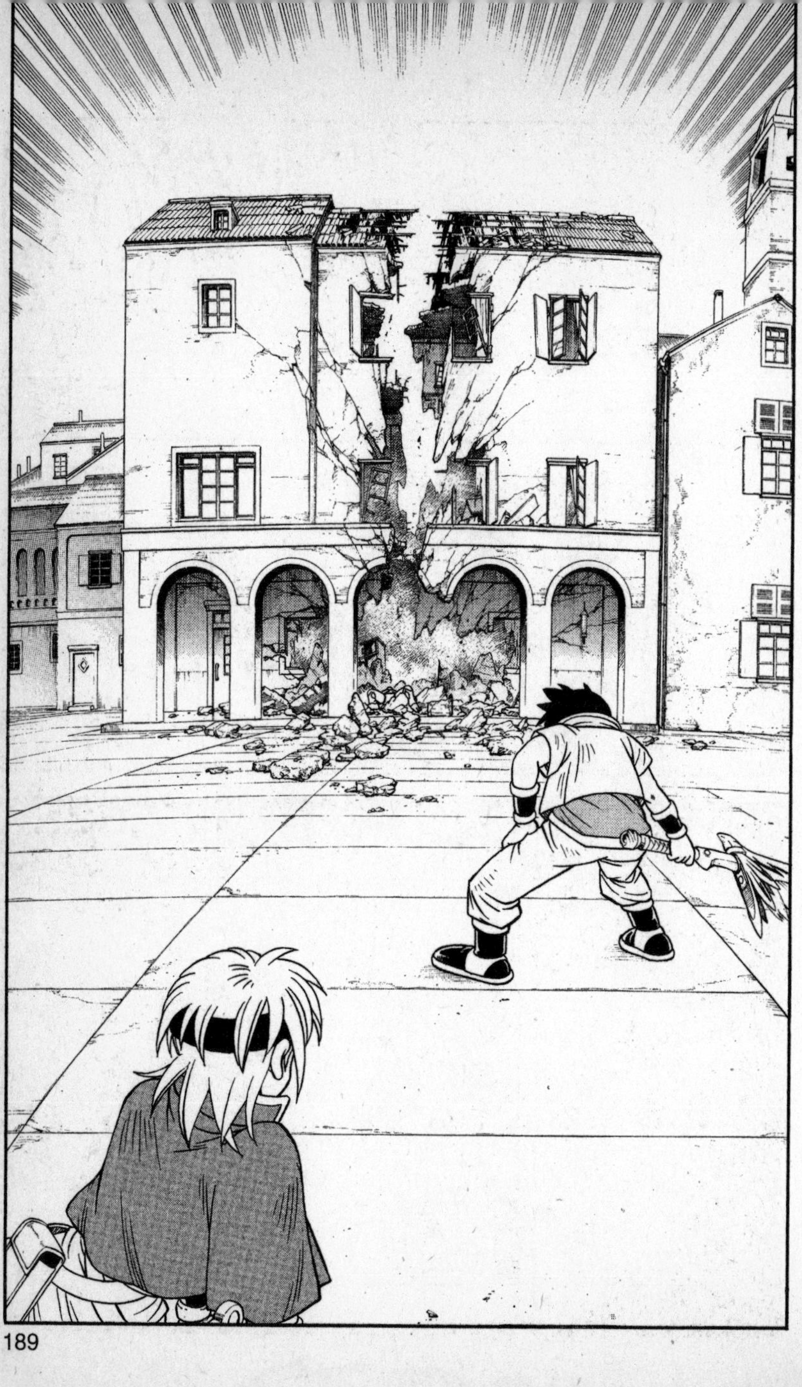

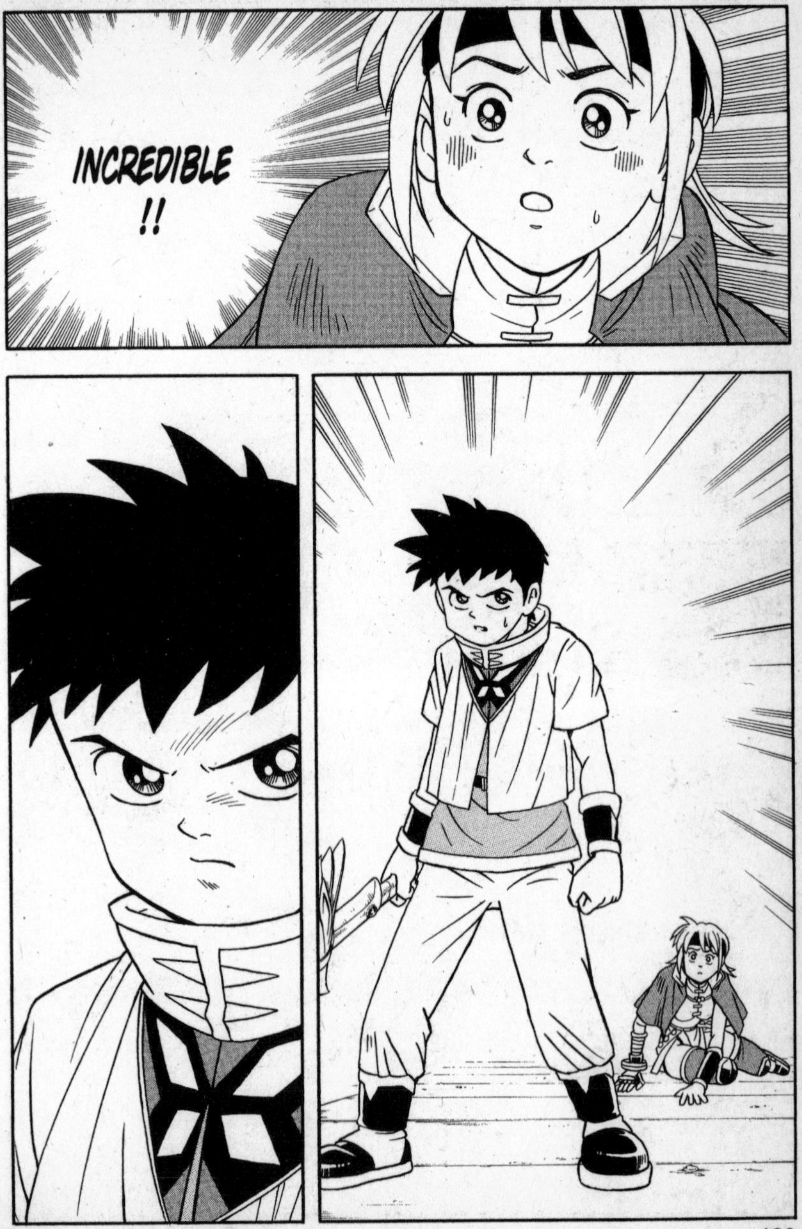
INCREDIBLE
!!

READ THIS WAY

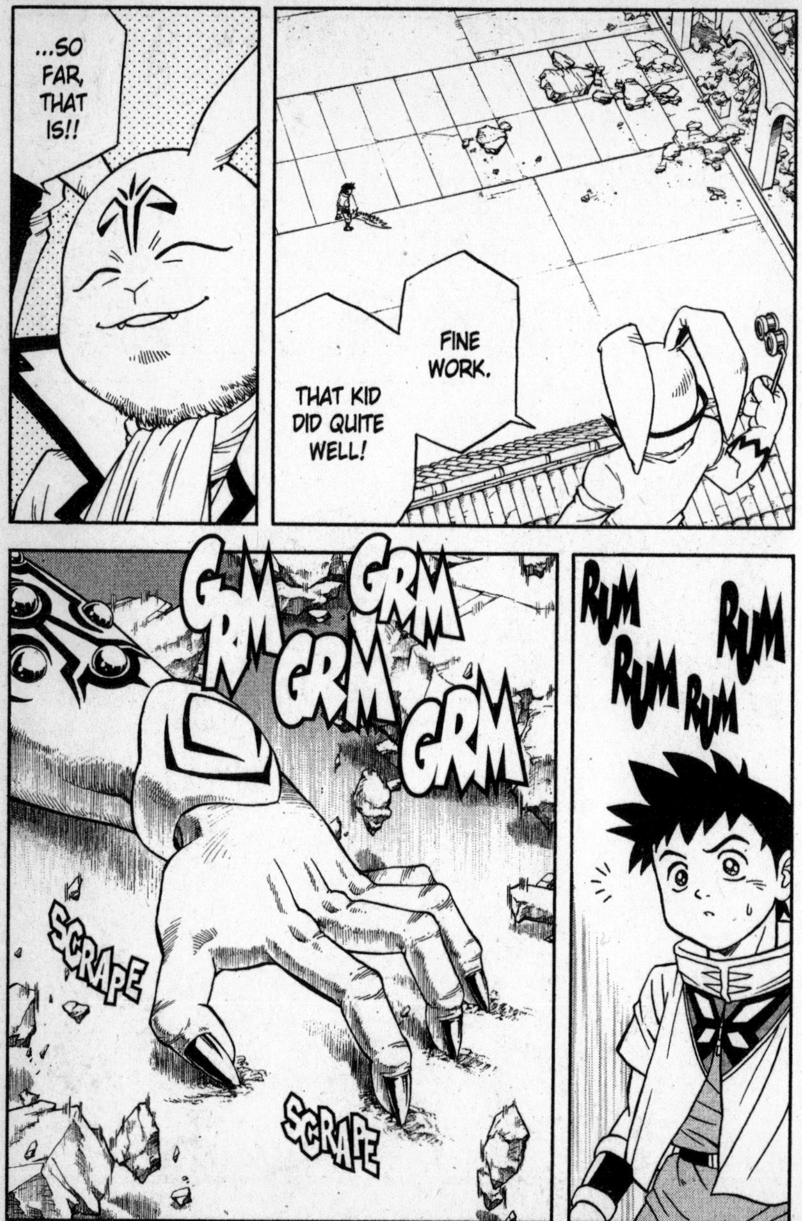

FINE WORK.
THAT KID DID QUITE WELL!
...SO FAR, THAT IS!!
RUM RUM RUM RUM
GRM GRM GRM GRM GRM
SCRAPE
SCRAPE

TO BE CONTINUED IN VOLUME 3!

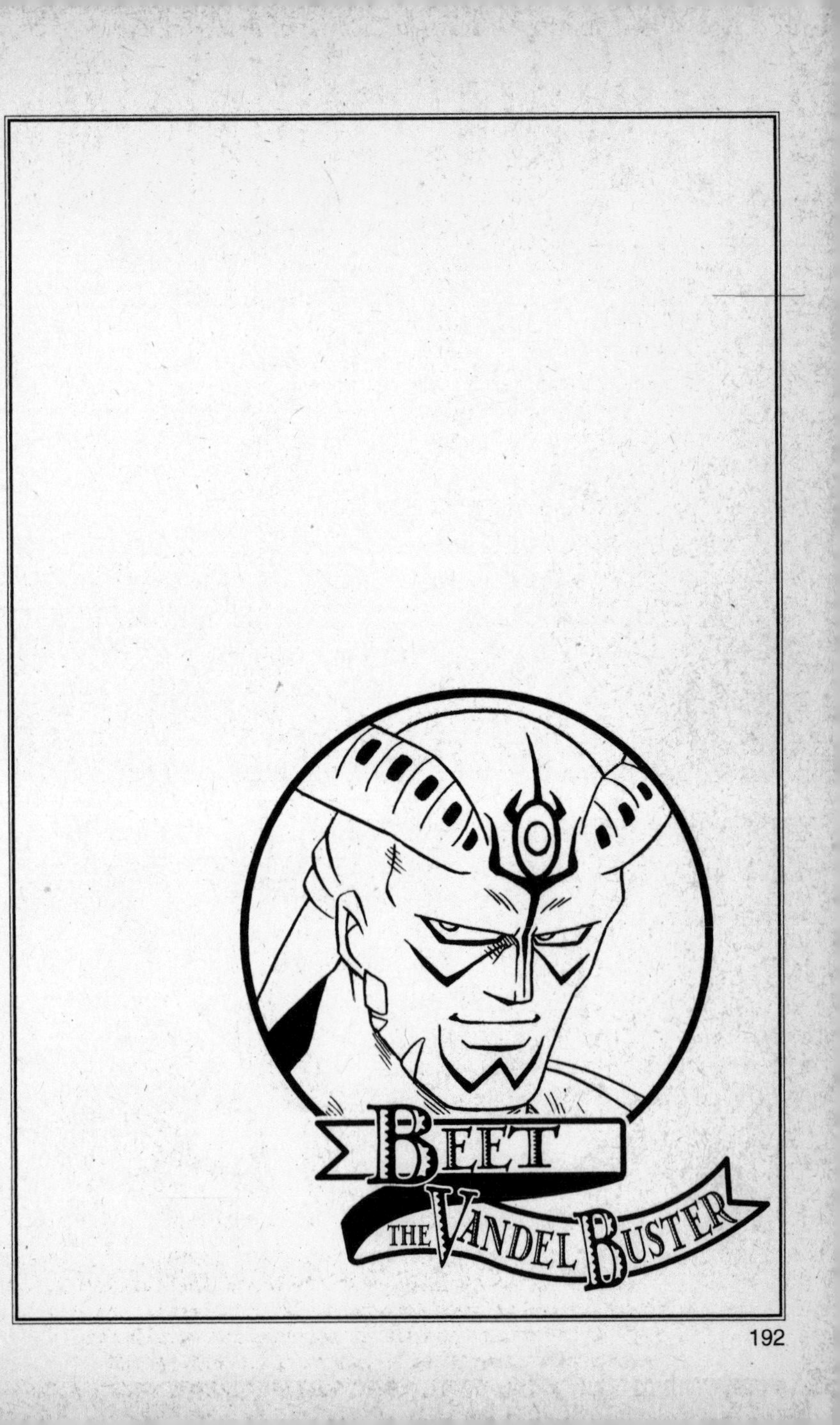
BEET
THE VANDEL BUSTER

BEET THE WORLD

THE WORLD OF
BEET the VANDEL BUSTER • PART 2

With the introduction of powerful Vandels, the world of Beet is expanding
even more! This end-of-the-book special examines this world in detail.
To meet popular demand, we're presenting you with part 2!!

DIVINE ATTACK

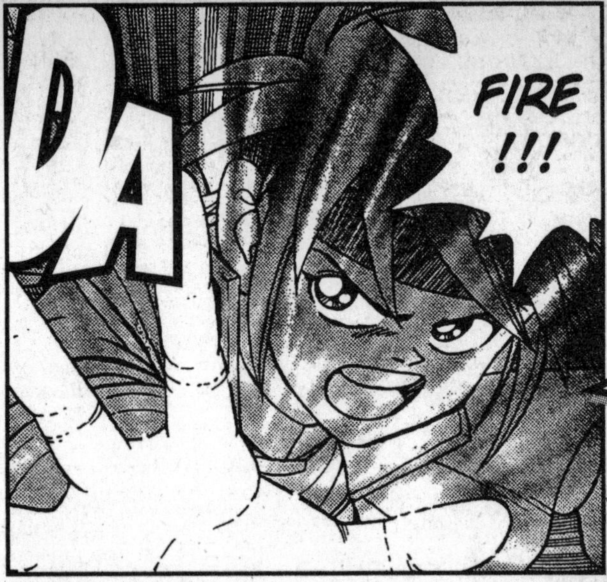
FIRE !!!
DA

The power that can control the energy in the atmosphere is called "Divine Power," and when it's transformed to attack the enemy, it is called "Divine Attack." It is the standard method people in this world use to attack the powerful Vandels, who have superhuman abilities. Every human has some Divine Power. However, to be able to increase and control this Divine Power and enable the Divine Attack, it's necessary to have special aptitude, as well as training. There are many people who carry out their daily routine without knowing how to use the strong Divine Powers they possess. Most people learn about their aptitude for Divine Power only after they visit an Appraiser's House and become Busters.

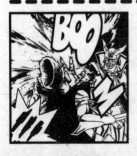

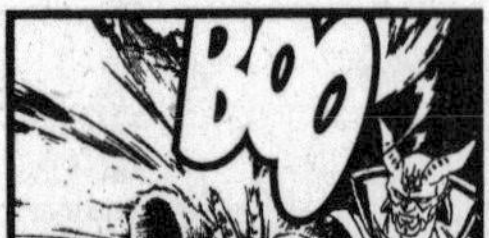
BOO
M

▲ The Vandels' Dark Attack uses five elements, just like the humans' Divine Attack.

The Divine Attacks are divided into five elements — fire, water, wind, thunder, and light — based on their attributes. Each element can unleash overwhelming destructive power. Most of the warriors have preferences based on their ability to use each element, and it's very rare for a single human to be able to use every element well. When forming a warrior group, it is better to team up with warriors who specialize in different elements. This way, the group can initiate a balanced attack.

THIS IS AN EXTRAORDINARY ATTACK THAT HUMANS LAUNCH USING DIVINE POWER RECEIVED FROM ABOVE!

THE DIVINE POWER TRANSFORMS THE FIVE ELEMENTS, CREATING FIVE DISTINCT FORMS OF SUPER-POWERFUL ASSAULTS!

FIVE ELEMENTS OF DIVINE ATTACK

火 FIRE

This is a type of Divine Attack that generates fire, sparks and high heat. Despite its immense power, it is easy to control and many learn to channel this element first.

水 WATER

This attack produces the effect of a water spurt and cold air. It can freeze an opponent or be used as an antidote against poison. It also works well in defensive maneuvers.

風 WIND

This type of attack generates gusts of wind and cyclones. It can pierce through an opponent's defenses and blow him or her away. It also increases the user's attack speed.

雷 THUNDER

The lightning attack, which produces the power of a thunderbolt, is very effective. Its electric shock inflicts massively painful physical damage on opponents. Of all the Divine Attacks, this is the most powerful.

光 LIGHT

This mysterious power is considered the highest of the Divine Attacks. Its lightning attack can destroy and annihilate all evil. Very few people can use it.

DIVINE ATTACK: FIRE

This is the most basic form of the fire-based Divine Attack. With the Divine Power of fire, the energy in the atmosphere is synthesized into a ball of fire. The size and temperature of the fireball are not fixed. The power of the fireball will vary depending on the strength of the user.

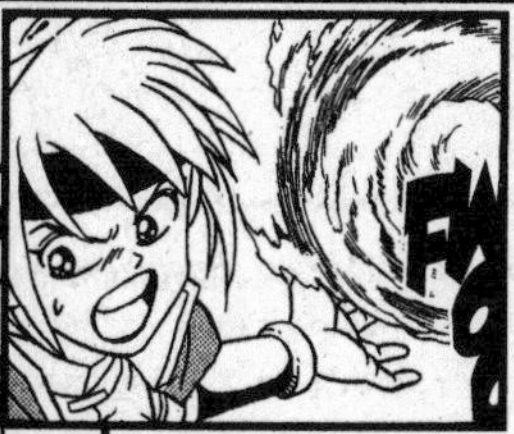

▲ This is the Divine Attack Poala uses frequently.

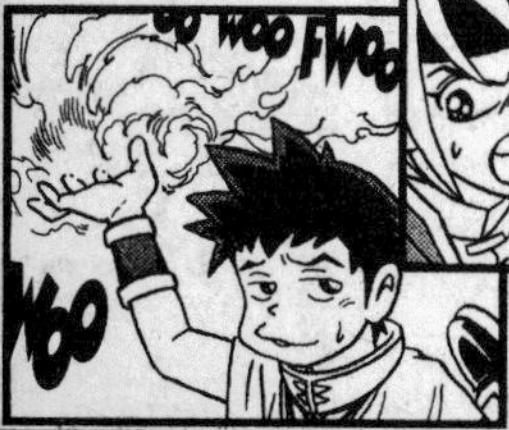

▼ Beet is not good at this Divine Attack, and he can't even master it.

DIVINE ELEMENT ATTACK: FIRE POLE

This is an advanced form of the fire-based Divine Attack. The fire energy is sharpened like a spear and thrown at the opponent. This arrow of fire pierces through the opponent's defenses and explodes, annihilating the opponent. Among the regular Divine Attacks that use the element of fire, this is one of the strongest.

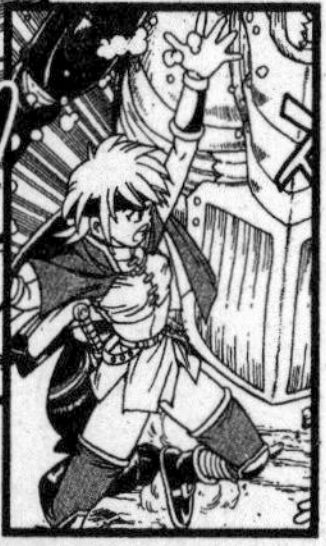

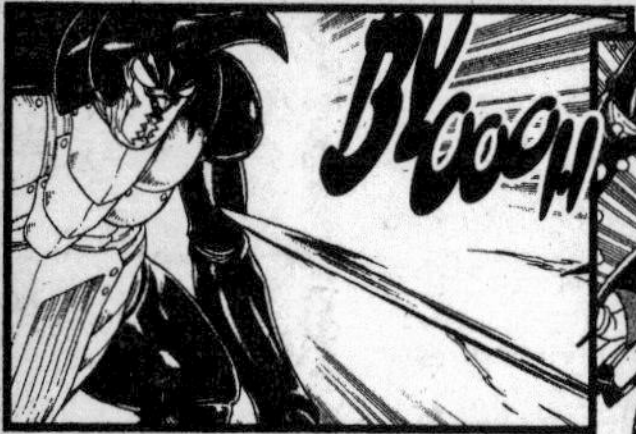

▲▶ Currently, this is the Divine Attack Poala resorts to in her time of greatest need.

DIVINE ATTACK: HAIL BULLET

This is the most basic form of the water-based Divine Attack. The energy is transformed into a small, dagger-sized icicle, which is thrown at the opponent. Once struck, the spot it hits becomes frozen. Like the fire-based Divine Attack, this has an advanced form, called Ice Pole. The attack has many other variations, such as Icy Rain, Snow Storm, and Avalanche.

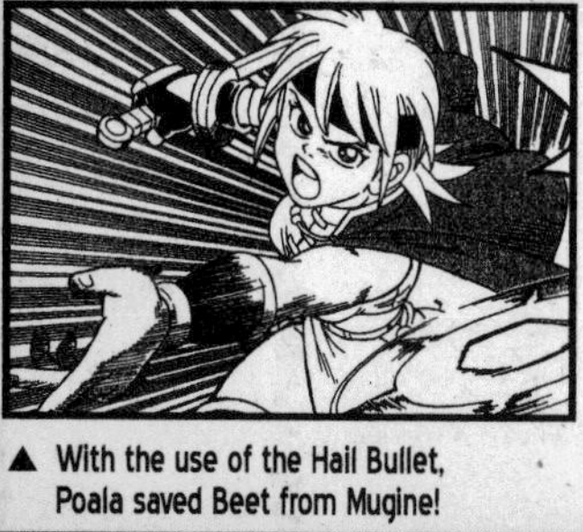

▲ With the use of the Hail Bullet, Poala saved Beet from Mugine!

DARK HOUSE of SORCERY

THIS IS A FOUNTAIN OF EVIL THAT EXISTS AT THE END OF THE WORLD. IT IS THE PLACE VANDELS GATHER TO OBTAIN MONSTERS.

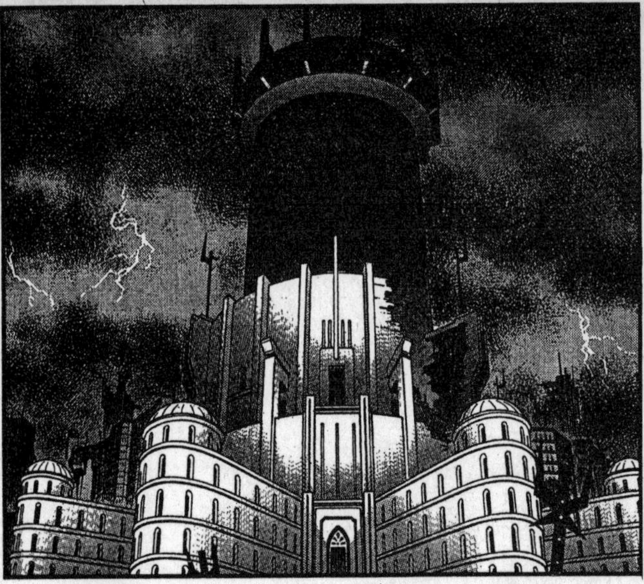

If a Buster's centers of activity are the various Appraisers' Houses, the Vandels' centers of activity are their individual castles and hiding places. However, the Vandels also have a single headquarters they all use together. That place is the Dark House of Sorcery.
All of the monsters that appear on the earth are generated there. Vandels receive Sorcery Bills for inflicting damage on human society, and they use the Sorcery Bills to purchase monsters as their subordinates. This system applies to all Vandels. If a Vandel wants to expand his power base, he has no choice but to use the service provided by the Dark House of Sorcery. All monsters that are ordered by Vandels are delivered within a few days. Once delivered, they become the subordinates of the Vandels and start inflicting destruction around the world.

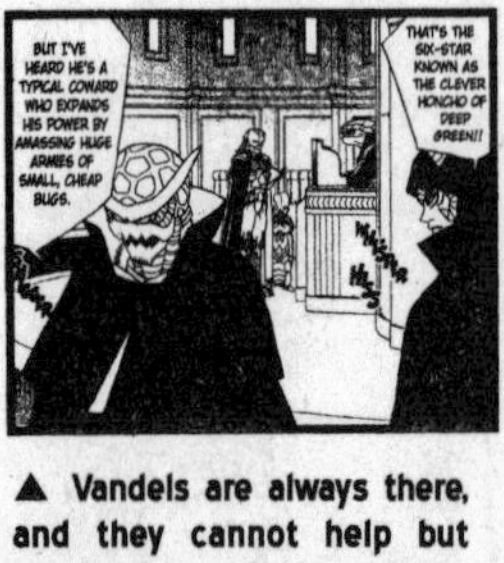
THAT'S THE SIX-STAR KNOWN AS THE CLEVER HONCHO OF DEEP GREEN!!
BUT I'VE HEARD HE'S A TYPICAL COWARD WHO EXPANDS HIS POWER BY AMASSING HUGE ARMIES OF SMALL, CHEAP BUGS.

▲ Vandels are always there, and they cannot help but gossip amongst themselves.

That's why so many Vandels visit this place. The Dark House of Sorcery provides amenities to visiting Vandels, such as the conference rooms, recreation rooms, and reference rooms. Because of this, many Vandels seek this place for relaxation between battles. Gossip flies about the latest and strongest Vandels around the world, and each Vandel vigilantly watches the other Vandels as they purchase their monsters. The place is a true paradise of demons.

DARK HOUSE of SORCERY, CENTRAL RECEPTION

LET'S EXAMINE THE MAIN ROOM OF THE DARK HOUSE OF SORCERY!

● **CENTRAL HALL**
Leads deep into the Dark House. What's hidden in that darkness? Right now, it's still a mystery.

● **ELEVATOR FLOOR**
This is the floor where Vandels receive monsters. If a Vandel orders expensive monsters, they can be delivered to the place the Vandel designates.

● This is the sitting area set up for the Vandels who visit to order or receive monsters. Usually, good-looking female staff members provide assistance. They typically report directly to the Chief of the House.

● This is a Vandel named Tarotos. He is the managing officer responsible for overall reception and the Second Chief of the House. He is in charge of accepting orders from all Vandels and functions as the main organizer of the Dark House of Sorcery.

SHAGIE CHIEF OF THE DARK HOUSE OF SORCERY

He is a Vandel, although his facial features resemble those of a rabbit. He looks distinctly different from all other Vandels. He is the Chief of the Dark House of Sorcery and is also responsible for evaluating and supervising all Vandels; thus he is known as the world's busiest Vandel. He is a strange character whose job is to monitor every Vandels' action by moving around the world, using a door that appears from below ground.

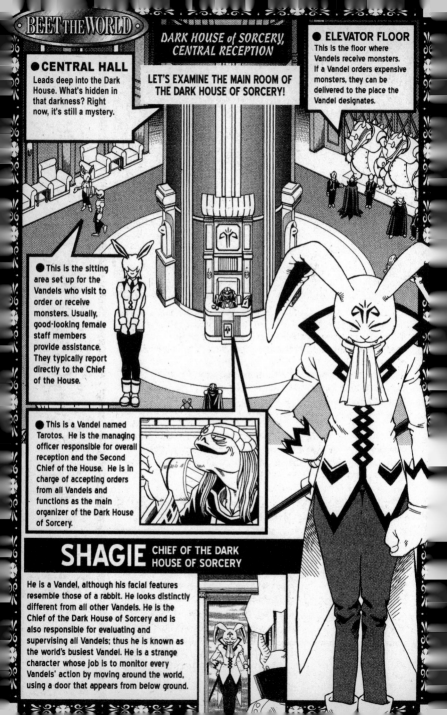

ENCYCLOPEDIA of MONSTERS

THIS IS THE ENCYCLOPEDIA OF HELL, CONTAINING EVERYTHING ABOUT MONSTERS.

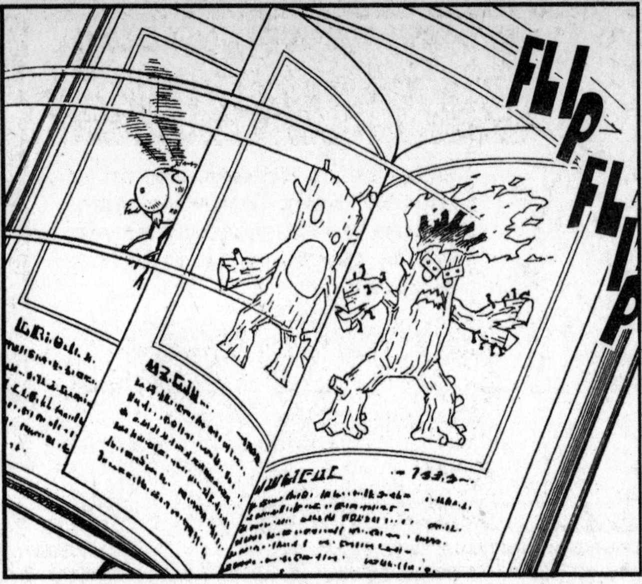
FLIP
FLIP

The Encyclopedia of Monsters is a book that describes every monster the Dark House of Sorcery can produce. The encyclopedia is divided into several sections, such as the wood section, bog section, and cave section, and details each monster's characteristics, ability and price. Vandels use this as reference to order suitable monsters and pay for them with Sorcery Bills. Once purchased, these monsters become subordinates of their owner. Naturally, the stronger the monster, the more expensive it is. This systematically limits monster production. The Vandels' personalities also affect how monsters are selected. Some Vandels are selective and choose their subordinates with great care, while the other Vandels expand their armies with numerous but weaker monsters.

SORCERY BILLS

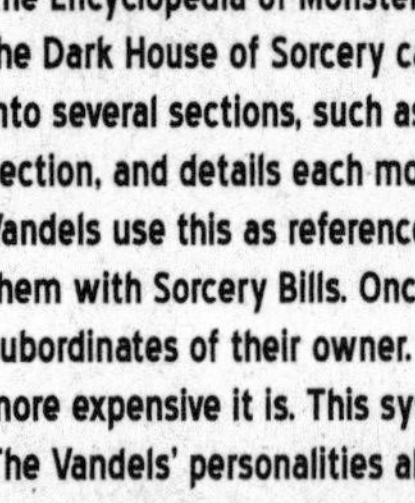

▲ Because the Sorcery Bills are produced with special magic, no one can make counterfeits.

By inflicting massive damage to humans, Vandels receive an honorary distinction in the form of stars. Vandels also receive practical rewards in the form of Sorcery Bills. In the human world, only coins are used as money, while among Vandels, only bills are used. Sorcery Bills are used to purchase monsters, construct castles, and fulfill the other needs of Vandels.

The ENCYCLOPEDIA of MONSTERS: WOOD SECTION

Perhaps because Grineed himself has an insect-like aspect, he tends to gather monsters from the wood section and make them his subordinates. Let us introduce them here.

Dangowl is Grineed's right-hand man.

He takes care of Grineed, almost like a steward. He used to be a monster called a Protector Bug, but Grineed gave him a unique name and the ability to use language.

CRIMINAL TORCH

This is a burning torch monster made of flames. Its fire is powerful.

JAGARM

This is a centipede type monster that hides underground and waits for humans.

GIANT BEETLE

This is a gigantic insect monster, with a flexible and super-strong outer shell.

KODA MANBO

This monster makes odd noises and confuses people. It's a very weak torch-type monster.

GURUME ANTS

This is a termite-like monster that can instantly gobble up people's homes.

PEN BARRY

This is a scout-type monster that can draw whatever it sees with perfect accuracy.

Coming Next Volume

Because he received the Zenon Army's five mystical saiga weapons, Beet thinks he has it made as a Vandel Buster. Yet, he can never quite defeat his arch-enemy, Beltorze. Worse yet, the Vandel knows it. But Beet and Poala meet a new ally who helps them stay alive, while Beltorze has to deal with a rival Vandel who is as powerful as he is. No matter which one comes out on top, you can bet it means big trouble for Beet!

Available in February 2005!

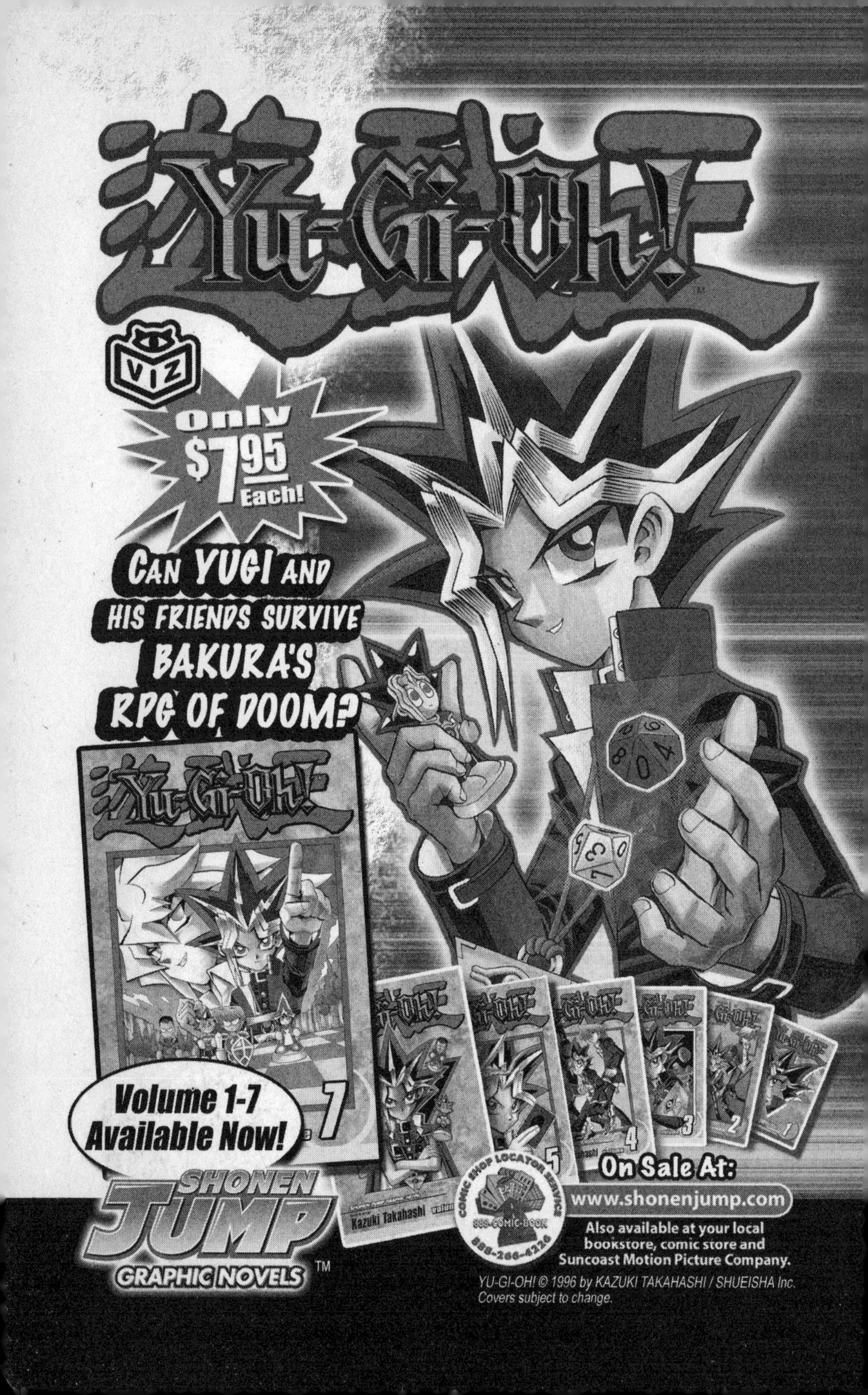
YU-GI-OH!
VIZ
Only $7.95 Each!
CAN YUGI AND HIS FRIENDS SURVIVE BAKURA'S RPG OF DOOM?
Volume 1-7 Available Now!
SHONEN JUMP GRAPHIC NOVELS
On Sale At:
www.shonenjump.com
Also available at your local bookstore, comic store and Suncoast Motion Picture Company.
COMIC SHOP LOCATOR SERVICE
888-COMIC-BOOK
888-266-4226
YU-GI-OH! © 1996 by KAZUKI TAKAHASHI / SHUEISHA Inc.
Covers subject to change.

DRAGON BALL Z™
VIZ
Vol. 18 on Sale January 11th!
FIGHT, GOKU... OR THE EARTH IS DOOMED!
DRAGON BALL Z
SHONEN JUMP GRAPHIC NOVEL
Story & Art by Akira Toriyama
volume 18
Vol.1- 17 on Sale Now!
DRAGON BALL ©1984 by BIRD STUDIO / SHUEISHA Inc.
Cover Art Subject to Change

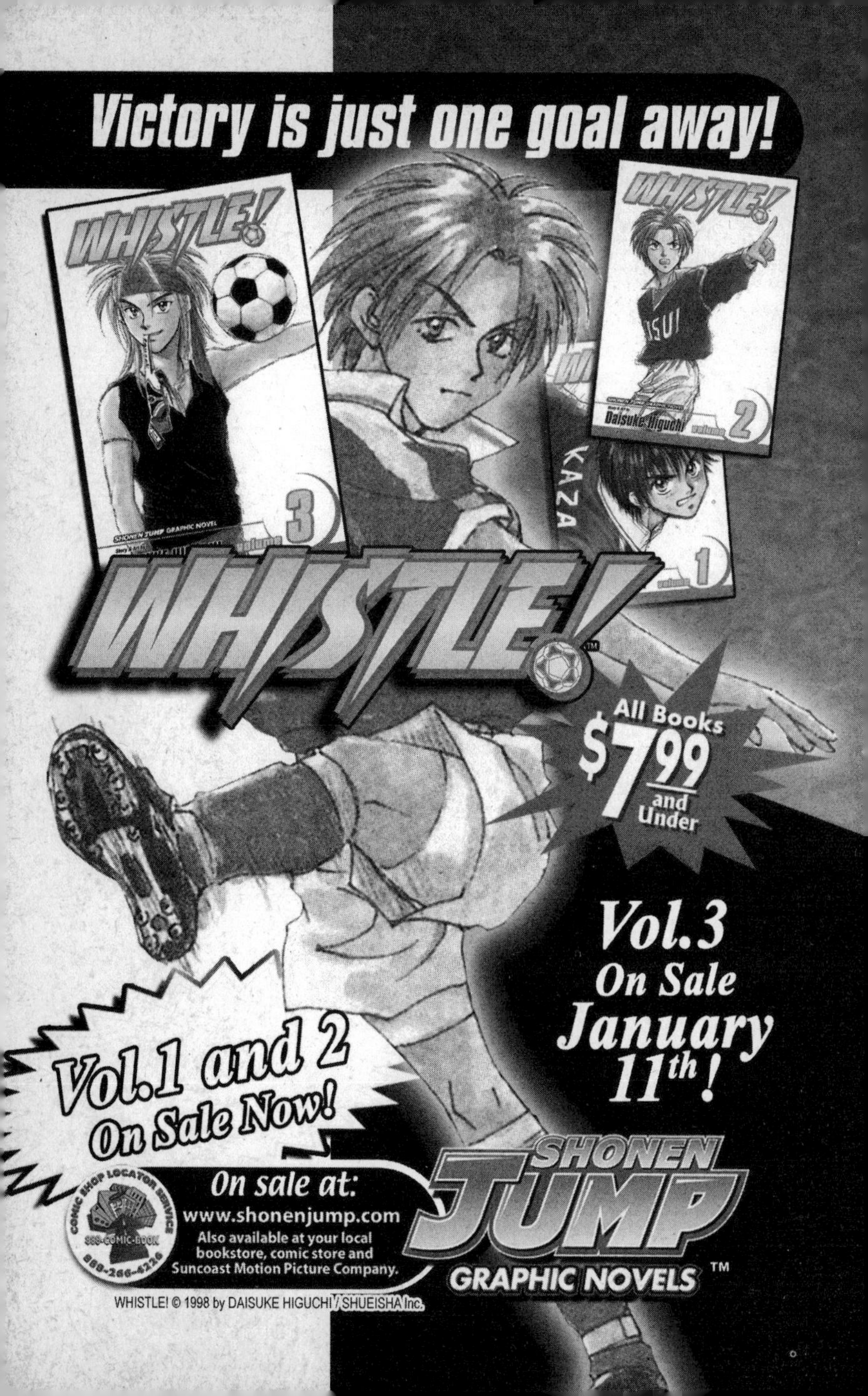

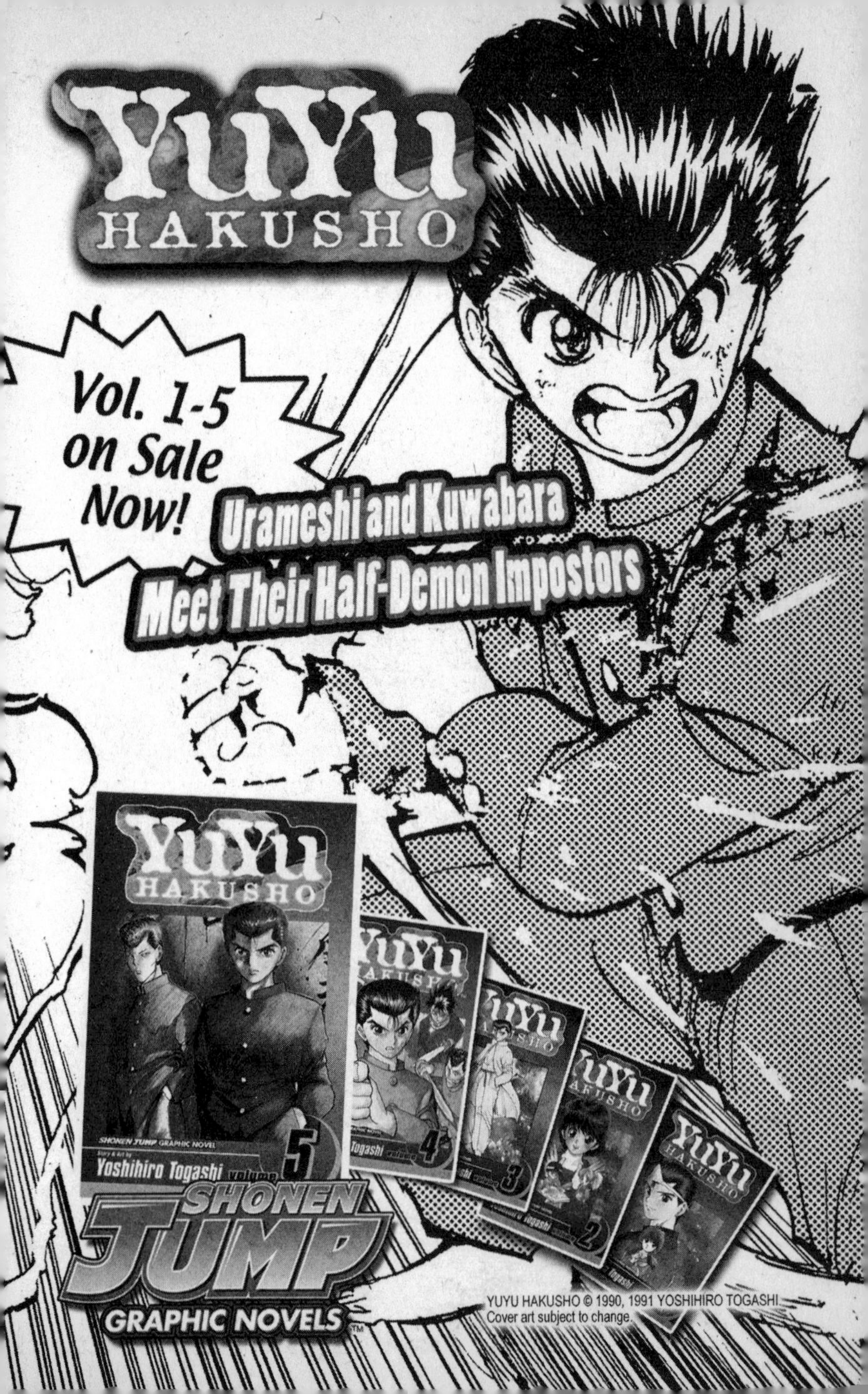
YuYu HAKUSHO
Vol. 1-5 on Sale Now!
Urameshi and Kuwabara Meet Their Half-Demon Impostors
SHONEN JUMP GRAPHIC NOVEL
Story & Art by Yoshihiro Togashi
SHONEN JUMP GRAPHIC NOVELS™
YUYU HAKUSHO © 1990, 1991 YOSHIHIRO TOGASHI
Cover art subject to change.

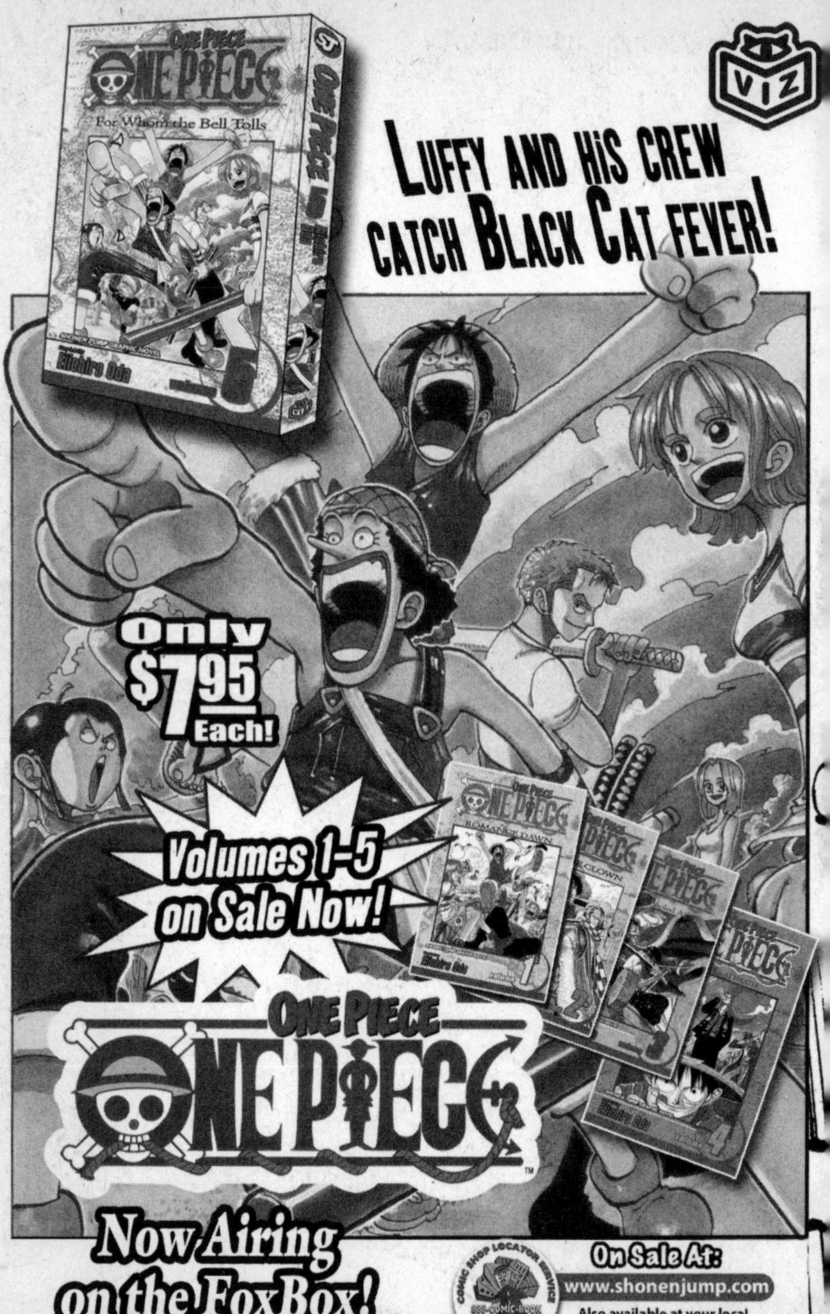

LUFFY AND HIS CREW
CATCH BLACK CAT FEVER!
VIZ
Only $7.95 Each!
Volumes 1-5 on Sale Now!
ONE PIECE
Now Airing on the FoxBox!
On Sale At:
www.shonenjump.com
Also available at your local bookstore, comic store and Suncoast Motion Picture Company.
COMIC SHOP LOCATOR SERVICE 888-COMIC-BOOK 888-266-4226
ONE PIECE © 1997 by EIICHIRO ODA / SHUEISHA Inc. Covers subject to change.

UNDER PRESSURE: AKIRA, HIKARU AND SAI!
VIZ
HIKARU NO GO
VOL. 1-2 ON SALE NOW!
SHONEN JUMP GRAPHIC NOVELS
www.shonenjump.com
Also available at your local bookstore, comic store and Suncoast Motion Picture Company.
COMIC SHOP LOCATOR SERVICE
888-COMIC-BOOK
888-266-4226
HIKARU-NO GO © 1998 by YUMI HOTTA, TAKESHI OBATA / SHUEISHA Inc.

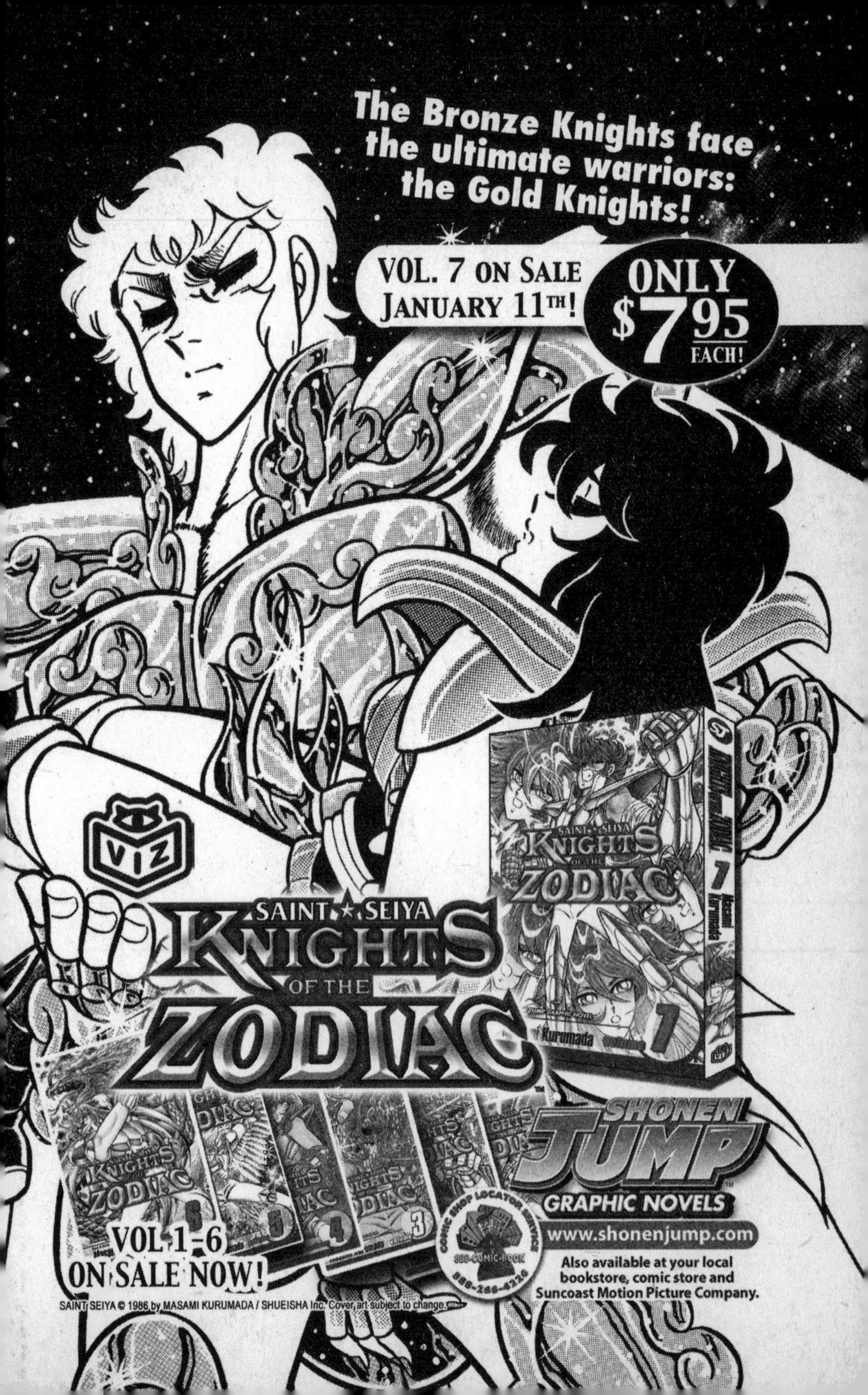
The Bronze Knights face the ultimate warriors: the Gold Knights!
VOL. 7 ON SALE JANUARY 11TH!
ONLY $7.95 EACH!
SAINT SEIYA KNIGHTS OF THE ZODIAC
VOL. 1-6 ON SALE NOW!
SHONEN JUMP GRAPHIC NOVELS
www.shonenjump.com
Also available at your local bookstore, comic store and Suncoast Motion Picture Company.
COMIC SHOP LOCATOR SERVICE 888-COMIC-BOOK 888-266-4226
SAINT SEIYA © 1986 by MASAMI KURUMADA / SHUEISHA Inc. Cover art subject to change.

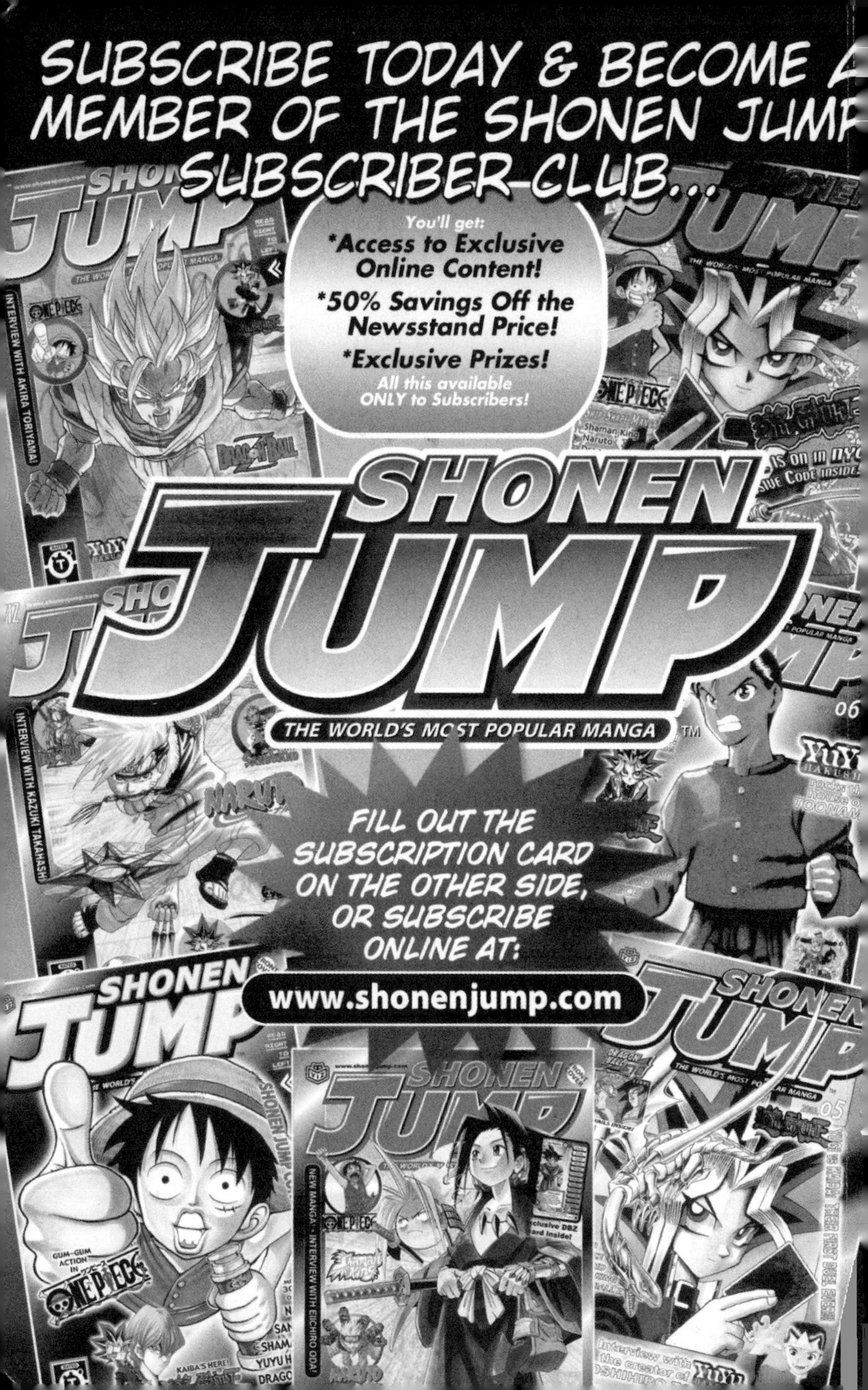
SUBSCRIBE TODAY & BECOME A MEMBER OF THE SHONEN JUMP SUBSCRIBER CLUB...
You'll get:
*Access to Exclusive Online Content!
*50% Savings Off the Newsstand Price!
*Exclusive Prizes!
All this available ONLY to Subscribers!
SHONEN JUMP
THE WORLD'S MOST POPULAR MANGA ™
FILL OUT THE SUBSCRIPTION CARD ON THE OTHER SIDE, OR SUBSCRIBE ONLINE AT:
www.shonenjump.com

SHONEN JUMP
THE WORLD'S MOST POPULAR MANGA

COMPLETE OUR SURVEY AND LET US KNOW WHAT YOU THINK!

☐ Please do NOT send me information about VIZ and SHONEN JUMP products, news and events, special offers, or other information.

☐ Please do NOT send me information from VIZ's trusted business partners.

Name: ______________________________

Address: ______________________________

City: ____________ **State:** ________ **Zip:** ____________

E-mail: ______________________________

☐ **Male** ☐ **Female** **Date of Birth (mm/dd/yyyy):** ___/___/_____ (**Under 13? Parental consent required**)

What race/ethnicity do you consider yourself? (please check one)

☐ Asian/Pacific Islander ☐ Black/African American ☐ Hispanic/Latino

☐ Native American/Alaskan Native ☐ White/Caucasian ☐ Other: __________

What SHONEN JUMP Graphic Novel did you purchase? (indicate title purchased)

____

What other SHONEN JUMP Graphic Novels, if any, do you own? (indicate title(s) owned)

____

____

Reason for purchase: (check all that apply)

☐ Special offer ☐ Favorite title ☐ Gift

☐ Recommendation ☐ Read in SHONEN JUMP Magazine

☐ Read excerpt in the SHONEN JUMP Compilation Edition

☐ Other ______________________________

Where did you make your purchase? (please check one)

☐ Comic store ☐ Bookstore ☐ Mass/Grocery Store

☐ Newsstand ☐ Video/Video Game Store ☐ Other: __________

☐ Online (site: ______________________________)

Do you read SHONEN JUMP Magazine?

☐ Yes ☐ No **(if no, skip the next two questions)**

Do you subscribe?

☐ Yes ☐ No

If you do not subscribe, how often do you purchase SHONEN JUMP Magazine?

☐ 1-3 issues a year

☐ 4-6 issues a year

☐ more than 7 issues a year

What genre of manga would you like to read as a SHONEN JUMP Graphic Novel?
(please check two)

☐ Adventure ☐ Comic Strip ☐ Science Fiction ☐ Fighting

☐ Horror ☐ Romance ☐ Fantasy ☐ Sports

Which do you prefer? (please check one)

☐ Reading right-to-left

☐ Reading left-to-right

Which do you prefer? (please check one)

☐ Sound effects in English

☐ Sound effects in Japanese with English captions

☐ Sound effects in Japanese only with a glossary at the back

THANK YOU! Please send the completed form to:

VIZ Survey
42 Catharine St.
Poughkeepsie, NY 12601

All information provided will be used for internal purposes only. We promise not to sell or otherwise divulge your information.